KT-167-475

PENGUIN BOOKS

THE MONKS OF WAR

Desmond Seward was born in Paris and educated at Ampleforth and Cambridge. Since the first edition of *The Monks of War* appeared in 1972 he has become a Knight of Malta, which has deepened his knowledge of the military religious orders. His other books include a study of the Wars of the Roses, which examines the impact of the wars on the lives of five men and women; and *Richard III: England's Black Legend*, which is also published in Penguin.

THE MONKS
OF WAR

The Military Religious Orders

DESMOND SEWARD

PENGUIN BOOKS

PENGUIN BOOKS

Published by the Penguin Group
Penguin Books Ltd, 80 Strand, London WC2R 0RL, England
Penguin Putnam Inc., 375 Hudson Street, New York, New York 10014, USA
Penguin Books Australia Ltd, 250 Camberwell Road, Camberwell, Victoria 3124, Australia
Penguin Books Canada Ltd, 10 Alcorn Avenue, Toronto, Ontario, Canada M4V 3B2
Penguin Books India (P) Ltd, 11 Community Centre, Panchsheel Park, New Delhi – 110 017, India
Penguin Books (NZ) Ltd, Cnr Rosedale and Airborne Roads, Albany, Auckland, New Zealand
Penguin Books (South Africa) (Pty) Ltd, 24 Sturdee Avenue, Rosebank 2196, South Africa

Penguin Books Ltd, Registered Offices: 80 Strand, London WC2R 0RL, England

www.penguin.com

First published 1972
This extensively revised edition published in Penguin Books 1995
10

Set in 10/12.5 pt Monotype Baskerville
Typeset by Datix International Limited, Bungay, Suffolk
Printed in England by Clays Ltd, St Ives plc

For Peter Drummond-Murray of Mastrick,
Slains Pursuivant of Arms

CONTENTS

ILLUSTRATIONS AND MAPS

ACKNOWLEDGEMENTS

Since this book was first published in 1972 scholars have shed
new light on the history of most military religious orders, while
considerable changes have taken place within those which survive.
I am more than ever conscious of my temerity in attempting to
provide an introduction to a subject which ranges over so many
centuries and so many countries.

I still recall with gratitude the advice and encouragement
given to me by Professor Jonathan Riley-Smith and Dom Alberic
Stacpoole of Ampleforth Abbey when I was writing the first
edition, although I realize that the former may not agree with
every conclusion which I have reached in this new version.

My first debt is to Monsignor A. N. Gilbey, a Conventual
Chaplain Grand Cross *ad honorem* of the Sovereign Military Order
of Malta, who persuaded me to revise the book. I must also thank
Peter Drummond-Murray, the SMOM's Delegate for Scotland,
for help at every stage and for reading the proofs. Other British
Knights of Malta whom I would like to thank are Julian Allason
and Charles Wright for their comments on the typescript and for
supplying me with otherwise unobtainable information.

In addition I am indebted to Count Ciechanowiecki, Vice
President of the SMOM's Polish Association; to Fra' John
Macpherson, former President of the SMOM's Canadian Associa-
tion, and to Dr Robert Pichette, the Canadian Association's
Historian. I am no less indebted to Pater Dr Bernhard Demel,
OT, Archivist of the Teutonic Order's Zentralarchiv at Vienna.

I am grateful to HSH Franz Prince Lobkowicz, Lieutenant
Grand Prior of the SMOM's Grand Priory of Bohemia, for
photographs of its church and palace at Prague; to the Bailiff

Prince Guy de Polignac, President of the SMOM's French Association, for a photograph of his Knights at Versailles; and to Sir Reresby Sitwell for the photograph of the seventeenth-century painting of a galley of the Order of Malta in the collection at Renishaw.

There could have been no more supportive editor than Janice Brent nor a more expert picture-researcher than Lily Richards.

ABBREVIATIONS

C.A.R.H.P.	*Collecçam de documentos e memorias da Academia Real da Historia Portuguesa (*Lisbon 1720*)*
Dugdale	*Monasticon Anglicanum,* ed. W. Dugdale, 8 vols (London 1817–30)
H.R.S.E.	*Historiae Ruthenicae Scriptores Exteria,* 2 vols (Berlin 1841)
M.L.A.	*Monumenta Livoniae Antiquae* (Riga and Leipzig 1835–47)
M.P.L.	*Patrologiae cursus completus. Series Latina,* ed. J. P. Migne, 221 vols (Paris 1844–55)
R.H.C.	*Recueil des historiens des croisades* (Paris 1841–1906):
R.H.C. oc.	*Historiens occidentaux,* 5 vols (1844–95)
R.H.C. or.	*Historiens orientaux,* 5 vols (1872–1906)
R.H.C. arm.	*Documents arméniens,* 2 vols (1869–1906)
R.H.C. Lois	*Lois. Les Assises de Jérusalem,* 2 vols (1841–3)
S.R.L.	*Scriptores Rerum Livonicarum,* 2 vols (Riga and Leipzig 1848–53)
S.R.P.	*Scriptores Rerum Prussicarum,* 6 vols (Leipzig 1861–74)

AUTHOR'S NOTE

In order to emphasize the brethren's monasticism, the title *Fra'* is used throughout (except for *Frey* when writing of Spanish Knights). This is an abbreviation of the official Latin *Frater*, for which *Br.* is hardly satisfactory; *Fr.* was the normal usage in most military orders but is too easily confused with 'Father'. I have therefore employed *Fra'*, which is still the prefix for professed brethren of the only military order to survive in anything like its original form, the Knights of Malta. It is worth emphasizing that Middle English could refer to the Hospitallers and the Templars as 'freres' or 'friars' – the Templars were sometimes called 'Red Friars'.

For the sake of clarity, in the chapters on the Iberian orders I have used Castilian, Portuguese and Catalan names rather than English since Juan, João and Joan, Alfonso, Afonso and Alfons are an aid to identification amid a multitude of Johns and Alfonsos. For the same reason, the Portuguese branch of the Order of Santiago is referred to throughout as '*São Thiago*'.

I

INTRODUCTION

Rejoice, brave warrior, if you live and conquer in the Lord, but rejoice still more and give thanks if you die and go to join the Lord. This life can be fruitful and victory is glorious yet a holy death for righteousness is worth more. Certainly 'blessed are they who die *in* the Lord' but how much more so are those who die *for* Him.

Bernard of Clairvaux

I

THE MONKS OF WAR

This is an introduction to the military religious orders, the first general history of them since the beginning of the eighteenth century. It concentrates on the period up to the Counter-Reformation when they were monks with swords. However, many of these orders still exist, notably the Knights of Malta; although nowadays occupied exclusively with charitable works, they cherish their history and traditions. An account of their later role is given in the last chapter.

The knight brethren of the military orders were noblemen vowed to poverty, chastity and obedience, living a monastic life in convents which were at the same time barracks, waging war on the enemies of the Cross. In their chapels one saw monks reciting the Office, but outside they were soldiers in uniform. The three great orders were the Templars, Hospitallers (Knights of Malta) and Teutonic Knights, though Santiago and Calatrava were no less formidable. Most of them emerged during the twelfth century to provide the Church with stormtroopers for the Crusades. They were the first properly disciplined and officered troops in the West since Roman times.

On many occasions they tried, literally, to fight their way into heaven. During countless wars they never doubted that theirs was a religious calling. 'Who fights us, fights Jesus Christ,' claimed the Teutonic Knights. For the Holy War was once an ideal admired by all Western Christians, and the crusade an inspiration which endured for centuries.

The brethren fought and prayed in many lands – and on many seas. As Edward Gibbon wrote, in Crusader Palestine, 'the firmest bulwark of Jerusalem was founded on the Knights of the Hospital of St John and of the Temple of Solomon; on the strange association of a monastic and a military life which fanaticism might suggest but which policy must approve'. Because of their sacrifices, Outremer, land of the Crusades – and in some ways precursor of Israel – endured for nearly two centuries. After the kingdom of Jerusalem had finally fallen, the Hospitallers, first from Rhodes and then from Malta, devoted themselves to guarding the shores of the Mediterranean and protecting Christian merchantmen against Turks and Barbary Corsairs.

The soldier monks waged another holy war in northern Europe, against the pagans of Latvia, Lithuania and Estonia, where they played a vital role in shaping the destinies of Germany and Poland. All these countries were influenced by them – racially, economically and politically. The heritage of the *Drang nach Osten*, today's Oder–Neisse line, was largely bequeathed by the Teutonic Knights whose lands, the *Ordensstaat*, reached almost to St Petersburg. It was they who created Prussia, by conquering the heathen Baltic race who were the original Prussians and by the most thorough colonization seen in the entire Middle Ages. Their forest campaigns against the Lithuanians have been called the most ferocious of all medieval wars. The Polish Corridor was a legacy of the Knights' seizure of Danzig (Gdansk) from Władysław the Dwarf in 1331. The first Hohenzollern ruler of Prussia was also the last '*Hochmeister*' to hold sway in that country. Field Marshal von Hindenburg's victory over the Russians among the Masurian lakes in 1914 was deliberately named Tannenberg after a battle there five centuries earlier, in which a Hochmeister had been killed and his Knights almost wiped out by Slavs. Their black-and-silver cross was chosen as the model for the Iron Cross and is still the emblem of the German Army.

In Spain the brethren of Santiago, Calatrava and Alcántara spearheaded the Reconquista. They consolidated the Christian advance, ranching sheep and cattle on the lonely *meseta* where no peasant dared settle for fear of Moorish raiders. From Portugal other brethren initiated the expansion of Europe with expeditions which were half-missionary and half-commercial. Enrique the

Navigator, Master of the Knights of Christ – successors to the Portuguese Templars – presided over a research centre at Sagres where he employed the foremost geographers of the day and from where he sent out ships on voyages of discovery under the Order's flag.

It is surprising that so few historical romances have been written about them. The *Götterdämmerung*-like fight to the death by the Templars and Hospitallers at the fall of Acre in 1291, Hochmeister Ulrich von Juningen's refusal to leave the doomed field of Tannenberg, and the Knights of Malta too badly wounded to stand waiting in chairs at the breach of Fort St Elmo for the Turks' final assault are only the best known among many scenes of epic heroism. The end of the Templars – whose last Master, Jacques de Molay, was burnt alive over a slow fire – has inspired the odd novel, but it needs an opera to do it justice. (Of the other twenty-one Masters of the Temple, five died in battle, five of wounds and one of starvation in a Saracen prison.) Eisenstein made the Teutonic Knights' defeat on the ice of Lake Peipus in 1242 the plot for his film *Alexander Nevsky*. There is also Henri de Montherlant's play, *Le Maître de Santiago*, but little else.

Whatever their order, the Knights' inspiration was the same on the banks of the Jordan or the Tagus, on the Mediterranean or the Baltic. They were as much a part of monasticism as the friars – if mendicant brethren preached the Gospel, military brethren defended it. 'Take this sword: its brightness stands for faith, its point for hope, its guard for charity. Use it well . . .' says the Hospitaller rite of profession. The Bible may tell us that those who live by the sword shall perish by the sword, but the Knights saw themselves as warriors of Christ. They do indeed deserve the title 'monks of war'.

II

LATIN SYRIA
1099–1291

The Crusades and the international orders:
Templars – Hospitallers – St Lazarus –
Montjoie – St Thomas

. . . such are they whom God chooses for himself and gathers
from the furthest ends of the earth, servants from among the
bravest in Israel to guard watchfully and faithfully his
Sepulchre and the Temple of Solomon, sword in hand,
ready for battle.

Bernard of Clairvaux

2

THE BIRTH OF A NEW VOCATION

The three greatest military orders, the Templars, the Hospitallers and the Teutonic Knights, were founded in the twelfth century, an earlier renaissance which saw the birth of Gothic architecture, the zenith of papal monarchy, and an intellectual revolution that would culminate with Aquinas. Perhaps its most outstanding figure was the Cistercian monk Bernard of Clairvaux, last of the Fathers of the Western Church. The Templars had been in existence for a decade when he met their founder, Hugues de Payens, in 1127 but this meeting was the real moment of the military brethren's genesis, for St Bernard at once understood how Hugues's inspiration matched the conflicting vocations of chivalry and the cloister.

The Abbot of Clairvaux, the greatest moral force of his day, proclaimed the superiority of love to knowledge and presided over the change in religious emotion when the humanity of Christ was at last fully appreciated: a crucifix of the tenth century has a figure of Christ the King in majesty, *Christos Pantocrator* the terrible judge, while one of the twelfth has a compassionate representation of the tortured man. Later Francis of Assisi brought this message to the masses with explosive results, but in the first half of the century popular enthusiasm found an outlet in new monastic orders, especially the Cistercians. Bernard joined them in 1113, when they were confined to one monastery, Cîteaux, and at his death in 1153 there were 343 such houses.

The ascetic impulse produced a papal revolution. Gregory VII (1073-85) set the papacy firmly on a course towards the position of leader and judge of Western Christendom, demanding that temporal power be subordinated to spiritual just as the body depends on the soul, envisaging a papal army, the *militia Sancti Petri*. Europe listened with new respect. When in 1095 Pope Urban II called upon the faithful to recover Jerusalem – occupied by the Moslems since 638 – his appeal inspired extraordinary enthusiasm. Palestine's importance was heightened by the new appreciation of Christ's humanity; the scenes of the Passion were still pointed out at Jerusalem. That His City should belong to infidels was contrary to the law of God. Fortunately the Moslem world was in chaos, from India to Portugal. Syria was more vulnerable than it had been for a century, broken up into principalities ruled by Turkish atabegs, while the Fatimid Caliphate at Cairo was in terminal decline. The Crusaders stormed Jerusalem in July 1099.

Those who stayed in Palestine were adventurers, mainly French, with nothing to go back to, and the state they created reflected the feudalism of their own land. It came to include four great baronies: the principality of Galilee, the county of Jaffa and Ascalon, the lordship of Kerak and Montréal, and the lordship of Sidon, together with twelve smaller fiefs. There were also three lesser states: the principality of Antioch and the counties of Tripoli and Edessa. Without the assent of the Haute Cour, or great council of the realm, in theory no political action was valid, though the king was extremely powerful. Outremer was shaped like an hour-glass, extending for nearly five hundred miles from the Gulf of Aqaba on the Red Sea to Edessa, which lay east of the Euphrates. At the centre, Tripoli, it was only twenty-five miles broad and never more than seventy miles across in the south. There was a chronic shortage of manpower, while the desert frontier was far from impenetrable, holding water and fodder. The 'Franks' put their trust in sea power and fortresses. Genoese, Pisan and Venetian fleets soon controlled the sea, eager for commerce as the lure of spices, rice and sugarcane, of ostrich plumes from Africa and furs from Russia, of carpets from Persia, of inlaid metalwork from Damascus, of silks and of muslin from Mosul, and of countless other luxuries attracted merchants who settled in the coastal towns.

There was a large native Christian population, Maronite, Melkite, Syrian and Armenian. In about the year 1120, Fulcher de Chartres wrote of how 'Some of us have married Syrians, Armenians or even baptized Saracens . . .', and how his people were no longer Frenchmen but Palestinians who were accepted by the natives as fellow countrymen.[1] Morfia, the queen of Baldwin II himself, was the daughter of an Armenian prince. Many officials and merchants were Christianized Arabs, while great barons employed Moslem secretaries. But if European visitors talked of *poulains*, Syrian-born Franks, it is too much to say that a new Franco-Syrian race had been born. The local Christian churches were treated with contemptuous tolerance, patriarchs of the Latin rite being installed at Jerusalem and Antioch. French was the language of administration, and the ruling classes remained French.

Nevertheless, to the Franks Jerusalem was home. The king dressed in a golden burnous and keffiyeh, and gave audiences sitting, cross-legged, on a carpet. Nobles wore turbans and shoes with upturned points, and the silks, damasks, muslins and cottons that were so different from the wool and furs of France. In the towns they lived in villas with courtyards, fountains and mosaic floors, reclining on divans, listening to Arab lutes and watching dancing girls. They ate sugar, rice, lemons and melons and washed with soap in tubs or sunken baths, while the women used cosmetics and glass mirrors, unknown in Europe. Merchants, grown accustomed to bazaars, veiled their wives, and professional wailers were seen at Christian funerals. Coins had Arabic inscriptions. Yet this success in sinking roots vitiated the brutal missionary urge necessary for a detested minority to survive on the edge of a vast and hostile world empire. It was not only a higher civilization which softened the Franks. The climate, with its short but stormy winters and long, sweltering summers, and the new diseases, caused heavy mortality despite Arab medicine.

Now, for the last time, the neighbouring Eastern Empire was reviving under the Comnenoi emperors. The Franks were overawed by Constantinople with its million inhabitants, although

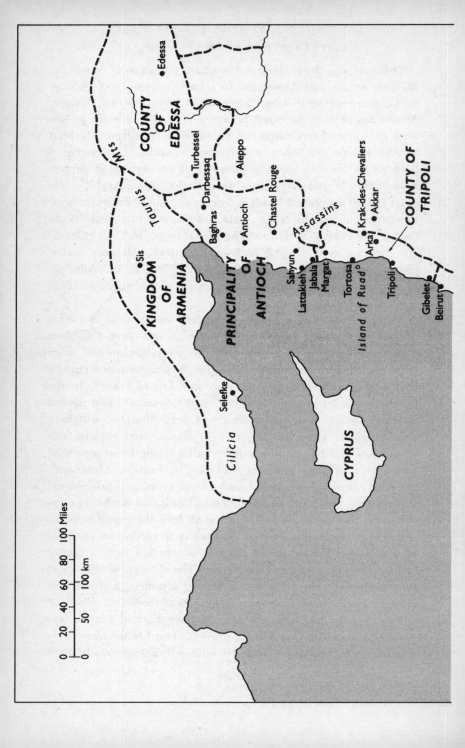

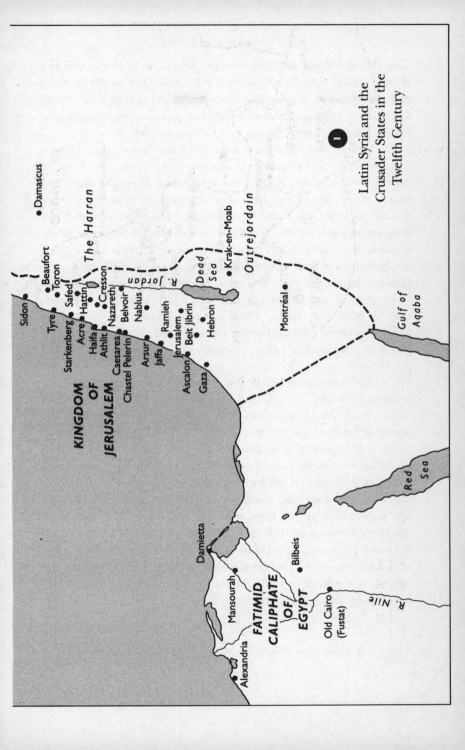

Latin Syria and the Crusader States in the Twelfth Century

Damascus

Beaufort
Toron
Safed
Sidon
Tyre
Starkenberg
Acre
Haifa
Athlit
Caesarea
Chastel Pelerin
Arsur
Jaffa

The Harran

Cresson
Hattin
Nazareth
Belvoir
Nablus
Ramleh
Jerusalem
Beit Jibrin
Hebron
Ascalon
Gaza

R. Jordan

Dead
Sea

Krak-en-Moab

Outrejordain

Montréal

Gulf
of
Aqaba

KINGDOM
OF
JERUSALEM

Damietta

Red
Sea

Mansourah

FATIMID
CALIPHATE
OF
EGYPT

Bilbeis

Old Cairo
(Fustat)

Alexandria

R. Nile

they thought them soft and corrupt. Schism with Rome was not yet an accomplished fact, but the West had little understanding of Eastern Christendom. The Byzantine army was still extremely formidable, consisting almost entirely of mercenaries, English and Danish infantry and Patzinak and Cuman cavalry.

At this date the Armenians were still fierce mountain warriors, though their old kingdoms in Greater Armenia, the land of Mount Ararat where Noah's Ark rested, had been absorbed and their princes murdered by the Byzantines so that they were unable to resist the Seldjuk onslaught. The 'Haiots'* did not despair, and throughout the eleventh and twelfth centuries many trekked down to Cilicia, the southern shore of Asia Minor. Led by Ruben, a cousin of their last king, they carved out a new country among the glens and crags of the Taurus mountains, half wrested from the crumbling imperial administration, half conquered from the Turks. They welcomed Outremer and their nobility married Frankish ladies and acquired a feudal character.[2] But if an ally against Islam, Armenia was nevertheless a rival of the Latin states.

Frankish success in battle depended on skilful use of specially equipped cavalry over carefully chosen ground.[3] Infantry with spears, long Danish axes and crossbows provided cover until the moment for a single decisive charge.[4] There were two sorts of cavalry, knights and sergeants, the former's armour consisting of a conical steel helmet, a chain-mail tunic with sleeves and hood worn over a quilted undershirt, padded breeches and a kite-shaped shield. Later the shield became smaller, the conical helmet was superseded by the helm covering the whole face, and mail stockings were adopted, with a burnous and keffiyeh to ward off the sun. They carried a lance held under the arm, a long, two-edged cutting sword and occasionally a mace. On the march the knight rode a hack or mule, mounting his carefully trained war-horse when action was imminent. These 'destriers' were enormous

* The Franks called them 'Hermins' and their country of Cilicia 'Erminie'.

animals, often seventeen hands high, more akin to a dray-horse than a cavalry charger, and taught to bite, butt and kick. Sergeants were similarly armed but did not wear the chain hauberk. They charged with the knights, riding in the rear ranks.[5] To time the charge correctly, restraining troops beneath blistering sun and the enemy's arrows, demanded real leadership.

Their Turkish opponents used classic Turanian tactics, highly manoeuvrable mounted bowmen shooting from the saddle; they never attacked frontally but tried to divide and surround the enemy, before closing in with short sabres or yataghans. Their arrow fire was extremely rapid and they liked to attack the Franks on the march, aiming at the horses and leaving their opponents no time to prepare defensive formations. There were some armoured cavalrymen, but even these rode Arab ponies chosen for speed.[6]

The Franks had a certain admiration for the Turks, but little for the Egyptians.[7] The caliph at Cairo – whom the Franks called King of Babylon – was the pope-emperor of the Shias, who did not bear allegiance to the Caliph of Baghdad, head of the other great Moslem sect, the Sunni. Fatimid armies were made up of Arab horsemen, who charged home with the lance or waited to receive the Frankish charge, and Sudanese archers on foot. Their discipline was wretched. However, just before their conquest by Saladin's family, the Egyptians began to employ cavalry of Turkish type, recruited from Caucasian slaves known as Mamelukes.

Battles between Frank and Turk were like the combats of bull and matador, but when the bull got home the effect was shattering, victories being won in the face of incredible odds.[8] Not only were the Franks and their horses bigger and heavier, but they were better at in-fighting and could deal out terrible punishment. The perennial problem of Outremer was to muster enough of these tank-like noblemen.

When the first king of Jerusalem, Baldwin I, died in 1118 the land was still in wretched disorder, infested with criminals; with some justice Latin Syria has been compared to a medieval Botany Bay.[9] Many Franks had been sent on the crusade as penance for atrocious offences such as rape and murder, and they reverted to their unpleasant habits. Pilgrims were a natural prey, though one of the principal objects of the crusade had been to make the Holy Places safe for them. Baldwin's successor, Baldwin II, had no means of policing the kingdom. The English merchant, Saewulf, wrote of the miseries of pilgrims in 1103; and about the same time the German abbot, Ekkehard, recorded robberies and martyrdoms as daily occurrences. William of Tyre observed that in the early days of the kingdom the Moslem peasants of Galilee kidnapped solitary pilgrims and sold them into slavery.

Hugues de Payens was no mere adventurer but lord of the castle of Martigny in Burgundy, a cousin of the counts of Champagne, and may have been a relative of St Bernard, whose family home was near Martigny. Hugues arrived in Syria in 1115, and by 1118 had become a self-appointed protector of pilgrims on the dangerous road from Jaffa to Jerusalem, harried ceaselessly from Ascalon. This ragged eccentric persuaded seven knights, also from northern France, to help him, all taking a solemn oath before the patriarch to protect pilgrims and observe poverty, chastity and obedience. They looked very odd, dressing only in what old clothes were given to them, but King Baldwin was impressed and gave the 'Poor Knights' a wing of the royal palace, the mosque of al-Aqsa, thought to be the Temple of Solomon. He also joined the patriarch in subsidizing them.[10]

Even before the crusade there was a hospital of St John the Almoner for pilgrims at Jerusalem, near the Church of the Holy Sepulchre; it was both an infirmary and a guest house.[11] It had been founded about 1070 by some merchants of Amalfi. In 1100 a certain Fra' Gerard, about whom little is known, was elected master. Probably he arrived before the crusaders. After the kingdom's establishment, the increased number of pilgrims necessitated a reorganization and Gerard abandoned the Benedictine rule for St Augustine's while another more important St John was adopted as patron, the Baptist himself. The new order became deeply respected, acquiring estates in many European countries,[12] and in 1113 Pope Paschal II took them under his special protection.[13] Possibly Gerard employed Poor Knights to protect his hospitals, which spread throughout Outremer.

King Baldwin must have lost many men in the bloody victory of Tel-Shaqab in 1126. The solution appeared to be another crusade. Not only did Hugues de Payens have some link with St Bernard, but Hugues, Count of Champagne, founder of the abbey of Clairvaux, had joined the Poor Knights, while another recruit may have been St Bernard's maternal uncle. In 1126 two brethren were sent to France with letters for St Bernard from the king, and the next year Hugues de Payens himself came to ask Bernard for a new crusade.

Other founders of religious orders had asked the abbot's advice, St Norbert of the Premonstratensian canons and the English Gilbert of Sempringham. Indeed there was a spate of new vocations during this period: Carthusians, Grandmontines and Tironians, besides those of Savignac and Fontevrault. Cistercians and Templars were produced by the same wave of asceticism. However, Hugues and his companions did not see themselves as a religious order until they met the great abbot. A document of 1123 refers to Hugues as 'Master of the Knights of the Temple'* but his little band was merely a voluntary brotherhood; recent research seems to indicate that they were having difficulty in finding recruits and were on the verge of dissolution.[14] Hugues had come about another crusade, not to ask for a rule.

St Bernard took a strong liking to Hugues, promising to compile a rule for him and find recruits. 'They can fight the battle of the Lord and indeed be soldiers of Christ.' In 1128 a council was convened at Troyes and, on Bernard's advice, Hugues attended it. Though the abbot was not present he sent a rule, which was debated and endorsed by the council. Copies of the Templar constitutions survive from the thirteenth century and these state that the first part of the rule was 'par le commandement dou

---

* '*Magister Militum Templi*' – it is perhaps significant that 'Magister Militum' had been the title of the Commander-in-Chief of the later Roman Empire.

concile et dou venerable père Bernart abbés de Clerevaus'.[15]

Bernard thought of Hugues's new brethren as military Cistercians. Significantly, brother-knights wore a white hooded habit in the cloister, like Cistercian choir monks, while lesser brethren wore brown, as did Cistercian lay brothers. On active service this habit was replaced by a cloak. An emphasis on silence, even to the extent of using signs in the refectory, came from the same source, while the simplicity of Cistercian altar furnishings was paralleled by the plainest weapons and saddlery possible, with no trace of gold or silver. Brethren slept in dormitories in shirt and breeches, as Cistercians still do today. Unless on night duty, attendance at matins was strictly enforced, for they said Office together in choir, not the full Roman Office, but the Little Office – psalms and prayers easily memorized by men who could not read; on campaign, thirteen 'Pater Nosters' were said in lieu of matins, seven for each canonical hour and nine for vespers. Religious services alternated with military exercises. There were two main meals, both eaten in silence with sacred reading from a French translation of the Bible, special emphasis being placed on the Books of Joshua and the Maccabees. All found inspiration in the ferocious exploits of Judas, his brothers and their war-bands in reconquering the Holy Land from cruel infidels. Brethren ate in pairs to see that the other did not weaken himself by fasting. Wine was served with every meal and meat three times a week; their mortification was the rigours of war. Each knight was allowed three horses but, with the symbolic exception of the lion, hawking and hunting were forbidden. He had to crop his hair and grow a beard, being forbidden to kiss even mother or sister, and no nuns were to be affiliated to the Order. His Master was not merely a commanding officer but an abbot. For the first time in Christian history soldiers would live as monks.[16]

St Bernard's rule was the basis of those of all military orders, even if only indirectly, whether the framework was Cistercian or Augustinian, for he had defined a new vocation. Its ideals were set out in a pamphlet, *In Praise of the New Knighthood*,[17] written to attract recruits. The Templars found themselves heroes almost

T. VI. P. 21

1. A Templar in his everyday habit

overnight and donations poured in from the kings of Aragon and Castile, from the Count of Flanders and many other princes. Hugues was especially well received in England and Scotland[18] while in France the Archbishop of Rheims instituted an annual collection. Europe was thrilled by these holy warriors who guarded the throne of David.

When Hugues returned to Palestine in 1130 he began to erect a system of preceptories or commanderies. This evolved slowly, ultimately depending on temples in the front-line territories, Jerusalem, Antioch, Tripoli, Castile–León, Aragon and Portugal, each ruled by a master who owed allegiance to the Master at Jerusalem. However, centralization was not complete until the next century. Temples, with preceptories, were also set up in France, England (including Scotland and Ireland), Sicily (including Apulia and Greece) and Germany. These were used to administer estates, as training or recruiting depots, and as homes for elderly brethren. It was very different from the days when the Templars' only resources had been a scanty portion of the bishop's tithes.

By the mid-thirteenth century the hierarchy would comprise a Master; his deputy, the Seneschal; the Marshal, supreme military official; the Commander of the Land and Realm of Jerusalem, who was both treasurer and in charge of the navy and estate management; the Commander of the City of Jerusalem, who was hospitaller; and finally the Draper or keeper of the wardrobe – a sort of quartermaster general. The Master was chosen by an elaborate combination of vote and lot designed to ensure impartiality, a procedure which recalled the election of the Venetian Doge. Powerful though he was, important decisions were taken by the General Chapter. Provincial Masters had all the Grand Master's rights in their own lands save when he was present in person. The Marshal was the Order's third most important officer and provincial Marshals were responsible to him. This organization took many years to evolve, but it became increasingly necessary, for there were many recruits. Their number was swollen by confrère knights, who served for only a short period, donating half their property, and who could marry. Cistercian *confratres* were the model for these auxiliary brethren.[19]

The Order's ecclesiastical privileges were very great, since, though it soon acquired its own clergy, priest brothers, it was exempt from episcopal visitations, being responsible to the pope alone; the bull *Omne datum optimum*[20] allowed these chaplains to celebrate Mass and dispense the sacraments during an interdict. As clerics, brethren could be tried only in ecclesiastical courts: it has been said that they were both a Church within a Church and a State within a State.

The new brethren had joined the Order not just to fight but to pray. They saw nothing contradictory in their vocation. In St Bernard's words, 'killing for Christ' was *malecide* not *homicide*, the extermination of injustice rather than of the unjust, and therefore desirable; indeed, 'to kill a pagan is to win glory since it gives glory to Christ'. Long before the Crusades, Popes Leo IV and John VIII had declared that warriors pure in heart who died fighting for the Church would inherit the kingdom of God. Death in battle was martyrdom, a road travelled by 20,000 Templars during the next two centuries.

Yet basically their ideals were those of contemplative monasticism. A monk abandons his will and his desires to search for God; the monastic life is often described as a martyrdom in which the monk must die to be reborn. Many of the early brethren ended in contemplative houses, and it is no exaggeration to call the first Templars military Cistercians. Active service – usually of a fire brigade nature, galloping off at a moment's notice to deal with Turkish razzias – was the only interruption in an essentially ascetic existence. The worst hardship of monastic life is not self-denial or celibacy, but obedience to a superior's least command; a Templar was not even allowed to adjust his stirrup without permission. In battle they neither gave nor asked for quarter and were not allowed to ask for ransom. 'They neglected to live, but they were prepared to die in the service of Christ', full of that holy delirium which, according to Ekkehard, filled the first crusaders.[21] These soldiers with cropped hair and hooded white mantles were unmistakable. They faced death if captured; after the Field of Blood in 1119 the atabeg Togtekin gave Frankish prisoners to his soldiers for archery practice or hacked off their legs and arms, leaving them in the streets of Aleppo for the townsmen to finish off, though this was before the days of the brethren, who suffered much worse. For a brother to lose the black-and-silver gonfalon, 'Beau Séant', meant expulsion from the Order. This was the ultimate penalty, also inflicted for desertion to the Saracens, heresy or murdering a fellow Christian.

Frequently they were reminded by popes and theologians that the Holy War was not an end in itself and that bloodshed was intrinsically evil. From the very beginning there were Western Christians who mistrusted the ideal. An English mystic, the Cistercian abbot Isaac of Etoile, wrote in St Bernard's lifetime:

... this dreadful new military order that someone has rather pleasantly called the order of the fifth gospel was founded for the purpose of forcing infidels to accept the faith at the point of the sword. Its members consider that they have every right to attack anyone not confessing Christ's name, leaving him destitute, whereas if they themselves are killed while thus unjustly attacking the pagans, they are called martyrs for the faith ... We do not maintain that all they do is wrong, but we do insist that what they are doing can be an occasion of many future evils.[22]

However, most contemporaries admired this new vocation, and when Hugues de Payens died in 1136 – in his bed – the Temple had a rival, the Order of the Hospital of St John the Baptist. Gerard had been succeeded as Master in 1120 by Fra' Raymond du Puy, an organizer of genius. The Order's nursing work had already made it rich and popular, more than a thousand pilgrims a year being accommodated in Jerusalem, while its hospitals and guest-houses spread throughout the kingdom. It received grants of land from Godefroi de Bouillon and also acquired property in France, Italy, Spain and England. Raymond was expert in providing an administration for these European possessions, setting up houses whose revenues were spent in forwarding food, wine, clothes and blankets for hospital use; some were specifically charged with providing luxuries, such as white bread, for the sick. The papacy gave the Hospitallers many privileges: Innocent II forbade bishops to interdict Hospitaller chapels; Anastasius IV gave them their own priests; and the English Adrian IV gave them their own churches. In 1126 a constable of the Order is mentioned, suggesting some sort of military organization, but the first firm date for armed activity is 1136, when King Fulk gave them land at the key position of Beit Jibrin, on the road from Gaza to Hebron. This was the first of their huge fortresses, the castle of 'Gibelin'. The Hospitallers owed an enormous debt to St Bernard, who had made it possible for them to take up arms. Christian war had not only become spiritually respectable but a means of self-sanctification. Without the great Cistercian, the brethren of St John would never have evolved into a military order. By 1187 they controlled more than twenty great strongholds in Outremer.[23]

The rule developed very slowly. A Christian must love Christ in other Christians, and this command was the basis of the Hospital's nursing vocation. In the rule of the Temple it was laid down that a brother must be expelled from the Order for killing a Christian but only reprimanded for killing a Saracen slave; Christ did not live within Saracens. Nursing made the Hospitallers more humane, while the presence of women within the Order must also have had a softening influence. Fra' Raymond seems to have taken the Augustinian rule as a framework and then experimented with various ideas from the Poor Knights' constitutions.[24] The brethren took vows of poverty, chastity and obedience; they were to expect only bread and water for sustenance, and to obey the orders of the sick whom they visited every day. There was provision for surgeons who messed with the knightly brethren, while much attention was given to the maintenance of the hospital. As with the Templars, there were four classes: knights, sergeants, serving brethren and chaplains. Similarly there was provision for confrère knights. A bull of Alexander III of 1178 states that 'according to the custom of Raymond' the brothers could carry arms only when the standard of the cross was displayed – to defend the kingdom or attack a pagan city. The habit was a black mantle with a white cross on the chest, shaped like a bell-tent and very clumsy in battle, and a black skull cap (though outside the house brethren sometimes wore a white turban).[25] There were also nursing sisters attached to each hospital. In the twelfth century fighting was only a secondary activity for Hospitallers (not even being mentioned in the Order's statutes until 1182), and militarization was a long and slow process.

Eventually the structure came to resemble the Templars, and knights ruled the brotherhood. The bailiffs, as the great officers were known, included the Master, elected by the same process as the Master of the Temple, and the only bailiff to hold office for life; the Grand Preceptor (sometimes called Grand Commander) of Jerusalem, the Master's lieutenant; the Treasurer; the Marshal; the Draper or quartermaster general; the Hospitaller; and finally the Turcopolier, who commanded the 'Turcopoles', light native horse.[26] Commanderies were small units of knights and sergeants administering adjoining groups of properties. In Syria the commanders were directly responsible to the Master, but elsewhere the system was more complex, European commanderies being grouped into priories, and the priories into provinces corresponding to countries. Like the Templars, supreme power lay with the General Chapter. A smaller assembly, the conventual chapter which was reminiscent of a cabinet, assisted the Master, acting as a secret privy council for affairs of state and as a full public council to hear appeals. A quorum constituted 'the venerable chamber of the treasury'. Each province, priory and commandery had its own chapter.[27]

Day-to-day routine was no less monastic than that of the Templars, the Little Office being said. The Psalms of the *Little Office of the Dead* clearly meant a good deal to warriors who were generally outnumbered, anticipating death as much as facing it. Thus Psalm 26, *Dominus illuminatio mea*: 'Whom shall I fear? The Lord is the protector of my life: Of whom shall I be afraid? . . . If armies in camp should stand together against me, my heart shall not fear. If a battle should rise up against me, in this will I be

38

T. III. p. 82.

2. A Hospitaller in his habit

confident.' Or Psalm 17, *Diligam te, Domine*: 'And thou hast girded me with strength unto battle: and hast subdued under me them that rose up against me. And thou hast made my enemies turn their back upon me; and thou hast destroyed them that hated me. They cried: but there was none to save them . . . And I shall beat them as small as the dust against the wind: I shall bring them to nought, like the dirt in the streets.' They were recited fervently by little squadrons riding out against overwhelming odds, by tiny garrisons besieged in undermanned fortresses.

Like non-military religious, brethren received the sacraments more frequently than layfolk – it was said that when they had received the Body of the Lord they fought like devils. Yet the Hospitallers' spiritual life was deepened by their devotion to the sick, for wherever they had estates they also had hospitals and guest-houses. Then, as now, accommodation was hard to find and pilgrims had cause to be grateful. Caravans were regularly escorted from the coast up to Jerusalem. Here there was a hospital with beds for 1,000 patients, for Syrian-born Franks as well as visitors were weakened by frequent ptomaine poisoning and plagues of insects, afflicted by sand-fly fever, ophthalmia, desert sores or endemic septicaemia. It has been suggested that the brethren's great hospitals were founded on Byzantine models, but their latest historian believes that the brethren owed more to Arab medicine.[28] Certainly they took the place of a field medical corps for, after a battle, besides the wounded there were always casualties suffering from terrible bruises beneath their chain mail, from shock or from heatstroke. This twofold vocation, to nurse and to fight, gave them an important role in the life of Latin Syria and, like the Templars, they were exempt from episcopal control.

As front-line troops, the brethren required a vast financial outlay. Equipment and supplies had to be purchased, strongholds maintained and revictualled. In consequence, many members of the Order had to live in Europe in order to run the estates given to them by pious benefactors and send the revenues out to Outremer. They were governed by priors and commanders, generally knights – more rarely chaplains or sergeants – who had been sent back from Palestine in middle life.

The rule of the Temple specifies that a knight who catches leprosy must leave the Order and join the brethren of 'St Ladre'.[29] Leprosy, which included all forms of skin disease, was prevalent in Syria. The Hospitallers of St Lazarus were the first military order to emerge after the Temple and the Hospital. Probably there had been a leper house of St Lazarus at Jerusalem before the conquest, run by Greek or Armenian religious who observed the Basilian rule, the Eastern equivalent of St Benedict's. Early in the twelfth century it was taken over by Frankish Hospitallers following the Augustinian rule.* A tradition that St Lazarus' first Master was that Gerard who was also first Master of St John could mean that he supplied brethren to found a specialized nursing order; the Hospitaller customs state that those who contract leprosy must lose the habit – like Templar lepers, these may well have joined 'St Ladre'. There is also a strange legend that the early Masters were always lepers. They administered a network of 'lazar houses' in both Syria and Europe, organized on a commandery framework similar to that of St John. After the Second Crusade, Louis VII established a house at Boigny, near Orléans, while Roger de Mowbray founded another at Burton Lazars in Leicestershire;[30] many leper hospitals in France and England depended on these commanderies, who in turn depended on the great house of the Order at Jerusalem. This had itself been richly endowed, and Raymond III of Tripoli was a confrater of the brotherhood. Probably the habit was black and resembled that of the Hospitallers; its green cross was not adopted until the sixteenth century. The Lazar Knights were never numerous and had only a handful of non-leper brethren for protection, though no doubt in times of crisis unclean knights also took up arms.

* Professor Riley-Smith believes that the tradition of a Basilian rule may stem from the fact that a considerable number of the Order's first brethren were Greek-rite Italians – many names from southern Italy are found witnessing the earliest known charters of St Lazarus.

This always remained primarily a hospitaller order even if it took part in several battles.

The only other fighting brotherhood in twelfth-century Outremer was the Knights of Our Lady of Montjoie.[31] A bull of Alexander III of 1180 recognized them as an order who followed the Cistercian rule and who, besides ransoming captives, took an oath to fight Saracens, a quarter of their revenues being set aside for this purpose. Montjoie was a hill castle outside Jerusalem which took its name from the pilgrims' cries of joy when they saw the Heavenly City from its summit. The actual founder was a Spaniard, Count Rodrigo, a former knight of Santiago, who gave the new brethren lands in Castile and Aragon, while King Baldwin IV entrusted them with several towers at Ascalon. Their habit was white with a red-and-white cross. Rodrigo himself, an unstable character, was the first Master, and the Order did not prosper. It had difficulty in attracting recruits, as most Spaniards preferred to join their great national orders. After 1187 the remnants retired to Aragon, where they became known as the Order of Trufac, their Castilian commanderies being appropriated by the Templars.

3

THE BULWARK OF JERUSALEM

The county of Edessa was the most exposed of the Frankish territories, lying on both sides of the Euphrates, a Mesopotamian march rather than a Syrian state. Despite its rich cornland it had few castles, being scantily furnished with the indispensable Frankish knights. Everything depended on the count. Joscelin I was a brilliant captain of heroic character whose very presence warded off raiders. However, his half-Armenian son, who succeeded him in 1129, was cowardly and irresolute. Joscelin II preferred to live in the pleasant castle of Turbessel on the west bank of the Euphrates rather than in his perilous capital, whose protection he left to a sort of town guard recruited from the Armenian and Syrian merchants. Suddenly, in November 1144, the 'blue-eyed devil' of Aleppo, the terrible atabeg Zengi, laid siege to Edessa and stormed it on the day before Christmas Eve.

Western Christendom was appalled. Bernard of Clairvaux used his last energies to preach the Second Crusade, and by the autumn of 1147 two armies had reached Anatolia, one led by the Emperor Conrad III, the other by Louis VII of France. In October the Germans were cut to pieces in a Turkish ambush at Dorylaeum and they fled to Nicaea, where the French joined them. Conrad fell ill and returned to Constantinople, but Louis continued through Anatolia, relentlessly harried by the Turkish bowmen. By January, lashed by winter storms and short of food, his men's morale had collapsed. After a particularly murderous attack in which Queen Eleanor was almost captured and Louis nearly killed, the king lost all confidence in his powers of generalship and handed over the command to the Templar Master.

Everard des Barres was an ideal Poor Knight, half fervent

religious, half skilled soldier. He had joined Louis in France with a detachment of 300 Spanish Templars, many of whom had probably joined the Order only for the duration of the crusade, which they were allowed to do on payment of a premium. For the first time Templars wore the red cross on their mantles. The king was impressed both by Everard's diplomatic skill in dealing with the Byzantines, and by his brethren, who alone retained their discipline. The Master restored order, bringing the battered army through to the coast, where Louis took ship with his cavalry, leaving the infantry to struggle on.

Though thousands had perished, Conrad rejoined his men, and the joint army – French, German and Syrian – assembled at Acre in June 1148. Raymond du Puy was summoned to the council of war, an acknowledgement of his brethren's military importance. A disastrous decision was taken, to attack the emir Unur of Damascus, the one Saracen prince anxious for a Frankish alliance, an error which eventually led to the unification of Moslem Syria. The attempt failed amid mutual recriminations; crusaders considered the barons of Outremer, the *poulains*, to be half-Turk, while Latin Syrians regarded their northern cousins as dangerous, unwashed fanatics. By 1149 the Second Crusade had petered out, having done irreparable harm to Frankish prestige.

The survival of Jerusalem was largely thanks to the ability of Baldwin III (1143–62) and his choleric brother, Amalric I (1162–74). Syrian-born, with Armenian blood and married to Byzantine princesses, they were fully alive to their native land's growing danger. Energetic warriors, they hoped to extend their territory. Already Frankish castles had been built on the Gulf of Aqaba across the caravan-route from Baghdad to Cairo. King Baldwin's capture of Ascalon in 1153 was the occasion of a peculiarly unedifying display by the Templar Master, Bernard de Tremelay. The detachment of 'the avenger who is in the service of Christ, the liberator of Christian people' had breached the city wall, whereupon Fra' Bernard, posting guards to prevent other Franks entering, went in with forty hand-picked brethren. They were killed to a man, but the Master's rashness was attributed to greed rather than gallantry.[1] On the other hand the king's decision to persevere with the siege was due to Raymond du Puy's persuasion. The Hospitallers were becoming soldiers too.

Together the brethren could now put nearly 600 knights into the field, half the total muster of the kingdom, while their possessions accumulated steadily. Count Raymond II (1137–52) of Tripoli was a Hospitaller confrater and in 1142 he entrusted his brothers-in-religion with the key position of his county, the enormous fortress of Qalat al-Hosen, which they rebuilt as Krak-des-Chevaliers. Raymond III (1152–87) was also a confrater of the Hospitallers and during his long captivity they acquired the strongholds of Arka, Akkar and many others. With these they were the greatest landowners in the county, though rivalled by the Templars, who had large possessions in the north. In Antioch there was a similar division of territory, while many castles in the kingdom itself were handed over to them. Their constitutional role grew accordingly, both Masters sitting as members of the Haute Cour, the commanders of Antioch and Tripoli doing likewise in their local courts. The three keys of the royal treasury, in which was deposited the crown, were entrusted to the patriarch and to the Masters of the Temple and the Hospital, an apt symbol of their power. The princes continued to endow them with fiefs. Many lords preferred to retire to some luxurious villa on the coast, while the brethren had the money and men to run the Syrian fortresses and besides dealing with such problems as finding husbands for heiresses or furnishing wards with guardians. Donations and recruits poured in from Europe in a steady flow.

Their chief critics were the local clergy. These military orders were almost a church within a church, whose priests were not only exempt from diocesan visitations but also from any financial obligation. Brethren wrangled with bishops over dues, tithes and jurisdictions and were accused of admitting excommunicated men to their services. When in 1154 the Patriarch of Jerusalem ordered them to desist, the Hospitallers interrupted his sermons, shouting him down and shooting arrows at his congregation. Templars contented themselves with merely shooting at his church door. In 1155 the patriarch travelled to Rome to ask the pope to place the military brethren under his authority, but Fra' Raymond followed him, obtaining a confirmation of all Hospitaller privileges. Reluctantly the clergy of Outremer accepted the brethren's independence, but their chroniclers always gave them a bad press.

The brethren were remarkably adaptable, turning their hands to many skills. Some learnt Arabic (great officers kept Saracen secretaries) and the brothers' spy service was unparalleled. They had to fill such institutional vacuums as banking, for only they possessed the necessary vaults, organization and integrity. The Templars became professional financiers; all moneys collected for the Holy Land were conveyed by them from their European preceptories to the temple at Jerusalem, while pilgrims and even Moslem merchants deposited their cash at the local temple. Brethren needed money for arms and equipment, to build fortresses, to hire mercenaries and to buy off enemies, so the funds in their strongrooms could not be allowed to lie idle; the Church's embargo on usury was circumvented by adding the interest to the sum due for repayment, and Arab specialists were employed for dealings in the money markets of Baghdad and Cairo, while an excellent service of bills of exchange was provided. In many ways the military brethren foreshadowed the great Italian banking houses.

Both Templars and Hospitallers found it cheaper to transport troops in their own ships, and passages were available to pilgrims; at one time the Templars conveyed 6,000 pilgrims each year.[2] Their boats were popular, for they maintained a flotilla of escort ships and could be trusted not to sell their passengers into slavery at Moslem ports, as did certain Italian merchants. It was natural to use empty space for merchandise so they exported spices, silk dyes, porcelain and glass, taking full advantage of their exemption from customs dues, and they soon rivalled the Levantine traders who banked with them.

Such activities hardly harmonize with the name of 'Poor Knights'. As Jacques de Vitry pointed out, the Templars owned

3. The head of St John the Baptist adapted from the seal of a thirteenth-century Hospitaller Prior of England

no individual property, but in common they seemed anxious to possess everything. Nevertheless their life was as ascetic as ever. Certainly by this time purely contemplative orders were no strangers to high finance; Cistercian techniques of agriculture brought great wealth to the white monks – the entire wool crop of many English abbeys was often sold for years ahead. Although rivalry over revenues made for little love between Poor Knights and Knights of St John, yet none the less both would unite in times of real danger.

In 1154 the young Fatimid caliph was murdered by his homosexual favourite, Nasr, who fled to Syria and was captured by the Templars. To save his skin he asked for instruction in the Christian faith. He did not deceive the unsympathetic brethren. They accepted Cairo's offer of 60,000 dinars for him, and Nasr was taken home by the Egyptians in an iron cage, to be first horribly mutilated by the caliph's four widows and then, still living, crucified at the Zawila Gate, where his rotting corpse hung for two years. At least one contemporary chronicler appears to have been disturbed by the brothers' business acumen.

Certainly one Armenian joined the brethren as a knight and probably many more were admitted to the sergeant class (which also numbered Christian Arabs). The Templars had an unfortunate experience with Fra' Mleh, a member of the Cilician ruling family, 'hom pleins de grant malice et trop desleaus'. After taking vows as a Poor Knight he attempted to murder his brother, Prince Thoros, then fled to Damascus where he turned Moslem. In 1170 he came back with Turkish troops to conquer Cilicia, after attacking the Templar stronghold at Baghras. 'Ce desloial Hermin' cherished a venomous hatred for his former co-religionists and treated Templar prisoners with particular cruelty. At last, outraged by their prince's apostasy, his own people killed him.[3]

Fra' Raymond died in 1158. He was succeeded as Master of the Hospital by Fra' Gilbert d'Assailly. Until 1168 King Amalric's Egyptian policy had been a realistic one of alliance with the viziers of the Shia caliph against the Sunni Nur ed-Din who now ruled Aleppo and Damascus. However, it was clear that the Fatimid regime was near its end and Amalric negotiated an alliance with the Emperor Manuel; the Byzantines would attack by sea while the whole muster of Jerusalem struck overland. Success depended on the co-operation of the emperor, who was busy campaigning in Serbia. Amalric was prepared to wait, but Fra' Gilbert intervened with an offer of 500 knights and 500 Turcopoles, in return for the town of Bilbeis.[4] At this the barons refused to wait any longer before enjoying the fabulous riches of Cairo. Fra' Bertrand de Blanquefort, the Templar Master, refused to support the expedition; there was not sufficient manpower to wage a campaign and at the same time cope with the counter-attack which was certain to come from the north-east.

The Franks captured Bilbeis, but the troops got out of hand and a massacre, including the local Christians, took place. The Egyptians were panic-stricken and the caliph himself wrote to Nur ed-Din for help, whereupon the atabeg sent his Kurdish general Shirkuh with 8,000 horsemen; they by-passed Amalric and entered Cairo. Shirkuh was proclaimed vizier but soon afterwards ate himself to death and was succeeded by his nephew, Salah ad-Din Yusuf ibn Ayub, better known as Saladin. Within two years the last Fatimid caliph was dead and Shia Egypt had returned to the Sunni fold; the Frankish protectorate was replaced by a Cairo–Aleppo axis, the most formidable coalition yet to threaten Outremer.

The Hospital was nearly bankrupt as it had staked all available funds on a successful outcome. Fra' Gilbert was not noted for stability, and the failure of his gamble unbalanced him. He appears to have had a nervous breakdown in the summer of 1170, when he retired to a cave in the Hauran to become a hermit. Eventually he was coaxed out but, despite the General Chapter's pleas, abdicated; later he was drowned while crossing the English Channel. The Hospitallers had suffered a grievous setback and it took them years to recover their losses in money and manpower.

In 1173 'the new Machabees', as the English pope Adrian IV called the Templars, had a fierce quarrel with the king over the Assassins. These *Hasishiyun*, 'eaters of Hashish', were an extremist sect of the Shias, whose founder had placed an excessive emphasis on the doctrine of Jihad – that paradise was the reward for death in combat against unbelievers. Their weapon was the poisoned knife, flat cakes their trade mark, and they terrorized Moslems and Christians alike. The sect's organization had a superficial resemblance to the brethren's. They had several 'eagle's nests' in the Nosairi mountains of the Lebanon, whose governor was called the Sheikh al-Gebel, the Old Man of the Mountains. In 1173 this was Rashid ed-Din Sinan, who was much alarmed by the recent extinction of the Fatimid caliphate. Suddenly he sent an embassy to King Amalric, announcing his imminent conversion to Christianity and asking to be relieved of the tribute imposed by the Templars. The king knew just how much belief to place in Rashid's conversion, but peace in the Nosairi and the use of the Assassin intelligence network were worth having. He remitted the tribute, announcing that his own ambassadors would visit the Sheikh. As the Assassin envoys were returning home they were ambushed by some Templars, under the one-eyed Fra' Gautier de Mesnil, and decapitated. Amalric was so furious that to his courtiers he appeared to be out of his senses.[5] He had had trouble from Templars before, hanging ten for surrendering a castle without permission. He ordered the Master, Eudes de St Amand, to hand over the culprit. Fra' Eudes refused but offered to send the erring brother to Rome – the pope alone could try the case. However, Amalric burst into the Master's quarters and seized Gautier, whom he flung into prison.

Next year Nur ed-Din died. Saladin now ruled Damascus as well as Cairo and was proclaimed King of Egypt and Syria in 1176, with the Caliph of Baghdad's official blessing. A Kurdish adventurer who hacked his way to the throne, once there he became a Moslem St Louis, something of a mystic, an ascetic who fasted, slept on a rough mat and gave alms unceasingly – in Gibbon's amusing phrase, 'while he emulated the temperance he surpassed the chastity of his Arabian prophet'.[6] His ambition was to restore the unity of Sunni Islam, which would include a Jihad against the Franks. Nevertheless, with his sensitive, inquiring mind he saw that there was much good in Christianity, even if it lacked the Third Revelation, and he was intrigued by the Frankish code of chivalry. The Franks had a deep respect for his bravery and magnanimity; there was even a legend that in his youth he had been knighted by the constable of Jerusalem.

Amalric died in the same year, succeeded by perhaps the most gallant figure of the whole Frankish venture, the leper king, Baldwin IV (1174–85), who inherited the throne at thirteen, a year after his leprosy had been discovered. He literally dropped to pieces during his reign, a *via dolorosa* on which he showed, with moving courage, political realism and remarkable powers of leadership.

Outremer's strategic position was deteriorating rapidly. In 1176 the Seldjuk Sultan of Iconium wiped out the army of Emperor Manuel at Myriocephalum; Byzantium, finished as a military power, would never again intervene in Syria. Lesser Armenia was growing at the expense of Antioch, unedifyingly ready to ally with Moslem neighbours. Worse, however, was the kingdom's encirclement. Saladin would take Aleppo in 1183 and was steadily consolidating his empire.

In November 1177 Saladin led the whole of his army, 26,000 Turks, Kurds, Arabs, Sudanese and Mamelukes, in a raid on the plain between Ramleh and Ascalon. Blockading the leper king in Ascalon with a small garrison, he marched on Jerusalem. Baldwin broke out with 300 Knights and, joined by Eudes de St Amand with eighty Templars, circled Saladin by hard riding. The little force caught him off his guard in the ravine of Montgisard and, with the leprous youth and the Bishop of Acre carrying the True Cross at their head, the heavy Frankish horsemen smashed into the Egyptian army. It was a bloodbath, and Saladin and his troops fled into the Sinai desert, where they all but perished of thirst.

Next time Baldwin was not so lucky. On the morning of 10 June 1179 the king ambushed a raiding party, commanded by Saladin's nephew, at Marj Ayun. Resting, he himself was surprised some hours later by Saladin's entire army and was routed with heavy losses. The Templars charged too soon and Fra' Eudes was taken prisoner but, in accordance with his Order's rule, refused to be ransomed. William of Tyre abuses the fire-breathing Master, '*homo nequam superbus et arrogans*', '*fel et orgueilleus*',[7] but Eudes was a man of principle and died in prison the year after, probably from starvation.

The sinister Gerard de Ridefort became Master of the Temple in 1185. A penniless noble from Flanders, he had taken service with Raymond III on condition that he be given the hand of the heiress of Botrun. Raymond did not keep his promise and the embittered Gerard joined the Templars. His driving ambition and aggressive self-confidence soon took him to the top, but he embodied all his Order's worst faults. A Master had to live with princes, and an impressive household pandered to Gerard's pathological pride; his personal staff included bodyguards and Arab secretaries, with two great officers always in attendance.[8] It is interesting to compare Fra' Gerard with one of the companions of St Francis, Fra' Elias, Master General of the Franciscans, whose head was so turned by power that he would appear in public only on horseback. One may condemn Gerard without condemning his brethren.

One of the two co-heiresses of Baldwin who died in 1185 was his sister, Sibylla, married to Guy de Lusignan, a brainless adventurer gifted with good looks. When the child king, Baldwin V, died in 1185 many in Outremer hoped to enthrone Sibylla's younger sister, Isabella, who would leave affairs of state to the one man capable of saving the kingdom, the Regent Raymond III of Tripoli. However, an unscrupulous faction, including the patriarch and the vindictive Master of the Temple, rallied to Guy. Fra' Gerard extorted the third key of the royal treasury from the Hospitaller Master, Roger des Moulins, who flung it from his window but would have nothing to do with the coronation. Guy was crowned king, guarded by a phalanx of Poor Knights, whose Master commented 'ceste corone vaut bien le mariage dou Botron'.

Early in 1187 the Lord of Outrejourdain, Reynald de Chatillon, rode out from his desert stronghold, Krak-en-Moab, to slaughter a Damascene caravan with which the sultan's sister was travelling and which thought itself protected by the truce. Reynald was an archetypal robber-baron, a murderous throwback to the northern progenitors of the French aristocracy. His most lunatic exploit took place in 1182, when he transported ships, piece by piece, over the desert to the Red Sea and raided the pilgrims on their way to Mecca, earning the Franks the hatred of the whole Moslem world. Insanely brave and totally unscrupulous, he had much in common with Fra' Gerard. Outremer's affairs were exposed to the meddling of two irresponsible berserks at a time when the kingdom desperately needed wise and cautious leadership.

In May a raiding party of 7,000 Moslem cavalry was tackled at the Springs of Cresson near Nazareth by 150 Knights, comprising Fra' Gerard, 90 Templars, 40 secular knights, and the Master of the Hospital, Roger des Moulins, with his Marshal Jacques de Mailly and their escort. Ridefort taunted Fra' Jacques: 'Vos amez trop cele teste blonde'.[9] A Moslem eye-witness records how even the blackest head of hair went white with fright as the Frankish horsemen hurtled towards them. But the odds were too great. Fra' Roger went down, riddled with arrows, and only Fra' Gerard escaped with two brethren, all three badly wounded. It had been his decision to charge. He was a typical medieval man who believed in trial by battle – God always gave the victory to Christians unless they displeased Him, just as He had done with the people of Israel.

On 1 July 1187 Saladin crossed the Jordan with an army of 60,000 men. The whole muster of Outremer assembled, 1,200 knights and perhaps 20,000 sergeants, Turcopoles and foot soldiers. Of the knights about 300 belonged to the Temple, 250 to the Hospital. There was also a small detachment of the brethren of Montjoie, and possibly another from St Lazarus. Prince Bohemond III of Antioch sent his son with 50 knights. No more than 600 could have been provided by the kingdom, this being the total 'knight-service'. They were better equipped than the men of the First Crusade. Chain stockings and a mail shirt were worn in place of the long hauberk. The shield was smaller, and sometimes the helmet was flat-topped like a saucepan, with a grille to guard the face, though not yet the great barrel helm of the next century. Lay knights wore a keffiyeh and a surcoat, while the brethren had their white, brown and black cloaks. This was not an alien expeditionary force, but an army of *poulains* marching out to defend their homeland. Many brethren and most secular knights and sergeants had been born there; some were of mixed blood, Syrian and Armenian, or even pure Arabs. *Colons* and natives were united by their Christian faith and common peril.

Instead of trusting Count Raymond's experienced judgement, Guy relied on those two berserks, Reynald de Chatillon and Fra' Gerard. Saladin had captured Tiberias and was besieging Raymond's wife in the castle, but the count advised Guy to wait at

Saffaria where there was water. Gerard persuaded the king to change his mind, coming to the royal tent 'quant ce vint la nuit'[10] and telling Guy that Raymond was a traitor, that he would be disgraced before God and his subjects if he did not recapture Tiberias. Guy succumbed to the fanatic and gave the order to march. Friday, 3 July, was the hottest day of an unnaturally hot summer. After a grim trek through waterless desert, the Frankish army pitched camp on a hill called the Horns of Hattin. Its well was dry. Saladin could hardly believe his eyes, but gave thanks to Allah, while his troops encircled the hill. The Christians spent a terrible night without water, awaiting death.

At dawn the Moslems set fire to the scrub. Flames and smoke swept up the slopes, maddening men and horses tortured by thirst. The infantry soon broke and were slaughtered by the thousand, but the horsemen fought on in the appalling heat. After many charges over impossible ground and having beaten back attack after attack under a hail of arrows, King Guy's force was reduced to 150 dismounted knights, and surrendered. The Moslems captured the True Cross in its gold reliquary.[11] Saladin was merciful, treating the king with kindness. Most prisoners were spared, but there were two exceptions. Reynald de Chatillon, the harrier of pilgrims, was struck down by Saladin himself. At his express orders every Templar and Hospitaller was beheaded. He had them killed, explains the Arab chronicler Ibn al-Athir, 'because they were the fiercest of all the Frankish warriors'.

While the male population of Frankish Syria was driven off to the slave-markets of Damascus, Saladin proceeded to occupy their towns. Jerusalem had one man for every fifty women and children but, by putting up a gallant defence, was allowed to ransom a large proportion of its citizens, in humane contrast with the Christian sack of 1099. The Hospitaller and Templar financial officials were scandalously parsimonious, as there was not a single knight to take responsibility. However, Saladin let the penniless go free. Acre surrendered on the same conditions; within a month, apart from a few castles, only Antioch, Tripoli and Tyre resisted. A contemporary chronicler attributed the disaster of Hattin to the filth, luxury and adultery of Jerusalem; but, whatever the cause, Christendom had lost the 'City of the King of Kings' and with it the Temple and the Hospital.

Reduced to Tripoli, Tortosa, Antioch and Tyre, the kingdom at first seemed doomed. The conviction that God had deserted him could produce a sudden, staggering demoralization in medieval man, and Count Raymond died of a broken heart. However, Saladin concentrated on the few remaining strongholds inland which cut his supply lines. The brethren realized that resistance would help the coastal towns. In January 1188 the Hospitallers of Belvoir in Galilee cut to pieces a besieging army. For a whole year the Moslems invested Belvoir as well as the Templars at Safed, battering the two castles with rock-throwing mangonels and trebuchets, ceaselessly mining and mounting assault after assault. The winter's drenching rain and mud nearly defeated the besiegers, but at last, in December 1188, Safed surrendered, followed by Belvoir in January 1189. The sultan spent June 1188 before Krak-des-Chevaliers, but the Hospitallers were not easily frightened. He then invested Tortosa, where he was beaten off by the Templar garrison. Marqab, the Hospitallers' coastal stronghold, he left in peace. His caution was due to the arrival of 200 knights from Sicily, who relieved Krak at the end of July. In September, at Darbessaq, the Templars astonished the Moslems by standing motionless and silent in the breach. The castle resisted for a fortnight and then with Prince Bohemond's permission capitulated, as did Baghras, another Templar stronghold. Their garrisons retired to Antioch. These campaigns deflected Saladin from the reduction of Tyre, the centre of Christian resistance.

In July 1188 the sultan released King Guy, who swore he would never again bear arms against Islam, and shortly afterwards Fra' Gerard was allowed to ransom himself, a flagrant breach of the Templar rule. The Master found many brethren at Tyre, as well as Hospitallers who had come in haste from Europe. Then, in April 1189, a fleet arrived from Pisa with further reinforcements. The following August, Guy suddenly laid siege to Acre, whose garrison outnumbered his troops by three to one. Perhaps one may detect Gerard's baneful counsel in breaking the oath sworn to Saladin; sworn to an infidel under duress, it had no validity. The long siege of Acre has been compared to the siege of Troy but was the beginning of the Frankish recovery.

Saladin invested Guy's camp, and the besiegers found themselves besieged. Yet all the time reinforcements were arriving by sea – small parties of French, German and Danish crusaders. On 4 October Guy attacked Saladin for the first time since Hattin. It was a savage battle, though honours were even. Fra' Gerard, who commanded the advance guard, refused to leave the field and was taken prisoner. He was executed immediately on Saladin's express orders. Crusaders continued to arrive, including a contingent of Londoners, while since May 1189 Frederick Barbarossa had been marching to the Holy Land with 100,000 men. In 1190, however, while fording a river in Seleucia the old emperor was drowned and the German army disintegrated – not more than 1,000 reached Acre. The siege dragged on; the Franks could not take Acre, but nor could the Moslems dislodge them. Famine and plague broke out. By the spring of 1191 the crusaders were desperate.

On 20 April 1191 the fleet of Philip Augustus of France anchored off Acre, bringing food, men and siege engines. The Third Crusade had finally materialized. King Philip postponed an assault until the arrival of Richard I of England on 7 June and contented himself with concentrating a heavy bombardment on the Tour Maudite, Acre's principal bastion; both Templars and Hospitallers had their own mangonel. After recklessly overtaxing his subjects, Richard had made countless enemies during a leisurely journey, in the course of which he paused to conquer Cyprus, then a Byzantine island ruled by a rebel emperor. Yet in the Holy Land he became 'Richard Cœur de Lion', the hero that he is in Grétry's opera and Scott's novel. The 'Accursed Tower' crumbled. A series of ferocious assaults culminated in a particularly savage attack by the English on 11 July which broke the garrison's spirit; the next day Acre surrendered after negotiations conducted by the Hospitallers.

The French king installed himself in the Temple – upon which the brethren broke into vociferous complaints, led by their new Master, Frà' Robert de Sablé from Maine, who had been elected with Richard's support. The king soon moved out, a humiliating concession which shows the power of the brethren. At the end of July, Philip sailed for France, leaving Richard in undisputed command.

Saladin asked the Templars for their word that the prisoners would not be harmed but, knowing Richard's brutal, unreliable temperament, they refused it. On 20 August Richard ordered his English troops to butcher nearly 3,000 men, women and children. Two days later he marched on Ascalon down the coast road with the sea covering one flank, the Hospitallers for his advance guard and the Templars covering his rear. Later they changed places. Because of dense papyrus swamps the column was forced to turn inland, on to the plain before Arsuf.

Saturday, 7 September 1191, was a day of sweltering heat. The Moslems began a terrifying din: drums rolling, cymbals clashing, trumpets braying and dervishes howling. Horses began to fall beneath the arrow storm, but Richard was determined to wait until he could charge on as broad a front as possible. The Hospitaller Master, Fra' Garnier de Nablus, a former prior of England, whose knights were on the left, told him that they could not be kept back much longer; but Richard ordered them to hold, and they held. As the rearguard, the Hospitallers had suffered most of all. The order's Marshal could not restrain himself. The whole Frankish cavalry galloped with him. The Turkish squadrons disintegrated. For the Christians it was a victory of some significance; the sins which brought about the judgement of Hattin were forgiven and once more God was on their side.

The sultan started to evacuate coastal towns. Unfortunately, instead of marching on Jerusalem, Richard delayed to re-fortify Jaffa. In November he set out for the Holy City. By January he was only twelve miles away, but the winter rains were unusually heavy and Saladin's army was behind him, so Richard withdrew to Ascalon on the advice of the brethren and the *poulains*, a wise if melancholy decision. At the Templars' suggestion he set about re-fortifying Ascalon. The first months of 1192 were spent in deciding the future of the crown of Jerusalem. Queen Sibylla had died childless in October 1190 and the Syrian baronage was anxious to be rid of her lamentable husband. Her younger sister, Isabella, had her marriage to the weak Humphrey de Toron forcibly annulled and, protesting, she was married to Conrad of Montfer-rat in November. In July 1191 Guy, supported by Richard as a Poitevin, had won the right to keep the crown. Now the English king knew him better, and in April 1192 Richard summoned the Syrian magnates to a council. Unanimously they chose Conrad for their king. However, a week later Conrad was struck down by the Assassins. Within another week Isabella was married to Richard's nephew, Henry, Count of Champagne, young, able and popular, who was crowned in place of Conrad.

There remained the problem of the ex-king. On his way to Palestine, Richard had sold Cyprus to the Templars. They soon upset the islanders by their arrogant administration. In April 1192 there was a fierce uprising and the Templar commander, Fra' Armand Bouchart, fourteen brethren and a hundred troops survived only by taking refuge in the citadel of Nicosia. A few days later, Fra' Armand launched a lethal counter-attack which was successful, but the Templars returned the island to Richard. He sold it to Guy, who borrowed the necessary down-payment from the merchants of Tripoli, then left the Holy Land for ever.

In September Richard made a treaty with Saladin: peace for five years and the Franks to keep the coastal towns from Tyre to Jaffa. The Third Crusade had failed to attach Jerusalem to the narrow strip of land, ninety miles long and never more than ten miles wide, which was the new Outremer, a string of coastal towns. In October 1192 Richard left Palestine. The next year Saladin died the death of a saint at Damascus and his sword was buried with him, for, as the Prophet said: 'Paradise lies under the shadow of swords.' The Moslem counter-crusade slackened.

His heirs, the Ayubites, were busy disputing his inheritance and Outremer settled down under King Henry's capable government. The Temple of Solomon and the Hospital were lost with Jerusalem, so the brethren moved their chief houses to Acre.

In September 1197 Henry fell from a window fatally, and the wretched Isabella was married for a fourth time, to Amalric de Lusignan, Guy's youngest brother. Amalric had inherited Cyprus in 1194 on Guy's death and had recently been given a crown by the Emperor Henry VI. Amalric took up residence at Acre, a good friend of the orders: they had intervened on his behalf when he quarrelled with King Henry. At the same time, Amalric built a kingdom in Cyprus which endured for three centuries.

Lusignan Cyprus resembled Outremer in that it was ruled by a French-speaking king and had an aristocracy with an Italian merchant class. Castles and churches were built in the French style and the new Cypriot culture was Latin and feudal, Roman clergy being installed and Orthodoxy persecuted. Both Hospitallers and Templars founded commanderies, the most notable being at Kolossi whence the sweet St John wine still comes. However, the brethren never obtained the power they had in Syria, for the king was stronger and his thirteen barons weaker than in Jerusalem. Cyprus was a beautiful country and free from border warfare, yet ultimately it ruined Outremer. Settlers preferred its fertile soil, its lemon and orange groves and gentler climate, to the stones, heat and danger of Palestine, while the possession of Cypriot manors by the Syrian baronage lessened their stake in Jerusalem's survival.

The one important event in Amalric's reign was the abortive German crusade of 1197. Its sole achievement was to found the third great military order, the Teutonic Knights, in 1198; they were installed in the St Nicholas Gate at Acre. As the new brotherhood developed in the Baltic rather than in Palestine, its rise is dealt with in another chapter.*

* See Chapter 5, 'The Crusade on the Baltic'.

About this time another order was emerging, the Hospitallers of St Thomas of Canterbury at Acre, usually called Knights of St Thomas Acon. During the siege of Acre, William, chaplain to the Dean of St Paul's, moved by the English crusaders' misery, began nursing the sick and wounded. After the city's capture, aided by King Richard, he built a small chapel and purchased a cemetery, founding a hospital and a nursing brotherhood restricted to Englishmen.[12] Probably they did not turn military until the Fifth Crusade.

In 1229 the Bishop of Winchester ordered them to copy the rule of the Teutonic Knights. The habit was a white mantle and red cross, which had a white scallop shell on it. The new order acquired lands in Cyprus, Sicily, Naples and, later, Greece, while in England its headquarters was the Hospital of St Thomas Acon in London, on the site of what is now the Mercers' Hall.

The original house was the actual birthplace of Thomas Becket and had been presented to the brethren by his sister and brother-in-law. The brethren of St Thomas were always a small brotherhood, most Englishmen preferring to join the Hospitallers or the Templars.

The principality of the tough Cilician highlanders was expanding, and their ruler, Lavon II, had nearly succeeded in capturing Antioch with its half-Armenian baronage. Lavon had occupied the Templar castle of Baghras, which commanded the road from Antioch into Cilicia, after Saladin had evicted the brethren. He did not return it to the Poor Knights, who seem to have taken a very unecumenical attitude towards Eastern Christians in general and had unpleasant memories of Prince Mleh. Lavon then tried peaceful means, marrying his niece to Bohemond III's son, Raymond, to procure an eventual merger of the two principalities. He appreciated the advantages of both papal and imperial support. Something of a shotgun marriage was arranged and the Monophysite Armenian Church recognized the nominal supremacy of the pope's jurisdiction with little enthusiasm. The union was never very effective, though the Armenian bishops took to Western mitres and croziers, but in January 1198 at Sis, in the presence of a papal legate, the Jacobite patriarch and an Orthodox archbishop, Lavon was crowned King of Armenia by the Catholicos from Etchmiadzin. The Western coronation rite was used. Frankish influence grew stronger and the 'sparapet' became a 'cunstabl', the 'nakharar' a 'baron'. There was more intermarriage, and in old age Lavon himself married Amalric's daughter, Sibylla de Lusignan.

On the death of Bohemond III in 1201 the Templars and their new Master, Philippe du Plaissiez, opposed the succession of his baby grandson, Raymond-Ruben, whilst supporting his younger son, Bohemond of Tripoli. They would not tolerate an Armenian regency. In the ensuing war against Lavon the brethren were joined not only by the Antiochenes but also by Malik az-Zahir of Aleppo. However, the latter soon made peace after being badly mauled by the fierce Haiots. Then it was the turn of the Templars, a war of night raids followed by dawn pursuits in the hills along stony mountain paths, and of ambushes in the steep valleys of the Taurus. The struggle lasted for nearly twenty years, the Hospitallers supporting Raymond-Ruben, the Templars Bohemond. They were also fighting each other, and Innocent III reprimanded the Templar Master, saying that his Order's job was to fight Moslems, not Hospitallers.

The Armenians trusted the brethren of St John and gave them Selefke, the key fortress of Eastern Cilicia, from where they launched frequent razzias into Moslem territory, probably assisted by Teutonic Knights; it was no doubt on one of these that the Hochmeister Hermann Bart was killed in 1210. The Germans' presence exacerbated their feud with the Templars, who disputed their right to wear the white habit, chasing them out of Acre. The same year the Poor Knights allied with Malik of Aleppo and Kaikawas of Konya. Brethren and Turks rode together into Cilicia, where they captured the mountain stronghold of Partounk and even threatened Sis, the capital. Lavon was horrified and made peace, returning Baghras to the Templars, a triumph for their ruthless diplomacy. In 1213 Prince Bohemond's son,

Raymond, was stabbed to death by Assassins at Tortosa and the next year the patriarch of Jerusalem met the same fate. As he had been a loud critic of the Hospitallers, and the Assassins paid them tribute, some contemporaries suspected their connivance. At last, in 1216, Raymond-Ruben captured Antioch and its citadel from the Templars, installing a Hospitaller garrison under Ferrand de Barras, the castellan of Selefke, and handed over Jabala to Fra' Joubert, castellan of Marqab. But in 1219 the Antiochenes rose and brought back Bohemond, who confiscated all Hospitaller possessions. The Order appealed to Rome in vain, though the pope did succeed in reconciling Hospitallers and Templars in 1221. The latter were no longer active in Armenian politics, since their old enemy, King Lavon, had died and Raymond-Ruben had been murdered. Not until 1231 did Bohemond make peace with the Hospitallers.

King Lavon had left a daughter, Zabel, by Sibylla de Lusignan, and in 1222 the *cunstabl*, Constantine of Lampron, married her to Bohemond IV's younger son, Philip, who joined the Armenian Church, then out of communion with Rome. Nevertheless, the Hospitallers continued to support him. The new king behaved with such arrogance that he was murdered in 1226, Zabel being forcibly married to Constantine's son Hethoum. When the sixteen-year-old queen fled by night from Sis to the Hospitallers at Selefke, pursued by the regent, the castellan Fra' Bertrand sold both fortress and fugitive to Constantine, a cynical if practical decision. Later this Order supplied Armenia with an annual tribute of 400 horsemen while both Constantine and Hethoum became Hospitaller *confratres*. Happily Hethoum proved a kind husband and a great king, who reconciled his Church with Rome and followed a policy of alliance with Antioch. Firm government put an end to the brethren's intrigues.

The long struggle had shown them at their worst. Nevertheless one must see them as monks with a genuine sense of spiritual brotherhood, albeit monks living in barrack-room cloisters. They obeyed their Masters just as monks do an abbot and the good of their Order came before everything else. Their 'caravan priests' must have had considerable influence as spiritual directors — ideologists who decided difficult points of Christian dialectic, campaigning with the brethren rather like the commissars who rode with the Red cavalry in the Russian Civil War. Only they could hear the brother-knights' confessions.

They were not without writers — the fact that they were not intellectuals and could not read Latin did not mean that brother-knights were illiterate. The Templars produced several poets, *troubadors* and *trouveurs*, including one Grand Master, Fra' Robert de Sablé. Towards 1180 'the Templar of Temple Bruer' (a preceptory near Sleaford in Lincolnshire) was writing Norman French verse translations of 'Thais', and of Latin poems on Anti-Christ and on St Paul's descent into Hell; one is dedicated to his superior, 'Henri d'Arci, frère del Temple Salemun'. This unknown English poet of the Order also produced a prose translation of the 'Vitae Patrum'.[13] Such austere and didactic literature was obviously considered suitable for brother-knights. Undoubtedly their best mind was a Hospitaller, Guglielmo di San Stefano, who wrote a scholarly but brief history of his Order besides legal treatises which show considerable knowledge of the Nicomachean Ethics and of Roman law. In 1286 he commissioned a clerk at Acre to translate Cicero into French. It is significant that Fra' Guglielmo was not a chaplain but a brother-knight.[14] However, such men were probably exceptions rather than the rule; some clerical contemporaries sneered at the military brethren's lack of learning.

Innocent III launched the Fourth Crusade in 1204, as usual a mainly French affair. However, en route the Venetians' blind but exceedingly cunning Doge, Enrico Dandolo, persuaded the crusaders to help the pretender Alexius Angelus to secure the Byzantine throne. When the new emperor failed to make good extravagant promises of payment, the crusaders stormed Constantinople on 12 April. For three days they plundered and murdered their fellow Christians; even priests joined in the sack, which culminated in the desecration of Hagia Sophia, the Orthodox St Peter's, where a drunken prostitute was sat on the patriarchal throne. Then the conquerors elected a French emperor and a Venetian patriarch, carving out baronies and duchies. The second Rome had fallen at last. A horrified pope cried out that Greeks could not be blamed for hating Latins whom they knew only as treacherous dogs; but instead of reinstating the rightful patriarch, he confirmed the Latin usurper and the pseudo-emperor. Left in peace, the Eastern Empire might have revived, as so often in the past, to provide a strong bulwark against Islam; the ephemeral Latin Empire would soon fall before despised 'Griffons', to be overrun in turn by the Turks. But few Frankish colonists would set foot in Palestine while land could be had in Greece or on some Aegean island. For the barons 'Romania' was a paradise and the court of the princes of Achaia has been compared to Camelot. And the military brethren acquired many new commanderies.

On Amalric's death, Cyprus went to his son, Hugh, while Jerusalem passed to his young step-daughter, Maria, who in 1210 married John de Brienne, a soldier of fortune who at the age of sixty was surprisingly vigorous. Since 1201 the ruler of Saladin's empire had been the Sultan Saif ad-Din al-Adil, known to the Franks as Saphadin. Once an ardent champion of the counter-crusade and belonging to a Moslem military brotherhood distinguished by special trousers, he was now ageing. Exhausted by family quarrels, Saphadin adopted a peaceful policy towards the Christians.

For six years Outremer enjoyed peace largely because of the Albigensian crusade. Ostensibly a holy war against the melancholy and repellent sect of the *Catharii*, Manichaeans who abominated the flesh, it was a campaign by the nobles of northern France against those of Languedoc whose lands they coveted. The French commanderies of the Hospital and Temple took a small part in the campaign. At this time heresy menaced Catholic Europe, and Innocent III encouraged the foundation of fresh orders to cope with it. Extremist tendencies were either contained within the Franciscans or were combated by the Dominicans who staffed the new Inquisition. The mendicant friars' organization reflected that of military brethren, with provinces and Master Generals.

The Fifth Crusade materialized in 1217 to the secret dismay of Syrian Franks. In September King Andrew II of Hungary and Duke Leopold of Austria landed at Acre, joined in November by King Hugh of Cyprus. King John summoned his barons, including the Masters – the Templar Guillaume de Chartres, the Hospitaller Garin de Montaigu and the German Hermann von Salza. However, the next few months were frittered away in fruitless campaigns. Eventually King John decided that a hard blow struck at Egypt was more likely to regain Jerusalem than any direct assault. Accordingly, a Christian armada from Acre sailed up the Nile to invest Damietta in May 1218. The Egyptians attempted to cut the Franks off from the sea by placing a great iron chain across the Nile, but in August the Crusaders stormed the 'Tower of the Chain', opening the approach to the city walls. Old Saphadin died, his end hastened by mortification. More reinforcements arrived from Europe with an arrogant legate, Cardinal Pelagius. Damietta was bombarded, each order having artillery. On the night of 9 October 1218 the Egyptians made a surprise attack on the Latin camp but were beaten back by King John and the Hospital Marshal, Fra' Aymar de Layron, with only thirty knights, until sufficient help arrived to drive the Mamelukes into the Nile. On 29 August 1219 the Franks attempted to storm the town but were repulsed with very heavy losses, the Templars losing fifty brethren, the Hospitallers thirty-two, including their Marshal.

Finally Saphadin's son and successor, al-Kamil, offered the Franks all Moslem Palestine including Jerusalem if they would abandon the siege. King John and the Teutonic Order wished to accept, but Pelagius and the other brethren refused. On 5 November Damietta fell and the Franks held the town for two years. Kamil, alarmed by the news that Genghis Khan's hordes were making a bloody entrance into the Islamic world, again offered peace: Damietta for Palestine. This time all three Masters agreed with the king, but the greedy, overbearing cardinal refused. He wanted Cairo. John retired to Acre in disgust, but in 1221 Pelagius summoned him back. Once more Kamil offered generous terms, but in July the crusaders marched on Cairo.

Incredibly, they became bogged down in the network of canals in front of the great city and were surrounded by the Turks; starving and without hope of rescue, King John was lucky enough to save himself and his army in return for Damietta. Kamil, who lacked none of his uncle's charm, invited the crusader magnates to a banquet and sent provisions to their troops. When news came to Damietta that it must be surrendered, Italian merchants who hoped to use the town as a trading base rioted, one Templar being killed and a Teutonic Knight wounded during the uproar. Four years of crusade had been wasted through the arrogant folly of a prince of the Church.

St Francis of Assisi came to Outremer at this time and even obtained an interview with Sultan Kamil, who was intrigued by the Christian dervish. Francis was a testimony to the dynamism of Western Christianity. The triumph of the Church, however arrogant, took its force from this vitality, as did the fighting brethren themselves, who indeed had their own saints. The Hospitaller, St Hugh of Genoa, was a mystic noted for asceticism; he always slept in the hospital near the sick, performing the humblest duties such as washing patients or laying out corpses, yet to have attained the rank of commander of Genoa Fra' Hugh must have seen plenty of fighting. Nor were the brothers' good qualities confined to nursing. The diplomat St Gerland de Pologne, commander of Calatagirona, who had the unenviable task of representing the Master of St John at Emperor Frederick's court, was a legendary father to the Sicilian poor and was famed for his gift of mending broken friendships. There was another saint among the Hospitallers: a serving brother called Fra' Gerard Mercati, later a Franciscan, who died a hermit in 1241 still wearing the white cross on his grey habit. Even nursing sisters produced a saint – the much loved Ubaldesca. One must never underestimate the spiritual force of the brethren's vocation, to be, as the Hospitaller rite of profession put it: 'A servant of the gentlemen that are poor and sick and a person devoted to the defence of the Catholic faith'. The brethren were emulators of the Good Samaritan, including the Poor Knights.[15] The minnesinger Wolfram von Eschenbach visited Outremer during this period and was so overcome by admiration that in 'Parsifal' he compared the Templars to Knights of the Holy Grail.[16]

In Europe nursing sisters were at first attached to the Hospitaller commanderies, but were later grouped together in separate houses where they led a contemplative life, praying for their brethren who fought the infidel. Their habit was red with a white-crossed black cloak. The first convent was at Sigena in Aragon, which was occupied in 1188. The famous English convent of Buckland in Somerset, a former house of Augustinian canonesses, was founded by assembling all nursing sisters in England and was served by chaplain brethren. Such houses sent revenues to the Master like any commandery.

The papal monarchy had attained its zenith with Innocent III but was now over-reaching itself. Ultimately the struggle between empire and papacy destroyed both and was reflected in the next crusade, that of the Emperor Frederick II. He had inherited Sicily from his Hauteville mother and was more of a Norman than a Hohenstaufen, a 'baptized sultan' with Arab soldiers and a harem. The papacy was to call him 'Anti-Christ', yet he was loyally supported by the German Hochmeister, Hermann von Salza. For many years the latter was Frederick's most trusted agent, playing a key role in his master's policies, but never forgetting to exact privileges for his brethren. Against bitter Templar opposition, it was Frederick who secured from the pope the Order's right to wear a white mantle, and the Golden Bull of Rimini gave heathen Prussia to the German Knights. Probably it was Hermann who persuaded the emperor to acquire the crown of Jerusalem by marrying its heiress Yolande, John de Brienne's daughter. As soon as the marriage took place she was relegated to the harem while, after a surprisingly ineffective campaign in Italy against his unnatural son-in-law, John became Emperor of

Constantinople, a splendid climax to his career as professional monarch.

The Sixth Crusade was launched under inauspicious circumstances. The Holy Roman Emperor had just been excommunicated, while during a brief stay in Cyprus his arrogance and treachery alienated the Syrian baronage before his arrival in Palestine in 1228. There the clergy were ranged against him, with the exception of the Teutonic Order. Even so, he brought off a diplomatic tour de force. The emperor, who had Saracen subjects in Sicily and who spoke Arabic fluently, understood and liked Moslems, admiring Islamic culture. His adversary, Kamil, was a civilized, tolerant ruler who disliked war. The sultan was intrigued by news of this strange emperor who dressed like an emir, with the Koran embroidered on his silk robes. As a result Frederick obtained a treaty which gave him Nazareth, the castles of Montfort and Toron, and Jerusalem with a corridor from Jaffa, though the Moslems retained the Dome of the Rock and the 'Temple of Solomon'. No doubt Hermann had advised the emperor to save the sultan's face by yielding a little. The former had once written to a cardinal at Rome: 'Do not forget that before the loss of the Holy Land, in nearly all cities which belonged to the Christians the Saracens were free to practise their religion just as today the Christians in Damascus and in other Moslem lands still freely practise their religion.'[17]

The Masters of both the Temple and the Hospital, Pierre de Montaigu and Bertrand de Thessy, were infuriated by the treaty, ratified without their seals. Hospitallers and Poor Knights marched beside the emperor-king to take possession of the Holy City, not under his command but under orders given in the name of Christ, a typical piece of medieval chicanery. Frederick installed himself in the Hospital at Jerusalem and gave the old royal palace, Manoir-le-Roi, to the Teutonic Order. When 'Anti-Christ' wore the imperial crown at the Church of the Holy Sepulchre, he was alone save for the indispensable Hermann and his German brethren.[18]

Master Pierre de Montaigu of the Temple then wrote to the

sultan, suggesting that he assassinate Frederick on his way back to Acre. Kamil immediately forwarded this interesting letter to the emperor, who surrounded the Temple at Acre, but Fra' Pierre was safe inside and very wisely refused to emerge.[19] Frederick returned soon afterwards to Italy, where he confiscated all Templar preceptories. Their Syrian brethren retaliated by chasing the Teutonic Knights out of Acre. Frederick always believed that Pope Gregory was behind Pierre's plot, but, thanks to Hermann's inspired diplomacy, he made his peace with the papacy, which in 1231 recognized both the emperor and his son, Conrad, as kings of Jerusalem. The next decade in Syria was a struggle between their supporters and the barons, a condition best described as legalized anarchy. Yet it was also a period of territorial expansion, for the Franks recovered strongholds which they had not occupied since 1187. Al-Kamil, frightened by news of Moslem disasters in Persia and the terrible Mongols, was too preoccupied to care about infidels in Jerusalem.

The brethren's headquarters were in Acre, but their strongholds were outside the capital. The Germans had Montfort, which they called Starkenberg, near Acre; the Hospitallers had Marqab in Tripoli by the sea, and the Templars Chastel Pelerin. The latter, at Athlit, a fortified peninsula rather than a castle, was protected by sea on three sides with an immense wall of dressed stone on the landward end, and it had freshwater wells, woods, orchards, herds and even salt mines. All three of the chief Orders possessed many fortresses with names that still evoke Outremer's romantic quality: Chastel Rouge, Roche de Roissel and Belvoir, the last described by an Arab writer as 'among the stars like a falcon's nest'. At Starkenberg, one enormously tall watch-tower, separated from the main *enceinte*, dominated the landscape from its hill, while the conventual apartments were in a keep surrounded by a single curtain-wall. Perhaps the most famous of the castles was Krak-des-Chevaliers of the Hospitallers, 'the supreme achievement of medieval military architecture', ringed by massive curtain-walls and bastions. It contains a cloister, a chapter house, and a magnificent chamber – possibly the castellan's apartment –

whose delicate rib-vaulting and stone roses recall the monasteries of France.[20]

Medieval strategy was based on the capture and defence of strongpoints, the sole means of holding territory.[21] Throughout the history of Latin Syria large areas were controlled by strategically sited strongholds from which razzias or *chevauchées* could be launched: swift, hard-riding commando raids whose aim was to hit and run with any available loot – gold, slaves or livestock. The castellan was a senior commander with special military duties. Such fortresses were centres of administration and trade, halting places for caravans where taxes were paid.[22] The brethren spent much time garrisoning them; at Marqab the walls were always patrolled by four knights and twenty-eight sergeant-brethren. Sometimes they were magnificent, with mosaic floors and wall-paintings, especially the refectory and the castellan's apartments where visiting lords were entertained. As in non-military monasteries, guests sat at meals in silence, listening to devotional reading, but the food and table *équipage* before them were as splendid as any in Outremer.[23] The chapels were superb, and the Little Office was said punctiliously. Life in these frontier strongholds really was a military and monastic existence.

Whenever a serious crisis loomed, garrisons were reduced to a bare minimum, the brethren riding forth to join their Order's main army. If they failed to return, the isolated fortresses, though seldom more than ten miles from the coast, had little chance of discovering whether another 'Hattin' had taken place. Technically their defences were impregnable, but, although there was food, water and provisions for a thousand men, there were never enough troops to man the walls. The besieging army would give no quarter unless the garrison surrendered, while there was little likelihood of relief as the kingdom's forces were too small. Day by day the atmosphere in the great silent castles grew tenser. Assaults were constantly launched, accompanied by the cacophony of a Mameluke military band, the howling of enraged fanatics and the crash of missiles from the siege artillery. These 'bombs' included blazing barrels of Greek fire, a brew of sulphur and

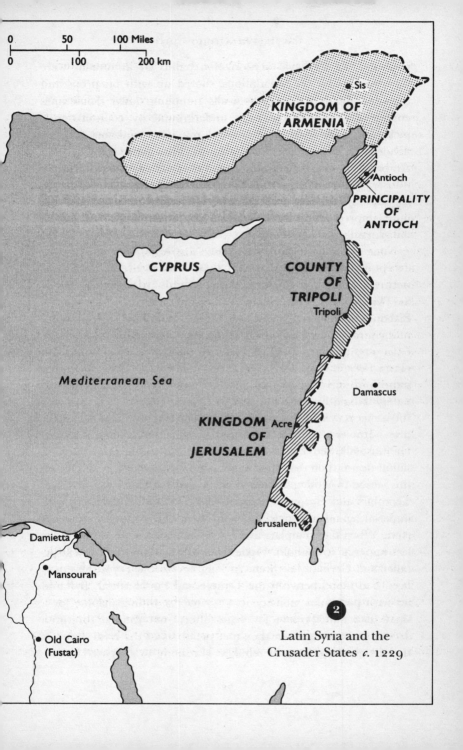

0   50   100 Miles

0   100   200 km

KINGDOM OF ARMENIA

Sis

Antioch

PRINCIPALITY OF ANTIOCH

CYPRUS

COUNTY OF TRIPOLI

Tripoli

Mediterranean Sea

Damascus

KINGDOM OF JERUSALEM

Acre

Jerusalem

Damietta

Mansourah

Old Cairo (Fustat)

Latin Syria and the Crusader States *c.* 1229

naphtha, the medieval version of napalm. Great tunnels were burrowed under the foundations, shored up with pit props and then set alight to bring the walls tumbling down. Sometimes engineers were attacked from underground by counter-mines, picks and knives, or were smoked out with stinkpots or even flooded out with water. Native troops, Armenians and Christian Arabs, were unreliable and prone to panic. Sieges quickly turned into wars of nerves so that fortresses rarely fell by storm but usually surrendered on terms; in 1187 Sahyun, reputedly the most impregnable of all the Frankish strongholds, yielded to Saladin after only three days.

None of the lesser orders possessed fortresses, with the possible exception of the Tower of St Ladre, next to the Lazar House between Athlit and Caesarea. Even so, the little brotherhood of St Thomas was making steady if modest progress. In 1231 the Bishop of Winchester, Peter des Roches, gave English brethren a new church at Acre and bequeathed them a large sum of money.[24]

In 1239 King Tibald of Navarre landed in Outremer with many French lords and over 1,000 knights, but that November some were surrounded and killed on a raid near Ascalon. Fortunately Tibald and the three great Orders had not accompanied them. Jerusalem was sacked by Moslem troops, who then withdrew. However, Tibald recovered Beaufort, Safed and Ascalon. He was followed by Richard, Earl of Cornwall, who through skilful negotiation recovered much land in the south-west. During this period of Moslem weakness when a real advance was possible, Templars and Hospitallers squabbled ceaselessly, intriguing with imperial agents and fighting each other in the narrow streets of Acre. When the Templars and the Syrian barons seized Tyre, the last imperial stronghold, Frederick was still supported by Hospitaller and German brethren. As long ago as the 1170s there had been bad blood between the Temple and the Hospital. It flared up with particular violence in 1197 over a trifling dispute for a small estate in Tripoli; for years afterwards younger brethren drew their swords when they met members of the rival order in the streets, despite papal rebukes. Harmony was secured briefly when Pierre de Montaigu, elected Master of the Templars in 1218, co-operated with his brother, Fra' Garin de Montaigu, Master of St John from 1208 to 1228, though relations deteriorated once more after their deaths.

The Poor Knights captured Nablus in 1242, massacring its inhabitants, including Christian Arabs, and in 1243 reoccupied the Temple of Jerusalem. They began to re-fortify the Holy City. However, Sultan Ayub had new allies in the Kwarismian Turks who were fleeing from the Mongols. In July of that year 10,000 savage tribesmen stormed Jerusalem, which was lost to the Franks for ever. In the meantime Outremer and the Moslem princes of northern Syria were mustering. The barons brought 600 knights and the Templar Master, Armand de Périgord, 300, as did the Hospitaller Master, Guillaume de Châteauneuf. There was a detachment of Teutonic Knights, even a few brethren of St Lazarus, together with knights from Antioch and Tripoli and several thousand Turcopoles and foot-soldiers. The Saracen princes brought a large force of Mameluke and Bedouin cavalry.

On 17 October 1244 at La Forbie near Gaza the allied army left a strong position to attack the Egyptian forces. Instantly they were charged by the ferocious Kwarismians, carrying lances with red streamers. On the right the Franks held out, but on the left and in the centre the wild onslaught proved too much for the Saracen troops who turned and fled. Together Kwarismian and Egyptian Turks surrounded the Franks and cut them to pieces. No fewer than 5,000 Christians fell, including Fra' Armand, his Marshal, Hugues de Montaigu, and 312 brethren; 325 Hospitallers perished, while their Master was taken prisoner and all the St Lazarus brethren were killed.[25] Only twenty-six Hospitallers, thirty-three Templars and three Teutonic Knights escaped.[26] Even if the Egyptian Sultan was too busy to complete Outremer's destruction, the little kingdom could never replace the loss of manpower. The Hospitaller Master spent the next six years in captivity at Cairo. Fortunately his Order had evolved machinery to deal with such cases and elected his Lieutenant, the Grand Preceptor of Jerusalem, Fra' Jean de Ronay as Vice-Master.

There was little central authority in the kingdom itself, though the regent, Henry of Cyprus, appointed various members of the Ibelin family as *baillis*. However, the Holy Land received a new God-sent leader who landed at Damietta in June 1249, Louis IX of France, the hero-king of the Christian West who once said that the only way to argue with an infidel was to thrust one's sword into his belly. His foreign policy, almost totally dependent on divine guidance, was noticeably inept. This forbidding character was relieved by magnanimity, kindness and a sense of humour, which explains some of his magnetic attraction for his contemporaries, Moslems included. He was never known to break his pledged word, even to Saracens.

Louis occupied Damietta with over 2,000 knights, including 400 from Frankish Romania, and a full complement of Templars, Hospitallers and Teutonic Knights. The king waited till the Nile floods had receded before advancing on Cairo. His progress was hampered by the network of canals, so in December he halted before the largest of the Nile's branches, the Bahr as-Saghir, near the town of Mansourah. On 8 February 1250, Shrove Tuesday, the army, led by the king's brother, Robert d'Artois, forded the river at dawn under strict instructions not to attack. Count Robert, arrogant and impetuous, charged as soon as he had crossed. The Egyptian army was taken by surprise and the Mamelukes fled in terror while their commander, the aged Vizier Fakr ad-Din, caught dyeing his beard, was cut down. Robert ordered a pursuit; the Templar Master Guillaume de Sonnac, 'bon chevalier preux et hardi', while trying to restrain him was called *poulain* and coward for his pains. The grim old man replied that neither he nor his brethren were frightened, that they would ride with him but that none of them would come back alive. The Turks rallied under a brilliant Kipchak captain, Baibars Rukd ad-Din '*Bundukdari*' (the Crossbowman), ambushing the Franks in the streets of Mansourah. Robert was unhorsed and killed, while Fra' Guillaume, who lost an eye, brought back five out of his 200 brethren.

Baibars then attacked Louis, and a terrible battle lasted until sunset, charge following charge. Eventually the Mamelukes were driven from the field; but the crusaders were exhausted, with little stomach left for an equally ghastly struggle three days later. Every time Turkish horsemen galloped forward the air was black with arrows and barrels of Greek fire from Mameluke catapults. Old Fra' Guillaume was caught defending a barricade that had been set ablaze by naphtha, but he fought on amidst the flames till he lost his remaining eye and fell, mortally wounded. However, inspired by Louis' almost supernatural heroism, the Franks held their ground and eventually beat off the dreadful Baibars.

In the next eight weeks the Christian army was stricken with dysentery and typhoid while its ships were captured by the Egyptian fleet. Louis decided to retreat in April, but his enfeebled troops were easily surrounded. After a hopeless resistance, the king, who was dangerously ill with typhus, surrendered. The poorer crusaders were slaughtered or herded off to the slave-market, but, after every sort of indignity, in May Louis and his knights were allowed to ransom themselves in exchange for Damietta and on payment of the huge sum of one million bezants. The king asked the Templars to lend him 60,000 bezants but the Commander, Etienne d'Otricourt, and the Marshal, Renaud de Vichiers, refused. For once Louis lost his temper and sent the faithful Joinville to collect the money from a Templar galley. Since the Templar Treasurer refused to deliver the keys, Joinville smashed the chests open with a hatchet.

King Louis spent the following four years at Acre administering the kingdom and he subjected the Templars' great officers to a humiliating punishment. Their Marshal, Hugues de Jouy, had negotiated a treaty at Damascus without the king's permission. Renaud de Vichiers, now Master, had to come before Louis, barefoot, and retract the treaty, kneeling in full view of the whole army. As a result Fra' Hugues was banished for life from the Holy Land.

The king obtained the release of many important prisoners, including the Hospitaller Master, Guillaume de Châteauneuf, with thirty of his brethren, fifteen Templars and ten Teutonic Knights, though negotiations nearly broke down when the Poor

Knights made their abortive alliance with Damascus. An attack on Jaffa by the Damascene army caused the Franks to launch a punitive expedition, during which the little detachment of Lazarus Knights came to grief.[27] Joinville describes the incident as follows:

While the king was before Jaffa, the Master of Saint Lazarus [Fra' Raynaud de Flory] had spied out near Ramleh, a town some three good leagues away, a number of cattle and various other things from which he thought to collect some valuable booty. So being a man of no standing in the army, and who therefore did exactly as he pleased, he went off to that place without saying a word to the king. But after he had collected his spoils the Saracens attacked him, and so thoroughly defeated him that of all the men he had in his company no more than four escaped.[28]

Louis' hopes of a Franco-Egyptian alliance came to nothing and his one lasting treaty was with the Assassins through the mediation of the Hospitaller and Templar Masters. Louis' mother, Queen Blanche, the Regent of France, died in 1254 and the king returned home. He left behind a seneschal, Geoffroi de Sargines, with a French 'regiment', but Latin Syria could not replace the losses in manpower it had suffered during his Egyptian campaign and the kingdom would never again know firm government. Not even a saint could save Outremer.

4

ARMAGEDDON

Latin Syria was now a mere string of coastal *entrepôts* in which commercial, municipal and clerical factions squabbled viciously, heedless of the Cypriot kings' futile efforts to assert their authority. Most barons had left for Cyprus, so military orders, holding what little territory remained inland, were the dying kingdom's last support, and even they quarrelled and fought with one another. Yet this self-destroying anarchy was menaced by a ferocious Mameluke state, the chimera of a Mongol alliance offering a sole, illusory hope of salvation. In 1256 the rivalry between the Genoese and the Venetians developed into civil war over the control of the monastery of St Sabas in Acre. The Venetians were supported by the Pisan and Provençal merchants, the Templars, the Teutonic Knights, and the brethren of St Lazarus and St Thomas. The Genoese were backed by the Catalan merchants, the Hospitallers and Philippe de Montfort, Lord of Tyre. There was a battle in the streets of Acre, ending in a temporary victory for the Hospitallers and the Genoese. An even bloodier battle followed, after which the Genoese withdrew to their own quarter of the town.[1]

Yet this period was one of important development for the Hospitallers under Fra' Hugues Revel, 'maistre prodome et sage',[2] who may have been an Englishman from Devon. Their militarization was complete, chaplains having been finally subordinated to knight-brethren, while their hierarchy was crystallizing. First came conventual *baillis* (great officers), then bailiffs of Syria, followed by ones from overseas. All priories and commanderies had to contribute one-third of their revenues for the use of the Order to offset losses in income from lands captured by the

Mamelukes. The increasingly aristocratic and military emphasis found expression in the Hospitallers' new uniform. By 1248 the cumbersome monastic cloak had been superseded by a black surcoat with a white cross, soon replaced by a red surcoat with a white cross. The original habit was retained for convent life. As early as 1250 the Templar rule stipulated that a postulant must prove himself a knight's son or the descendant of knights, and priest-brethren were restricted to fewer offices. Similar modifications appeared in the Hospitaller constitutions.[3]

The word 'knight' has a certain fairytale flavour which obscures the fact that such a man was a specialized fighting machine. They were often employed by a baronial household in administrative as well as military posts, or they plied for hire as mercenaries. The more fortunate acquired manors, but most were poor, their armour constituting the greater part of their wealth. The suit of armour was undergoing change, however. Plate knee-caps, gauntlets and leg-plates were beginning to be worn, and shields were smaller, while the helmet was the great barrel-helm, though some preferred a light steel-cap under a mail hood. The most curious innovations were ailerons, square pieces of *cuir bouilli* standing up vertically from his shoulders, on which the owner's coat of arms was painted. Naturally the brethren were provided with excellent equipment.

The Franks could afford to indulge in such petty squabbles as the 'War of St Sabas' only because their Moslem enemies were distracted by the threat of Mongol invasion. At the end of the twelfth century the nomadic tribes of the Gobi Desert had united under Genghis Khan, and the standard of the Nine Yak Tails had swept like a roaring whirlwind through Asia – 'the scourge of Heaven's fury in the hands of the merciless Tartars'. By the middle of the thirteenth century they had conquered Baghdad, throwing the last caliph, tied in a bag, into the river. Some of them were Nestorian Christians. The legend of Prester John, the great Christian potentate of the East, probably arising from rumours of the Coptic kings of Ethiopia, was well known in Latin Syria and resulted in much wishful thinking about the Great

Khan Mongka. King Louis had sent ambassadors to the '*kuriltai*' at Karakorum, while King Hethoum of Armenia went in person, acknowledging Mongka as overlord in return for military assistance. In 1259 the great Khan's brother Hulagu, Ilkhan of Persia, whose wife, Dokuz Khatun, and whose best general, Kitbuqa, were Nestorians, sent the horde into Syria, accompanied by a strong detachment of Armenian and Georgian Knights. Aleppo soon fell, followed by the other Moslem towns of the north. On 1 March 1260 three Christian princes, Kitbuqa, Hethoum of Armenia and Bohemond VI of Antioch, rode triumphantly into Damascus. At Baghdad, Hulagu had shown special favour to the Nestorian Catholics, and Kitbuqa was equally kind to the Christians in his new city. By now no great Moslem power existed east of Egypt.

Unfortunately Mongka's sudden death and the subsequent struggle for the throne forced Hulagu to withdraw most of his troops. Kitbuqa was left at Damascus with a small force, whereupon Sultan Qutuz of Egypt advanced into Syria with a large army. He asked the Christian lords for help and the Haute Cour discussed his appeal with some sympathy. The Tartars were uncomfortable neighbours who tolerated only vassals, not independent allies, and the *poulains* preferred civilized infidels to barbarous Christians. However, Hochmeister Anno von Sangerhausen warned them that the Saracens would turn on the Franks if they were victorious. Outremer remained neutral. On 30 September 1260 Mongols and Mamelukes joined battle at Ain Jalud – 'the Pools of Goliath'. Kitbuqa was surrounded, his troops wiped out and he himself captured and beheaded – Turkish captains playing polo with his head. Next month Qutuz was murdered by the sinister Baibars, who became sultan in his place, and ruler of Damascus as well as of Cairo.

'His Sublime Highness, the Sultan an-Nasr Rukn-ad-Din', the same 'Crossbowman' who had defeated St Louis, was a soldier of genius even if, in the words of a French historian, he was also a treacherous and ferocious beast of prey.[4] This former slave soon controlled all Saladin's former empire, building countless roads which gave the armies of the Mameluke sultans a mobility unknown to their predecessors. Determined to annihilate both Franks and Armenians, Baibars launched his first sledge-hammer blow in 1265. After taking Caesarea, he laid siege to Arsur, which the Hospitallers had recently bought from the Ibelin family. There were 270 knights in the town, and they fought bravely for forty days. Eventually the Mameluke heavy artillery and mangonels on movable towers breached the walls of the lower town. By now ninety Hospitallers had fallen. The citadel was crowded with refugees and unreliable native troops, and the castellan surrendered within three days. It was understood that he and his remaining knights would be allowed to withdraw to Acre, but Baibars dragged them off to Cairo in chains.

The following summer '*Bendocdar*' invested the Templar fortress of Safed in Galilee. The bleak stone stronghold controlled 160 villages. Again it was a story of local auxiliaries panicking. After three assaults had failed, Baibars offered a free pardon to all Turcopoles, who started to desert. The Templars began to lose their nerve and sent a Syrian sergeant, Fra' Leo, to negotiate terms with Baibars. He returned with a guarantee of safe conduct to the coast. The knights accepted and opened the castle gates, whereupon the sultan offered them a choice of Islam or death. Next morning, when they were paraded outside the walls to give their answer, the castellan stepped forward, begging his brethren not to apostatize. Baibars had him skinned alive and the brethren decapitated, after which he decorated his new possession with their rotting heads.

Meanwhile the emir Qalawun raided Cilicia. King Hethoum's two sons and the Templars from Baghras met them near Darbessaq. But they were too few and, after killing Prince Thoros and capturing Prince Lavon, the Mamelukes swept on to Sis, the Armenian capital, which they burnt to the ground. The little mountain kingdom was utterly laid waste and never recovered completely.

Three years later, after capturing Jaffa and the Templar fortress of Beaufort, Baibars attacked and stormed Antioch. Amid the usual atrocities one incident shocked even the Turks. The canon-esses of St John had cut off their own noses with scissors and gashed their cheeks in order to avoid rape. The appalled Moslems slaughtered them on the spot. Save for the isolated coastal town of Lattakieh, the principality had vanished. The Templars saw that northern Syria was lost and wisely withdrew their outposts at Baghras and La Roche de Roissel. As his subjects said, the sultan 'never destroyed the hiding place of error without giving it to the flames and drenching it in blood'. Baibars wrote a sardonic letter to Bohemond at Tripoli congratulating him on being absent. Gloatingly, the 'Crossbowman' went on to describe the desolation he had created, the butchery of Antiochene priests and citizens, the desecration of churches and how cheaply ladies had been sold in the slave-market.

The kingdom was tottering, though in 1269 Hugh III was crowned at Tyre, the first Levantine-born king since 1186. Baibars' relentless campaigns were sapping even the Hospital's resources; in 1268 Master Hugues Revel had written that his Order could muster only 300 knights in Syria. The sultan humili-ated them further in 1271. He had already taken Chastel Blanc from the Templars when on 3 March he laid siege to Krak-des-Chevaliers. The finest castle of the Christian world, which had defied Saladin, was garrisoned by the Hospitaller Marshal with 200 knights and sergeants of his order. A Saracen writer called this vast and lonely stronghold 'a bone stuck in the throat of the Moslems'. On 15 March mangonels breached the gate-tower of the first curtain-wall and on 26 March battered a way through the inner wall. Most brethren escaped to one of the great towers, but Baibars set up mangonels in the courtyard and their last refuge shuddered beneath a crashing barrage. On 8 April they surrendered and were conducted to Tripoli. An exultant Baibars wrote triumphantly to Hugues Revel: 'You fortified this place, entrusting its defence to the best of your men. All was in vain and you only sent them to their deaths.' In June the 'Crossbowman' surrounded Starkenberg. The castellan, Johann von Sachsen, had few knights, and his Turcopoles went mad with fear. After a week he yielded and was lucky enough to obtain a safe conduct to Acre for himself and his garrison.

There was no help to be had from Sicily or 'Romania'. The Latin Empire had fallen to the Greeks in 1261 and the Frankish lords of Achaia were fighting for survival. Even Cyprus was attacked by Egyptian galleys in 1271, though Mamelukes were poor seamen and their raid was easily beaten off. The Frankish paradise was at its zenith, with a way of life epitomized in the tournaments outside St Hilarion, the castle named *Dieu d'Amour* by the barons. Indeed it is remarkable that Cypriot kings tried to save their other, beleaguered, kingdom so often, when it meant leaving this beautiful land.

Providentially 'the Lord Edward' had arrived from England in May, but with fewer than 1,000 men. Had he had more, this cold, methodical giant would have proved himself a really effective crusader. King Hugh's Cypriots refused to help him, but the Ilkhan Abaga, who honoured Kitbuqa's memory, was more generous, and 10,000 Mongol horsemen galloped into Syria, where they taught the Mamelukes a bloody lesson. Unfortunately they were not strong enough to face the full might of Baibars, who was marching up from Damascus, and they withdrew. Edward did little more than lead a series of small and ineffectual raids, but he impressed the sultan sufficiently to conclude a ten-year peace with Acre. Baibars even paid Edward the compliment of trying to assassinate him – the legendary occasion when the prince's young wife was supposed to have sucked the poison from the stab-wound. Another less romantic story says that the English Master of the Temple, Thomas Berard, provided an antidote. Edward seems to have made much of the English order, helping the brethren of St Thomas build their new church at Acre and endowing them generously. It seems, from the letters they afterwards wrote to him, that their advice was always welcome. But in September 1272 he sailed away from Acre. For the rest of Baibars' reign the Franks were left in comparative peace.

Edward profited from his experience, which taught him how to conquer Wales. Previous English kings had been unable to cope with impassable terrain and fast-moving enemies, but he now employed Syrian methods: sea-to-land assaults, sea lines of communication, and advances consolidated by castle administration points, whose small garrisons could be switched quickly from place to place along the coast.* This strategy proved remarkably effective. While it is impossible to say whether his great fortresses like Conway or Beaumaris were copied from Palestinian models, the king had learnt how to use them in Outremer.

King Hugh III finally abandoned his ungrateful kingdom in 1276. The new Master of the Temple, Guillaume de Beaujeu,[5] a relative of the French royal family and an incurable intriguer, had systematically hindered the king's policies, and next year Charles of Anjou proclaimed himself king with the support of Fra' Guillaume. Hugh tried to return in 1279, but, though the Hospitallers were sympathetic, his attempt was frustrated by armed opposition from the Poor Knights. Returning to Cyprus, the angry monarch burnt out the Templar preceptories at Limassol and Paphos. However, Charles's government collapsed when he lost Sicily in 1282. King Hugh then returned, opposed by both Templars and Hospitallers, to die at Tyre in 1284. By now the kingdom was really a feudal republic in which merchants, brethren and barons quarrelled noisily. In 1279 the Knights of St Thomas had written to King Edward describing the alarming conditions in the Holy Land and their own gloomy forebodings. The Templars and their Master became involved in the deplorable squabble at Tripoli between Bohemond VII and Gui Embriaco, Lord of Gibelet. The Poor Knights, who were always baronial in their attitude to authority, consistently supported the rebel against his overlord, razing Botron to the ground (the castle once coveted by Gerard de Ridefort), and Templar galleys attacked those of the prince-count. This struggle lasted from 1277 to 1282, from the moment when Gui abducted an heiress until

* I must thank Dom Alberic Stacpoole for this analysis of strategy and tactics.

the day when he and his brothers were buried in a ditch up to their necks and left to starve.

Strategically the Frankish position never ceased to deteriorate despite some slight success. In October 1280 a Mongol army occupied Aleppo, while in the same month a raiding party of Hospitallers from Marqab, chased by 5,000 Turcomans, suddenly turned on its pursuers and cut them to ribbons. When the Mongols had withdrawn, 7,000 vengeful Saracens led by the Emir of Krak surrounded the great castle, but the garrison of no more than 600, led by brethren in red surcoats, galloped out to rout the astonished infidels. Another Tartar expedition entered Syria in the autumn of 1281, accompanied by King Lavon III of Armenia and a Georgian force. A detachment from Marqab joined them, including the English prior of St John, Joseph de Chauncy from Clerkenwell. However, the allied army was defeated outside Homs. Two years later the Mamelukes overran Lattakieh, the last remnant of the principality of Antioch. Outremer was crumbling piece by piece, its manpower dwindling with every battle.*

Without warning Sultan Qalawun and a vast army appeared before the mountain stronghold at Marqab on 17 April 1285. The Hospitallers had their own mangonels mounted on the wall towers and succeeded in putting the Mameluke machines out of action. However, on 23 May a mine brought an important tower crashing down. The castellan then discovered that other tunnels had been dug under the moat, reaching below the inner towers. Realizing that the castle was lost, he managed to obtain excellent terms from Qalawun. The garrison were allowed to withdraw to Tortosa, while the twenty-five Knights of St John in the keep were permitted to retain their arms and take away all personal

---

* For the last twenty years of Outremer we are largely dependent on the Chronicle of the Templar of Tyre (in the 'Gestes des Chyprois'). Its author was probably Gérard de Montréal who belonged to the Palestinian gentry and was not a Templar but merely 'écrivain sarrasinois' or Arabic secretary to Master Guillaume de Beaujeu.

property. Never again would the Office be said in the beautiful chapel.

Coastal Syria was still a western land, even if sadly shrunken. Most fiefs had been overrun, and the wealthiest class comprised the merchants and many nobles then living in the towns, like the mayor of Tripoli, Bartholomé Embriaco, who belonged to the Gibelet family, while younger sons often joined the military orders. At Beirut the Ibelins stayed on in their magnificent villa, with a rich income from local iron mines. Syrian Franks enjoyed comforts almost unknown in Europe. There were still farmers who not only cultivated the fields round the towns but also tilled those near the inland castles. Acre's architecture was splendid in the French style: the royal palace, the luxurious houses of the barons and merchants, the beautiful new Gothic Church of St Andrew, and the vast headquarters of the Orders. So imposing was the Hospitaller church that the city was called St Jean d'Acre. With double walls and many towers manned by hand-picked troops, a fortified promontory, it was inconceivable that infidels should take this strong seaport.

Perhaps thirty brother-knights were resident in its Hospital, the Temple holding as many Poor Knights. Most brethren were on garrison duty in the great castles or scattered throughout their wide properties, busy with estate management, collecting taxes and inspecting supply depots. It was not only diminished resources which sapped the strength of the military brotherhoods for, as with other religious orders, there was evidence of growing laxity. Knight-brethren no longer slept in dormitories but in their own cells, and senior officers enjoyed considerable comfort.

Acre was especially gay in 1286 when, after the coronation of Henry II, the epileptic boy who was also King of Cyprus, his court spent a fortnight celebrating. Nothing so lively or so decorative had been seen in Palestine since the old court at Jerusalem. There were tournaments and sumptuous banquets, while in the 'Herberge del Ospitau de Saint-Johan'[6] pageants of King Arthur and the Round Table were enacted, Syrian and Cypriot nobles playing the parts of 'Lanselot, et Tristan, et Pilamèdes', and other games 'biaus et délitables et plaissans'.[7] The king then returned to his other kingdom, leaving two Ibelin *baillis*. Yet the city was as turbulent as always and in 1287 Pisan and Genoese galleys fought in the harbour; the latter even attempted to sell their Pisan captives in the Moslem slave-market but were dissuaded by the outraged brethren.

In February 1289 Qalawun marched into Syria. The Templars' spies learnt from an emir in their pay that the sultan's objective was Tripoli. But the prosperous merchants did not want to believe this alarming news. Fra' Guillaume's weakness for political intrigue was too well known. To their incredulous horror Qalawun arrived in front of the city at the end of March with 40,000 cavalry, 100,000 foot soldiers and a menacing train of mangonels. Tripoli, with its famous schools, silk factories and fertile gardens, seemed strong enough, defended by Venetian, Genoese and Cypriot contingents. The Italians' galleys guarded it against any attack from the sea. There was also a large detachment of Templars, commanded by the Marshal Geoffroi de Vendac, and a smaller force of Hospitallers led by the Marshal of St John, the redoubtable Matthieu de Clermont. None the less many citizens prudently embarked for Cyprus. An incessant battering by nineteen mangonels eventually demolished two key towers whereupon the Venetians decided that the city was lost and sailed away. Soon after, on 26 May, the Mamelukes assaulted the undermanned walls with fanatic bravery and the defence collapsed. Most brethren died fighting, but the two Marshals escaped by boat. For the citizens it was a blood-bath in the style of Baibars. Nearly all were butchered and their families herded off to the slave-markets. Outremer was foundering, yet even now the Franks did not see their doom.

Not even a spectacular disaster could revive the crusader spirit. However, a band of out-of-work labourers from northern Italy volunteered and sailed for Acre, where they arrived in August 1290, a drunken rabble. There had been a fine harvest, caravans were coming down from Damascus, and the capital, gayer than ever, was crowded with Moslem visitors. The 'crusaders' had not been in the city very long before they rioted and cut the throat of every Saracen in sight, though the *poulains* and the brethren did their utmost to save them. Qalawun was infuriated and prepared to invade Syria. Once again Templar spies got wind of his plans and once again the Franks refused to listen to Fra' Guillaume's warning. He was so alarmed that on his own initiative he tried to negotiate with Cairo. Qalawun's terms were a gold piece per head of Acre's population. The Master was howled down by the citizens and accused of cowardice.

The sultan died in November but made his son, al-Ashraf, swear to destroy the Christian capital, and in March 1291 an enormous Mameluke army marched on Acre – 160,000 infantry and 60,000 cavalry. Their artillery was awe-inspiring, including no fewer than 100 mangonels. The two greatest were known respectively as *al-Mansour* (the Victorious)[8] and *Ghadaban* (the Furious) while the smaller, but almost equally lethal, catapults were called 'Black Bulls'. *Al-Mansour* threw stones weighing one hundredweight. On 5 April al-Ashraf invested the city.

By this time the Franks were not altogether unprepared. The Orders had thrown in every brother available so that, out of a population of fifty thousand, 14,000 were foot soldiers and 800 were mounted men-at-arms. There was no shortage of experienced leaders. All Masters were present, the Templar Guillaume de Beaujeu, the Hospitaller Jean de Villiers and the Hochmeister Konrad von Feuchtwangen. Unfortunately the latter had been able to bring only a few German brethren. St Lazarus provided twenty-five knights, while there were nine from St Thomas under their Master. Other troops included a Cypriot contingent, the Pisan and Venetian garrisons, the French regiment led by Jean de Grailly, a few Englishmen commanded by the Swiss, Otto de Grandson, armed citizens of Acre, and the Italian rabble who had caused the war. King Henry's young brother, Prince Amalric, was nominal commander-in-chief. The troops were divided into four divisions, each entrusted with a sector of the double walls. These and the twelve great towers were in excellent condition, while much of the city was protected by water, and, as the

Franks retained control of the sea, ships could arrive at any time with food and reinforcements.

On the night of 15 April Master de Beaujeu led 300 brethren and the English troops on a sortie to burn the Mameluke siege engines, but their horses became entangled in the enemy's tent-ropes and they were ignominiously chased back to Acre, losing eighteen knights. Later the Hospitallers launched another night-raid, this time in pitch darkness, but it was equally disastrous. Spirits sank, only to be restored on 4 May by the arrival of King Henry from Cyprus with 500 infantry and 200 knights.

But the young king and his advisers soon realized that the situation was hopeless. Turkish engineers were steadily undermin-ing the towers, which began to crumble beneath a ceaseless bombardment from the sultan's mangonels, a hail of enormous rocks and timber baulks. Lighter machines hurled pots of Greek fire or burning pitch which burst when they hit their targets, and the sky was ablaze with naphtha arrows. Henry tried to negotiate, but the implacable al-Ashraf would accept nothing but complete surrender. By 15 May the first wall and all its towers had been breached. Filling the moat with the bodies of men and horses as well as sandbags, the Saracens swept through the main gate, encouraged by 300 drummers on camels. Charging on horseback down the narrow streets, the Templar and Hospitaller brethren drove them out, but by evening the desperate Franks were forced to withdraw behind the inner wall. Next day, many citizens put their wives and children on board ship for Cyprus, but unfortu-nately the weather was too bad to put out to sea.

Just before dawn on Friday, 18 May 1291, the sultan ordered a general assault, announced by first one great kettle-drum, then by massed drums and a battery of trumpets and cymbals, 'which had a very horrible voice'.[9] Mangonels and archers sent an endless shower of fire bombs into the doomed city, the arrows 'falling like rain', while Mameluke suicide-squads led by white-turbaned officers attacked through the dense smoke all along the wall in deep columns. At the St Anthony gate they were hurled back by Marshal Matthieu de Clermont, the Hospital's chief battle commander, who then counter-charged at the head of a band of Templars and Hospitallers to recapture the 'Accursed Tower'.

He was unsuccessful, and after a short breathing space at the Temple, where he saw the Master's lifeless body brought in, Fra' 'Mahé' deliberately went out to find his own death. The Templar chronicler wrote that the Marshal returned to the battle taking all his brethren with him, for not one would desert him, and they came to 'la rue de Jenevés' and there he fought fiercely 'and killed, he and his companions, many Saracens and in the end he died, he and the others, like brave gallant Knights, good Christians, and may God have mercy on their souls'.[10]

The elderly Guillaume de Beaujeu had also attempted to recover the 'Accursed Tower', with only a dozen men. On the way there he met the Master of St John, who joined him, and the two stumbled grimly towards the Mamelukes, forcing a path through fleeing soldiers and over piles of dead and wounded, many horribly burnt by Greek fire, amid screams, groans, triumphant yells from the Turks and a few defiant shouts of 'St. Jean' or 'Beau Sire, Beau Séant'. But the little band in red-and-white surcoats could do nothing against the victorious horde and were so blinded by smoke, naphtha flames and dust from falling rubble that they could not see one another. Still the heroic old men and their bodyguards fought on, while a small group of Italians rallied to them. Finally a crossbow quarrel hit Fra' Guillaume beneath the left armpit, and he reeled back. The Italians pleaded with him to stay but the Master cried: 'Gentlemen, I can't go on because I'm a dead man – look at this wound.'[11] He collapsed and his aides took him into the Temple, where he soon died. Fra' Jean also was badly wounded and his brethren carried him, weeping and protesting, down to a ship.[12]

Acre was now lost irretrievably. The terrified population, women, children, babies and old men, ran to the harbour in frantic despair, though many able-bodied citizens died fighting. King Henry had already sailed for home and there were too few ships. Frenzied struggles took place on the crowded jetties, and overloaded boats sank. A deserting Templar, Rutger von Blum, seized a galley and made his fortune by extorting ruinous passage money from the ladies of Acre fleeing from rape, mutilation and death, or at best slavery. To add to the horror a great storm blew up. The Saracens soon reached the jammed quays to butcher the screaming fugitives. Every one of the Teutonic Knights except their Hochmeister died in the sack, as did all the brethren of St Thomas and St Lazarus. Among the few male prisoners taken by the Mamelukes were several Templars who apostatized; years afterwards, visitors to Cairo saw some slaves who had once been Poor Knights. However, most of their brethren who had not yet been killed held out in the Temple, by the sea.

The Order's Marshal, Pierre de Sevrey, was there to direct its defence. A large number of women and children had fled to them for protection and the Templars showed that they could be generous, putting as many refugees as possible aboard the Order's galleys and sending them off to join the king's fleet. There was not enough room for everyone, and all the brethren, even the wounded, stayed behind. An eye-witness who saw the ships leave wrote afterwards that 'when they set sail everyone of the Temple who remained raised a great cheer, and thus they departed'. After several days al-Ashraf offered good terms, which Fra' Pierre accepted, and some Mamelukes were admitted. They hoisted the crescent flag of Islam but then began to rape the women and boys, whereupon the infuriated Templars killed them. The infidel flag was torn down and 'Beau Séant' hauled up again. That night the Marshal sent away the Commander, Tibald Gaudin, by boat with the Temple treasury, the holy relics and some non-combatants. Next day the sultan once more proposed excellent terms, admitting that his men had got what they deserved, so Fra' Pierre went out to discuss surrender. He was immediately seized and beheaded. Some of the brethren were old men, most of them were wounded and all were exhausted, yet they decided to fight to the finish. They beat off assault after assault. 'They can fight the battle of the Lord and indeed be soldiers of Christ. Let them kill the enemy or die, they need not be afraid.' But the brethren had no reply to mangonel fire and the tunnels which riddled the foundations. On 28 May the mines were fired. Part of the massive wall collapsed and 2,000 Turkish troops poured in to meet a bloody reception. The weight was too much for the already badly damaged Temple, which came crashing down, and Saracens and brethren perished together in a flaming hecatomb.[13]

Outremer died with its capital. Tortosa, Beirut, Sidon, Tyre, Haifa and Chastel Pelerin remained to the Franks, but they had made their supreme effort at Acre and were exhausted. All these places were quickly abandoned, though the Templars at Sidon made some show of resistance. By the end of August only the waterless island of Ruad was left, two miles from the coast opposite Tortosa, with a small garrison of Poor Knights. The local Christians, including the Latin peasants, fled into the hills while 'la Douce Syrie' was methodically laid waste by the sultan's army, who dug up irrigation channels, felled and uprooted orchards, poisoned wells and devastated even the richest farmlands to make sure the accursed Franks would never return. Acre became a city of ghosts.* Those *poulains* and brethren who survived took refuge in Cyprus.

Historians differ in their judgements on the brethren in Latin Syria. Yet the most hostile cannot deny their good intentions, for the Holy Land meant everything to them. Certainly Templars were avaricious, Hospitallers scarcely less so, but both were prodigal of their treasure and their lives in defending a land which they loved passionately; they would hardly have been human had they refrained from politics, while to be combative and aggressive are necessary qualities in front-line troops. If their asceticism wilted during the thirteenth century, so did that of almost every monastic order.

---

* Israeli archaeologists have disproved an impression, based on contemporary chronicles, that Acre was completely destroyed; almost a third of the crusader city remains, including the Hospitaller refectory and several streets in the Genoese quarter. I owe this information to Professor Riley-Smith.

What has not been attempted – until now – is to contrast the Templars and Hospitallers in Syria with the Spanish military orders in their own land or with the Teutonic Knights on the Baltic; as will be seen, in Spain the Reconquista would have been impossible without such brethren, who alone could provide professional armies to consolidate the Christian advance, while in Prussia the *Deutschritter* built an entire new state. In this wider context it must surely be recognized that during that long, losing battle which was Latin Syria the contribution of the brethren of the Temple and the Hospital, who possessed all the gifts of their Spanish and German cousins, was beyond price.

III

THE CRUSADE ON THE BALTIC
1200–1560

German orders in Prussia and Livonia:
Teutonic Knights – Brethren of the Sword

Seven brethren from a Teutonic house together with a few noblemen built a fort in the Kulmerland beside a sacred oak tree. It is said that at first they had to fight a vast horde of natives, beyond number, but as time passed – perhaps fifty-three years – they drove them out [*exterminaverunt*] so that no one remained who would not bow his neck to the yoke of faith; this with the help of the Lord Jesus Christ who is blessed for ever and ever. Amen.

Petrus von Dusburg
'Chronica Terre Prussie' III, 3 (in *S.R.P.* vol. I)

5

THE CRUSADE ON THE BALTIC

Throughout the history of the *Deutschritter* the German genius is very evident, romantic idealism implemented with utter ruthlessness. Tradition claims that a Hospital of St Mary of the Germans had been founded at Jerusalem in 1127. After the débâcle of 1187, members of this establishment were included in a new foundation, a field hospital set up in 1190 by merchants from Bremen and Lübeck during the siege of Acre. Their first headquarters was a tent, made from a ship's mainsail, on the seashore.[1] In 1198 some noblemen who had come with the abortive German crusade joined these brethren to form a military order, 'the Teutonic Knights of St Mary's Hospital of Jerusalem'. Heinrich Walpot von Bassenheim, a Rhinelander, was appointed Master, recruits were enrolled and the new Order was given statutes similar to the Templars' but with provision for hospitaller work. There were three classes of brother: knight, priest and sergeant. Brother-knights, who had to be of noble birth and German blood, wore a white cloak with a black cross over a white tunic; priests wore a longer-skirted version, while the sergeants' cloak was grey, its cross truncated with only three arms. In certain hospitals a fourth class existed – nursing women known as half-sisters.

The new brotherhood's hierarchy resembled that of the Poor Knights. Under the *Hochmeister* (*Magister Generalis*) were the *Gross-Komtur*, the *Ordensmarschall* (later called *Grossmarschall*), the *Spittler* (Hospitaller),* the *Tressler* (Treasurer) and the *Trapier* (Quarter-

---

* The Spittler's headquarters would later be at Elbing at the mouth of the Vistula – the modern Elblag – in western Prussia.

T.III · p · 142

4. A Teutonic Knight

master), who constituted the Grand Council. The General Chapter, which elected the Hochmeister, met every September on the feast of the Holy Cross. A commandery contained no fewer than twelve knight-brethren under a *pfleger* or *hauskomtur*. The houses of a province formed a *landkomturei* or *ballei*. In charge of German *balleien* was the *Landmeister* whose headquarters were at Mergentheim in Swabia.

Eventually this organization would be repeated in many parts of Europe. At first the Hochmeister stayed in the east, though later he moved his headquarters to Italy, then to Prussia and finally to Swabia. Elsewhere, since he was so far away, the Knights were ruled by Landmeisters, and not just those Knights in Germany but also those in Prussia, Livland (today's Baltic states), Greece and Italy. The headquarters of the *Italienische Landmeister* was at Venice.

The empire endowed the new brethren generously with lands in Germany, Sicily and southern Italy, while they were also given Greek estates by the Frankish lords of Achaia. Teutonic Knights could not hope to compete with Templars or Hospitallers in Syria, so they devoted their energies to Armenia, where their chief strongholds appear to have been Amouda – a plain keep of Rhineland pattern – and Haruniye. King Lavon the Great became a *halbbruder* or confrère. In 1210 most brethren perished with their third Hochmeister, Hermann Bart, on an obscure Cilician campaign. At that date the Teutonic Order numbered twenty at most.

Hermann von Salza, his successor, was the real founder of the Order's greatness.[2] Born in about 1170, in his youth he attended the court of the dukes of Thuringia, where he was supposed to have acquired distinguished manners, and certainly he knew how to win the favour of princes. In 1219 King Jean de Brienne awarded the Hochmeister the privilege of bearing the Gold Cross of Jerusalem under the Order's black cross in his achievement of arms to commemorate the knights' bravery at the siege of Damietta. In 1226 the Emperor Frederick II made Hermann and his successors Princes of the Empire, while the pope presented him with a magnificent ring, afterwards used at the inauguration of every Hochmeister. It is a testimony to Hermann's statesmanship that he succeeded in remaining on good terms with both papacy and emperor; at the 'coronation' of the excommunicated Frederick as King of Jerusalem in 1229, Teutonic Knights mounted guard in the Holy Sepulchre and Hermann read the emperor's proclamation in French and German. The sceptical, ruthless Frederick appears to have had a genuine regard for the dedicated religious, and encouraged his order's progress. In 1229 a second headquarters was built, Montfort (or 'Starkenberg'), north-east of Acre, whose original function was to defend the thin corridor which then connected Jerusalem with the sea. However, there is not sufficient space to deal fully with their activities in Palestine, where they were always overshadowed by Templars and Hospitallers. The German brothers were to find their true destiny in Europe.

King Andrew II of Hungary was worried about eastern Transylvania, savagely raided by heathen Kumans. In 1211 he gave its mountainous Barcasag district to the Teutonic Order. The brethren adapted methods of warfare learnt in Syria and Armenia, building a network of wooden fortresses, and the Turkish Kumans proved neither so numerous nor so skilful as their Anatolian cousins. By 1225 the 'Burzenland' had not only been pacified but settled with German colonists. King Andrew grew alarmed; in any case the Kumans were now being integrated with the Magyars. Suddenly he descended on the Burzenland with a large army and evicted the knights. After loud protests Hermann began to look elsewhere.

Livonia, the modern Estonia and Latvia, was peopled by pagan Baltic and Finnish tribes. To the east it was bounded by Russian princes, whilst to the north it was scantily settled at Reval by Danes. The idea of a Holy War in northern Europe was not new. In 1147 the ubiquitous St Bernard had summoned all Germans to a crusade against the heathen Wends, who lived across the Elbe. Livonia was a fair enough prospect for land-hungry Teutons. In 1201 Albrecht von Buxhövden sailed from

Lübeck with a great fleet of colonists to found Riga at the mouth of the river Dvina, in the land of the Baltic Livs. The town prospered and many Livonians were converted. Nevertheless the little colony could not afford to depend on stray crusaders for protection, and in 1204 Albrecht, now Bishop of Riga, founded the Sword Brethren, who took the Templars' rule. The habit was white, marked with a red sword and red cross on the left shoulder. Their purpose was the defence of 'Mary's land', commemorated in the lines spoken by the Master in the ceremony of profession:

> Dis Schwert entfange von meiner Hand
> Zu schützen Gotts und Marien Landt.

They are supposed to have admitted postulants of ignoble birth, but recent research seems to disprove this legend.[3] Master Wenno von Rhorbach was murdered by one of his own brethren in 1208,[4] yet they were fine soldiers. For Albrecht, colonization was as much a part of the crusade as conversion. First his *Schwertbrüder* built the castle of Wenden as a headquarters, then they invaded Estonia with an army half-German, half-Livonian, penetrating the deep pine forests to rout the natives and their Russian allies; in 1227 they conquered the island of Oesel (Saaremaa), shrine of the god Tarapilla. German burghers settled in the new towns and the colony rested on sound foundations when its bishop died in 1229.

The bishop, later Archbishop of Riga, was the true governor of Marienland, and at first a system of dividing conquered territory between bishop and brethren worked very well. ('Thus arose the first Order State,' observes their modern historian, Friedrich Benninghoven.) Large estates were given to German nobles, in return for military service. Shortly after Albrecht's death the Sword Brethren proclaimed a Holy War against 'the Northern Saracens' and made steady progress. They possessed six preceptories, each administered by a guardian or '*vogt*', their chief strongholds being Wenden and Fellin, though the Master's seat was the Jurgenhoff at Riga. They also had chaplains, according to the priest chronicler, Heinrich von Lettland. Soon they wrested sovereignty from the bishop, seizing church lands, while their stern rule embittered their subjects who rebelled more than once. In 1237 the second Master, Wolquin Schenk (probably a son of the Count of Naumberg), was defeated and slain with fifty of his brethren – 'cut down like women amid the marshes' – at Siauliai by the Kurs in alliance with the Lithuanian prince, Mindaugas.[5]

In the meantime Hochmeister Hermann von Salza had seen other opportunities. The seaboard from the Vistula to the Niemen and its hinterland of lakes, marshes, sandy heaths and pinewood were inhabited by the heathen *Prusiskai*, a Baltic people who spoke a language closely related to Lithuanian.[6] The latter, in the primeval forest north and east of Poland, resembled the Prussian tribes in everything except disunity and were now coming together under the able Mindaugas. Balts worshipped idols in sacred groves and fields, and attributed divine powers to the entire creature-world, including their own animals.[7] They practised human sacrifice, by burning or beheading, and buried animals alive at funerals; dead warriors were cremated astride their horses, while widows were often made to hang themselves. Stockades of towns and temples were adorned with animal skulls to ward off the evil eye, their grim shrines served by weird priests and soothsayers. The Prussians' domestic habits were as unpleasant as their religion. The old, the sick, the blind and the lame were invariably slaughtered. Drunkenness from mead and fermented mares' milk was a major pastime while tribesmen often drank the living blood from their horses' veins. Inter-tribal warfare was endemic. Hermann decided that Prussia would make a good training ground for the wars in Outremer.

Konrad, Duke of Mazovia, had become so demoralized by Prussian raids that he abandoned the entire province of Chelmo. In 1222 the bishops of Kujawia and Plock recruited a handful of German knights to form a new military order as protection, the Order of Dobrzyn, though it proved to be ineffectual. Konrad offered Chelmo to Hermann with any other territory his brethren might succeed in conquering. In 1223 the Hochmeister obtained a document from his friend the emperor, known as the Golden Bull of Rimini, later confirmed by the pope, which gave him full sovereignty over these lands with nominal papal suzerainty. Two knights arrived in 1229 and built the castle of Vogelsang ('Birdsong') on the Vistula but were soon killed by the Prussians.[8]

The year after, one of the Teutonic Order's great heroes came with twenty knights and 200 sergeants to take possession of Vogelsang. It was Hermann Balke, styled *Landpfleger* (Preceptor), whose skill in war was equalled by his modesty and generosity. It is no exaggeration to call Balke the Pizarro of the Baltic lands. Most of his troops were volunteers who regarded themselves as Crusaders, the brethren acting both as command structure and as panzers. The Emperor gave lands in Apulia to establish southern Italian commanderies, providing the necessary financial resources. Help also came from Bohemia and Silesia. Transport was supplied by the seafaring merchants of Lübeck. In 1231 Hermann crossed the Vistula and stormed a fortress-temple, hanging the Prussian chief from his own sacred oak tree. This *Landpfleger* used his enemies' tactics of forest ambush. At first the Prussians were scornful of his tiny force, but soon they came to dread it. White-robed horsemen attacked them even in the snow and, riding over frozen rivers or charging out of blizzards like winter ghosts, their great cloaks served for camouflage. 'Often under the weird glitter of the Northern Lights combat was joined upon the ice that covered the rivers and marshes, until the solid crust broke beneath the weight of the warriors and the men of both sides were engulfed to their chilly doom.'[9] Tribesmen who fought on horseback with sword and battleaxe or on foot with bows found the uncanny strangers' terrible charge irresistible, very different from undisciplined Polish levies. The '*Pruzzes*', as the Germans called them, retreated to simple forts which were easily overrun by the brethren who employed *ballistae*, huge stone-throwing catapults, and used crossbows to pick off the defenders on the walls. Balke allied with one tribe to defeat another, Prussians who submitted and accepted Christianity being left in possession of their lands and enlisted as auxiliary troops.

Systematically he reduced the territory between the Vistula and the Niemen, penetrating up the rivers and consolidating his gains by wooden blockhouses.

In 1232 the town of Kulm (Chelmno) was founded on the left bank of the Vistula, in 1233 that of Marienwerder. The same year a Northern crusade was launched, the brethren joining forces with Duke Konrad and Duke Swientopelk of Pomerellen, and a great victory was won on the Sirgune where 1,500 Prussians fell. In 1234 the Hochmeister himself came to inspect Kulm and Thorn (Thorun). The year after, the Order of Dobrzyn was united with the Teutonic Order. Elbing was founded in 1237 near the mouth of the Vistula, and brethren could now attack along the Frisches Haff. By 1238 Pomezanien and Pogezanien were completely subdued. A new polity had been created, the *Ordens-staat*, or Order-State, ruled by the brethren themselves; German colonists, not only noblemen and burghers but peasants too, were brought in and given land. After the disastrous defeat of the Sword Brethren in 1237[10] the survivors applied for affiliation with the Teutonic Knights, a union ratified by the pope. Hermann Balke left Prussia with sixty knights to become Landmeister of Livonia with a hierarchy of officers similar to the Hochmeister's. A Landmeister of Prussia was also appointed, though Livonian Landmeisters always enjoyed greater independence. Two years later he and Hermann von Salza died, leaving their Order an extraordinary and magnificent destiny. Already it controlled 150 miles of the Baltic coastline from which to launch its conquest of the interior.

The vocation of the Teutonic Knight in Prussia and Livonia differed from those of his comrades in Palestine, who were in contact with a superior civilization. Prussians were aggressively barbarous and their land of swamps and forests held no sacred associations. Extremely treacherous, the tribesmen were expert at ambushes and their ways with prisoners did not endear them. The Order's chronicles describe the fate of two knights. One was placed in a cleft tree-trunk held apart by ropes which were released, crushing the wretched brother, whereupon the tree was

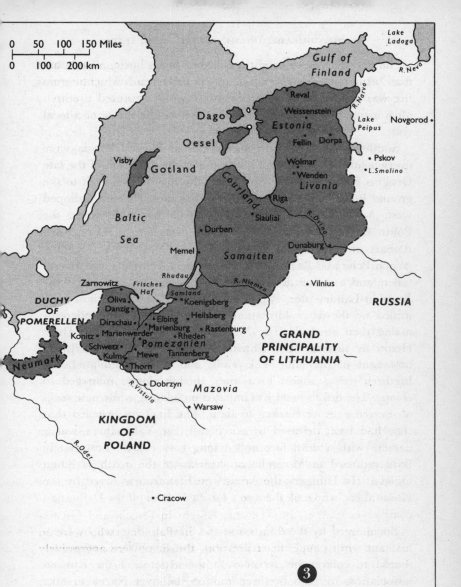

The Lands of the Teutonic
Order at their widest
extent, c. 1407

set on fire. The other knight was lashed to his horse, mount and man being hauled to the top of an oak underneath which a great fire was lit. The usual practice was to roast captured brethren alive in their armour, like chestnuts, before the shrine of a local god.

Suddenly in 1237 the principalities of Kievan Russia were overwhelmed by a Mongol horde under the grandson of the late Genghis Khan, Batu the Splendid, who burnt Kiev itself to the ground in 1240, massacring every living soul. He then galloped west. A division commanded by Baibars Khan destroyed the Polish army of Boleslav the Chaste in March 1241. On 9 April Baibars met the troops of Duke Henry of Silesia at Liegnitz: 30,000 Poles and Bavarians with a force of Templars and Hospitallers and a strong detachment of Teutonic Knights under the Prussian Landmeister, Poppo von Osterna. The Christians were misled by the dense formations of the Mongols and underestimated their strength. The Mongols seem to have taken Duke Henry by surprise. The Christians broke before the whirlwind onslaught of the Nine Yak Tails, and were annihilated, the brethren dying almost to a man, though Poppo managed to escape. The duke's head was impaled on a lance, while nine sacks of severed ears were taken to Batu. The fugitives believed that they had been defeated by witchcraft; the Yak banner was a demon 'with a devil face and a long grey beard'. Fortunately Batu returned to Mongolia on hearing of the death of Khan Ogodai. (In Hungary the Arpad royal family was saved by the Hospitallers, who took them to a fortified island off the Dalmatian coast.)

Encouraged by the disasters of the Slavs, undeterred by Liegnitz and with papal encouragement, the Livonian Landmeister sought to enlarge his territory at the expense of the Russian schismatics. In 1240 brethren crossed the river Narva to take Pskov; their objective was Novgorod, of whose wealth alluring reports had been brought by German merchants. There was little love between the Orthodox Christians of Russ and Catholic Teutons. Novgorod was ruled by Prince Alexander Yaroslavovitch, surnamed Nevsky after his victory on the river Neva in 1240 when he had defeated the Swedes. Alexander chose his ground with care. In April the Knights – outnumbered sixty to one if the *Livlandische Reimchronik* is to be believed – were manoeuvred on to the ice of Lake Peipus, which could support lightly armed Slavs but not heavy German cavalry. Twenty Knights died with their Landmeister, as did many of the troops who had accompanied them. Eisenstein's film *Alexander Nevsky* caricatures the scene, but does at least provide some idea of the dread which the brethren inspired among Balts and Slavs; their huge horses, faceless helmets, black-crossed shields and billowing white cloaks gave them a truly nightmarish appearance. The 'Ice Slaughter' put an end to Teutonic hopes of expansion into Russia beyond the Narva.

Although a Christian, the Duke of Pomerellen, Swientopelk, at first the brethren's enthusiastic ally, had become increasingly restive. Like Andrew of Hungary, he now realized that a dangerous power was emerging as his neighbour. Too many Germans had settled in Pomerellen. The building of Elbing on the lower Vistula and the Order's claim to the Vistula delta alarmed him as much as the Germanization of his erstwhile Prussian enemies. Liegnitz and Lake Peipus gave him his chance to redress the situation. In late 1242 he attacked the brethren without warning, using his fleet of twenty ships to strike at them from the river. At the same time, aided by their untamed kinsmen in the east, the Prussian tribes revolted and relapsed into paganism. In the Kulmerland (Chelmno) alone 40,000 Germans perished. One tribe, the Pomezaniens, stayed loyal, but only Thorun and a few castles held out.

Livonia was laid waste by Mindaugas and his savage Lithuanians. He had united them under his leadership, killing or cowing rival princes and making himself king. He equipped his mounted warriors with chain mail and swords captured from Germans or Slavs and with short throwing spears; they employed Mongol-style tactics but, instead of shooting arrows, hurled their javelins at short range. His infantry were armed with pikes, axes and crossbows.

He put his entire domain on a military footing, every able-bodied male being recruited to raid and lay waste in carefully planned campaigns. He increased his territory steadily at the expense of the Slavs, who submitted to his rule or else paid tribute. The dynasty he founded would continue his formidable organization and his aggressive policies.

However, the Teutonic Order now had commanderies all over Germany with the manpower to cope with the situation. A hundred commanderies from the German bailiwicks attended the chapter-general of 1250. Nevertheless, it took a full-scale crusade to rescue their beleaguered brethren in Prussia. In 1254 an army of 60,000 Germans and Czechs marched to their aid, led by Rudolf of Habsburg and Ottokar II of Bohemia. The most thickly populated region of Prussia, the Samland peninsula north of the Pregel estuary, was overrun and the Sambians, the foremost Prussian tribe, were conquered. Königsberg was founded, named after King Ottokar. Hochmeister Poppo von Osterna finally restored order and by 1260 had overcome all the western tribes as well.[11]

In Livonia the Lithuanians were beaten off, while two capable Landmeisters, Gruningen and Struckland, tamed the Kurs – Memel being built to stop arms from reaching the Kurs. Mindaugas made peace, seemingly converted to Christianity; with the pope's blessing he was crowned King of Lithuania. The brethren's aim was now to join Livonia to Prussia by conquering the Lithuanian seaboard. However, in 1260 Livonia was raided by tribesmen whom Mindaugas declined to control. Through the Kurs' treachery Landmeister von Hornhausen was ambushed at Durbe, perishing with 150 Knights who included the Marshal of Prussia. Mindaugas threw off Christianity and attacked, joined by Russians who seized Dorpat. The Kurs and Estonians rose in revolt. In 1263 Mindaugas's nephew Treniota crushed the Livonian brethren outside Riga and swept on into Prussia. But by some providence Mindaugas, Treniota and Alexander Nevsky all died later that year. By 1267 the Kurs had at last been brought to heel.

Even so, Durbe had precipitated a Prussian rebellion which went on for thirteen years, the 'great apostasy' as brethren termed it. The tribes united under Herkus Monte and Glappon, two able leaders who had lived in Germany and who understood the Knights' tactics, the possibilities of wooded terrain and how to besiege castles. They acquired crossbows and stone-throwing catapults, then they cut the waterways. Almost every command-ery fell, even Marienwerder; Königsberg had to be rescued by the Livonian Landmeister. To survive, brethren acted on the axiom 'who fights the Order fights Jesus Christ'. Double apostates who worshipped snakes could not hope for any mercy.[12] Tribes disap-peared without trace, their villages obliterated, Prussian *capitanes* (leaders) being kidnapped or hunted down. Brethren copied Prussian tactics, sending raiding parties deep into the forest, guided by friendly tribesmen.[13] No quarter was given. By 1273 the Prussian Landmeister Konrad von Thierberg, having broken his rebellious subjects for good, went on to conquer hitherto untamed tribes. Their last leader, Skurdo, laid waste his own lands and took his people to Lithuania. By the end of 1283 only 170,000 Prussians remained in Prussia.[14]

No doubt the Knights found justification in the Old Testament. 'So Joshua smote all the country of the hills and of the south and of the vale, and of the springs, and all their kings: he left none remaining, but utterly destroyed all that breathed as the Lord God commanded. And Joshua smote them from Kadesh-Barnea even unto Gaza and all the country of Goshon even unto Gibeon. And all these kings and their land did Joshua take at one time, because the Lord God of Israel fought for Israel.' Many Land-meisters must have seen themselves as Joshuas.

These early Teutonic Knights were famous for a meticulous observance of the Order's rule.[15] Self-renunciation was absolute, the only possessions allowed being a sword,[16] a habit and a right to bread and water; no brother was allowed to use his family coat of arms – the black cross was the sole blazonry permitted, though Livonian banners bore the Virgin.[17] Fur coats, indispensable in Baltic winters, had to be of goat or sheep skin. Beards were

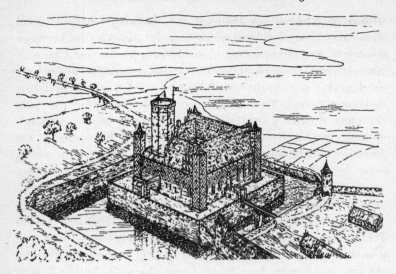

5. The commandery of the Teutonic Knights at Rheden in West Prussia as it must have appeared at the end of the thirteenth century. The four wings form chapel, dormitory, refectory and chapter house, fortified on the outside, while the cloisters are on an upper floor in case enemies should penetrate to the courtyard

compulsory. Brethren slept by their swords, fully clothed, rising in the night to say Office. No meat was eaten in Lent or Advent, when the diet was restricted to porridge with an occasional egg. The Bible was read at all meals. Self-flagellation took place every Friday; to curb the flesh still further, a mail shirt was sometimes worn next to the skin. On campaign the Knights heard Mass daily, before dawn in the Marshal's tent, where the Office was recited at the prescribed hours. Silence was kept on the march as in the cloister. On the battlefield the Marshal enforced discipline with a club. It was scarcely surprising that this strict observance began to relax during the later thirteenth century.

Triumph on the Baltic was offset by Outremer's collapse. In 1271 Starkenberg was lost, in 1291 the German Hospital vanished with Acre. Armenia was falling to the Mamelukes, Greece to the Byzantines. The Hochmeister waited in vain at Venice for a crusade to recover the Holy Land. In 1308 the Archbishop of Riga, hoping to regain control of the city, asked Pope Clement V to suppress the Teutonic Order because of its luxury, cruelty and injustice; accusations of sodomy and witchcraft followed. In 1309 Hochmeister Siegfried von Feuchtwangen moved the Grand Commandery to Marienburg, the Prussian Landmeister's post being merged with that of Hochmeister.

6

THE ORDENSLAND:
AN ARMY WITH A COUNTRY

Marienburg (known as 'Malbork' since 1945) was the symbol of the Order: a combination of fortress, palace, barracks and monastery. It dominated the Vistula, down which not only Prussian but Polish trade reached the Baltic. Like all military religious, the celibate brethren had a deep and tender devotion to the Virgin Mary, an enormous yet gracious statue of whom dominated the castle. None the less the splendour of their court was greater than that of many of the visiting European kings. It was presided over by the reigning Hochmeister, whose white habit was embroidered with a great black-and-gold cross, charged with the Hohenstaufen eagle and the lilies of St Louis. He was always escorted by four carefully chosen knights-in-waiting, the *Hochmeister companiones* who stood at his side to prevent a repetition of the tragedy of 1330. (That year Werner von Orselen, a demanding superior noted for piety, had severely punished a certain Johann von Biendorf for gross immorality; one dark November evening as the Hochmeister was attending Vespers in his private chapel the revengeful knight stabbed him to death.) Hochmeisters more than rated such semi-regal state; their Prussian and Livonian lands were outside the empire so they were real sovereigns. Under Hochmeister Luther, Duke of Brunswick, a talented musician, the great castle became another Wartburg, the setting of scenes worthy of *Tannhäuser*. There were frequent song-contests and on one occasion a pathetic figure appeared from the past, a Prussian harpist who sang in his own almost forgotten tongue. Jeering, the knights awarded this ridiculous ghost a prize, a sack of rotten walnuts, before sending him back to the forest and his sacred oak trees. Marienburg was a truly Wagnerian capital and indeed the minnesinger Tannhäuser seems to have been a *Deutschritter* for a short period.

A young knight might serve some years in a frontier blockhouse, but the greater part of his career was passed in the commanderies. He could be posted to the Levant – Greece or Armenia – while there were commanderies in Italy and even France, though after the thirteenth century few brethren lived outside Germany or the Baltic lands. It has been suggested that Hermann von Salza himself gave the Order a bureaucratic tradition derived from Norman Sicily, and certainly the administration followed a uniform pattern from the Mediterranean to the Baltic.[1] Officials developed the art of scientific book-keeping; financial and legal experts were employed and archives meticulously kept, including a personal dossier on each brother. Chaplains and sisters ran sixty hospitals and refuges for the destitute. Each Landkomtur was responsible for his district's colonization, later tax collection and the maintenance of roads and schools, as well as defence, while he was also president of the provincial Landthing. The chief relaxation of all brethren was hunting; not for pleasure but the necessary extermination of primeval fauna – wolf, bear, lynx, elk, aurochs and bison – which terrorized the settlers or ruined their crops. If elderly or infirm, brothers retired to a kind of Chelsea Hospital at Marienburg. Most came from the Rhineland or Westphalia – Westphalians predominating in Livonia. The latter, more dour and reserved, disliked the Rhinelanders' noisy volatility and tended to think them frivolous. Celibacy did not seem so ghastly a privation to the medieval mind as it does to the modern, and the Order offered an adventurous career to landless younger sons; a fair number of ne'er-do-wells took the habit in order to avoid criminal proceedings. For fear of nepotism the brotherhood would not admit Prussians, whether German or Balt, after about 1400.

The settlement of Prussia was the outstanding colonial achievement of the Middle Ages, the most successful economically. Nearly a hundred towns and a thousand villages were established under the brethren's auspices. Cultivation spread inland from the

Baltic and up the lower Vistula until the southern and south-eastern borderlands came under the plough. German and Dutch peasants, led by a *locator*[2] who combined the functions of immigration agent and village mayor, were given freeholdings in return for rent in kind. Marketplaces were set up. There were no labour dues, and peasants were not tied to the soil. Noblemen came too, and were granted estates, forming the new gentry.[3] An alliance was forged with the Cistercians, the White Monks who had a genius for transforming forest and swamp into fertile farmland. Most Prussians were reduced to serfdom though steadily Germanized. Marshes were drained, sea walls built, forests cleared and the sandy soil conquered by the heavy German plough. Customs duty was levied, but there were no inland tolls on the well-kept roads or the rivers, which were patrolled by the brethren. Understandably, there was little brigandage. By the fourteenth century, Prussia had the most contented peasant freeholders in Europe.

The Knights had learnt the value of commerce in the Levant and kept a fleet of merchantmen. They copied Templar banking methods, bills of exchange being accepted at larger commanderies. They enforced a uniform system of weights and measures, and minted their own coinage. In 1263, at the height of the Prussian rebellion, they obtained papal permission to trade, exporting grain in vast quantities from their estates. The *Gross-Schaffer* ('Grand Shepherd'), directly responsible to the Gross-Komtur at the Marienburg, was in effect a Minister of Trade; he managed the cornlands of West Prussia, employing salesmen to buy and sell grain. The Gross-Schaffer of the Grossmarschall at Königsberg supervised those of East Prussia and also the export of yellow amber, much prized for rosaries, of which the Order had a monopoly. In addition, the Ordensland exported silver, timber, salt, cloth, wax, furs, horses and falcons. It imported iron, copper and wine from western Germany, wool and, later, cloth from England. As a member of the Hanseatic League, the Hoch-meister was well able to sympathize with the ambitions of his merchants, who grew rich and had every reason to be grateful to the Order. They belonged to 'weapon clubs', riding fully armed with the Knights in emergencies.

Every landowner, whether German noble or Prussian chieftain, held his land from the Order in return for military service. He also had to pay annually a bushel of grain, with another bushel for every 'plough' of land. (A plough was four hides, a hide being the minimum needed to feed a family.) Immigrant smallholders paid tithes in grain and silver – as much as a mark of silver per hide. The annual levy on millers could be fifty marks of silver in addition to payments in grain. Innkeepers paid four marks. Even the poorest Prussian serf, farming a single hide, had to contribute two-thirds of a bushel of wheat, rye or oats and had to perform specified labour dues on the Order's land.

When a Hochmeister died, the Gross-Komtur summoned the Land-Komturs (senior commanders) of Germany, Prussia and Apulia as the first stage in an electoral system designed to avoid lobbying. They nominated a president who selected twelve electors – seven knights, four sergeants and a priest – each one joining in the process of selection as soon as he was chosen. When the twelve were complete, they elected the new Hochmeister. He was a limited monarch, whose bailiffs comprised a council rather like a modern cabinet of ministers and whose household revenues were kept separate from those of the *Ordensstaat*. One law governed Prussia, that of the Hochmeister and his council, applying to laymen and clerics alike. The Church was very much the servant of the knights' state. There was no archbishop, and all four bishops were priest-brethren of the Order. It is this uniformity of law and administration, co-ordinating foreign policy, internal government, church affairs, trade and industry, which gives substance to the claim that Prussia was the first modern state.

The Ordensland could boast a literature, although, like most contemporary princes, many of its rulers could neither read nor write.[4] Several brethren wrote biblical commentaries, among them Heinrich von Hesler (*fl. c.* 1300) and the Ermeland canon Tilo von Kulm (*fl. c.* 1340). Heinrich's commentaries, *Evangelium Nicodemi* and *Apocalypsis*, are interesting for their criticism of the landowners' harsh treatment of the peasants. Hagiography was not neglected, and Hugo von Langenstein (*fl. c.* 1290) wrote a life of St Martina which was much admired in its day. He also compiled the *Mainauer Naturlehre*, a strange work which deals with geography, astronomy and medicine. The Order's mystics did not emerge until the end of the fourteenth century, though its first great historians were at work much earlier. The tradition begun by the *Chronica Terre Prussie* of Petrus von Dusburg – translated into rhyming German by Nikolaus von Jeroschin and continued up to 1394 by Wigand von Marburg, the Hochmeister's herald – would reach its height in the fifteenth century with the 'Annals' of Johann von Pusilge.[5] The chronicle of Petrus (*fl. c.* 1330) has an introduction in which each weapon is sanctified by its scriptural precedents, giving holy war an almost sacramental quality. There were also various translations of the Old Testament, especially of Job and the Maccabees, which, like the chronicles, were read in the refectories.

Chroniclers also flourished in Livland. Conquest and settlement, the union of the *Schwertbrüder* with the Teutonic Knights and the early years of 'Marienland' were vigorously recorded as the *Chronicon Livonicum Vetus* by Heinrich von Lettland (d. 1259). In the next century the story was continued by Hermann von Wartberge. One should also mention a short chronicle in German, *Die Riterlichen Meister und Brüder zu Lieflant*, by Dietleb von Alnpeke. These early Livonian chronicles strike a noticeably grim note, compounded of savagery and anxiety, even when compared with those of Prussia, which are harsh enough. The German presence on the shores of the northern Baltic was far more precarious than in Prussia – at times the 'Crusaders', both brethren and colonists, saw themselves as a beleaguered garrison.

The Teutonic Knights' one real aesthetic achievement was their architecture. A typical '*domus conventualis*' was a combination of austerity and strategic necessity. By 1300 there were twenty-three of them in Prussia alone. At first these houses consisted of a strong watch tower on the Rhineland pattern, with curtain-walls enclosing wooden conventual buildings, the whole surrounded by

6. Brass of the Teutonic Knight Kuno von Liebenstein, *c.* 1396

moats and earthworks. However, towards the end of the thirteenth century they began to build commanderies of a specific
design. Chapel, dormitory, refectory and chapter house formed
four bulky wings, fortified on the outside, often with a free-
standing watch tower. There were cloisters, but these were on an
upper floor in case enemies should enter the courtyard. The
brethren's architects evolved a style which, although borrowing
from Syrian, Italian, French and even English sources, remained
their own.

Marienburg was the outstanding example. Here, the original fortified monastery grew into four great wings of several storeys enclosing a courtyard with arcaded galleries on two storeys against such rooms as chapel, chapter house, dormitory, kitchen and armoury. Square towers at the corners were linked by a crenellated rampart along the roof. In the days of the Prussian Landmeisters, the *Hochschloss* followed the basic pattern: a quadrangle with cloisters enclosing a courtyard, strengthened by towers at each angle. The Marienburg one was built in stone, but the later outworks, the *Mittelschloss* and the west wing, were of brick. The *Mittelschloss* contained the great refectory with star-shaped vaulting resting on delicate, attenuated, granite pillars. The Hochmeister's apartments were in the west wing and his personal dining-room, the charming 'summer refectory', centred round a single pillar whose stem supported a mass of decorative brick vaulting. This graceful mingling of brick and stone produced an ethereal, almost mystical effect. The nineteenth-century Romantic poet Eichendorff was so moved by its 'light diaphanous quality' that, standing in the summer refectory, he coined the phrase 'music turned to stone'. There were other great castle-commanderies at Thorun, Rheden, Mewe, Königsberg and Heilsberg. At Marienwerder the bishop's palace was both castle and fortified cathedral in one vast, yet undeniably elegant, red-brick building. The Ordensburgen's sombre history was relieved by the gaiety of their exquisite architecture.

The commanderies dominated the landscape of the *Ordensland*. However, there were other buildings in the brethren's distinctive style: walled towns and churches such as the Marienkirche at Danzig with its fantastic red gables. In Livonia, stone was plentiful, and brick was seldom used, but otherwise its architecture was very similar to that of Prussia. Towns were strengthened with massive citadels. At Reval and Narva there were tall towers named *Langer Hermann*, perhaps to commemorate the brave Landpfleger. The independent-minded Livonian bishops built castles in emulation of their Prussian colleagues, similar to the *domi conventuales* of the brethren, as the requirements of a dean and chapter were very like those of a *Haus-Komtur* and his twelve brother-knights. (The twentieth-century SS named their own fortresses *Ordensburgen.**)

Livland differed from Prussia in many ways. The Archbishop of Riga and his four bishops disputed power with the Order, frequently appealing to the pope and sometimes even to the heathen Lithuanians. So independent of Prussia was the Hochmeister's viceroy, the Landmeister, that some historians do not appreciate that he and his thirteen komturs were no longer Sword Brethren but Teutonic Knights. (He was appointed from two names submitted to the Hochmeister by the Livonian komturs.) His authority was far from absolute and often he had to seek approval from the province's *landtag* (assembly). However, the settlers were well aware that they depended on the Order for their survival. Largely confined to the towns, they formed a tiny percentage of the Livonian population, being always overwhelmingly outnumbered by the Baltic and Finno-Ugarian inhabitants.[6] Riga and the great commanderies of Dunamunde, Uskull, Lennewarden, Ascherade, Dunaberg, Wenden and Fellin were linked by water so that reinforcements could be rushed in should the natives rebel. During the night of 22 April 1343 the Estonians murdered 1,800 German men, women and children before attacking Reval. There they were routed by Landmeister von Dreileve, who swiftly restored order.[7]

The Teutonic Order's inspiration has been mistakenly seen as German nationalism by Slav, Balt and German historians alike. If Latin or German were used exclusively in administration, it was because the Baltic languages were unwritten. Prussians were forbidden to live in German villages because they were bad farmers who did not use the heavy German plough. Intermarriage was prohibited because too many natives remained pagan, not in order to avoid diluting German blood. In Samland, Christianized

---

* Oddly enough, Hitler's *Wolfschanz*, from where he directed his own *Drang nach Osten*, was near the site of the Teutonic Order's *Komturei* of Rastenburg.

Prussian chiefs were thoroughly assimilated, becoming indistinguishable from the German nobles whose daughters they married, building manor houses and adopting coats of arms. By the end of the thirteenth century, Prussians and Pomeranian Slavs were being admitted into the Order, some becoming komturs. The brethren's prejudices were religious and economic, not racial. They were Catholic Christians first and Germans second. The *Ordensstaat*'s primary purpose was the extirpation of paganism. The Knights could be ruthless enough when their interests were at stake. In 1331 King Władysław the Dwarf of Poland called them in to repress a rebellion at Danzig, whereupon they kept the town for themselves. The Poles routed the Knights at Płowce the following year, but proved unable to defeat them decisively. Casimir III abandoned the struggle in 1343, ceding Danzig and Pomerania to the Order by the Treaty of Kalisz.

The paganism of Lithuania was the Teutonic Order's *raison d'être*. Under Grand Duke Gediminas (1315–41), secure in his forests, the Lithuanians absorbed the Ukraine as far as Kiev, creating the largest state in Europe. Their Ruthenian neighbours began to civilize them, some becoming Orthodox Christians,[8] while Gediminas encouraged Polish merchants and artisans to settle in Lithuania. He began to build a more centralized government and his warriors acquired cannon. Nevertheless, as high priest of such deities as Percunos the Fire God, Potrempa the Water God and, most sinister of all, Dverkos the Hare God, the Grand Duke continued to serve the sacred green snakes and the holy fire of sweet-smelling amber in the magic oak-grove next to his palace at Vilnius.

There was unending war between the Order and the subjects of Lithuanian Grand Dukes. Its terrain was the '*Wiltnisse*' or Wilderness: primeval forest, heath and scrubland with innumerable lakes and marshes. The Knights attacked from the sea, sailing up the rivers; their clinker-built cogs were bigger than any Lithuanian boat and could carry 500 troops. Alternatively they raided through the dense woods and fens after being trained in woodcraft by Prussian trackers. They took their armour and provisions with them on pack-horses; the armour, heavier now with plates for limbs and shoulders, could be worn only when they reached the banks of the Niemen. Besides all the hazards of ambush, they sometimes lost their way beneath the pine trees which hid the sun and the stars, and died from starvation; it was not unknown for brethren to go mad from forest 'cafard'. If taken prisoner, they were sacrificed to the Lithuanian gods, captured komturs being invariably burnt alive in the sacred oak-groves – like Markward von Raschau in 1389. Seventy expeditions were launched from Prussia between 1345 and 1377, and another thirty from Livland.[9]

The most important were in the summer, the 'sommer-reysa', waged jointly by the Hochmeister from Prussia and the Landmeister from Livland, synchronized by the Ordensmarschall's careful staffwork – which included scouting, establishing supply depots and assembling ships. The 'winter-reysa' in December and January was a much smaller affair, seldom involving more than 2,000 horsemen who made quick raids from a makeshift camp in enemy territory; there was always the danger of blizzards, which could be even more dangerous than Lithuanians. Summer or winter, if successful, the Knights would return with cattle and prisoners.

The brethren were dreaded by their adversaries. When in 1336 they besieged and stormed a fort at Pilenai on the Niemen, rather than be captured the Lithuanians burnt all their goods in a great funeral pyre, killed their women and children, and then beheaded each other. An old priestess decapitated more than 100 warriors with an axe before splitting her own head as the Knights broke into the stockade.

Samaiten, the Lithuanian seaboard, was inhabited by a ferocious tribe who prevented the union of Prussia and Livland. The Knights had a man equal to the task, Winrich von Kniprode, who had joined them as a boy of ten and was Hochmeister from 1351 to 1382.[10] A jovial Rhinelander, he was elected after an already brilliant military career and soon introduced reforms which revitalized the entire Order. Imposing as Marienburg was,

Winrich built a new palace, the superb *Mittelschloss* with its beautiful gardens. Here he presided with true south German gaiety over a splendid court, welcoming a never-ending stream of foreign visitors for whom he provided sumptuous banquets and entertainments, with music and jugglers. Among those who came were Knights of Rhodes, from their own Order's German commanderies.[11] Tournaments (in which, as religious, the brethren did not take part) were frequently arranged. However, there was wisdom in the Hochmeister's extravagant hospitality, for the papacy had promised the full spiritual privileges of a crusader to those who assisted the Order, and throughout the fourteenth century the princes and noblemen of Europe flocked to fight the Lithuanians. The blind king, John of Bohemia, who died at Crécy, had lost his eye in Samaiten; he was accompanied in Prussia by his secretary, the composer Guillaume de Machaut. Marshal Boucicault, the French paladin, fought at the brethren's side,[12] while Henry of Derby, later Henry IV of England, paid two visits to the Hochmeister's court, though this was after Winrich's day.[13] No doubt he was enrolled as a *halbbruder*, a confrère knight. A young Yorkshireman, the twenty-year-old Sir Geoffrey Scrope – brother of a future Archbishop of York – fell fighting at Winrich's side in 1362 and was buried in Königsberg cathedral, where for centuries a window commemorated him.[14] Many English and Scots took part in the wars of 'the High Master of the Dutch Knights', while Chaucer's reference to such an episode in the career of his knight is well known:

> Ful ofte time he hadde the bord bigonne
> aboven alle naciouns in Pruce
> In Lettow hadde he reysed and in Ruce
> No Cristen man so ofte of his degree.

The Ordensland's campaigns had the attraction of big-game hunting in the nineteenth century. The courtly, charming Hochmeister understood how to make the best use of such enthusiasm.

Winrich tried to raise the spiritual and educational level of the Order. There were to be two learned brethren in every *komturei*, a theologian and a lawyer. A law school was set up at Marienburg, and the Hochmeister at one time contemplated founding a University of Kulm. So many recruits joined the brethren that there were not enough posts for them; there were probably 700 knights in Prussia by the end of Winrich's reign. He solved the problem by setting up convent houses as well as commanderies. These consisted of twelve knights and six priest-brethren, emphasis being put on the Office and spiritual life. There were four such houses in Marienburg alone.

More junkers were employed in official posts and their levies organized into a formidable militia. However, Winrich protected the peasantry against them, and indeed earned the title of the peasants' friend.[15] He was equally jealous of his burghers' privileges, defending them from foreign competition and issuing an excellent new coinage.

Winrich was determined to exterminate 'the skin-clad Samogitians' of Samaiten and their deities, to whom human sacrifice was far from unknown. Two extremely able grand dukes, Algirdas and Kestutis, led the enemy during thirty years of unbroken warfare, but the crisis came in 1370 when a vast army marched on Königsberg and was beaten back by the Hochmeister himself at Rhudav (Rudawa). He lost his Marshal[16] with 26 komturs and 200 other brethren, but the Lithuanians, who had lost their standard, never dared face him again. He played off one grand duke against another and kept on friendly terms with Poland. Always an innovator, he introduced ship-borne cannon for the *winter-reysa* of 1381. By the time Winrich died in 1382 he had secured Samaiten and seized Trakai, a mere fourteen miles from Vilnius. It was the Ordensland's zenith.

But in 1386 Grand Duke Iogaila became a Catholic, married the Polish Queen Jadwiga, and was crowned King Władysław II of Poland and Lithuania. The holy fire at Vilnius was extinguished for ever, and next year Iogaila set about converting his subjects. However, the Order claimed, with some justice, that many were still heathen or Orthodox schismatics. Only recently, in 1377, Grand Duke Algirdas had been cremated with his horses in the forest. As late as 1413 a French visitor, Guillebert de Lanoy, noted that some tribesmen still burnt their dead, splendidly dressed, on oak pyres within the sacred groves.[17]

The *Ordensstaat* was strong enough to defy Iogaila's vast empire, as his viceroy in Lithuania, Grand Duke Vitautas, took an independent line and even allied with the brethren, abandoning Samaiten, though the natives still held out in their swamps and forests. Konrad von Juningen, Hochmeister from 1394 to 1407, was an able statesman. He saw clearly that the Polish–Lithuanian Empire would only be united by opposition from the Order, and encouraged Vitautas to expand eastwards. In 1399 the grand duke rode against the Golden Horde, over the Russian plains, with a great army of Lithuanian and Ruthenian boyars. Amongst them, oddly assorted, were the exiled Tartar Khan, Toktamish, and a detachment of 500 men from the Teutonic Order. Tamberlane's lieutenant, Edegey Khan, met them on the river Vorskla, a tributary of the Dnieper. He used the tactics employed at Liegnitz and slaughtered two-thirds of Vitautas's army, pursuing him mercilessly over the steppes. This ended 'Mad Witold's' hopes of conquering the lands of the Golden Horde. He turned on the *Ordensstaat*. Desperately Konrad tried to keep the peace, besides attempting to secure an alliance with the Khan of Kazan. The brethren possessed fifty-five towns and forty-eight fortresses, and their subjects were prosperous and contented. The *Ordenstaat* could triumph, so long as it avoided a general conflict with all its enemies. But the peace-loving Konrad died in 1407, his death from gall-stones supposedly hastened by spurning his doctor's remedy – to sleep with a woman.

The untameable Samogitians overran Memel in 1397, occupying the fortress-town which linked the *Ordensstaat*'s two halves, but the brethren recaptured it in 1406. This was the limit of their territorial expansion. They had purchased the Neumark of Brandenburg from Emperor Sigismund in 1402, and their control of the Baltic coastline was not to be equalled until the Swedish empire of the seventeenth century. In 1398 the brethren had landed an army on the island of Gotland, occupied by Swedish pirates, the 'Sea Victuallers', who preyed on the Hansa ships. These were driven out and the seas patrolled. The island was then seized by the Danes, and so the knights returned in 1404 with 15,000 troops and retook it, as well as 200 Danish ships, installing the Hansa in Visby, the capital. Finally, in 1407, the new Hochmeister, Ulrich von Juningen, gave it back to Margaret of Denmark in return for a guarantee to protect the Hansa.

King Władysław did his best to provoke the Order. Polish merchants were forbidden to trade with the burghers of Prussia and Livland, who were already made restive by the Hansa's decline and resented the Order's private trading ventures. At Władysław's request, the Duke of Pomerania blockaded the roads from Germany. Władysław also fanned discontent among the Prussian junkers, resentful of komturs most of whom came from the Rhineland, besides persuading the Samogitians to rebel. Konrad's dying words had been a plea not to elect his brother in his place, since Ulrich was notoriously proud and foolhardy. In 1409 the smouldering border disputes broke into open war. Władysław and Vitautas assembled 150,000 troops, every man they could muster, together with large contingents of Tartars and Cossacks, and also of Czech, Vlach and Hungarian mercenaries under Jan Zizka (the future military genius of the Hussite wars). The Order's entire force – Knights, mercenaries and volunteers – totalled 80,000. Apart from his Polish chivalry, Władysław's army consisted chiefly of light horse, while the Order's was mainly heavy cavalry save for a few arbalestiers with the new steel crossbows and some artillery brought from Tannenberg. The Livland brethren could not come in time, but the Knights seem to have been confident of victory.

The two armies met at Tannenberg in Prussia, among the Mazurian marshes, on 15 July 1410. True to his role as God's champion, the Hochmeister scorned the suggestion of a surprise attack. The Poles sang the battle-hymn of St Adalbert, whereupon the brethren replied with the Easter song, 'Crist ist enstandin',[18] the guns spoke briefly, then the heavy Ordensland cavalry, in plate armour and hounskull helmets, attacked, roaring the old

7. Hochmeister Ulrich von Juningen, killed at Tannenberg, 1410

war cry, 'Gott mit uns', a hammer-like mass of gleaming steel. It shattered the left wing of Czechs and Lithuanians, nearly smashing the right. However, the Poles held stubbornly in the centre and their allies rallied. His left wing had not yet reformed, but Ulrich charged with the entire reserve, weakened by the treacherous desertion of Kulmerland junkers. The Poles still held. After many more charges, at the end of a long day, the knights were outflanked, and the battle degenerated into a sword and axe mêlée while Tartars surrounded the brethren. Their grim and stubborn Hochmeister refused to leave the 'Götterdämmerung' he had brought about, fighting on in his gilt armour and white cloak beneath the great battle banner, white and gold with its black cross and eagle,[19] till he was cut down (when found, his body had been mutilated almost beyond recognition).[20] 18,000 of the Ordensland's army were said to have been killed, including the Grosskomtur, the Ordensmarschall and many komturs, 205 Knights in all. It was claimed that 14,000 of their host were taken prisoner, including a large number of Knights – most of whom were tortured or beheaded – while fifty of their standards were hung up as trophies in Cracow cathedral. Whatever the exact figures for casualties, the battle of Tannenberg was indisputably the Teutonic Order's Hattin.

Heinrich von Plauen, Komtur of Schwetz, galloped from Pomerania to Marienburg with 3,000 men, and, to prevent it affording cover, burnt the beautiful town to the ground. A vast army surrounded him, the captured guns of Marienburg battered the walls and, worst of all, the Order's subjects, even the bishops, gave the Poles a triumphant welcome while Kulmerland gentry sent him insulting messages.[21] Yet Plauen held on with cold courage. His brethren's morale had collapsed but was miraculously restored by a vision of Our Lady. After two months Władysław raised the siege and at the First Peace of Thorn in 1411 the Order lost only the Dobrzyn land (south-east of the Kulmerland) to Poland and Samaiten to Lithuania. But it was the end of the Baltic crusade.

THE CRUSADERS WITHOUT A CAUSE

Tannenberg marked the end of the belief that 'who fights the Order fights Jesus Christ'. No longer could Teutonic Knights count on a martyr's crown if they fell in battle, since their Lithuanian enemies were no longer pagan. The consequences of their defeat were compounded by severe economic troubles. Depopulation resulting from recurrent outbreaks of plague throughout Europe had steadily reduced the demand for wheat which had been the bedrock of the Ordensland's prosperity.

In *The Crutched Knights*, the Polish novelist Henryk Sienkiewicz imagines a Polish nobleman's visit to Marienburg in the fourteenth century and his horror at the local Prussian peasantry's down-trodden appearance. In reality they enjoyed better conditions than Polish serfs, many of whom fled to the Ordensland where lords were not allowed to flog them. But by 1410 many Prussian land-holdings were deserted and, because of an increasing shortage of labour, the Knights and the Prussian gentry had difficulty in cultivating their estates. Only the brethren could resort to forced labour, which made the gentry resentful. As early as 1397, those in the Kulmerland had formed 'The League of the Lizard' (*Eidechsenbund*) to express their grievances.

Just when its revenues were ruinously depleted, the Teutonic Order found itself with insufficient money to meet the indemnity demanded by the Poles at the Peace of Thorun. In 1412 Heinrich von Plauen, who had become Hochmeister, established a *Landesrat* (general assembly) of the Estates of Prussia, composed of twenty noblemen and twenty-seven burghers. Hoping to persuade them to pay higher taxes, he promised that in future no taxes would be imposed or wars declared without their agreement. But neither nobles nor burghers supported him.

More than a few Knights were angered by the establishment of a *Landesrat* and resented the way in which brethren who had taken refuge in Germany were brought back to Prussia in chains. Plauen had many enemies within the Order. He also had enemies outside it, especially in Danzig where he had beheaded the leading burghers for welcoming the Poles after Tannenberg.

King Władysław sent a stream of raiding parties into Prussia, and eventually the young Hochmeister, goaded beyond endurance, instructed the Grossmarschall to attack the Poles, but consulted none of his great officers, as he was bound by the constitutions. The Grossmarschall refused to march, forcing Plauen to summon a chapter. This met in October 1413 and deposed the tyrannical Hochmeister.[1] During his brief rule he antagonized all his subjects, knights and laymen. He saw his role as that of a visionary prince, not as the governor of an ecclesiastical corporation, and his arrogance cut at the roots of the Order's discipline. It is significant that his supporters were mainly Rhinelanders, his opponents north Germans. Regional prejudices were already sapping the Order's vitality.

His destroyer and successor, the elderly Grossmarschall, Michael Kuchmeister von Sternberg, who led the brethren in the war of 1414–22, knew the Order could not risk a pitched battle. The knights stayed in the impregnable Ordensburgen, riding forth on vicious raids by night. The Poles counter-attacked, entire districts of the Ordensland being depopulated by massacre or famine.[2] The pope even listened favourably to complaints by the Poles at the Council of Constance, though the Order's spokesman managed to avert condemnation. The war culminated with a full-scale Polish invasion of Prussia in 1422. Hochmeister Paul Bellizer von Rusdorf made peace, ceding Samaiten and also Nieszawa – the first town given to the Order by the Poles in the thirteenth century. The Deutschmeister (Landmeister of Germany) reproached him bitterly.

In 1430 Hochmeister Bellizer made a final attempt to break the Polish–Lithuanian alliance. There were two claimants to the Lithuanian throne: Svitrigaila, supported by the Orthodox boyars of the east, and Zigmantas, backed by the Poles who led the Catholic magnates of the west. Paul allied with Svitrigaila and in 1431 attacked Poland. In 1433 the Livonian Landmeister and his new friends carried all before them, only to be destroyed by plague,[3] while in 1455 the supporters of Zigmantas wiped out Svitrigaila's army, together with most of the Livonian brethren. It took years for the Order to recover its strength in the north.

Bohemia, convulsed by religious war, was not the ally against Poland she had been in the previous century. The Hussites were angered by the brethren's part in Emperor Sigismund's disastrous crusade against them. Hussite armies raided the Ordensland from Bohemia, their strange battle-wagons rolling deep into Prussia. They sang a grim war song, 'We, warriors of God', which ended 'slay, slay, slay, slay them every one' – perhaps they also brought their war drum whose skin was the skin of their blind and terrible leader, the dead Zizka. In 1433 Jan Czapko sacked Dirschau and Oliva.[4] The *wagenburgs*, laagers of armoured farm carts linked by chains, from behind which the peasant brigands shot with small hand-guns before sallying out with flails and scythes, proved as effective as modern tanks. Taborite heretics, the Bohemian scourge, enjoyed ravaging this clerical state, laying waste, torturing priests and junkers to death, and carrying the common people away to captivity. Then came plague, bad harvests and famine. The roads were left to brigands. In any case trade was dying, for the Hansa was already in decline when the Scanian herring fisheries failed in 1425. Medieval currency was based on a bi-metallic standard, and a growing scarcity of silver brought about a steady debasement of the coinage. The Livonian staple in Novgorod was undermined, while Prussian towns were ruined by imports. Restrictions imposed by the brethren, customs dues and a monopoly of the grain trade infuriated the bankrupt burghers of the Ordensland. Flat, sandy Prussia with its mournful mists had always been a gloomy land, but now it was becoming a desert.*

By 1450 the Teutonic Order's membership had dropped by a third. Men of inferior quality were being admitted. In at least one commandery anybody coming to complain would have his face slapped by the komtur and be told, 'Get out, son of a bitch. So far as you're concerned, I'm the Hochmeister.' Yet there were still Knights who lived their calling. In the fifteenth century an anonymous priest of the Frankfurt house wrote the *Theologica Germanica*, a handbook of mysticism based on Meister Eckhart, which enjoyed great popularity.† Even in the bewildering days of the Reformation, brethren were to remain faithful to their vows. It is probable that in most commanderies the rule was kept with a fair degree of regularity and much respect for tradition.

By 1430 the Emperor Sigismund II, whose domains included Hungary and Croatia, was increasingly alarmed by Osmanli attacks. He therefore proposed to Hochmeister Bellizer that the brethren transfer their headquarters to Transylvania. *A komturei* was set up at Severin (on the Yugoslav border of modern Romania) under Klaus von Redwitz to defend the Danube. Unfortunately Sigismund then killed a project which might have revitalized the Order, by foolishly suggesting that its Prussian lands be shared out among neighbouring princes. Immediately the whole plan became suspect, and after a few years the brethren abandoned Severin.[5]

The foreign policy of Livonian Landmeisters had always differed from that of Prussia, as their opponents were the Russian princes rather than the Lithuanians. During two centuries they fought no fewer than thirty wars with the land of Russ. The Order had never ceased to covet Pskov and Novgorod the Great, especially the latter's vast commercial empire. In 1444, Livonian

---

* Conrad Bitschin was so heartbroken that he composed a lament filling nearly a page of his chronicle and entitled 'Exclamacio dolorosa contra maliciam Hussitorum'.

† A work which would one day have great influence on Martin Luther.

brethren began a skilful campaign against the republics. Small raids whose primary purpose was psychological were launched across the river Narva. In 1445 able diplomacy nearly succeeded in bringing the Danish king into the war to overawe Novgorod. The merchant state was blockaded, cut off from its trade with the Livonian towns. The Order made use of its monopoly to forbid the import of grain to Novgorod. However, though well conceived, the campaign failed and in 1448 the knights made peace with the Russians. The war had disastrous consequences, ruining the Livonian staple and harming the Prussian ports.

In 1440 junkers and burghers met at Marienwerder to found the *Preussische Bund*, which became a real state within a state, levying its own taxes. The Order was powerless to suppress the *Bund*, and the Hochmeister tried to reach a *modus vivendi*. This proved impossible, for he could not share political power with the Prussian nobility without undermining the whole concept of the *Ordensstaat*, while it was equally difficult to alleviate the burghers' troubles. An explosive situation developed. Hochmeister Ludwig von Erlichshausen appealed to Frederick III in 1453, and the latter solemnly declared the *Bund* dissolved. He could not enforce his decree.[6] In February 1454, after the mysterious murder of their employer's ambassador, the *Bund* – which included twenty-one towns – renounced allegiance to the Hochmeister, and the country rose. Within two months fifty-six castles were in rebel hands and a ringleader of the revolt, a renegade knight, Hans von Baisen, journeyed to Cracow to offer the 'crown' of Prussia to Casimir IV. The real object was to win the anarchic freedom possessed by the Polish upper classes.

King Casimir came to Prussia but, instead of a welcome, found a war which was to rage for thirteen years. The Ordensland tore itself to pieces, junker fighting junker, burgher warring with burgher. In Königsberg sailors and townsmen battled mercilessly in the narrow streets and along the quays, while the merchant princes of Danzig, bitter haters of the Order, sent its supporters to the galleys. Casimir had few troops. However, the *Bund* gave him plenty of money, as did the Danzig oligarchy, and he hired mercenaries, Czechs and Heyducks – wild Hungarians or Croats – who harried and burnt the wretched Ordensland.

Yet the Order could still produce another Plauen, the Spittler Heinrich Reuss von Plauen, a cousin of the tragic Hochmeister.* In September 1454 he marched to the relief of Könitz, besieged by King Casimir with an army, 40,000 strong, of Poles, mercenaries and Prussian Leaguers. The Spittler had only 9,000 men, but narrowed the front by a skilful use of marshy ground and, finding a point where the enemy's light troops were exposed, charged in with 1,000 heavy cavalry. Casimir's army disintegrated and the king himself barely escaped, leaving his banner in the brethren's hands.

There were now few sergeants and the ratio of brethren to levies or mercenaries in the squadrons was probably about the same as that of officers and senior non-commissioned officers to other ranks in a modern infantry regiment. Crossbowmen were being replaced by foot soldiers with hand-guns, and war carts were used by the Bohemian troops. There were none of the romantic adventurers of Winrich's day. Tannenberg had destroyed the Order's prestige, while the Lithuanian wars had ceased to be crusades. There was little point in travelling to northern Europe to obtain experience which could be found nearer home. Only the wolfish freelances came, with scavenging camp-followers, greedy for pay and plunder. This 'Thirteen Years War' was one of sieges and raids, but few pitched battles. Towns were sacked and burnt, villages destroyed, cornfields laid waste, peasants massacred in droves.

The mercenaries, always open to a good offer, changed sides frequently. To pay them, the Hochmeister attempted to sell castles and manors, even towns, but without success. Landed property was no longer profitable and capital was scarce. Rents and taxation had ceased to exist. The German Landmeister,

*The enthusiastic author of the near contemporary 'Historia Brevis Magistrorum Ordinis Theutonici . . .' calls Heinrich 'alter Hector et Achilles'.

Ulrich von Lentersheim, came to fight at the Prussian brethren's side and gave some financial help, but his advances were soon swallowed up. The desperate Ludwig guaranteed his troops' pay with twenty towns and castles, which they promptly occupied. The Livonian Landmeister tried to buy back Marienburg but failed,[7] and in 1457 the Bohemians sold it to Casimir. The miserable Hochmeister escaped in a small boat to Königsberg, whose sympathetic burghers sent him a barrel of beer but no money. The Spittler persuaded the loyal Burgomaster of Marienburg, Bartholomaus Blumen, to open the gates to him. Together and with only a small band they defended it desperately against the Poles, who surrounded the city and occupied the citadel. Finally in 1460 they were overwhelmed and Burgomaster Blumen was beheaded. But Plauen escaped to fight on.

The brethren's defeat at Zarnowitz (Puck) in August 1462 by a smaller force has been described as the turning-point of the war.[8] The composition of the Order's troops is of interest: 1,000 fully equipped heavy cavalry, 600 light cavalry, 1,300 militia and 400 foot soldiers. Much more important was the sea-battle the following year at the mouth of the Vistula. The brethren sent forty-four ships against the Danzigers, whose own fleet was paid for by the jewels of the merchants' ladies. But the Elbingers, the allies of Danzig, arrived and the Order lost all its ships and 1,500 men. It was a strategic disaster, for it blocked the water route into west Prussia. Yet the brethren still resisted without troops, without money, without hope, their fortresses holding out, with no possibility of relief, and falling one by one.

When the Hochmeister finally surrendered in 1466 he had spent sixteen million Hungarian florins, and both sides had lost over 100,000 men. At the Second Peace of Thorun it was agreed that Poland should take Danzig and the western *balleien*, henceforth to be known as 'Royal' Prussia. The Order kept the east, while in future no fewer than half of the Teutonic Knights were to be Poles. The Hochmeister had to pay homage for his Prussian lands to the Polish king, a humiliating ceremony which the unhappy Ludwig performed in the Guildhall at Thorun, 'weeping, and with torn garments'. The Grand Commandery was now at Königsberg.

The treaty divided the Order. It was difficult for the brethren outside Prussia to obey a Polish vassal who sat in the *Sejm* at the king's left hand. The Livonian Knights were confirmed in the habit of electing their own Landmeister, while the German Landmeister adopted the title *Deutschmeister* and became more independent. Livland remained formidable. In 1471 Ivan III, Grand-Prince of Moscow, annexed Novgorod, whereupon the brethren tried to seize Pskov as a counter-stroke, waiting until 1480 when Ivan was fully occupied by the last invasion of the Golden Horde. Landmeister Bernhard von den Borch led a large and well-equipped force[9] through the snow and sacked the small town of Visgorod on 1 January 1480, returning at the end of the month to encircle Pskov with one army and systematically devastate the countryside with another. Bernhard retreated when a Muscovite army raided Livonia, but on 1 March he chased the men of Pskov off the ice of Lake Peipus and then sacked and burnt the town of Kobyle, killing nearly 4,000 inhabitants before withdrawing. The Landmeister's raids had profoundly shaken Pskov's morale. In August he returned without warning at the head of '100,000 men', threatening Pskov. The republic was desperate, but Bernhard again withdrew. Unfortunately the Golden Horde's invasion failed and Ivan was now free to protect Pskov.

Prussian brethren were determined to regain their independence. In 1498, they elected a powerful prince as Hochmeister, Friedrich of Saxony, the elector's brother. Königsberg was transformed into a semi-regal court administered by Saxon officials, and the Hochmeister-Duke's wealth provided an illusory splendour. He refused to pay homage to the Polish king, demanding the return of west Prussia.

By the end of the century Livland was ailing, split into three camps – bishops, towns and brethren – the latter distracted by feuds between Rhinelanders and Westphalians. Riga, Reval and Dorpat had lost their staple rights at Novgorod when Ivan III expelled the Hansa and all Germans. In any case the burghers of

8. Friedrich of Saxony, the last Hochmeister but one to reign in Prussia

both Livland and Prussia had abandoned the Hansa after 1467. The Order always maintained good relations with the Tartars, sending ambassadors to Kazan and Astrakhan, but the Golden Horde was in its final decline. Ivan had married a Byzantine princess and Moscow was quickly becoming the third Rome. Its grand-prince wanted an outlet to the Baltic and threatened Narva from his fortress of Ivangorod. Yet Marienland was to enjoy an Indian summer, often called its Golden Age. Wolther von Plettenberg, born in Westphalia in 1450 and elected Landmeister in 1493, was a ruler of Kniprode's calibre. A handsome man of distinguished manners, a gallant soldier and a gifted diplomatist, he seems to have stepped from the Order's heroic age into its twilit dusk. He restricted admission in Livland to Westphalians and controlled the cities and bishops by playing one against another, taking care to cultivate a special relationship with the Archbishop of Riga. Caspar Linde, archbishop from 1509 to 1524, was a close friend and sympathizer. Even burghers were grateful for Wolther's benevolent rule, which lasted nearly half a century.[10]

In 1499 Muscovy and Mengli Gerei, Khan of the Krim Tartars, declared war on Grand Duke Alexander of Lithuania, who allied with the Tartar Khan of the Volga, Sich Achmed, and the Order. In 1501 the Russians defeated and massacred the Lithuanian army, invading Livonia. Alexander sent no help and Sich Achmed was delayed. On 27 August, Plettenberg attacked the Russians alone on the Seritsa river. He had 8,000 foot and 4,000 cavalry. The Russians – Muscovites and the army of the Prince of Pskov – numbered 40,000. Using a murderous combination of artillery and heavy cavalry, Wolther practically wiped them out. The Landmeister fought like a devil, though twice surrounded and once beaten to his knees. According to the chronicler Balthasar Russow, his 12,000 soldiers killed most of the 40,000 Russians, the remainder fleeing to Pskov. But a severe outbreak of dysentery forced him to withdraw.

In November 1501 the Russians returned: 100,000 Muscovites and 30,000 Tartars[11] commanded by Ivan's best general, Prince Daniel Shchenya. They joined battle with the Order's main army, based on the fortress of Helmed outside Dorpat and, despite the Knights' superior artillery, annihilated them. Not even a messenger got through to warn Plettenberg. Then the Muscovites devastated eastern Marienland, 40,000 Livonians being killed or dragged into captivity. The Landmeister was undismayed. In the spring of 1502 he launched several swift raids into the Pskov country, culminating in September with the siege of Pskov itself. He retreated before the relieving Muscovite army, luring his pursuers into a deathtrap at Lake Smolino. Again he used cavalry and skilled gunners to terrible effect. Many brethren also died, but Plettenberg's army was allowed to withdraw without further challenge. Shortly afterwards, Grand Duke Alexander made peace with Ivan, and in May 1503 the Order's ambassadors concluded a fifty years' truce with the Russians. Russian and German chroniclers differ about the honours of the war, claiming the same battles as victories.[12] Whatever the truth, the brethren did remarkably well to tie down a much larger army for so long and to emerge with their territory intact. The achievement is comparable to that of the Finns in the Winter War of 1940.

In 1512 another prince of the empire was elected Hochmeister, the twenty-one-year-old Albrecht von Hohenzollern, Margrave of Brandenburg-Anspach, poor, ambitious and without scruples. He refused to admit Poles to the Order and in 1517, after allying with Denmark and Grand-Prince Vassily III, demanded not only the return of Royal Prussia but also compensation for fifty years' occupation. Finally, in 1519, he attacked his uncle, King Sigismund of Poland, in a campaign of sieges, forays and burnings, but no pitched battles. Only the ravening *Landsknechts* profited, and in 1521 Albrecht, an indifferent general, agreed to a four years' truce.

But a new foe, Protestantism, now confronted the Order. In 1523 Martin Luther wrote to Hochmeister Albrecht: 'Your Order is truly a strange order and especially because it was founded to fight against the infidels. For this reason it must make use of the worldly sword and must act in a worldly manner and yet it should be spiritual at the same time, should vow chastity, poverty and obedience and should keep these vows like the members of other monastic orders.' With habitual invective Dr Luther went on to describe the Order as a hermaphrodite institution. On Christmas Day 1523 the Bishop of Samland, George von Potenza – who was a member of the Order – publicly accepted Lutheranism in a sermon at Königsberg cathedral: 'This day Christ is born anew.' The doctrine had already spread among the burghers, even among the knights.

Albrecht met Luther at Nuremberg during the Imperial Diet of 1524 and was converted. On 8 April 1525 the Hochmeister signed the Treaty of Cracow. Henceforth he held Prussia from the Polish king as a hereditary duchy. Next day he did homage to King Sigismund (his mother's brother) in Krakow marketplace.[13] There was little opposition, for he had deliberately left vacant the offices of Grosskomtur and Ordensmarschall, and summoned only a quorum of the 55 Knights in Prussia to the last chapter at Königsberg. Erich of Brunswick-Wolfenbüttel, Komtur of Memel, was the sole commander who tried to resist. Others were unhappy but did nothing. Phillip von Kreuz, Komtur of Insterberg, wrote a *Relatio* in which he described the coup as 'a dirty business', comparing his brethren to the frogs who took a stork for their king in the fable of King Log; he admits that he himself acquiesced in order to keep possession of his commandery. A few Knights married, founding Prussian noble families, but others returned to Germany. Duke Albrecht reigned prosperously until his death in 1568 and his son until 1618, when their Hohenzollern cousins of Brandenburg inherited the Duchy of Prussia.

Walther von Cronberg was elected Deutschmeister at Mergentheim in 1527 – the year after the Peasants' Revolt when this new Grand Commandery had been sacked by a rabble – then Hochmeister in 1530. The following year Charles V created the *Hoch- und Deutschmeister* a Prince of the Empire. The brethren gave the emperor help, if on a small scale, during the religious wars of the Schmalkaldic League. Plettenberg, the obvious choice, was not chosen, because of his Westphalian bias, certainly not because of a leaning towards Lutheranism as was suggested by one historian of the Order. He was indispensable in Riga and seventy-five years old. In 1526 Charles V made him a Prince of the Empire.

Luther's teachings spread quickly among Livonian burghers, though not, apparently, among the brethren. To a man of Plettenberg's diplomatic temperament an understanding between Lutheranism and the papacy then seemed far from unlikely and he arranged public debates between Catholics and Lutherans. At the Diet of Wolmar in 1522 Lutheran burghers and even a few brethren protested against Luther's excommunication, and in 1524 there were anti-Catholic riots in Riga and Reval. Churches were desecrated, priests and religious expelled from the cities. In 1526, at the second Diet of Wolmar, the assembly asked their ruler to follow Hochmeister Albrecht's example by renouncing his cross and becoming Duke of Livonia. But Plettenberg refused, amicably enough, and his refusal was respected. There was always the shadow of Moscow. In 1533 Wolther, eighty-three years of age, died a good Catholic at his favourite castle of Wenden after a reign of forty-four years.[14]

For twenty years the Landmeisters remained undisturbed,* but at last in 1557 Ivan IV the Terrible denounced the brethren as criminals 'who had deserted the Christian faith and burnt Russian ikons'. The tsar's army was more efficient than his grandfather's, and he had already conquered Tartar Kazan and Astrakhan. In January 1558 Prince Ivan Kurbsky invaded eastern Estonia, burning and slaying. Young people aged between ten and twenty were dragged off to the Tartar slave-markets, goaded on with iron rods; but, apart from these, every German was put to death horribly, the women having their breasts cut off, the men their limbs. No fewer than 10,000 were slaughtered before the gates of Dorpat. In May 1558 Kurbsky captured Narva; in July, Prince Shuisky stormed Dorpat. The Russians occupied twenty towns by September, but then retired for the winter, leaving garrisons.

The ailing Furstenberg abdicated and the komtur of Dunaburg, Gotthard Kettler, was elected Landmeister. The last army of the Ordensland marched out to war, to the music of trumpets and kettledrums, under the battle banner of the Blessed Virgin. Yet though brethren still wore the black cross piped with silver on their tunics, with a black enamelled silver *Ritterkreuz* hanging

---

*Westphalians continued to dominate the Order, even during this period. One of the last Landmeisters was Heinrich von Galen, whose family also provided a Prince-Bishop of Munster and, in our own day, Cardinal Count Clemens von Galen, Bishop of Munster, notable for his defiance of the Nazi regime.

from each neck, and though everyone was ready to roar 'Gott mit uns', they had only 2,000 cavalry as well as a few arquebusiers and pikemen. Kettler took advantage of the winter weather to overrun several garrisons. Ivan reacted swiftly, and in January 1559 the Russians returned, in the snow, with 130,000 men. This time not even babies were spared.

Twenty years later, Sir Jerome Horsey, travelling through Livonia on his way to Moscow for the Russia Company, spoke to eye-witnesses. He wrote: 'Oh, the lamentable outcries and cruel slaughters, drowning and burning, ravishing of women and maids, stripping them naked without mercy or regard of the frozen weather, tying and binding them by three or four at their horses' tails, dragging them some alive, some dead, all bloodying the ways and streets full of carcases of the aged men and women and infants.'[15] Ivan, however, now feared an invasion by the Krim Tartars and gave the Order an armistice, demanding that the Landmeister come to sue for peace in person.

When the Poles asked the tsar to end his war with the knights, Ivan replied, 'by the all powerful will of God since the days of Rurik, Great Prince of Russia, the Livonian lands have been part of the realm'.[16] In 1560 the Russians invaded Livland once more, inflicting further atrocities and devastation. To add to the bloody confusion the wretched Estonian peasantry rose. The brethren, bankrupt, almost without troops, defended their fortresses grimly, to no avail. Fellin, the residence of von Furstenberg, was stormed by Prince Kurbsky in August, though garrisoned by a strong detachment of knights with a train of heavy artillery, and the former Landmeister was carried off to Moscow. Ivan seriously considered restoring him as puppet head of a vassal state. But it was too late. The golden age of Marienland was over in a smoking holocaust of the sort which four centuries later marked the end of the Third Reich.

The Ordensland fell to pieces. In 1562 one last victory was won in the style of Balke and Plettenberg: at Weissenstein, after a siege of five weeks, a young brother, Caspar von Oldenbock, with only 2,000 men beat off a Russian force of 30,000.[17] But now, at the urgent request of the merchants of Reval, the Swedes occupied northern Estonia, while the Danes took the offshore islands. Gotthard gave up the hopeless struggle, ceding all lands of the Order to Poland at the Treaty of Vilnius in November, though he kept his title of Landmeister until 1562. Poles, Swedes, Danes and Livonians united to drive out the Russian tsar. The brethren were disbanded. Some departed sadly for Germany, others stayed, turning Lutheran and marrying, including Kettler himself, who retained the south-west of Livland, becoming Duke of Courland (now Kurzeme), a charming coastal province, which he held as an independent fief from the Polish king (which his descendants ruled until the eighteenth century). So perished the *Ordensstaat*, which has been described with some justice as medieval Germany's greatest achievement. The baneful rewriting of history by subsequent regimes has obscured the real motives of the Teutonic Knights. In no way were they protagonists of Treitschke's brutal 'Prussianism', let alone of the Third Reich's racial madness. No doubt much blood was shed but, even so, they were missionaries, not exterminators. So long as the pagans of the Baltic would accept their rule and become Christians, the Knights governed them decently enough. Crusaders who fought for another Outremer, in their own way they had sought to build a new Jerusalem. Indeed, their spiritual inspiration was so enduring that the Teutonic Order still survives today.

IV

THE RECONQUISTA
1158–1493

Spanish and Portuguese orders:
Calatrava – Santiago – Alcántara – Aviz – Knights
of Christ – Montesa

To avoid confusing our warriors with that soldiery which
belongs to the Devil rather than God we will now speak
briefly of the life these Knights of Christ lead on campaign
or in the Convent, what it is they prize, and why soldiers of
God are so different from those of the world.

Bernard of Clairvaux 'De Laude Novae Militae'

8

THE RECONQUISTA

The Reconquista was Outremer's story in reverse, when Christian natives drove out Moslem invaders, though one which lasted eight hundred years. In Spain, military brotherhoods evolved by a long process, not being created to meet the needs of the moment as in Syria; yet their sonorous names – Calatrava, Alcántara and Santiago – were even more celebrated among Spaniards than those of the Temple or the Hospital. They were the perfected instrument of five centuries of warfare with Islam, given their final shape by the Templars' example.

The Moslem invaders, Arab, Syrian and Berber, crossed the Straits of Gibraltar in 711; within five years they had conquered the whole peninsula, with the exception of a few barren mountains in the north. In 753 the Umaiyad, Abd al-Rahman, arrived in Spain to create a unified Cordoban monarchy whose northern frontier ran from the Ebro to the Tagus, from Coimbra to Pamplona. By the eleventh century five Christian kingdoms had appeared: Galicia (with Portugal), León, Castile, Navarre and Aragon, whose people lived in dread of razzias. Every year the Christian territories were devastated, crops burnt, fruit trees cut down, buildings razed, livestock driven off and the inhabitants herded back to the slave-markets. Those who escaped were cowed by ingenious atrocities, the victims' heads being salted as trophies to impress the caliph's unruly subjects. Yet the barbarous princes with their puny kingdoms never forgot they were rightful lords of Spain. The Reconquista was a holy war. The body of St James had been discovered in Galicia and, as *Santiago Matamoros* (St James the Moor Killer), came down from heaven to lead the faithful – his shrine at Compostella becoming the greatest centre of pilgrimage in Western Europe and his war a crusade long before the Franks marched on Jerusalem.

'Castilian' conjures up patrician pride, but the first Castilians were rough pioneers who colonized the southern lands, protecting themselves by the towers from which their kingdom took its name. These were often refugee rebels, whose hunger for land constantly drove them further south. Naturally there was close contact between Moors and Castilians, and even today Arab traits are found in the Spanish character: dignity and courtesy, the sacred duty of hospitality, fantastic generosity, intolerance, an inability to compromise, and a ferocity which is not so much cruelty as indifference to physical suffering.

Al-Andalus could be united only by a despot. In 1031 the caliphate broke up into *taifas* (small city-states) and within a few years the military initiative had passed to the Christians, who took Toledo, the ancient capital of the Visigoths, in 1085. The *taifa* princes played a last card and asked the Berber 'Almoravids' (*al-murabbitun* – 'those who gather in the fortress to wage the holy war') to rescue them. This fanatical sect, which had united the barbarous Saharan tribes, came quickly and al-Andalus was added to its empire. *Ribats* were set up – fortified 'monasteries' where tribesmen performed ascetic exercises and fulfilled the religious duty of holy war; their border patrols, the *rabitos*, became as dreaded as the razzias of the caliphs. The Christians none the less managed to hold the frontier of the Tagus. Within two generations the Almoravids succumbed to Spanish wine and singing girls, but again 'Ilfriqiya' came to the rescue. The Berbers of the Atlas mountains had formed another sect, the 'Almohads' (*al-muwahhidun* – 'unitarians'), who also saw holy war as a religious duty, their caliphs always going into battle with an entourage of fakirs. In 1147 Abd al-Moumin invaded al-Andalus; more Berbers were brought in and the cities re-fortified. Christian Spain was once more menaced by a united Andalusia.

In the decade after 1130 the Templars founded many preceptories. Even before that date the Hospital had set up several houses, but these were concerned only with hospitaller work and dispatching money and supplies to their Syrian brethren. When Alfons, *lo Batallador*, died in 1134, he left his kingdom of Aragon to the Templars, the Hospitallers and the Canons of the Holy Sepulchre. The Poor Knights were installed in the royal palace at Sanguera, and obtained many castles. No doubt they were aided by the Count of Barcelona, Ramón Berenguer IV, a Templar confrère. In 1143 the Poor Knights were given a great stronghold at Monzon, while in 1146 they established headquarters at Punta la Reyna, but they were less powerful in Castile. They had a castle in Portugal at Soure as early as 1128, setting up outposts in the wild country near Pombal and Ega.

The Hospitallers also established themselves. In 1148 they acquired the port of Amposta at the mouth of the river Ebro, which became the headquarters of their Aragonese brethren. Four years later they founded the Castellany of Amposta (later moved to Saragossa), 'Castellan of Amposta' being the title borne by future Priors of Aragon. Yet, if heavily fortified, Amposta was an embarkation point for the Holy Land rather than a frontier stronghold. In Castile by contrast the Hospitallers held exposed border castles such as Olmos from 1144 and Consuegra in La Mancha from 1183 – the district around Consuegra becoming known as the 'Campo de San Juan'. In Portugal too they played a frontier role, building a fortress at Belver on the north bank of the Tagus in 1194. Nevertheless, the Hospitallers' real concern was Outremer and they could not pay sufficient attention to the Moors. The Reconquista required a native solution.

Armed brotherhoods had long existed in Christian Spain. At first these *hermangildas* were little more than small bands of local farmers. Later, however, emulating the Almohad *rabitos*, they acquired a quasi-religious character and their members may have taken certain vows such as temporary celibacy and an oath to protect Christians. The *hermangildas* undoubtedly contributed to the rise of purely Spanish orders.

Toledo, the Castilian capital, was protected by mountains, but between this range and the Sierra Morena, which guarded Córdoba, lay the open plains of the *meseta*. Razzias could gallop

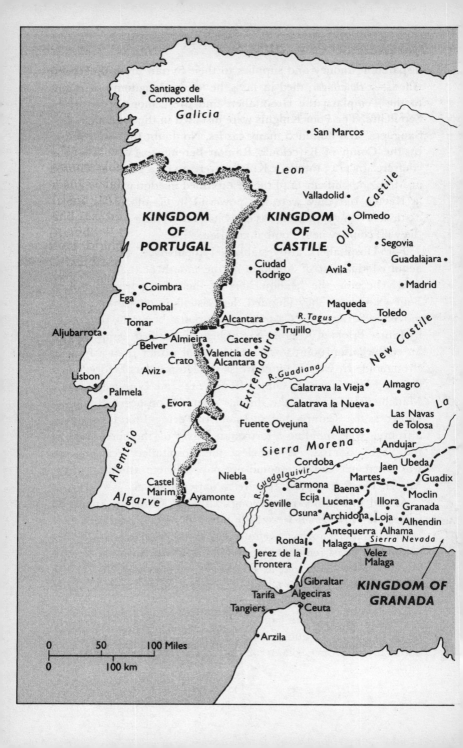

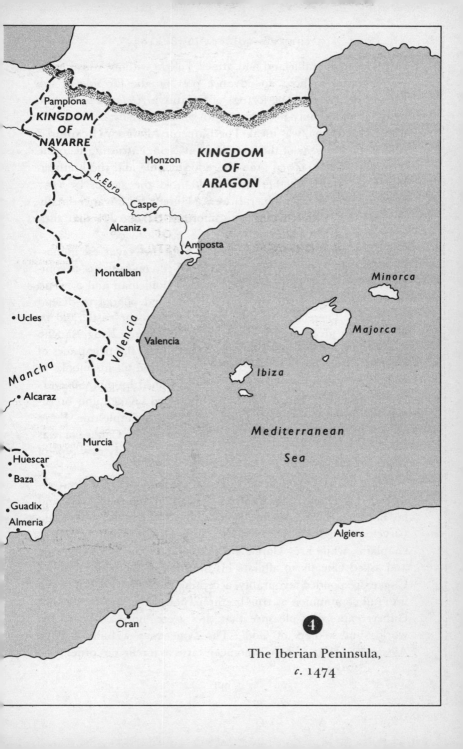

Pamplona

KINGDOM OF NAVARRE

Monzon

KINGDOM OF ARAGON

R. Ebro

Caspe

Alcaniz

Amposta

Montalban

Minorca

Majorca

• Ucles

Valencia

Valencia

Ibiza

Mancha

• Alcaraz

Mediterranean

Murcia

Sea

Huescar

• Baza

Guadix

Almeria

Algiers

Oran

4

The Iberian Peninsula,
c. 1474

swiftly over the tableland and attack Toledo without warning. It was essential to hold an advance post on the far side of the Montes de Toledo. The fortress of Calatrava (*Qalat Rawaah*, 'the castle of war'), sixty-five miles south on the marshy banks of the upper Guardiana, was ideal. The Emperor Alfonso VII captured it in 1147, the year of the Almohad invasion, entrusting it to the Templars. Later, *rabitos* grew more formidable and the brethren began to doubt whether they could hold the castle. In 1157 rumours that African generals were planning an advance finally decided the Poor Knights, who informed Sancho III that they were evacuating Calatrava.

A Cistercian abbot, Ramón Sierra, from the Navarrese monastery of Santa María de Fitero, was in Toledo on business, accompanied by the monk Diego Velásquez, a nobleman and a friend of Sancho. The abbot went to the king and offered to defend Calatrava. There was no alternative; in 1158 the castle and its lands were given to the community of Fitero, King Sancho exhorting the community to defend them from the pagan foes of Christ's Cross. Ramón immediately transferred all his monks to Calatrava, preaching a crusade. He was joined by many Navarrese soldiers, and Diego Velásquez organized laymen and brethren into an effective fighting unit, compiling a simple rule. From a *ribat* garrisoned by monks and an *hermangilda* Calatrava was transformed into the first commandery of an entirely new type of military order.[1]

When Ramón died in 1164 Calatrava had still not been attacked. The choir monks elected a new abbot, but the knights and lay brethren chose a Master, Don García. The monks withdrew to Cirvelos, though Diego stayed, recruiting secular priests to serve as chaplains, while Frey García swore to observe the Cistercian rule and asked Cîteaux to affiliate his brethren to the white monks.[2] Cîteaux responded favourably, accepting these *freyles* of Calatrava into full communion as true brethren, not just as *confrates*, Abbot Gilbert expressing pleasure that they were 'not soldiers of the world, but soldiers of God'. The same year a bull of Pope Alexander III gave them canonical status as a religious order.

T. VI. P 36

9. An early Knight of Calatrava

The basic organization of the Knights of Calatrava was complete within twenty years, though its constitutions were not finalized until the fifteenth century. The mother house was staffed by *freyles clerigos*, who prayed for success in battle, but the normal Commandery contained twelve *caballeros freyles* and a chaplain. The election of the Master resembled a Cistercian abbot's, with a certain flavour of the Visigothic war-band. When he died, his lieutenant, the Grand Commander (*Comendador mayor*), summoned all knights and chaplains to Calatrava within ten days to choose a successor. The new *Maestre* was raised on high and given the Order's seal, sword and banner, while his *freyles* sang the *Te Deum*. Then, after swearing loyalty to the King of Castile, he was seated on the magistral throne to receive his brethren's homage amid the pealing of bells, after which there was a High Mass in thanksgiving. As Calatrava was attached to Morimond in Burgundy (the mother house of Fitero), like any dependent priory of white monks the latter's abbot confirmed each Maestre's election, performing an annual visitation. The Maestres' headquarters were in one of the larger commanderies, the castellan of Calatrava being the third great officer, the *Clavero*, who was assisted by a *Sub-Clavero* and an *Obrero*, the latter a kind of quartermaster responsible for the house's maintenance. Next came the Order's senior clerical officer, the Grand Prior, supported by a *Sacrista* or procurator. Always a French Cistercian from Morimond, as heir to Ramón, the Grand Prior wore a mitre and carried a crozier, residing at Calatrava, where he held a chapter of the house's *freyles clerigos* each day. These lived a life almost indistinguishable from the white monks', using the Cîteaux breviary.

Their habit was a hooded white (later grey) tunic. That of the *caballeros* was shorter than that of the *clerigos*, to facilitate riding. On active service knights wore a long sleeveless mantle like a Templar's, but with no cross, and sometimes a fur-lined cloak. Armour was always black. Indoors both *freyles* and *clerigos* donned the full habit of a Cistercian choir monk, including his 'cowl', a pleated over-tunic with wide sleeves.[3] Professions were made to the Prior, later to the Master 'as though he were abbot' after a year's novitiate, who 'clothed' the brethren; there was a single vow of obedience in which those of chastity and poverty were implicit. Each brother was constantly reminded of a Christian's seven obligations, *'comer, bever, calcar, vestir, visitar, consolar, enterrar'* (to feed, give drink to, shoe, clothe, visit, console the sick, poor or afflicted and bury the dead). Meat was eaten only three times a week, and such offences as fornication were punished by flogging. Silence was kept in chapel, refectory, dormitory and kitchen, while every *caballero* recited the psalter ten times each year. However, knights sometimes sang the whole office with the chaplains, and after 1221 were allowed to sit with the choir monks in any monastery of the Cîteaux obedience, entering refectories and chapterhouses forbidden to lay brethren.[4] On campaign they recited a specific number of 'paters' and 'aves'.

A chapter general was held at Calatrava, at Christmas, Easter and Pentecost, when all *caballeros* were bound to attend and receive the sacraments. Each commandery was inspected annually by a knight and a chaplain to ensure that the rule was kept and fortifications maintained. These commanderies, manned by twelve experienced *freyles*, served as a blockhouse for their district, all able-bodied fighting men rallying to the commander in times of danger. In 1179 a commandery was founded in Aragon, at Alcañiz, to fight the Moors of Valencia. This became one of the Order's great houses, with many chaplains, and its conventual life resembled that at Calatrava.

Shortly after Abbot Ramón began his great enterprise, a *hermangilda* near Cáceres had offered its services to the Canons of St Eloi in León for the protection of pilgrims travelling to Compostella. About 1164 the knights of Cáceres were given Uclés to defend on the Castilian frontier south of the Guardiana, and in 1171 the papal-legate, Cardinal Jacinto, presented them with a rule, while Alexander III recognized them as the Order of St James of the Sword in 1175.[5] By 1184, when their first Maestre, Frey Pedro Fernández de Fuente Encalato, was killed during the siege of Cáceres, the new brethren had made rapid progress. In Portugal they received several castles from Sancho I, including Palmela, and later acquired lands in France, Italy, Palestine, Carinthia, Hungary and even England. Alfonso IX, *'el Baboso'* (the Slobberer), endowed it with a tenth of all money coined in León. There were five Grand Priors for León, Castile, Portugal, Aragon and Gascony. The priors of Uclés and San Marcos (León) were mitred, ranking as abbots.

Santiago based its rule on St Augustine's, evolving a structure of remarkable originality. Canons looked after the spiritual welfare of the knights, who took vows of poverty, chastity and obedience,[6] while canonesses tended pilgrims in separate guesthouses and hospitals. Each commandery contained thirteen brethren, representing Christ and His Apostles, as did the Great Council, the *'Trezes'*, all celibate commanders who elected the Maestre; in chapter these wore the black habit of their canons. What made Santiago so unusual was its incorporation of married knights, not just as *familiares* or confrères, but as full members who gave up their *patria potestas* and whose goods and families became technically part of the Order.[7] At certain times of the year they made retreats in the commanderies and during Lent and Advent slept apart from their wives, but otherwise lived a normal married life.* Knights wore a white habit with a red cross on the shoulder, the bottom arm of which resembled a sword blade. This distinctive cross, the *espada*, was nicknamed the *Largetto* or Lizard. The *Santaguistas'* ferocious motto was 'Rubet ensis sanguine Arabum' (May the sword be red with Arab blood) and they appropriated the old battle-cry, *'Santiago y cierra España'* (St James and close in Spain!).†

Before 1170 a small *hermangilda* was operating on the Leonese frontier 'in the jaws of the Saracen'. This brotherhood, 'the Knights of San Julián de Pereiro', would one day become the

---

* Chastity was interpreted as 'coniugal castidad': the Rule comments that 'It is a better thing to marry than to be burnt in the flames'. (Clause 1.)

† The Rule states that 'The intention of all shall be to defend the Church of God, in order to give souls to Jesus Christ and to go against the Moors not for plunder but for the increase of the Faith of God'. (Clause 34.)

Order of Alcántara. The brethren's historians afterwards con-
cocted a legend that it was an earlier foundation than that of
Calatrava; a certain Suero Fernández Barrientos came from
Salamanca in 1156 to San Julián (about twenty-five miles from
Ciudad Ródrigo), where a hermit showed him a site for a
fortress, his ambition being to save his soul by fighting Moors,
but soon after he was killed in battle. Certainly the brotherhood
existed a decade later.[8] In 1176 their leader, Frey Gómez Fernández, was granted lands by Ferdinand II of León, and Pope
Alexander recognized them as an Order with the right to elect a
prior. Frey Gómez received the title of Maestre in 1183 from
Lucius III. By 1187 the 'Sanjulianistas' had placed themselves
under the protection of Calatrava, developing similar constitutions, though their prior was elected and was not a Cistercian.
Brethren were divided into caballeros and clerigos, wearing a plain
white habit.

The Portuguese 'brethren of Santa María' claimed to have
been founded by the first king of Portugal's brother, Dom Pedro
Henriques.[9] There is evidence that a hermangilda of this name
guarded the open plains of the Alemtejo province in 1162. Four
years later the brethren obtained a house at Évora, a hundred
miles south of Lisbon, adopting the Benedictine rule suitably
modified by a Cistercian abbot, João Zirita. But although the
brethren took the title 'Knights of St Benedict', their inspiration
was from Cîteaux, and they accepted the Abbot of Tarouca's
visitation. Later they too came under Calatrava's control, copying
its constitutions. However, Évora was so weak that King Afonso
returned it to the Templars, who in 1169 were promised a third of
any land they might conquer. Through this grant they obtained
their famous stronghold at Thomar.[10]

The military orders combined to guard the invasion routes
along which the Moors might always come at any moment.
'Thus Alfonso VIII tried to defend the southern approaches to
Toledo by placing the friars of Santiago in Mora and Piedra
Negra, and the Calatravans in Calatrava, Alarcos, Malagón and
Aceca,' writes Derek Lomax in The Reconquest of Spain. 'To hold

the eastern approaches he gave Zorita and Almoguera to Calatrava, and Uclés, Oreja and Fuentidueña to Santiago. On the Seville–Salamanca road, the friars of Santiago received Cáceres, Monfragüe and later Granadilla; and to the south of Lisbon, Palmela and the whole peninsula between the Tagus and the Sado.

The brethren raided enemy territory constantly, sometimes with the king but usually by themselves. The second Master of Calatrava, Frey Fernando Escaza, was a particularly good frontiersman. On one occasion, after raiding Muradel and storming the castle of Ferral, the Moors caught up with him and he was besieged in the keep for ten days. However, the *freyles* galloped from Calatrava to his rescue, and he returned home in triumph with many prisoners and a great herd of cattle. Border warfare consisted mainly of razzias and skirmishes, often degenerating into mere horse-stealing and rustling. His successor, Frey Martín Pérez de Siones, an Aragonese, launched many savage expeditions. His most famous exploit took place after the Moors had captured the fortress at Almodovar and killed seventy knights. He pursued them and took 200 prisoners, promptly cutting their throats. Santiago suffered a temporary setback, losing Uclés to the Moors in 1176, but recovering it the same year, whereupon its Maestre made a pilgrimage of thanksgiving to the Holy Land.[11] Nor was San Julián idle, despite scanty resources. Frey Gómez gave valuable assistance to Ferdinand II of León, and the next Maestre, Benito Suárez, captured Almeida. Later, led by the Archbishop of Toledo, the Sanjulianistas carried out a particularly destructive razzia on the district between Jaén and Córdoba.

In 1194 King Alfonso VIII of Castile challenged Caliph Yakub ibn-Yusuf to come to Spain and fight. The Almohad, a fine soldier, marched out from Marrakesh the following year with an enormous army, accompanied by a host of slave-dealers, and, crossing the straits to al-Andalus, advanced north. Alfonso hastened to meet them, but the kings of León and Navarre failed to join him, supposedly insulted by his boast that Castilian Knights could do the job alone. However, the Masters of Calatrava and Santiago, Nuño Pérez de Quiñones and Sancho Fernández de Lemos, who had sworn a pact of brotherhood, rode with him. Outnumbered, they advanced to meet the caliph.

Spanish weapons and armour were those used throughout Europe: sword and lance, steel helmet, chain tunic and shield. Tactics were based on the single, decisive charge, though there was a tendency to wear lighter equipment and ride Arab horses. Auxiliary cavalry had little more than a lance, javelins and a knife. Infantry consisted of spearmen, slingers and archers carrying swords or axes. A rich man's arms were often jewelled and damascened in the Saracen fashion, especially the superb swords from Toledo, while Andalusian mantles were worn and some knights preferred to use Moorish scimitars.

Almohad cavalry, Berber or Andalusian, wore mail shirts and spiked onion helmets, charging with spears held overarm or hurling javelins. Their swords were light scimitars, their shields heart-shaped, their armour often gilded or silvered, and they used lassos or hooked lances to pull opponents from the saddle. The infantry were usually Negroes with broad-bladed stabbing spears and enormous hide shields, supported by archers and slingers who could discharge lethal clay bullets from a surprising distance. Moorish horsemen frequently swamped Spanish cavalry by sheer numbers, preventing them from choosing suitable ground or assembling their elaborate formations. If the Christians did manage to launch a charge, its impact was often absorbed by a dense mass of infantry sometimes roped together.

On 18 July 1195 Alfonso's army met the Berber horde outside the Moorish castle of Alarcos near Ciudad Real. Yakub made skilful use of his numbers and, amid shrill war-cries and the throbbing of drums, the Castilians were annihilated; 25,000 were killed or taken prisoner, among them Frey Sancho and many brethren, though the king and the Master of Calatrava escaped, hotly pursued by Berber cavalry, to the commandery of Guadalherza which they just managed to hold. Another group including some *freyles* tried to make a stand in a pass near La Zarzuela and were slaughtered to a man. Yakub advanced slowly north; within two years he had captured Guadalajara, Madrid, Uclés and Calatrava – whose chaplains were put to the sword and whose chapel was turned into a mosque. But he failed to take Toledo, and his triumph would prove only a temporary setback for the Christians.

9

THE GREAT ADVANCE

Alarcos must have seemed an irreparable disaster, for by 1197 two Orders had lost their mother houses and most knights were dead or slaves. When Calatrava's brethren set up a new headquarters at Salvatierra nearby but well inside Moslem territory, calling themselves 'Knights of Salvatierra', they nearly succumbed to an Aragonese plot. Though Frey Nuño, a Leonese, had survived, the brethren of Alcañiz tried to secede, electing their commander, García López de Moventi, as *Mestre*; Innocent III forced them to end this abortive schism, but Aragonese discontent still simmered, and in 1207 Maestre Ruy Díaz de Anguas was to recognize the commander of Alcañiz as his Order's special representative to the King of Aragon.[1] The brotherhood was strong enough to endure both defeat and internal dissension. Islam was faced by a really effective fighting machine which knew how to fall back on prepared positions.

Kings were learning to depend on the *freyles*, and even on the international Orders, though probably these could seldom put more than twenty brethren in the field. Local Templar Masters and Hospitaller Priors had to be approved by the king, who frequently appropriated revenues intended for *Ultramar*.[2] Apart from the priory of Castile, the territorial boundaries of the *caballeros de San Juan* never corresponded to those of the kingdoms, the Portuguese priory including Galicia and the Navarrese northern Aragon, while Valencia was to become a separate unit under the castellan of Amposta. Though a bailiff was sometimes styled 'Grand Commander in Spain' his overall jurisdiction was only theoretical. For promotion, caravans against the Moors were reckoned equal to those served in the Holy Land.

When the Almohads had invaded southern Portugal in 1190 and only Évora and Gualdim Paeis' Templars at Thomar held out, King Sancho I learnt a valuable lesson, afterwards erecting many commanderies on the far side of the Tagus for the brethren of St Benedict. In 1211 Afonso II was to give the town of Aviz to the fourth recorded *Mestre* at Évora, Fernão Rodrigues Monteiro, whose brethren became known as Knights of Aviz.[3]

Meanwhile, frontier warfare continued with unflagging ferocity. The news of Salvatierra's evacuation in 1211 warned the pope that a massive Almohad offensive was imminent, and he proclaimed a crusade while Rodrigo Jimenez de Rada, Archbishop of Toledo, preached the Holy War. Next summer a large army assembled with detachments from all Iberian kingdoms save León, the Orders contributing many squadrons. There was also a large number of French and Italian crusaders, the Archbishop of Narbonne bringing 150 knights. Everyone, including the Kings of Aragon and Navarre, placed themselves under the command of the same Alfonso who had been defeated at Alarcos. They marched out from Toledo in June 1212, Archbishop Rodrigo riding at their head, carrying his cathedral's great silver cross. On 1 July Calatrava was recaptured and restored to the brethren. Then a temporary shortage of provisions disgusted the foreign crusaders, who turned back. Weakened and discouraged, the Christian army continued its advance.

The Moorish army, both African and Andalusian, was thought to number 460,000, and though this figure is impossibly high it must still have been enormous. The young Caliph Muhammad III ibn-Yakub, melodiously named 'Miramamolin' by the Spaniards, selected a position at Hisn al-Uqab, afterwards known as Las Navas de Tolosa, which could be approached only through a narrow mountain pass, where he hoped to ambush the *Nasrani*. However, on the night of 15 July the Christians forced the pass and reached open ground suitable for heavy cavalry. Next morning they assembled their battle order. The centre was commanded by King Alfonso, the right wing by Sancho VIII of Navarre, the left, which included the Orders, by Pere II of

Aragon. Here the Hospitallers were led by the Prior of Castile, Frey Gutierre de Armildez, the Templars by their Castilian Master, Frey Gómez Ruiz, and Calatrava by Frey Ruy Díaz. Santiago's Master, Frey Pedro Arias, rode with the centre as the host's standard-bearer. The battle began badly. The Christians' charges were beaten back, the Moors concentrating on the centre and left, encouraged by their caliph who directed operations from a red velvet tent, wearing his ancestor's black cloak, scimitar in one hand, Koran in the other, surrounded by fakirs and hedged by a bodyguard of gigantic Negroes linked with iron chains. When Frey Pedro was slain, Alfonso began to lose heart. The Aragonese *Templarios* were killed to a man and their Castilian brethren suffered ghastly losses; the *freyles* of Calatrava were decimated and Frey Ruy lost an arm. However, the Almohad onslaught was halted, whereupon King Sancho smashed the Africans with a final decisive charge, breaking through to the caliph's pavilion and cutting down his guard.[4]

Al-Andalus was doomed, for the victory opened up the valley of the Guadalquivir, exposing the Córdoban heartland. Military Orders were the shock troops of the inevitable offensive, the Masters acting as strategic advisers. Their scouts and spy service gave them an unrivalled knowledge of the terrain and enemy fortifications. Not only did the kings use *freyles* as panzers, but they employed them to consolidate the advance, endowing the brethren with vast tracts of land. Before, it had been difficult to attract settlers to the south; Moorish razzias on border villages were conducted with great slaughter. To desperate peasants holding out in the village church against a *rabito* the brethren's arrival must have seemed like divine intervention. Colonists were protected by their patrols, while chaplains converted *mudéjares*.[5]

Commanderies tended to be priory towns rather than isolated strongholds, the actual commandery usually being centred on a rectangular Spanish keep, or *torre del homenaje*, with extravagantly machicolated corner towers to facilitate arrow-fire and oil-pouring. Often there was a watchtower outside the walls, a *torre alberrano*, connected only by a plank bridge with the commandery, as at Zorita de los Canes (Calatrava). Chapels were always of particular magnificence, like that of Calatrava la Nueva with its great rose window. Built of stone or yellow brick, the architecture frequently reflected Moorish influence, though the commandery castle of Maqueda (Calatrava), north-west of Toledo on the road from Madrid to Extremadura, was in the French style – a square bastille with massive round towers. At Calatrava la Vieja a castle of this sort with rectangular bastions overlooked the town, flanked by the conventual buildings and another smaller fortress; the style was plain and typically Cistercian though, later, *mudéjar* arcades with horseshoe arches were added, while the chapel was a converted mosque. At Aviz a town grew up beside the castle and priory, which were separate in the peninsular fashion. Iberian Orders never evolved a specific pattern of *domus conventualis*, even if a few commanderies were fortress monasteries, like Alfama in Valencia and Osuna (Calatrava) near Seville, but usually castle and conventual buildings were separate, as at Alcañiz, a compound enclosed by a curtain-wall.

In 1217 Alfonso of León gave Alcántara, which guards the great Roman bridge (*al-Cantara* – the bridge) over the Tagus near the Portuguese border, to Frey Martín Fernández de Quintana, the new Master of Calatrava; but next year Frey Martín made a pact with the Master of the Sanjulianistas, Frey Nuño Fernández, ceding the town and all possessions of Calatrava in León. San Julián, sometimes called the Order of Trujillo, was renamed Alcántara. Its second house was Magazella, also a priory-commandery. In 1218 Calatrava transferred all Portuguese properties to Aviz, preferring to consolidate its main territory, which eventually ran from Toledo to the Sierra Nevada, including La Mancha and the upper waters of the Guardiana and Guadalquivir. In 1216 the mother house was moved to Calatrava la Nueva in the Sierra de Atalayo, as Calatrava la Vieja had lost its strategic value. Here the crippled Maestre Ruy Díaz, who had abdicated on the battlefield of Las Navas, spent his last days with great saintliness.

The *freyles* not only cultivated their estates with *mudéjar* slaves but also exploited the barren *mesetas* in true Cistercian style, ranching cattle, horses, goats, pigs and, in particular, sheep, all half-wild, driving them into the high sierras during the summer. They owned some of the best pastures in Spain. Directed from the commanderies, their serving brothers made excellent herdsmen, and the wool, meat and hides fetched good prices. Business became still more profitable when Merino sheep were introduced from Morocco about 1300. Spanish landowners were to copy the knights' *haciendas* and bring them to the New World, and so the monkish frontiersmen could claim to be the first cowboys.

In 1217 the Spanish St Louis became King Fernando III of Castile. *Fernando el Santo* resembled the Frenchman in his grim orthodoxy and hatred of infidels. A Franciscan tertiary who wore a hair shirt, fasted and spent long hours in prayer, he claimed to fear the curse of a single poor Christian woman more than the anger of a whole Moorish host. But the Castilian was also a ruthless statesman and brilliant general. He saw the Reconquista as a war no less holy than the Syrian crusade, and when Louis asked him to come to Outremer, Fernando replied, 'There is no lack of Moors in my own country.' He spent the night before each battle in prayer and his character was typical of those who entered military Orders.[6] As Derek Lomax observes, Ferdinand's campaigns were genuine Crusades, within the strictest definition of the term.

1217 was also a year which saw impressive co-operation between the orders. Together, *freyles* of the Hospital, the Temple, Santiago and Calatrava laid siege to the Moslem city of Alcácer do Sal in southern Portugal, digging mines beneath the walls and attacking from siege towers; a fleet invested it from the river Sado. The Moors of Seville, Jaén and Badajoz attempted to relieve it, but were routed. Alcácer do Sal surrendered, to be given to the Knights of Santiago, who used it as a headquarters from which to conquer the surrounding region.

In 1221 the Knights of Santiago agreed that in operations on the far side of the Despeñaperros pass they would fight under the leadership of the Grand Commander of Calatrava. Both orders promised to help each other if attacked by Moslems, regardless of any treaties made by the Christian king, swearing to act as one in both war and peace.

Now that African rule in Andalusia had collapsed, *taifas* reappeared. The king promised the brethren new lands. They raided ceaselessly, returning with severed heads dangling from their saddles, for they had learnt Moorish ways. It was the Moslems' turn to complain of butchered women and children. By 1225 rival claimants were squabbling bloodily for the Almohad throne, and the Castilian army, whose real objective was Córdoba, raided Jaén, while the *freyles* of Calatrava captured Andújar. Fernando then intervened in the Almohad succession, sending an army to Morocco which gained Marrakesh for his ally, Mamoun. The king's strength was doubled by his succession to the Leonese throne in 1230. Each year he conquered more territory. In 1231 he took Trujillo with assistance from the Master of Alcántara and, though Frey Pedro González, Master of Santiago, was killed in 1232 besieging Alcaraz, it fell to his successor.

Next year the king faced a capable opponent at Jerez de la Frontera, Ibn Hud, Emir of Murcia: only ten Christians died in the battle, but Moors were slain by the thousand. In 1234 Fernando drove the infidels out of Ubeda, where the *freyles* of Calatrava and Santiago distinguished themselves. When at this time the king summoned the Master of Alcántara he came with 600 horse and 2,000 foot; his Order was growing steadily more formidable. Meanwhile the Castilians were enlarging their bridgehead near Córdoba.

The Aragonese Reconquista was entirely separate from the Castilian struggle. The Moorish war had been neglected until the Albigensian crusade put an end to aspirations north of the Pyrenees. Then Jaume the Conqueror stormed the pirates' nest of Majorca. Minorca surrendered four years later, while Ibiza was taken by the Archbishop of Tarragona in 1235. Although the kings endowed Templars and Hospitallers generously, especially the latter's convent at Sigena, their attempts to found an

Aragonese brotherhood failed dismally.* The obscure Brothers of
St George of Alfama were founded in about 1200, following the
Augustinian rule and sporting a white habit, but they achieved
little. By 1233 a Provençal nobleman, Pere Nolasco, had organized a confraternity of 'Mercedarians' to ransom penniless Christian slaves; as these must be rescued by every means, including
war, the new Order was given a military organization. Its habit
was white, like all Iberian military orders, while a small shield
bearing the royal arms of Aragon hung from the neck. Clerical
brethren had gained control by 1317, when the Order ceased to
be military, though honorary knights continued to be appointed.
In practice these Mercedarians were probably never more than
supernumerary troops.

After the defeat of Ibn Hud, King of Murcia, at Jerez in 1231,
the brethren began to conquer south-western Spain in earnest.
The Master of Calatrava, Frey Gonzalo Yañez, took Trujillo in
1233, while Santiago's Grand Commander of León, Frey Rodrigo
Yañez, captured Medellin in 1234. Every year more Moslem
towns fell to the brethren.

In 1236 Christian troops raiding the suburbs of Córdoba
discovered that it was almost undefended. Immediately the king
was informed. He arrived quickly with reinforcements, including
a detachment from Calatrava. The Murcian ibn-Hud tried to
save the ancient capital of Abd al-Rahman and al-Mansur, but
dared not face the Castilian army and rode off in despair.
Fernando ordered those who would not accept the true faith to
leave Córdoba, then he marched into the deserted city. He
turned the mosque into a cathedral, dedicating it to the Blessed
Virgin.

Meanwhile the Aragonese were proving equally successful.
King Jaume burst through the Valencian mountains in 1233,
reaching the Sierra de Espadan, and was soon in front of the

---

* In 1221 King Fernando ordered that Monfrac – the rump of Montjoie – should
be incorporated with Calatrava.

capital. The only brethren present were twenty Templars. After a long siege, Moorish Valencia, the city of the Cid, surrendered in September 1238, 'King Zayne' recognizing Jaume as the kingdom's ruler north of Xuxcar; but by 1253 the latter controlled the whole country. The Reconquista of the east coast was complete.

These spectacular advances had a tactical explanation. The Almohad collapse took away the Moors' numerical superiority, so that enveloping tactics became impossible. Now the Christians used their own light cavalry to hold down the Moors and, having chosen the terrain, each charge achieved the maximum impact. Almost invariably this broke the Moorish battle-order, rolling over their small Arab horses and riding the infantry into the ground.[7]

A determined attack was made on Murcia in 1243, and, seeing no hope, the wali of the capital surrendered. Fernando went on to capture Jaén and Carmona, before investing Seville in 1247. Surrounded by hills covered with olive orchards, with its beautiful mosque, the pink *Giralda*, its libraries, pleasure gardens, orange groves and luxurious baths, and guarded by the river Guadalquivir, flanked on each side by lighthouses with gilded roofs, the former capital of the Almohads recalled the splendours of Córdoba under the caliphs. Its junta had neglected to ally with other *taifas* and found itself isolated. Wisely the junta entrusted its beautiful city's defence to the brave wali of Niebla, Abu Ja'far. Ramón Boñifaz, Castile's 'emir of the sea', destroyed the Moorish fleet in the Guadalquivir, cutting off all hope of African relief. An Andalusian army gathered in the hills among the villages, 'which gleamed like white stars in a sky of olives', but was cut to pieces by Fernando and Muhammad ibn-al-Ahmar, ruler of Granada; Abu Ja'far must have watched the rout from the great tower-minaret. Assault parties, in which *freyles* of Santiago and Calatrava were prominent, hammered at the Sevillanos night and day. The city's once-crowded wharves, divided by the river, were joined by a bridge of boats, but during a storm the Christians broke it in two, ramming the light craft with heavy-laden ships.

Then they burst into Tirana, the northern suburb, whose inhabitants fought to the death. Finally, after a siege of sixteen months, Seville surrendered. Many of its grief-stricken citizens departed to Granada or Africa.

First to enter were 270 *Santaguistas* whose Master planted the red damask standard of St James and the white horse high on the city walls.[8] Fernando rode in to dedicate the mosque to Our Lady and to celebrate Christmas. It was here that the noblest Spaniard of the Middle Ages chose to be buried, in a Franciscan habit, when he died in 1252.

There were many new commanderies and priories to pray for his soul, including convents of nuns. Those of Calatrava followed the Cistercian rule. However, some sisters of Santiago were married; these did not have the white cloak but wore a black habit, like the Order's chaplains who ranked as canons regular. Mother superiors were known as *comendadoras*.

Fernando's successor, Alfonso X, had ambitions of playing 'Solomon' to his father's 'David'. Learned rather than wise, *el Sabio* was a patron of lawyers and astronomers but was no politician, reigning with great pomp and singular ineptitude. None the less the early years of his reign saw the destruction of what remained of western Andalus. By 1251 the Orders (notably Portuguese Santiago under Gonçalo Péres, Grand Commander of Palmela) had finally conquered and subdued the eastern Algarve, while in 1262 Castile captured the strong city of Niebla and then the port of Cadiz and, a year later, Cartagena.

There were urgent problems of administration and resettlement. The only solution was to grant large estates to the nobles and the Orders. As early as 1158 Abbot Ramón had brought peasants from his domain at Fitero. Maestres and *ricos hombres* attracted colonists by *fueros*, charters which offered both townsmen and peasants more freedom than elsewhere. Soon the south flourished again, though the crown derived scant profit. The great lords' sole obligation was to provide troops, and they ruled their vast *latifundios* like independent princes. *Freyles* benefited most of all.[9] Eventually Calatrava's lands reached to the Sierra Nevada, while Alcántara owned half Extremadura. Santiago's possessions equalled those of both Orders put together. Jewish stewards ran these estates very profitably indeed. In 1272 Frey Gonzalo Ruiz Girón, Master of Santiago, farmed his rents in Murcia, Toledo and La Mancha to the Jewish bankers Don Bono, Don Jacobo and Don Samuel.[10] None the less brethren themselves spent much time in estate management.

The *mudéjares* must have been heartened by the Mameluke victory in Syria at Ain-Jalud in 1260. Grasping settlers had goaded the Moorish landowners of Murcia beyond endurance, and suddenly in 1264 they rose without warning to massacre the Christians. Hundreds of towns and villages repudiated Castilian rule, and it took Alfonso two years, even with help from Aragon, to crush this desperate revolt.

Al-Andalus was now confined to the kingdom of Granada. The creator of this last *taifa* was a border chieftain, Muhammad ibn-Yusuf ibn-Ahmed ibn-Nasr, called al-Ahmar, who realized that, since the Sierra Morena and the Guadalquivir had been lost, Spanish Islam must find new frontiers. The mountainous region around Granada – where he installed himself in 1238 – was ideal, extending from the sea to the Serranía de Ronda and the Sierra de Elvira, with the Sierra de Nevada as a backbone, while its ports gave access to Africa.

Al-Ahmar came to terms with the Reconquista. When Ferdinand was besieging Jaén in 1246, the sultan suddenly rode into his camp to pay homage, and as Ferdinand's vassal he intervened decisively at Seville. His most remarkable innovation was European armour, and Granadine troops began to wear Spanish mail and ride heavier horses, attacking in dense formations. Supported by *jinetes*, the traditional light cavalry, this new army proved most effective. Granada was a microcosm of al-Andalus. Refugees had fled to it from all over the peninsula; many Granadine labourers were supposedly descended from Moorish noblemen. Its capital's glories are well known, especially the Alhambra with its Court of Lions and Court of Myrtles, but the seaports of Málaga and Almería were even richer. Peasants tilled and irrigated every inch of fertile soil, famous for wheat and fruit. Merchants exported silks, jewellery and slaves, returning with African and Asiatic spices, while a vigorous intellectual life produced many poets and historians.

When al-Ahmar died in 1273 a new Berber dynasty was established at Fez, the *Banu Marin*, which was under the gifted Yakub, a philosopher-warrior. Muhammad II of Granada offered him Tarifa, north-west of Gibraltar. Yakub arrived in 1275 with his Berber '*Guzat*', fanatical troops similar to the rabitos. The Moroccan horde swarmed up to Jerez in the old style, killing and burning. Yakub then retired, but he launched another raid in 1279. Christian Spain lived in dread of a further invasion.

The Reconquista made small progress during the reigns of Sancho IV (1284-94) and Ferdinand IV (1294-1312), though the former took Tarifa and the latter Gibraltar, attacking from the seaward side. The rock was too exposed to attract settlers, so Ferdinand granted it a *fuero*, giving asylum to all criminals, robbers, murderers and even women who had run away from their husbands. Then it was the turn of Islam. In 1319 the two Castilian regents perished in 'the disaster of the Vega' and the frontier towns were so horrified that they formed a league to make peace with Granada at any cost. Five years later, the Berbers took Baza and Martos, then in 1333 recaptured Gibraltar.

All this time the brethren continued to raid. The background was the hot yellow plains, their monotony broken only by rocks, olive orchards and the sheep which grazed on the parched, dusty scrub, the bleak sierras with deep valleys and high passes, or the carefully tilled Granadine *vega*. Towns were built of whitewashed mud-brick, their narrow streets resembling a Moroccan *souk*. Despite its dangers, the military vocation had become an attractive career; a commander was a rich landowner. Before, a desire for spiritual perfection had been the sole requirement for a postulant, but by the end of the thirteenth century Orders stipulated that he must show all four grandparents to have been of noble birth.*

Iberian Orders were proud of their history. A *frey caballero* of Santiago, Pere López de Baeza (*fl. c.* 1329), commander of Mohernando, wrote a brief chronicle of his brotherhood's origins. No doubt this was read in the refectories.

By this date Maestres were transformed into princes with rich commanderies in their gift; they could not only command the Orders' troops but hire mercenaries. Half of Calatrava's revenues, the *mesa maestral*, went to the Master, who on one occasion brought 1,200 lances to the field. A magistral palace was built near Ciudad Real at Almagro, in the centre of Calatrava's enormous domains; it became the administrative capital and, though its Gothic splendours have not survived, was probably the nearest approach to a Spanish Marienburg. At Alcántara *freyles* kept their court in a palace next to the castle. Maestres now spent too much time with the king, and the Chapter of Calatrava had to stipulate that their Master must visit Calatrava at least three times a year. In place of the Grand Prior, the Maestres of Calatrava began to profess knight brethren themselves, an innovation copied by Alcántara and Aviz. Masters were exposed to many temptations, for it was easy to defy authority. The feudal levies' disorderly appearance made the *freyles*' discipline all the more alarming. Inevitably they became involved in politics.

In 1287 the Portuguese Master of Alcántara took his *freyles* to the aid of King Dinis of Portugal, whose brother, the Infante Dom Afonso, was in revolt. By this date Portuguese São Thiago (Santiago), under pressure from Dinis, had become a separate order, electing its own *Mestre* at the headquarters in Palmela, though it was many years before Castile recognized the secession.[11] Aviz had received the visitation by Frey Martín Ruiz of Calatrava

---

* At the Chapter of 1259 Santiago reserved castellanries for *freyles* of noble blood, limited profession to candidates of knightly birth and reserved many privileges to brethren – lay and clerical – of knightly birth. Lomax (op. cit., p. 88) believes that before this date many *freyles caballeros* must have been of plebeian origin.

as late as 1238 but was, in practice, independent. Lack of strong authority and employment on purely secular campaigns weakened the vocation.[12] In 1292 Frey Ruy Pérez Ponce, Master of Calatrava, demanded payment from Sancho IV when asked to garrison Tarifa.

Unrest was perhaps highest at Alcántara. In 1318 some brethren, both *caballeros* and *clerigos*, complained to Master Garcia López de Padilla of Calatrava that their own Master, Frey Ruy Vásquez, was ill-treating them. Calatrava had the right of visitation, so Frey Garcia arrived at Alcántara with two Cistercian abbots, whereupon Ruy, his Grand Commander and the *clavero* barricaded themselves in the conventual buildings, protesting that the privilege had lapsed. However, a chapter of only twenty-two knights declared Frey Ruy deposed and stormed the commandery; Suero Pérez de Maldonado was elected Master in his place. Ruy Vasquez escaped to Morimond and appealed, but the abbot recognized the deposition's legality, forbidding Frey Ruy to leave France. This lamentable incident indicates spiritual decline, though the Master of Alcántara still remained a power in the land, and in 1319 Frey Suero attended the wedding of Ferdinand's sister to the King of Aragon, making a *hermandad* with the Masters of Calatrava and Santiago the same year.[13]

The suppression of the Templars gave the peninsula two new brotherhoods. King Dinis did not wish St John to become over-mighty in Portugal, and, as the pope would not agree to the crown's acquisition of the Poor Knights' property, the king created the Order of the Knights of Christ, simply deleting the words 'of the Temple' from their title. In 1318 the new brotherhood was installed in all former Templar preceptories, though it is unlikely that any Poor Knights were admitted. The first *Mestre* was a brother of Aviz, Dom Gil Martins, who by 1321 had sixty-nine knights, nine chaplains and six sergeants, with constitutions modelled on those of Aviz and Calatrava.[14] Under the *Mestre* was the *Prior Mor* – who summoned brethren to the castle-convent at Castro Marim for magistral elections – the Grand Commander, the *clavero* and the *alferes* or standard-bearer.

The Aragonese Order of Montesa was erected on the ruins of the Temple, with Frey Guillem d'Eril as *Mestre*; several Mercedarian Knights enrolled, now that their own brotherhood had ceased to be military. Like the Knights of Christ, the Order of Montesa was based on a headquarters house staffed by knight and chaplain brethren with a prior and *clavero*, and affiliated to the White Monks. Its first members, including Fra' Guillem, were mainly Aragonese *frares* of Calatrava, whose Grand Commander presided over its inauguration, assisted by Hospitallers, Mercedarians and Knights of Alfama. The brethren retained the white mantle but, unlike the Portuguese, exchanged their red cross for a black one. They took their name from their headquarters, a former Templar preceptory in Valencia where more Moslems remained than anywhere in Spain. Here they could deal with *mudéjar* revolts or pirate raids. Soon the new brethren numbered four or five times as many as their predecessors, which resulted in severe impoverishment, and they seem to have had difficulty in recruiting chaplains. Though rich and respected, the three orders – Montesa, Calatrava at Alcañiz and Santiago at Montalbán* – never dominated Aragonese politics.[15]

Alfonso XI (1312–50) was the leader who met and broke the Moslem resurgence. His subjects feared him even more than the Moors, for he used treachery and murder to intimidate the nobles, killing rebels without trial. They called him 'the avenger' or 'the implacable' but admired his grim courage. In the end they named him after his finest victory, '*el rey del Río Salado*'. He was determined to be a strong king and, as he could not merge the brotherhoods into a single royal military Order, he brought them firmly under his control. The beginning of his personal rule coincided with a peculiarly unedifying display on the part of Calatrava.

Since 1325 the aged Maestre of Calatrava, Garcia López, had

---

* Montalbán – confusingly spelt Montalaun by Rades – was the Grand Commandery in Aragon and was accompanied by a priory which was the only house of *Santaguista* canons in that kingdom.

been quarrelling with his Grand Commander, Juan Núñez de Prado, who disputed the *maestrazgo*, alleging that Frey Garcia had shown cowardice in the battle of Baena, abandoning the Order's standard.[16] After a pitched battle, the old man agreed to abdicate in return for the rich commandery of Zorita de los Canes. Frey Juan was duly installed in 1329 but then refused to honour the bargain. The indignant Frey Garcia thereupon set himself up as Master in Aragon and, though he died in 1336, the schism lasted until 1348, when Don Joan Fernández, the Grand Commander, recognized the Castilian Maestre, though Alcañiz remained semi-autonomous. Soon the Grand Commander had the authority of a separate *mestrat*.

Alfonso needed crack troops led by good generals, not a squabbling rabble under fractious grandees, and in 1335 he forced the abdication of Alcántara's Master, Ruy Pérez de Maldonado, precipitating a bitter struggle within the Order which lasted for over two years until, after a short but bloody siege, Valencia de Alcántara was stormed by royal troops and the Master, Gonzalo Martínez, beheaded and burned. Alfonso[17] then installed the obedient Nuño Chamiro. There was even greater interference with Santiago. When Maestre Vasco Rodríguez Coronado died in 1338, Alfonso ordered the *trezes* to elect his eight-year-old bastard by Leonor de Guzmán, Don Fadrique. Instead they chose Frey Vasco López, whereupon the king advanced on Uclés and Frey Vasco fled to Portugal. Alfonso forced the brethren to depose Frey Vasco and accept Leonor's brother, Alonso Meléndez de Guzmán, promising the succession to Fadrique. Frey Alonso was killed two years later, whereupon the ten-year-old boy was solemnly installed as Master of Santiago.

Alfonso was faced by an alliance between the able Sultan Yusuf of Granada and the formidable Marinid Abul Hassan, 'the Black Sultan'; both dreamt of recovering their 'lost land' just as did Henry V of France or Louis IX of Outremer. In 1340 the African fleet defeated the Castilian navy off Gibraltar, sinking thirty-two warships, whereupon Abul Hassan of Fez landed at Algeciras with the largest Moorish army seen in Spain since the

Almohads. Granadine troops hastened to join the Marinids, and Tarifa was invested. It took Alfonso six months to gather his army, which assembled at Seville by October. By northern standards Spanish troops were old-fashioned, their armour too light. The king had one modern asset – cannon, thick tubes of cast iron bound with iron bands, firing large stones; frequently these blew up, killing their gunners. Alfonso himself commanded the centre, accompanied by the Archbishop of Toledo, and all three Maestres, Nuño Chamiro of Alcántara, Juan Núñez of Calatrava and Alonso Meléndez de Guzmán of Santiago. Afonso IV of Portugal arrived with 1,000 lances and sent ships to the joint Castilian–Catalan fleet commanded by the Hospitaller Prior of Castile, Alfonso Ortiz Calderón. Tarifa still held out.

Though a few Granadines had European armour, most Moorish horsemen were lightly equipped *jinetes* and Abul Hassan relied on numbers and speed. On 30 October Alfonso attacked him at the river Salado, the Portuguese taking the Granadines, the Castilians the Moroccans. Suddenly a sortie from Tarifa burst into the unguarded enemy camp. The Moors panicked and the Christians proved heavy enough to break them, Berbers and Granadines fleeing with ghastly losses. Christian casualties were relatively light, though Frey Alonso died a glorious death. Santiago and the Hospitallers had ridden with the Castilians, Calatrava and Alcántara with the Portuguese. It was the end of the Marinid threat.

Alfonso invested the port of Algeciras in 1342, beginning a long siege during which two Masters of Alcántara died; one drowned fording the river Guadarranque at night, while his successor succumbed to wounds.[18] The straits of Gibraltar were again blockaded. Early in 1344 the Earls of Derby and Arundel arrived in Alfonso's camp, and he used them to impress a Moorish embassy, who were intrigued by the Englishmen's ornate crests – animals and perhaps even an odd Saracen's head modelled in boiled leather. Chaucer's knight was present at this siege, possibly in the earls' retinue.[19] The starving town surrendered the same year, in March.

One last Moroccan foothold remained – Gibraltar. In 1350 Alfonso advanced on the rock with a large army, but the Black Death came to its rescue and he died of bubonic plague. The Moors admired their savage enemy and a number joined the black-robed mourners of his funeral procession as it crossed the sands. This cruel, brilliant soldier was the last king of Castile able to unite his subjects in Holy War. Unfortunately he had involved the brethren even more deeply in secular politics. Now kings would use them to fight barons instead of Moors.

KINGS AND MASTERS

Alfonso's son, the boy Pedro III, inherited a kingdom which was almost impossible to govern. Great lords hired troops, keeping these private armies on a permanent footing, and even the townsmen's *cofradias* – municipal leagues – had their own soldiers. Alfonso had left a *maîtresse en titre*, Leonor de Guzmán, with five sons, the eldest being Enrique, Count of Trastámara, and Fadrique, Master of Santiago.[1] She was dangerous and ambitious for her children, and King Pedro murdered her in 1351. Next year Enrique rebelled, beginning a long and terrible struggle for the crown. The king's problem was to survive at all, for he had little money, few troops, no obvious allies and an uncontrollable nobility. Pedro therefore turned to treachery and murder.

Enrique of Trastámara schemed with implacable hatred. In 1354 a second rising was very nearly successful and the Maestre of Santiago joined his brother, but was reconciled with Pedro the following year. The king had to make sure of the Orders. Frey Fernán Pérez Ponce de León,[2] Alcántara's Maestre, would not submit and was deposed, as was his successor, Diego Gutiérrez de Zavallos, who proved equally unsuitable, the *freyles* being forced to take Suero Martínez as their superior. Old Juan Núñez of Calatrava had tactlessly criticized the royal mistress, Blanche de Padilla, and then intrigued with Aragon; he was arrested at Almagro and taken to the commandery of Maqueda, where his throat was cut.[3] He left two bastard sons but it was his nephew who avenged him, the Grand Commander, Pedro Estevañez Carpenteiro. The brethren elected Frey Pedro, whereupon the king ordered them to instal Blanche's brother, Diego García de Padilla. The Grand Commander proclaimed himself Master at the commandery of Osuna, mustering 600 lances and occupying Calatrava. The Order was split. When the anti-Master finally surrendered at Toro in 1355, he was brought to the royal palace, where the king personally butchered him in the presence of the queen-mother.[4] Finally in 1358 King Pedro lured Frey Fadrique of Santiago to Seville. The Master was hunted through the Alcázar by the arbalestier guards, who clubbed him to death with maces;[5] he was still breathing, and Pedro gave his own dagger to a Moorish slave to finish the job. Santiago then elected García Álvarez de Toledo with royal approval. The king now controlled the only real armies in Castile.

His power was at its zenith in 1362 when Pere IV, '*lo Ceremonios*', of Aragon, was all but defeated. Since Castile was now allied with England, the despairing Enrique had to take refuge in France. The Moors had become friends. When in 1359 the emir Abu Said seized power, the deposed Muhammad V fled to Fez, but, receiving no help from the Marinids, tried Seville. Pedro welcomed him, lent him troops and money and set him up at Ronda from whence he recovered Granada in 1362. In his turn Abu Said, 'the Red King', took refuge with Pedro, who promptly murdered him.[6] No doubt Diego García of Calatrava mourned him, as he had once been taken prisoner by Abu Said and released after a most hospitable entertainment.[7] Though Pedro kept the Nasrid crown jewels brought by his rash visitor, he maintained excellent relations with the Alhambra.

Martín López de Córdoba, to whom the king gave the *maestrazgo* of Alcántara in 1365, was *contador mayor* (royal treasurer) and from the same mould as the period's politician prelates, though none the less unswervingly loyal to Pedro. That year Enrique invaded Castile, having hired French mercenaries by making huge promises. The French, commanded by the great captain, Bertrand du Guesclin, proved invincible in their heavy plate armour, riding down the lightly armed Spaniards. Soon the Castilian nobility began to desert, and all three Orders divided into Pedro or Trastámara factions.

Meanwhile, as Enrique continued to advance, the king sent

Frey Martín, now Master of Calatrava,[8] to Edward III to beg for help; and then in 1366 fled to Bordeaux — murdering the Archbishop of Santiago en route. Next year he returned with Edward, Prince of Wales, whose seasoned companies could cope with the best French troops. On 3 April 1367 he met the Trastámara army at Nájera. Calatrava, Santiago and Alcántara had brethren fighting on both sides. As usual, the Black Prince routed his opponents, though Enrique escaped to Aragon. However, despite Pedro's considerable charm and the gift of the Red King's great ruby (actually a garnet), Prince Edward was infuriated by his inability to pay for the expedition and left Spain.

Then the Trastámara came back with du Guesclin, accompanied by *his* Masters of Santiago and Calatrava. Pedro's army was mainly *mudéjar* and Granadine *jinetes* and he dared not face the French cavalry. In the end he lost patience and marched to meet his enemies. In 1369 du Guesclin easily routed the Moors at Montiel. After the battle the two rivals met in the Frenchman's tent. On entering, Pedro the Cruel rushed at his half-brother, but a page tripped him and as he lay on the ground Enrique pulled up the king's belly armour and stabbed him in the stomach. The Maestre Martín López, legal guardian of Pedro's daughters, held out for them at Carmona until May 1371. He was beheaded in the marketplace at Seville despite Enrique's sworn word.[9] Helped by his Frenchmen, King Enrique II (as the Trastámara was now called) overcame all opposition by recklessly mortgaging the *realengo* (the royal domains), granting lands, privileges and titles in wild profusion.

Between 1355 and 1371 no fewer than sixteen Masters or anti-Masters had occupied the three Castilian *maestrazgos*, of whom six died a violent death, three being murdered. Not only had they waged purely secular battles, but brethren had fought brethren. The last quarter of the fourteenth century saw a series of visitations which attempted to restore discipline. Calatrava was the daughter house of Morimond, whose abbot possessed the right of visitation. Similarly Alcántara, Aviz and Montesa were subject to Calatrava's visitation; either the Master came in person or sent a deputy. Pride was the *freyles'* worst vice but fornication followed close. Ballads often refer to beautiful Mooresses, and since Christian Spain had taken over slavery from the Moors there were many temptations. In 1336 Abbot Renaud forbade suspicious-looking women to be admitted at Alcañiz after nightfall, ordering that a reliable man act as porter. The Order's statutes contained savage punishments for lapses of chastity,[10] including flogging, which meant 'the discipline' every Friday, besides eating one's food off the floor for a year. In practice concubinage seems to have been common and in 1418 Abbot Jean IV of Morimond ordered that brethren who kept mistresses must forfeit their offices; none the less several Masters left bastard children.

In Portugal the brethren's power had increased steadily, even if the Cortes complained of their rapacity. Hospitallers were frequently employed as ambassadors to Rome. Their priory of Crato, which included Galicia, had its headquarters at Belver. Towards the middle of the fourteenth century Prior Álvaro Gonçález Pereira built a castle at Almiéria which still stands, its *donjon*, the largest of four square towers, serving as keep. The Portuguese Hospitallers enjoyed greater power than their Spanish brethren, but it was the brothers of Aviz who had the most decisive impact on domestic politics.

In 1383, King Fernando died. His heir was Beatriz, wife of the Castilian Juan I. The Portuguese, especially the merchants and peasants, after countless atrocities had a real loathing for their neighbours, so with much popular support a bastard half-brother of the late king was proclaimed Governor and Defender of the Realm. This new ruler was a brother-knight, João, Mestre of Aviz, his supporters being led by 'the Holy Constable' Nun' Álvarez Pereira, one of the Hospitaller Prior's thirty-two sons. Their cause was described by a contemporary as 'a folly got up by two cobblers and two tailors', opposed by the majority of *ricos-homems* who included the *claveiro* of Aviz and the Constable's brother, Pedro, Prior of Crato.[11] The first Castilian invasion, in 1384, was a failure, and two successive Masters of Santiago died of plague besieging Lisbon. After João, dispensed from his vows, had been proclaimed King of Portugal, King Juan returned in 1385 accompanied by 20,000 cavalry and 10,000 foot, among whom were detachments from Alcántara, Calatrava and Santiago. More nobles had now joined the popular cause, including Fernão Afonso de Alburquerque, Mestre of São Thiago, the new king's ambassador to London and original architect of the Oldest Alliance. None the less, João had pitifully few troops.

On 14 August 1385 the royal Mestre and the Holy Constable met the Castilians at Aljubarrota as they were advancing on Lisbon. The Portuguese army was mainly infantry, with 4,000 spearmen and slingers, 800 crossbowmen and a small company of English archers. Though some brethren were present, João had only 200 horse. Nun' Álvarez employed classical tactics, his foot soldiers giving way in the centre before the Castilians, who pressed in towards the young king's banner. This allowed archers and crossbowmen a clear field of fire, shooting point blank at the enemy, till the Portuguese cavalry broke the demoralized rabble of cursing men and screaming horses. Juan's forces were completely routed, with very heavy casualties, among them the Master of Calatrava, and the king fled to Seville. Shortly afterwards Nun' Álvarez invaded Castile and smashed the army of Alcántara at Valverde, killing Pedro Múñiz of Santiago. Thus began the dynasty of Aviz.

Castile suffered another disaster ten years later. The Master of Alcántara, Martín Yáñez de Barbudo, once *claveiro* of Aviz, proclaimed a crusade in 1394 and led an expedition into Granada. The Nasrid kingdom was difficult country to invade, mountainous and without water. The *vega* was rich enough, but there were only small areas under extensive cultivation while cattle had to be imported from north Africa or rustled from the infidels. An enemy would find his supply lines cut in this inhospitable land and the Moors' favourite tactic was to ambush raiders in the mountain passes. Muhammad VI's soldiers surrounded Frey Martín's over-confident troops, then massacred them.[12]

Calatrava was undergoing radical reforms. Though Gonzalo Núñez, a former Master of Alcántara, was not untouched by scandal – there were stories of a secret marriage – he was a gifted administrator. By now the offices of Grand Commander and *Clavero* had become elective, but the Maestre could still allot benefices. Frey Gonzalo introduced *priorados formados* for the chaplains, whose superiors ranked as priors. Life in the new houses reflected that at Calatrava and Alcañiz, though there were no resident *caballeros*. In 1397 the visiting Cistercian abbot confirmed this innovation. The reason was financial rather than spiritual, as religious needed funds to support themselves, being no longer content with bare necessities. Calatrava now possessed about forty commanderies. The number of *freyles caballeros* is not known, though Abbot Martin, who visited Calatrava in 1302, noted that over 150 knights were present. At its peak Santiago, the largest order, may have numbered – without its Portuguese offshoot – nearly 250 *freyles*. However, with no more than four *caballeros* to every commandery – communities of twelve had long been abandoned – each military brother had a reasonable chance of obtaining a commandery.

The Aragonese Brotherhood of Montesa was exceptionally poor and its brethren were advised to obtain financial assistance from relations while waiting for a commandery; on one occasion ten gold *libras* was stipulated.[13] Less rigorous qualifications for admission may be attributed to this poverty: only two proofs of nobility, while sometimes candidates of ignoble birth were accepted. The problem was partly solved by union with Alfama in 1400. The joint order was henceforth known as that of Our Lady of Montesa and St George of Alfama, its *freyles* wearing a red cross.

Afonso IV had obtained papal permission for Aviz to bear a green cross, while Knights of Christ bore a double one of red and silver.[14] São Thiago's cross was red, like that of its Spanish parents, but the bottom arm ended in a fleur-de-lis, not a sword. In 1397 Calatrava adopted a red cross fleury which evolved into a curious and distinctive shape, the petals of the lis bending back until they touched the stem to form a Lombardic 'M' – for María. Shortly afterwards Alcántara began to use a green cross of similar design.

Modifications in dress reflected the decline of primitive ideals. In 1397 the chapter general at Calatrava obtained papal permission for *freyles caballeros* to stop wearing hood and scapular. From 1400 the cut of a brother's clothes resembled an ordinary nobleman's – a short grey tunic with a cross embroidered on the breast. He was clean-shaven and wore linen, though he continued to sport the great white mantle. Later, Santiago brethren adopted a black tunic with a prominent red *espada* on the chest. Despite sartorial indulgence, the Cistercians watched carefully over their military brothers' spiritual welfare, their visitations continuing with much fulmination against fornication.

Sometimes the brethren proved bad lords. Lope de Vega has a play, based on an incident in Rades y Andrada's *Chrónica de las tres Órdenes*, which is called 'Fuente Ovejuna' after the remote Extremaduran town of that name near Córdoba. Here, in 1476, the townsmen rose against a tyrannical commander of Calatrava, Frey Fernán Gómez de Guzmán, who was too fond of their wives and daughters and even of their brides. After his servants had been killed, the commander was hurled from his castle window on to spears and pikes held by women waiting below.

In the red palace beneath the perpetual snow of the Sierra Nevada Nasrid sultans still reigned in splendour. Granada both repelled and fascinated its neighbours. Embassies from the north wandered under the coral turrets and through the strange courts of the Alhambra and the Generalife, past fountains and date palms, through gardens of mimosa and almond blossom or lemon groves and orangeries, shaded by cypresses. Many brethren had visited Granada as captives, ambassadors or even guests and acquired a taste for such oriental luxuries as sherbet, soap, carpets and steam baths. They were taught to fight in the Moorish way, as *jinetes* or on foot with axes, and to ride Arab ponies, and they employed *mudéjar* Turcopoles and secretaries.

Muhammad VI's attack on Murcia in 1406 provoked a furious Christian reaction. In 1407 the Regent of Castile, Don Fernando, led the royal army into western Granada, accompanied by many *freyles* including Enrique de Villena, the eccentric Master of

Calatrava. After a siege of only three days the brethren of Santiago stormed Zahara, then Ayamonte; but Ronda proved too strong, even though the regent had brought St Fernando's sword with him. However, he returned in 1410 to invest the rich town of Antequerra.[15] A relieving party came down from the hills in May and attacked a Christian division, mistaking it for the whole army, whereupon the Castilian vanguard charged the Moors from behind and cut them to pieces. Sultan Yusuf III abandoned all hope of saving his beleaguered subjects, who tried to assassinate the regent. But on 18 September Christian troops scaled the walls, though the citadel was not taken for another week. Don Fernando came back to Seville in triumph, with Moorish prisoners in chains. Yusuf made peace, ceding Almería, a valuable salient for future raids.

It has been claimed that by 1400, because of the decline of feudal cavalry, the brotherhoods were no longer a military asset, while the new mercenary companies had by now acquired a higher degree of discipline. But brethren knew how to adapt themselves, and *freyles*, besides hiring troops, left their squadrons to officer crossbowmen, artillery or infantry. The fifteenth century saw them more formidable than ever. Each Maestre controlled one of the three most numerous, best-equipped, best-organized, best-paid, best-led and most dangerous professional armies in Castile.

The sons of *ricos hombres* or *escuderos*, most brethren had a natural bent for estate management, though they were assisted by the indispensable Jews. Probably conventual life was ill-observed in the smaller houses as some of them were left to stewards.[16] High officers were magnates who dominated local society, while the Master of Santiago was *ex officio* treasurer of the *Mesta*, a confederation of sheep-ranchers which constituted the richest and most powerful corporation in medieval Spain. Many noble families owed their wealth and prestige to a relative's tenure of a *maestrazgo*; the Figueroa dated their rise to fortune from Lorenzo Suárez's mastership of Santiago, as did the Sotomayor from Juan and his nephew Gutierre's occupation of Alcántara.[17] A Master could bring massive patronage to his kinsmen's aid, obtain 'mercies' for them from the king, including lordships and lucrative posts, win friends by granting benefices, intimidate their enemies with his soldiers, and in general give them unlimited opportunities of advancement. Fifteenth-century Maestres either came from great families like that of Guzmán, the most powerful in Spain, or founded new dynasties.[18]

Though an excellent steward to young King Juan II, the regent coveted these princedoms for his sons. In 1409 Alcántara became vacant. Its brethren elected their *clavero* as Master despite Fernando's known wishes, but the election was quashed on a technical hitch. The regent wrote two letters to each commander and in January 1409, with papal dispensation, his eight-year-old son was solemnly clothed with the habit and then installed as Maestre.[19] The same year Ferdinand obtained the mastership of Santiago for his even younger son, Enric. However, Don Fernando himself found promotion in 1410, being elected to the throne of Aragon. The coronation at Saragossa, postponed until 1414, was organized by the king's friend and cousin, Enrique, Marqués de Villena, Maestre of Calatrava.

In 1404 King Enrique III of Castile forced the election of this twenty-year-old dilettante who was not even a member of the Order, and was married. His wife Doña María conveniently announced that her husband was impotent and that she would enter a convent. Rome granted an annulment, together with a dispensation from the novitiate, and 'Frey Enrique' was enthroned. After King Enrique died in 1407, a group of *freyles* hopefully elected Frey Luís de Guzmán, the Grand Commander, but, seeing the regent's determined support for his relative, he fled to Alcañiz, that haven of dissident Castilian *caballeros*. The 'impotent' Master had now resumed living with his wife; he seems to have had little taste for the military vocation, intellectual interests and women taking up all his time. The Guzmán faction persisted, and eventually in 1414 the Chapter-General at Cîteaux declared Enrique's election invalid. Luís became Maestre, Villena retiring happily enough with his wife to Madrid, where he died in 1434. He is the supreme example of an intellectual Master, his interests including literature, alchemy, medicine and gastronomy. Popular tradition also credits him with practising black magic.[20] He made the first translation of *The Aeneid* into a vernacular language and the first Castilian translation of Dante. He also wrote on verse form, astrology, leprosy and the evil eye, and compiled the first Spanish cookery book, the *Arte Cisoria*. So bizarre are the latter's recipes that some historians believe they hastened his early demise. If his writings are pompous, his interests eccentric and superstitious, Villena was nevertheless one of Spain's earliest humanists.

Maestres have an admirable record of patronage. Villena's supplanter, Luís de Guzmán, himself commissioned a Spanish translation of the Hebrew Old Testament (now known as the *Alba Bible*) from Rabbi Moshe Arragel of Guadalajara, which is also a triumph of the illuminator's art; its frontispece shows the Master seated on his throne, holding the Order's sword and wearing a grey tunic and a great white cloak with the red cross, while below him his brethren in grey, red-crossed but without cloaks, are depicted fulfilling the seven duties of a Christian. The Rabbi had toiled at his task for ten years, in the commandery of Maqueda. Like all grandees, each Master kept 'his Jew' who combined the roles of financial adviser, land agent, accountant and even tutor.

It was the Portuguese Orders which made the most use of science. King João, once Master of Aviz, procured the Knights of Christ's *mestrat* for his third son, Dom Enrique, that of Aviz for his youngest, Dom Fernando.* In 1414 Enrique persuaded his father to revive the Holy War, and the following year, in July, an expedition sailed for Ceuta; incredibly, this strong seaport, which had so often menaced the Reconquista, fell within five hours, the young Mestre fighting throughout in full armour beneath the terrible sun with unflagging determination. The chronicler Zurara wrote that Enrique the Navigator's object was 'to extend the

---

* Before sailing for Ceuta King João appointed Dom Fernando Rodrigues de Sequeira, Mestre of Aviz, to be Regent of the Realm.

Holy Faith of Jesus Christ and bring it to all souls who wish to find salvation'. The Master was not concerned with the expansion of Europe but with the expansion of Christendom.* To this end he sought for 'a Christian kingdom that for love of Our Lord Jesus Christ would help in that war'. His whole life shows that the military vocation was still a living ideal; like a Carthusian, he wore a hair shirt and his devotions were almost excessive. However, he exploited every modern method. At Sagres his staff included geographers, shipwrights, linguists, Jewish cartographers and Moorish pilots. The team studied map-making and how to improve navigational instruments, the astrolabe and compass. Islam had conquered the Spains; Christianity would conquer Africa, then Asia. By 1425 his brethren had colonized Madeira and the Canaries. In 1445 they settled the Azores. The systematic exploitation of the west African coast began in 1434, made possible by the new caravels, the most seaworthy ships of their day. Rigged with many small sails instead of one or two huge spreads of canvas as hitherto, these new ships were much easier to handle – a smaller crew made provisions last longer.

Juan II of Castile reached his majority in 1419 but for most of his reign the real ruler would be his favourite, Álvaro de Luna. Poor, a bastard of a great family and greedy for possessions, he was a brilliant statesman. First he had to overthrow Enric, Master of Santiago, Don Fernando of Antequerra's son. This wild adventurer had abducted Doña Catarina, Juan's sister, with 300 troops, forcibly married her, then seized the king who gave him the lands that had once been Enrique de Villena's. In 1422 Álvaro persuaded Juan to escape and imprisoned the Master for three years until his brothers, Alfons, King of Aragon, and Juan, King of Navarre, obtained his release. The Constable of Castile made the grand gesture of invading Granada in 1421. The Orders went with him, including Frey Luís de Guzmán, and a

---

* Strictly speaking, Dom Enrique was the Order's *Regidor*, or administrator, to which office he had been appointed in 1418.

base was set up in the Sierra Elvira, whence the Castilian army raided the *vega* outside the Nasrid capital. The incensed Muhammad VII attacked them, but was heavily defeated in a memorable battle at Higuerela, after which a young commander of Santiago, Rodrigo Manrique, took the town of Huéscar, where no Christians save captives had entered for seven centuries. The glory was saddened by an ambush in which fifteen commanders of Alcántara and many *caballeros* were slaughtered.

In 1437 the Orders of Christ and Aviz sent an expedition against Tangier, led by the latter brotherhood's Master, Dom Fernando. It landed in August and was quickly surrounded by the Moors. The Mestre surrendered, yielding his banner of Our Lady carrying the Order's green cross. Dom Enrique went to the Sultan of Fez, offering Ceuta for his brother, but the *'infante santo'* died in captivity. Enrique returned to his ships. Lagos was reached, serving as a base for further explorations. Soon African gold, Negro slaves, ivory, monkeys, parrots and strange animals filled Lisbon's markets and swelled the Order's coffers. Trading posts were established, defended by brethren, while the Templar's red cross continued to sail south. In 1452 an Ethiopian ambassador visited Portugal. The Order of Christ grew steadily richer. Dom Enrique obtained the Cape Verde Islands, and his brethren introduced sugar cane to their Madeira estates. In 1460 Afonso V granted them a levy of 5 per cent on all merchandise from the new African discoveries. If Knights of Christ were busy overseas, at home São Thiago proved no less politically minded than Castilian Santiago; in 1449 its Mestre, the Count of Ourem, was largely responsible for the battle of Alfarrobeira, when his supporters killed the Regent, Dom Pedro.

Castilian Orders were as fractious as ever. Luís de Guzmán, growing old, virtually abdicated his responsibilities in 1442, whereupon the Order's Grand Commander, Frey Juan Ramírez de Guzmán, advanced on Calatrava with 500 horsemen and 1,200 foot. The *Clavero*, Fernando de Padilla, acting on the Master's instructions, met the attacking force at Barajas with 1,200 cavalry and 800 infantry, and inflicted a complete rout, taking Frey Juan prisoner. When Luís died, shortly afterwards, the brethren chose Frey Fernando, but the constable wished to instal Don Alfons of Aragon, and so the Master-elect withdrew from Almagro to Calatrava where, besieged by the royal army, he was killed by a missile thrown by one of his own supporters. However, the constable turned against Prince Alfons in 1445 and Calatrava now had three aspiring superiors: Alfons in Aragon, Juan Ramírez de Guzmán supported by the Andalusian commanderies and, at the mother house itself, a new contender, Pedro Girón.[21] Then Enric of Santiago returned to Castile with his nephew, Alfons of Calatrava, hoping to make the *maestrazgo* of Santiago into a hereditary duchy, but was crushed by the constable at Olmedo. Enric was mortally wounded though Alfons escaped. The *Trezes* elected Rodrigo Manrique, commander of Segura, but Luna took this greatest of masterships for himself; a contemporary portrait shows 'Frey Álvaro' at prayer in his white cloak and gilt armour. Meanwhile Pedro Girón made good his claim to Calatrava, Juan Ramírez yielding while Alfons remained helpless at Alcañiz. In 1450 the latter raided Castile with 300 cavalry, only to retreat hastily before the formidable Frey Pedro, who crossed the Aragonese border, burning and slaying.

Don Álvaro's arrogance had made him many enemies including Juan Pacheco, Marqués de Villena, and his brother, Pedro Girón. Suddenly they united and seized the constable in the summer of 1453, executing him on a charge of bewitching the king. Pacheco now became the strongest magnate in Castile, and his power grew even greater when the remorseful Juan II died the next year. He had been young Enrique IV's tutor and remained his friend and favourite. *El Impotente* was weak, stupid and unstable. The monarch was probably not a homosexual (a smear intended for Pacheco) for he slept with ladies of the court despite his supposed impotence.[22] His time was spent shambling after favourites through the Alcázar of Segovia with its silver walls, marble floors and gilded statues or at his beloved, obscure *mudéjar* Madrid, or on endless hunting parties. Dressed like a Nasrid emir and wearing the Granadine fez, Enrique received audiences, cross-legged on a carpet ringed by Moorish crossbowmen. Soon Pacheco filled Álvaro de Luna's position, supported by a clique which comprised his Calatravan brother, his uncle Alonso Carillo, Archbishop of Toledo, and three young men: Juan de Valenzuela, later Castilian Prior of St John; Gómez de Cáceres and the Andalusian Beltrán de la Cueva – the last two future Maestres. Although the king's brother, Alfonso, was appointed Master of Santiago, Pacheco increased his strength, remorselessly extracting huge grants from the crown.

In 1462 the queen gave birth to a daughter, Juana. In view of the king's impotence this was something of a surprise, and so, as the queen doted on Beltrán de la Cueva, the child was popularly named *la Beltraneja*. Yet Don Beltrán became royal favourite. An armed opposition, among them Frey Pedro Girón, demanded full recognition of the king's brother as heir to the throne. But the infante's deprivation of Santiago, which was given to Beltrán, made even Pacheco join the rebels. Enrique compromised, restoring Alfonso to his *maestrazgo*, Don Beltrán being compensated with a duchy, but the revolt continued. Frey Pedro Girón occupied Toledo, whence he ravaged the royal lands. The monarch was universally execrated, not least on account of his Granadine arbalestier guards who 'forced married women and violated maidens and men against nature'. In 1465 at Ávila de los Caballeros Enrique's crowned effigy was enthroned outside the walls, then solemnly stripped of its regalia by a group of nobles and hurled to the muddy ground amid the vilest abuse.[23] The Master of Alcántara, Gómez de Cáceres y Solís, a former favourite, had a prominent role in the macabre ceremony. The infante Alfonso, Master of Santiago, was proclaimed king. Deadlock ensued until Pacheco made a surprising offer which the king eagerly accepted. Pedro Girón was to be dispensed from his vow as a *frey-caballero* and given Alfonso's sister, the Infanta Isabella, as wife. In return he and Pacheco would kidnap Alfonso, join the royal army and break the revolt.

The Master of Calatrava had few qualms about marriage; his reputation for womanizing was well earned – on one occasion he had tried to seduce Isabella's mother. The future Isabella the Catholic, sixteen years old, was so appalled by the news that she spent a day and a night in prayer. But once the papal dispensation arrived, the former Frey Pedro set out from the magistral palace at Almagro, escorted by a strong troop of his former brethren. The wedding was to be in Madrid. However, the bridegroom was alarmed on his journey by a strange omen: an uncanny flock of white storks hovering over a castle where he was to rest. Next day he took to his bed with a quinsy and three days later he was dead.[24]

The Master seems to have made a pious and resigned end, dictating a will full of admirably devout sentiment. He had built a splendid chapel at Calatrava for his tomb, which bore a proud but simple inscription.[25] Indeed the last twelve years of his life had been spent mainly in battle against the Moors. The Granadine wars of Enrique IV were discredited by the king's antics, particularly by the ludicrous *promenade militaire* of 1457 when the queen and her disreputable ladies dressed as 'soldiers'. Yet Pedro and his brethren took part in serious expeditions every year from 1455 to 1457 and from 1460 to 1463, six raids being launched between 1455 and 1457 alone, while in 1462 the Master captured Archidona, though this success was eclipsed by the Duke of Medina Sidonia retaking Gibraltar the same month. Pedro was succeeded as Master by his bastard son, Rodrigo Téllez Girón, only eight years old, Morimond stipulating that the Order must be ruled by four guardians until the boy came of age. These had little power, as Pacheco became coadjutor in 1468 but, even so, Abbot Guillaume III took the opportunity to revise the *freyles'* statutes, issuing definitive constitutions in 1467 and conducting a visitation the following year.

In 1458 Afonso V, 'the African', of Portugal revived the Holy War in North Africa. Landing 25,000 men with contingents from all Orders, the king quickly captured the little town of Alcacer-Sehgir, a valuable base for further operations. Tangier was attacked three times in 1463 and 1464, while Portuguese troops even raided mountain villages. When the Marinids of Fez finally collapsed in 1471, Afonso brought up 30,000 men to storm Arzila and, at last, Tangier itself. Triumphantly he proclaimed himself 'King of Portugal and the Algarves on this side and beyond the sea in Africa'.

The second bloody battle of Olmedo in 1467, when the *Clavero* of Calatrava commanded a rebel division, did little to resolve Castilian strife, but in the following summer 'Alfonso XII' died. Pacheco then reconciled the two factions. For himself, this brilliant schemer obtained the *maestrazgo* of Santiago, remaining virtual dictator of Castile for the rest of his life. The remainder of King Enrique's sad reign was distracted by the *freyles'* noisy quarrels. In 1472 the Maestre of Alcántara, Gómez de Cáceres, insulted his *Clavero*, Alfonso de Monroy, at a wedding breakfast. The infuriated brother struck his Master, who promptly imprisoned him. Frey Alfonso managed to escape, gather supporters and seize Alcántara.[26] Gómez speedily returned to retrieve his headquarters, accompanied by 1,500 horse and 2,500 infantry, but was ambushed and killed. Monroy was elected to the *maestrazgo*, though he still had to contend with the late Master's supporters, led by his nephew, Francisco de Solís, who held the priory-fortress of Magazella. The latter eventually agreed to surrender the great commandery. Unwisely Frey Alfonso came to take possession with an inadeqate bodyguard and was arrested at dinner, whereupon Francisco proclaimed himself Maestre.[27] Then the Duchess of Plasencia set up her son, Juan de Zúñiga, as a rival candidate.[28] In 1474 Alfonso de Monroy escaped from captivity – after breaking his leg in a previous attempt – and there was war between the three contenders, an unedifying conflict which continued for the rest of the decade. Juan Pacheco died in the same year; the Master of Santiago and coadjutor of Calatrava had used his two Orders to dominate the Castilian state, the climax of the *freyles'* political influence. Three brethren now claimed Santiago: young Diego Pacheco, Alonso de Cárdenas, chosen by San Marcos, and the valiant old warrior, Rodrigo Manrique, elected at Uclés. The third and certainly the worthiest candidate soon became undisputed Master. Enrique IV expired in December 1474, to be succeeded by Isabella the Catholic who, with her husband, Prince Ferdinand of Aragon, was to unite Spain. However, Alfonso of Portugal was betrothed to his niece, *la Beltraneja*, and claimed the Castilian throne. Among those who recognized Juana as queen was the young and popular Frey Rodrigo Téllez Girón. His *Clavero*, Frey Garci López de Padilla, stood with Isabella, as did Rodrigo Manrique of Santiago and Francisco de Solis of Alcántara. In February 1476 the decisive battle was fought at Toro, when the Portuguese were annihilated. Isabella was firmly established and Ferdinand became King of Aragon in 1479.

When the veteran, Rodrigo Manrique, died in 1476, his succession was disputed between the Conde de Paredes and the Grand Commander of León, Alonso de Cárdenas. Paredes, however, died suddenly, and Frey Alonso marched on Uclés. The *Trecenazgo* assembled for his election. Isabella, hearing the news at Valladolid, 150 miles away, rode to Uclés, scarcely leaving the saddle for three days, and burst in upon the astounded *Treces*, beseeching them to leave the choice to her husband. They consented, but Ferdinand allowed them to elect Cárdenas. Juan de Zúñiga became undisputed Master of Alcántara in 1487. Francisco de Solis had been murdered during the Portuguese wars; lying wounded on the battlefield, he was recognized by a former servant of his old rival, Monroy, who promptly cut his throat. Frey Juan proved the most intellectual of all Maestres, a keen humanist who attended lectures at Valladolid. The revival of classical Latin in Castile was inaugurated by Antonio de Nebrija, whom Juan installed in his palace at Zalamea, while a Jewish scientist, Abraham Zacuto, was employed to teach the Master astronomy and advise him on the less reputable science of astrology, as Juan was writing a treatise on the subject for the guidance of Alcántara's physicians. Though Calatrava's schism lasted until the end of the Portuguese wars, Rodrigo Téllez Girón, who possessed all his family's charm and ability, was then confirmed in the *maestrazgo* by Ferdinand and Isabella, and reconciled with his

Clavero, Frey Garci López. He served the crown loyally for the remainder of his short life.

Something of the Castilian brethren's mentality may be learnt from the elegy which Jorge Manrique wrote on the death of his father, the Master of Santiago, '*tanto famoso y tan valiente*'. In 1474 Frey Jorge, commander of Montízon, had himself become one of the *trecenazgos*, or great officers of the Order, because of his prowess and bravery. His melancholy and haunting poem is one of the best loved in all Spanish literature:

> What became of the King, Don Juan?
> And the Infantes of Aragon,
> what became of them?
> What became of the gallants all?
> What became of the feats and deeds
> that were done by them?
> The jousts and the tournaments,
> the trappings, the broideries,
> and the plumes,
> were they vanity alone,
> no more than springtime leaves
> of the gardens?

He speaks of '*la dignidad dela grand cavalleria del Espada*' and, significantly, of how lasting joy can be obtained by monks only through prayer and weeping or by knights through hardship and battle against the Moors. The tone is one of aristocratic pessimism:

> Nuestras vidas son los rios
> Que van a dar enla mar
> que es el morir . . .[29]

Three years later, in March 1479, Frey Jorge, fighting for Queen Isabella against *la Beltraneja*, was mortally wounded in a skirmish before the fort of Garc-Muñoz. He was buried at Uclés. One would like to think that he resembled his brother knight in religion, el Doncel, killed in battle against the Moors in 1486, of whom there is a striking effigy in the cathedral at Siguenza.

The military orders had reached their ultimate political development during Enrique IV's reign, but even under Ferdinand and Isabella they at first retained their dominant position, possessing armies far beyond royal resources. During all the decades of weak central government they had acquired a stranglehold over the administration which was consciously exploited by ambitious politicians. Since Álvaro de Luna's day, Santiago was a perquisite of the chief minister, dispensations by-passing the novitiate; and a determined faction could even appropriate the celibate masterships of the other Orders.

3. The minnesinger Tannhäuser – the original of Wagner's hero – in the habit of a Teutonic knight *c*. 1300. From the Manessa Codex at Heidelberg University. (Photo: AKG London)

4. Frey Don Álvaro de Luna, Master of Santiago (1445–53), kneeling at prayer, with St Francis. Over the gilded armour of a Master, Frey Alvaro wears the Order's habit – a white mantle with the red *espada* and a red bonnet. From the *retablo* by Sancho de Zamora in the chapel of Santiago at Toledo Cathedral. (Photo: MAS)

5. Frey Don Luís de Guzmán, Master of Calatrava (1414–43). This miniature, *c.* 1430, shows the Master seated on the magistral throne and holding the sword of Calatrava. He wears the Order's white mantle and red cross. Beneath him, seven of his brethren are depicted fulfilling the seven basic duties of a Christian, while the others applaud a new translation of the Bible. All wear the black or grey tunics with the red cross. From the Alba Bible. (Photo: MAS)

6. Frey Don Juan de Zúñiga, Master of Alcántara (1478–94), attending a lecture by Elio Antonio de Nebrija, author of the first Spanish grammar. Both Don Juan and the *frey-caballero* seated at bottom right are wearing the Order's habit – white with a green cross on the left breast. From the frontispiece to Nebrija's *Institutiones Latinae*. (Photo: MAS)

7. A doorway at the Priory of the Order of Christ at Thomar. (Photo: MAS)

8. Fra' Luis Mendes de Vasconcellos, Grand Master of the Knights of Malta (1622–3). The habit is still unmistakably monastic. (Photo: Malta Tourist Office)

9. Monarchical pretensions – Grand Master Manuel Pinto de Fonseca (1741–73) in all but regal robes. (Photo: Malta Tourist Office)

10. A seventeenth-century galley of the Knights of Malta with a life-size statue of their patron, John the Baptist, on the poop.

11. The Auberge of Castile in Valetta, remodelled by Grand Master Fra' Manuel Pinto de Fonseca (1741–73). (Photo: Malta Tourist Office)

12. The Palace of the Grand Priory of Bohemia, Prague, recently returned to the Knights of Malta by the state.

13. Church of the Bohemian Knights of Malta, Prague. The two towers once guarded a predecessor of the Karl Bridge. (Photo: © Milan Kincl)

14. Archduke Karl (the only man besides Wellington to defeat Napoleon) being invested as a Teutonic Knight in 1801 by Archduke Maximilian-Franz, whom he later succeeded as Hoch und Deutschmeister.

15. Corpus Christi procession of Teutonic Knights and Knights of Malta at Vienna, 1934. At left the former Hoch und Deutschmeister, Archduke Eugen of Austria; in the centre Fra' Karl, Baron von Ludwigstorff, Prince Grand Prior of Bohemia (Order of Malta); and at right Friedrich, Count von Belrupt-Tissac, who later became a priest of the reformed Teutonic Order.

16. King Alfonso XIII of Spain and Queen Ena in 1924 with the Prince of the Asturias who wears the *habito* of a Knight of Santiago. (Photo: Hulton Deutsch)

17. Knights of Malta in their military uniform. The Prince de Polignac, President of the French Association, at an investiture at Versailles in 1990.

18. Knights of Malta in choir dress, 1994. Fra' Matthew Festing, as Grand Prior of England, taking the oath of allegiance to the Grand Master's delegate, Fra' Anthony, Viscount Furness, in the presence of the Papal Nuncio.

TRIUMPH AND NEMESIS

In 1476 Muley Hassan, the aged but ferocious sultan of Granada, refused to pay tribute to Castile, telling its ambassador that 'Granadine mints no longer coin gold – only steel'. Isabella asked the pope for a crusading indulgence in 1479, but the Moors moved first. On the night after Christmas 1481, during a blinding storm, they broke into Zahara, massacring most of its population. It was more than a century since a frontier town had been captured by Moors. Isabella immediately sent the Master of Calatrava to Jaén and the Master of Santiago to Écija, ordering all *adelantados* and commanders to reinforce their garrisons. In February 1482 a small Castilian force surprised and stormed the rich town of Alhama, holding it against furious attempts at recapture by the enraged sultan, who slew the messenger bringing the news. It was the turn of the Granadines to be horrified. The Christians had thrown their victims' corpses over the walls for dogs to eat the rotting remains. Muley Hassan retreated, to find his son, Abu Abdullah, proclaimed sultan. The humiliated old man took refuge at Málaga, where his brother, az-Zagal – the Valiant – was alcalde. A popular ballad made '*el rey Moro*' – Muley Hassan – lament

> *Que Christianos, con braveza*
> *Ya nos han tomado Alhama,*
> *Ay de mi Alhama!*

King Ferdinand was so encouraged that he attacked the city of Loja, in mountainous country perfectly suited to the Moors' style of fighting. The *cadi*, Ali-Atar, surrounded the Castilians on the heights of Albohacen, driving them into a ravine. Moorish cavaliers rode in and out, cutting down the unhorsed. Frey Rodrigo of Calatrava was killed by two arrows; many brethren had their heads taken to adorn Granadine saddles. Losing his siege-train, Ferdinand managed to withdraw over the rocky hills but only with the greatest difficulty.

Fortunately there were men who knew how to repair Castilian morale. The *Clavero* of Calatrava, Garci López de Padilla, elected to take Rodrigo's place, was flesh-and-blood testimony to the military vocation's survival, who said his Office in choir every day and really lived the rule; noted for his devotion to the Order's founder, St Ramón Fitero, he spent much of his time in prayer before his relics. In battle Frey Garci was a skilled and popular soldier.[1]

After defeating the Master of Santiago in the Axarquia in March 1483, the Moors launched a counter-raid by Sultan Abu Abdullah himself. 'Boabdil' rode out with nearly 10,000 hand-picked cavalry, including his gallant father-in-law, Ali-Atar, to attack the town of Lucena but was ambushed by a force of only 1,500 lances. In the rout Ali-Atar was slain and the sultan taken prisoner. Immediately Muley Hassan's supporters, led by az-Zagal, seized the kingdom. After much deliberation Ferdinand and the royal council decided, with inspired cunning, to release Boabdil; the Granadines were divided against each other and eventually Boabdil took Almería, his father retaining the capital. Yet until 1484 the war seemed no more than another incident in the Reconquista. The Christians employed the traditional tactics of the *cavalgada*, with heavy cavalry and lightly armed *escaladores* – footmen carrying ladders and grappling-hooks, knives and axes in their belts, their task being to scale castle walls quickly and silently. The Moors too retained their customary style of fighting. Even if hand gunners were replacing slingers, their favourite soldiers were still *jinetes* on Arab ponies or Berber footmen, including savage Negro *gomeres*, while even the poorest Granadine kept his crossbow. Two-thirds of Granada was mountainous, protecting the coastal plain whose strong towns were supplied by sea from the Maghrib. The sierras were inhabited by pugnacious mountaineers who cut Castilian supply-lines climbing the misty passes. Armies could not live off waterless rocks, and even in the *vega* invaders starved when the Moors deliberately destroyed their own crops. Winter made conditions impossible. This little Spanish kingdom was the jewel of Islam and its people had no sense of doom.

However, with the resources of a united Spain, Ferdinand and Isabella hired specialist mercenaries from all over Europe. German and Italian gunners brought 'bombards', firing iron or marble cannon-balls weighing up to 160 lb., as well as fireballs, lumps of tow soaked in oil, gunpowder and stone shells which were not as primitive as they sound, splintering on impact, with an effect like shrapnel. Siege engineers came from Italy to train corps of sappers. In 1485 'Switzers', the first pikemen, appeared in Spain, carrying the great eighteen-foot spear and using the hollow square. French crusaders, men-at-arms – heavy cavalry in plate armour – came too, though the English Earl Rivers brought archers and billmen, 300 veterans from the Wars of the Roses. New troops were accompanied by new tactics. Campaigns were directed at each of the three chief cities in turn, Málaga in the west, Almería in the east and finally Granada itself. Captured towns became bridgeheads, garrisoned during the winter, so that no ground had been lost when the advance was resumed the following spring. Light troops systematically devastated the *vega* on a scale hitherto unknown, while the Castilian and Catalan fleets blockaded the coast, their war-galleys chasing Barbary merchantmen away from Granadine ports.

By 1484 Muley Hassan was near death. His brother, az-Zagal, rode into Granada, with the heads of Calatravan *freyles* dangling from his saddle, and seized the throne. Again Boabdil fled to the Christians and again he was released to fight his uncle. However, in the spring of 1485 King Ferdinand set out from Córdoba with 29,000 troops, accompanied by the Masters of Santiago and Alcántara. Their objective was Ronda, the second city of the western province. Hitherto it had been thought impregnable, built on a hilltop and surrounded by deep ravines. But sappers dragged the new artillery up the mountains facing Ronda, until the great bombards were trained on the city. The inhabitants were not at first alarmed. Then on 5 May the bombardment began, with gunners firing down into the city. The Rondeños were terrified by the fireballs with their blazing tails but, on seeing their ramparts splinter and crumble, towers collapse and houses demolished, were more appalled by the cannon shot. To reply they had nothing heavier than arquebuses. After only four days the outer walls fell and the suburbs were stormed, whereupon guns were brought up to hammer the inner ramparts at point-blank range, while more traditional weapons, stone-throwing catapults and battering rams, set to work. On 15 May the garrison surrendered unconditionally.

The bombardment of Rónda doomed the Granadines. Nearly 100 strongholds surrendered. By the end of the year half of western Granada, as far as the mountains guarding Málaga, was in Christian hands. Desperately the *Ulema* tried to make peace between the sultan and his uncle, but neither would agree. Meanwhile their supporters fought savagely. Loja, Boabdil's residence, was the target selected by Ferdinand in May 1486; his artillery battered it into submission. It was soon followed by the towns of Mochin and Illora, the 'shield and right eye' of Granada, controlling the western roads to the capital. Once more Boabdil was released. The following year, 1487, the Castilian army concentrated on Málaga, 'the hand and mouth of Granada' and second city of the kingdom. In the spring they first took Vélez Málaga and then, with 70,000 men, besieged the great port itself. A fierce emir, Hamet el Zagri, and a strong Berber *guzat* were in command of the city, which had two vast keeps, the Gibralfaro and the Alcazaba. The Christians were in larger force than ever before, with bigger and better artillery. As an ultimate refinement of psychological warfare they brought carillons of bells which played havoc with devout Moslem sensibilities.

The surrender of Málaga meant that the Nasrid capital would become untenable. The dying kingdom was now split in two, the north ruled by Boabdil from the Alhambra, and the eastern province of Almería ruled by az-Zagal at Baza, Granada's other great artery. In the summer of 1488 Ferdinand attacked Almería unsuccessfully. The Moors were filled with joy, for at last they had beaten back the Christians. But in the following year the king returned with an army of nearly 100,000 men. This city, protected by woods and a network of canals, held a garrison of 20,000 carefully chosen warriors who were commanded by a redoubtable general, Cidi Yahya. The siege, which was drawn out for five months, cost the Spaniards 20,000 casualties through plague and sorties. In August the rains turned the battlefield into a swamp, the bombards being bogged down in mud. By November, though the cidi wished to carry on, the Moors were near breaking point. A high officer of Santiago, the commander of León, negotiated a truce and Yahya sent to az-Zagal, asking leave to yield. The old emir gave way to pious resignation. In December Yahya surrendered Baza. Az-Zagal then gave up his strongholds of Guadix and Almería and retired to the Maghrib, where he was blinded by the Sultan of Fez. Moslem Spain's last great warrior ended a beggar in the *souk*.

Boabdil never believed his terrible uncle could fail and had promised to surrender Granada in return for a vassal principality. But even this degenerate could not abandon the city of his ancestors. He refused, and once again Moors raided La Frontera, inciting their enslaved brothers to rise. King Ferdinand led two savage *cavalgadas* into the *vega* during 1490, but the Moors gained a victory by annihilating a small force of English bowmen at Alhendin. Finally, in April 1491, the beautiful Moslem capital, filled with refugees, was invested by the Christians, for the last time, with 50,000 men. The Granadines foresaw their own doom, yet like the *poulains* at Acre they fought magnificently. The crusaders nearly lost heart, but then Queen Isabella arrived to build the city of Santa Fé (Holy Faith). The town was built of stone, not wood or canvas, opposite Granada as a sign of invincible determination. In November Boabdil despaired. Negotiations were concluded principally through Frey Gonsalvo de Córdoba, a commander of Santiago who spoke fluent Arabic.* Weeping, the last Sultan of al-Andalus greeted his destroyers on 2 January 1492 before riding off to a small domain in the desolate Alpujarras. Then the Christian army entered.

On the Torre de la Vela of the red Alhambra, Frey Diego de Castrillo, Grand Commander of Calatrava, erected a crucifix and, when the Master of Santiago set up the crimson banner of St James with the Moor slayer on his white horse, the whole army greeted it with a roar of 'Santiago y cierra España'. The holy land of the apostle James was cleansed of Babylonians, its captivity brought to an end. The brethren had consecrated the Reconquista, and now it was complete. The entry into Granada was their apotheosis.

The Catholic sovereigns had no wish to destroy the military Orders; they simply wanted to control them. The Portuguese expedient of nominating infantes to the masterships had been successful. By careful pressure on the curia the Aragonese Pope, Alexander VI Borgia, was persuaded to ratify the Crown's assumption of the *maestrazgos*, of Calatrava (when Garci López de Padilla died in 1487) and of Santiago (when Alonso de Cárdenas died in 1493). These were not extinguished but were merely administered by the king as a provisional measure. Then, in 1494, Juan de Zúñiga of Alcántara was persuaded to abdicate. The next step was the nomination, instead of election, of *claveros* and Grand Commanders, the latter becoming royal lieutenants. But although the *mesa maestral* was appropriated to purposes of state, life in the commanderies changed little.[2] Juan de Zúñiga retired to a commandery with three knights and three chaplain brothers to observe the rule properly, and, if Alexander VI dispensed all Spanish military brethren from celibacy, it was a dispensation rather than a reform and merely brought them into line with Santiago. Alexander VI had given as reason the need

---

* This *frey caballero* later became one of Spain's greatest generals in the Italian wars.

'to avoid the scandal of concubinage', but many brethren remained celibate.

No strong government could tolerate these immense corporations. Soon after 1500 it was estimated that Santiago possessed 94 commanderies with an annual revenue of 60,000 ducats, and Alcántara 38 commanderies with 45,000 ducats. Estimates for Calatrava vary, but there seem to have been between 51 and 56 commanderies with 16 priories, yielding an income of between 40,000 and 50,000 ducats, the Orders' estates comprising not fewer than 64 villages with 200,000 inhabitants.[3] For the Renaissance mind such wealth was better used as an instrument of royal rather than clerical patronage. Now that the Reconquista was complete, the Spanish Orders' decline became inevitable. The new centralized monarchies took over the brotherhoods, with royal councils to administer their masterships. This decline, however, was only gradual; in 1508 Cardinal Ximenes proposed that Santiago's headquarters be moved to Oran, while as late as 1516 the *Trecenazgo* at Uclés attempted to elect a Maestre. Then in 1523 Charles V officially embodied administration of the masterships of Santiago, Alcántara and Calatrava in the Crown, and in 1527 he pledged their revenues to the Fuggers. By mid-century military Orders were hardly more than civil lists to provide royal favourites with titles, palaces and pensions, even if canon law regarded them as religious. The Iberian military vocation was dead, though it remained a splendid ghost for many years.

By contrast, while the Iberian Orders began their long decline, the Knights of Malta began to play an even more prominent role in Spanish and Portuguese life. Membership of their order became far more sought after than that of Santiago or Calatrava. The Grand Priors of Castile and the Castellans of Amposta were often royal princes, as were the Priors of Crato in Portugal.

In 1500 it seemed that the Portuguese Knights' vocation still had a future in Africa or the Indies, although brethren of Aviz and of Christ were allowed to marry after 1496 'on account of concubinage' and in 1505 were dispensed from their vow of poverty. Aviz had 48 commanderies and 128 priories, but this was nothing in comparison to the riches of the Knights of Christ. King Manoel reassumed his mastership, encouraging members of other Orders to transfer. His brethren possessed 454 commanderies by the end of his reign, in Portugal, Africa and the Indies. Their wealth was reflected in the Order's headquarters. Built on a hill overlooking Thomar, the priory's size and splendour make it easy to believe that the Knights of Christ was the richest corporation in Europe.

Unfortunately, an attempt to reform the Order was too extreme. The Hieronimite priest Antonio de Lisboa made impossible conditions, restoring all the old vows, while chaplains had to resume conventual life at Thomar, following the arduous Cistercian rule. The innovations for knights proved impracticable and were soon discarded. When Prior Antonio began to observe the new constitutions in 1530, he had only twelve *Thomaristas* with him. The reform drove a wedge between knights and chaplain brethren, destroying any sense of vocation which remained to the former.

Yet as late as 1536 Santiago rebuilt its second commandery, San Marcos at León. This Renaissance Ziggurat, its massive court surrounding an elaborate conventual church, was a palace barracks rather than a fortress, and a witness to the brethren's staggering wealth as well as to their confidence in the future. By the middle of the century Santiago, Calatrava and Alcántara all possessed university colleges at Salamanca and a real attempt was made to reform chaplains, not drastically as in the purging of Thomar, but as a rational improvement. The brethren produced their greatest writer, a *frey clerigo*, Rades y Andrada, whose *Chrónica de las tres Ordenes*, published in 1572, still remains the standard work on Spanish military Orders.* He was an excellent historian, conscientious and methodical, who carefully collated

---

* This deals only with Santiago, Calatrava and Alcántara, but in the following year Rades published a little book containing the Statutes of Montesa, though it does not include a chronicle.

charters and compiled lists of Masters and commanders. Every military Order produces chroniclers, but Rades was outstanding. Unfortunately, as in Portugal, the chaplains' revival cut them off from the *caballeros*.

Much of Spanish history cannot be understood without some knowledge of the brethren. They had become the Reconquista itself and helped form their country's military tradition, that compound of unspeakable ferocity and incredible gallantry. It was this spirit and the techniques of the Reconquista which overcame Aztecs and Incas, creating the Spanish Empire, while Portuguese brethren transformed the crusading ideal into a movement of colonization which ended with Europe dominating the world.

READJUSTMENT
1291–1522

The end of the Templars and the Hospitallers'
new role: Secularization in Europe – Rhodes –
the later Crusades

Never do they idle or wander where fancy takes them. If
not campaigning – a rare occurrence – instead of enjoying a
well-earned reward these men are busy repairing their weapons and clothes, patching up rents or refurbishing old ones
and making good any shortcomings before doing whatever
else the Master and the Community may command.

Bernard of Clairvaux
'De Laude Novae Militiae'

READJUSTMENT AND THE TEMPLAR
DISSOLUTION

In 1303 the island of Ruad was captured by Mamelukes and its Templar garrison taken in chains to Cairo to be shot to death with arrows. The brethren had raided Alexandria unsuccessfully in 1300, while two years later they had tried and failed to re-establish themselves at Tortosa; now the last toehold on the Syrian coast had been lost. Burdened by exorbitant taxes, Europe was reluctant to donate yet more money for Holy Wars and its kings were too busy to go on crusade. None the less, the military orders were blamed for losing Outremer.

St John's new headquarters were the Hospital at Limassol; the Grand Commandery of Cyprus at Kolossi, a formidable stronghold six miles away, had always been their richest house in the Levant. As the island's chief seaport, Limassol made an excellent base for war galleys – in 1299 the Admiral became a great officer of the Order.[1] However, in 1302 the total strength of this Cypriot convent was only sixty-five brother knights, five of them English.[2] The Poor Knights also transferred their headquarters to Limassol; apart from the Grand Preceptory, their main house in Cyprus seems to have been Templos, near Kyrenia, and they had nearly fifty estates on the island. Naturally the two great brotherhoods squabbled. Nor was it long before Templars began meddling in Cypriot politics. Forbidden by King Henry to acquire more land, they plotted to replace him with his brother, Amalric; Henry was seized by the brethren and imprisoned in Armenia, an unwilling guest of King Oshin.[3] St Lazarus soon abandoned military activities as too expensive for a poor brotherhood, while it is far from clear whether the Master was the prior of Capua or the preceptor of Boigny, though the latter was recognized by English and

Scottish brethren. Probably it had never been an exempt Order – i.e. free from episcopal control – like the Templars and Hospitallers, and local bishops may well have been anxious to make use of what revenues it possessed, reducing the role of knight brethren. The Hospitallers of St Thomas suffered a similar decline but managed to maintain a preceptory in Cyprus throughout the fourteenth century.

The European strength, however, of all Orders was unimpaired. In England, St John possessed thirty commanderies, each possessing a chapel or a church, sometimes patterned on the Holy Sepulchre. Such houses usually contained three brethren (knight, chaplain and sergeant) and novices; postulants entered at sixteen but could not serve in the East until reaching the age of twenty. Conventual life was observed, the Office said in choir every day. Occasionally a lesser commandery was given to a chaplain, more rarely to a sergeant. Several smaller houses or manors were attached to each commandery, often occupied by a steward with a secular priest. In all there were probably forty-five establishments. Whether a commandery was in the depths of the country or in a town, the commander had to entertain the local notables, while remaining a man apart under vows.

The superior was the Prior at Clerkenwell. His territory included Wales, which had a single commandery, Slebeche, in Pembrokeshire. The Prior of Ireland – whose grand commandery was Kilmainham – came under Clerkenwell's jurisdiction, though this was never very effective as Irish brethren had a lamentable tendency to embroil themselves in tribal warfare. Scotland had only one commandery, Torphichen in Midlothian, though its incumbent was always known as Prior of Scotland. He too was subordinate to London. The Prior of England, 'My Lord of St John's', given precedence before all lay barons, was an important figure in English life, not least because of his magnificent residence with its household of knights and chaplains. Clerkenwell was the second richest monastic establishment in London, owning the great wood of St John's and the manor of Hampton Court.

Like St John, the Poor Knights had houses from Sicily to

Scandinavia, grouped in provinces; all obeyed the Temple of Jerusalem – now at Limassol – but were also subordinate to the Master of the Paris Temple where the 'Chapter of the West' was held. Under the Provincial Masters, usually known as Grand Preceptors, came the priors who commanded groups of preceptories. The Grand Preceptor of England – second senior officer in Europe – was in charge of the Grand Preceptors of Scotland and Ireland but had little control in practice. Life in British preceptories was very like that in Hospitaller commanderies, though, apart from houses for elderly brethren, they did not maintain hospitals. 'Red Friars' took an even more prominent part in public life than St John, and Temples always outshone Hospitals in splendour. The London house derived an income of £4,000 from its preceptories, an enormous revenue for the period. However, avarice earned the Templars much unpopularity. The most notorious incident was the Eperstoun affair. A husband had bought a corrody (board and lodging annuity) at the preceptory of Balentrodach with his life interest in his wife's property. When he died the Poor Knights claimed the widow's house. She refused to leave, clinging to a door post, so a brother hacked off her fingers with a knife. Edward I restored the unfortunate woman's property, but later her son was murdered by Templar troops, whereupon the brethren took possession. They also took part in civil wars, Irish brothers joining in the local chieftains' squabbles while Scots brethren helped Edward I defeat Wallace at Falkirk.

By contrast St John maintained many hospitals, dispensing food and accommodation to pilgrims and the sick poor. There were also nearly 200 leper hospitals in medieval England, perhaps twenty of them administered by the Burton Lazars' preceptory, where there was provision for a Master and eight brethren as well as leper brothers. Usually houses dedicated to St Lazarus or Mary Magdalene belonged to the Order of St Lazarus but not all have been identified. Its London house was at St Giles-outside-the-City. The preceptor of 'La Mawdelyne' at Locko in Derbyshire depended directly on Boigny.[4] St Thomas had its Master and twelve brethren at the headquarters in Cheapside[5] besides hospitals at Doncaster and Berkhamsted.[6]

Even during the days of St Bernard and Hugues de Payens there had been criticism of the Templars. At the end of the twelfth century a German, Otto of Blasien, accused both Templars and Hospitallers of having reached a secret understanding with the Moslems and, as time went by, criticism of all military orders became widespread. Towards 1250 the English chronicler Matthew Paris wrote that the Templars and Hospitallers received such enormous revenues 'merely for defending the Holy Land' that they were in danger of being dragged down to Hell; he also alleged that they deliberately discouraged fresh Crusades which, if successful, might put them out of a job. In 1258 the Teutonic Knights were accused of trying to prevent the conversion of Prussians or else of enslaving those who had converted, charges which almost certainly emanated from their hostile Polish neighbours. During the 1260s the Franciscan Roger Bacon argued that the same order's aggressive attitude impeded the preaching of the Gospel, a charge which would also be made against the Templars by Archdeacon Walter Map in 1289. None of these attacks appears to have done the military orders any harm. They were far too much a part of the establishment of the Roman Church.

However, everything changed when Acre fell. The brethren had always insisted that they alone could save the Holy Land and now, very unfairly, they were blamed for failing in their self-appointed task. Pope Nicholas IV said publicly that the quarrels between Templars and Hospitallers had contributed to the disaster, suggesting that the two Orders should be merged. At least one Christian king began to turn covetous eyes on their vast wealth.

For many years there had been strange rumours about the Templars, who had developed a mania for secrecy. Minds darkened by hostility were only too ready to credit sinister accusations; 'suspicions among thoughts are like bats among birds – they ever fly by twilight', and the brethren became enveloped in a miasma of poisonous gossip. In France the Poor Knights were especially pretentious. Their Master, Fra' Jacques de Molay, was godfather to Philip IV's son and, though in 1287 Philip had declared forfeit all Templar property acquired since 1258, he did not implement the decision. They supported him against Pope Boniface VIII, confirming a secret treaty for alliance in 1303, while in 1306 the king took refuge for three days in the Paris Temple to escape a furious mob. This sanctuary was also the royal treasury. Perhaps Philip's enforced sojourn aroused his cupidity; he had already organized a vicious pogrom against the Jews, seizing their property, besides extracting forced loans from the Lombards. Indeed he had good reason to appreciate the brethren's wealth, having borrowed large sums (on special terms), including a dowry for his daughter, Isabella, the 'she-wolf', when she married the future Edward II. The Paris Temple constituted something like a European money market. Preceptories were the safest banks available and credit rates compared favourably with those of Jews or Lombards, Templar bills of exchange being accepted everywhere. It seems that the brethren preferred money to landed property; in about 1250 Matthew Paris estimated the Hospitallers' wealth at 19,000 manors, the Poor Knights' at 9,000. Yet the latter was undoubtedly the richer order. All orders had *confratres*, who led an ordinary life but spent certain periods in the houses, coming to the brotherhoods' assistance in a crisis. Both Templar and Hospitaller rules made provision for married *confratres* to live at preceptories with their wives in special quarters, though in practice this was very rare. All *confratres* received valuable privileges, and consequently there were several thousand honorary Templars in Europe, many of them rich men.

Philip 'le Bel' of France was famous for his good looks, but beneath the thick yellow hair his pale blue eyes reflected a chilly inhumanity. Secretive by nature, he was an enigma to his courtiers. His ambition was that France should take the empire's place; for this he needed a subservient papacy and money.

Several writers had produced plans for the Holy Land's recovery; the most practical came in 1305 from the Aragonese Dominican, Fra' Ramon Llull: European kings were to pool resources under a single 'war-leader king', the *Rex Bellator*, who would organize the campaign, while military brethren were to be combined in a single order 'the Knights of Jerusalem'. This scheme received very serious consideration and the papacy contemplated the appointment of Fra' Foulques de Villaret, Master of St John, as head of the new brotherhood. An earlier project had been Pierre Dubois' *De Recuperatione Sanctae* written about 1300, also advocating the union of military Orders; a secret appendix showed how the king might obtain control of the whole Church through the cardinals. Philip solemnly proposed to Rome that he himself should become *Rex Bellator*, that the French kings be appointed hereditary Masters of the brethren of Jerusalem, that the surplus revenues of *all* Orders be placed at the *Rex Bellator*'s disposal, and that the new Master should have four votes at the conclaves which elected popes. The brethren, however, firmly rejected any suggestion of amalgamation.

The fall of the imperial monarchy had opened the way for national monarchies; never again could a pontiff depose princes, arbitrarily summon Europe to a crusade or protect clergy against an irate king. Philip's destruction of Boniface VIII marked the final collapse of papal pretensions. They quarrelled over clerical dues, the conflict ending with Boniface's death after his seizure by French troops. Clement V, a former archbishop of Bordeaux, who became pope in 1305, moved the papal court to Avignon where it remained for over seventy years – 'the Babylonish captivity'. This new Vicar of Christ, weak, racked by ill-health, was desperately afraid of his former sovereign who had secured his election by heavy bribes.

The decision to destroy the Templars was probably made by Philip's chancellor, Guillaume de Nogaret, a lawyer whose parents had been burnt at the stake as Albigensian heretics. He had little love for Rome and, during the struggle with Pope Boniface, was the king's chief instrument. He was also responsible for the royal finances. Suggestions that Philip feared a Templar *coup d'état* are unrealistic; the Order's combat troops were in Cyprus. Nogaret needed 'evidence'. His first source was Esquiu de Florian of Béziers. This medieval Titus Oates, once Templar prior of Montfaucon, had been expelled for irregularities and during his efforts to obtain 'justice' had committed at least one murder. In 1305 Esquiu offered to sell King Jaume of Aragon his former brethren's 'secret', accusing them of blasphemy and horrible vices. The king was unimpressed, but French agents saw possibilities in Esquiu, who was asked to make a legal deposition. Next year royal officials recruited twelve spies to join the Order. By 1307 Nogaret had sufficient material – of a sort – on which to base a prosecution.

Clement was weak and credulous but not dishonest. A crusade was being considered and on 6 June 1306 the pope wrote in all sincerity to the Masters of the Temple and the Hospital: 'We wish to consult you about a crusade with the kings of Cyprus and Armenia.' The Templar Master, Jacques de Molay, answered with a detailed memorandum, announcing that he would visit Clement to discuss the matter in detail; no doubt he hoped to wrest the crusade's leadership from the Hospital. He landed at Marseilles in early 1307 with sixty knight brethren and rode to Paris in great state. Among their baggage were twelve pack-loads of gold and silver, including 150,000 gold florins; later they were to regret this ostentation. King Philip gave them a warm welcome, but the Grand Preceptor of France knew something was in the wind. However, after seeing the pope at Poitiers and asking for a papal commission to investigate and dispel any hostile rumours about his Order, Jacques returned to the Paris Temple. On the night of Thursday, 12 October 1307, Philip's troops broke in to arrest Molay with sixty brethren, incarcerating some in royal prisons, others in the Temple's own dungeons. By the morning of Friday, 13 October, 15,000 people had been seized: knights, chaplains, sergeants, *confrates* and retainers – even labourers on the Order's farms. Probably not more than 500 were full members, fewer than 200 were professed brethren. By the weekend popular preachers were denouncing the Poor Knights to horrified crowds all over France.

The arrest was illegal; the civil authority could not arrest clerics responsible only to Rome. But Philip hoped to substantiate certain charges: denial of Christ, idol worship, spitting on the crucifix and homosexuality – unnatural vice was a practice associated with the Albigensians, and all these accusations were the stock-in-trade of heresy trials. The French Inquisition, staffed by Dominicans, 'Hounds of the Lord', was expert at extracting confessions. The brethren, unlettered soldiers, faced a combination of cross-examining lawyers and torture chambers whose instruments included the thumbscrew, the boot and a rack to dislocate limbs. Men were spreadeagled and crushed by lead weights or filled with water through a funnel till they suffocated. There was also 'burning in the feet'. Probably the most excruciating torments were the simplest – wedges hammered under fingernails, teeth wrenched out and the exposed nerves prodded. The Templars would have resisted any torment by Moslems but now, weakened by confinement in damp, filthy cells and systematic starvation, they despaired when the torture was inflicted by fellow Christians.

It is not surprising that thirty-six brethren died, or that, out of 138 examined, 123 confessed to the least nauseating charge, spitting on the crucifix, for medieval man was accustomed to swearing oaths under duress and then obtaining absolution once he was safe. Even Jacques de Molay stooped to this stratagem, humiliated by a charge of homosexuality which he furiously denied. However, though his 'confession' may have been politic it unnerved the brethren, while Fra' Hugues de Peyraud frightened them still more by admitting *every* accusation; 'made of the willow rather than the oak', the wily Treasurer co-operated with gusto, declaring he worshipped an idol in chapter. At Carcassonne two brethren agreed they had adored a wooden image called 'Baphomet' while a Florentine Templar named it 'Mahomet' and another brother said it had a long beard but no body. Royal agents hunted frantically for Baphomet and 'discovered' a metal-plated skull suspiciously like a reliquary. (The Baphomet story may have been inspired by the Hospitaller practice of venerating a representation of the severed head of their patron, John the Baptist; sometimes, flanked by the sun and the moon, this was painted on a panel like an icon, while it was also the seal of the Hospitaller Priory of England.)

These avowals of idolatry only served to discredit other evidence, for in extremities of pain and anguish men will say anything. Yet only three brethren would confess to homosexual practices, a refutation of 'indecent kisses'. It was alleged that in the rite of profession, postulants were required to kiss their superior on the navel or the base of the spine – possibly a few preceptors indulged in mumbo-jumbo, but it is highly unlikely. And intensive searches failed to find 'the secret rule'.

When one considers how the Templars fought and died throughout the crusades it seems hard not to believe in their innocence. Yet, until the discovery of documents relating to the trial of Aragonese brethren, most historians were inclined to find them guilty. Even today no less an authority than Sir Steven Runciman remains suspicious. At the end of his *History of the Crusades*, referring to the charges against the Order, he writes: 'It would be unwise to dismiss these rumours as the unfounded invention of enemies. There was probably just enough substance in them to suggest the line along which the Order could be most convincingly attacked.'[7] In *The Medieval Manichee* Sir Steven suggests the possible influence of Dualist ideas and usages. This indeed may be the clue. It is surely more than coincidence that the most strident accusations came from the heartlands of the Albigensian heresy; Nogaret was a Provençal, Fra' Esquiu a Catalan. Local brethren in these regions could well have turned isolated preceptories into Cathar cells during the previous century when the heresy was at its height, while the Order's bankers would have been quite capable of protecting fugitive heretics in order to obtain the Cathar treasure which disappeared just before their last stronghold fell in 1244. Admittedly Catharism was almost extinct by 1307; but vague memories from years before of heresy hunts within the Order, kept secret to avoid scandal, may have been the origin of tales of devil-worship, secret rites and sodomy which were all charges which had been made against the Cathars. Perhaps Pope Clement's confusion is not so surprising after all.

Surely the king, the chancellor, the grand inquisitor, the bishops and the archbishops could not all stoop to false witness? At first the pope had protested vigorously, suspending the Inquisition in France on 27 October 1307. But by now Philip was announcing sensational 'discoveries', including a letter of confession from Fra' Jacques, and so, at the end of November, Clement issued a second bull ordering the arrest of all Templars. Courts of inquiry were set up throughout Christendom. In January 1308, with some reluctance, England arrested its Templars. There were not more than 135 in the country – 118 sergeants, 11 chaplains, and only 6 knights. The Grand Preceptor, Fra' William de ia More, was immured in the Tower of London, his brethren in various prisons, though there was no interrogation for eighteen months. Irish and Scottish Templars were also rounded up. All but two Scottish brethren escaped; King Robert never legally ratified the Scottish Temple's dissolution.

Aragonese *Templarios* were not numerous but they were far too proud to surrender tamely;[8] Monzon capitulated only in May, and Castellat held out until November, while other peninsular fortresses resisted even longer. The Aragonese commission found the brethren innocent, and the Archbishop of Compostella pronounced the Castilian brothers also blameless, as did the Portuguese bishops their Templars. Prince Amalric, the Cypriot regent who had been installed by the Poor Knights, delayed until May before acknowledging receipt of the papal letter; his country too could ill afford to lose valuable fighting men. He seems to have warned the brethren, who surrendered on terms. Even when King Henry escaped from Armenia to recover his throne with Hospitaller aid, his courts acquitted the Templars.[9] Wild- und Rheingraf Hugo, *Pfleger* (preceptor) of Grumbach and twenty ritter, all in full armour and carrying swords, strode into the Archbishop of Metz's council.[10] The *Pfleger* cried that not only was the whole *Tempelherrenorden* innocent of such vile insults and his Grossmeister a man of piety and honour, but Pope Clement was an evil tyrant, unlawfully elected, whom he, Hugo, with his ritter, declared deposed. Further, all brethren would welcome ordeal by battle; all challenges would be accepted. The council dispersed hastily.

In France the situation had changed radically at the end of June 1308. In May, Philip came to Poitiers to discuss the affair with Clement, finally agreeing to surrender the Templars to a papal commission. In return the pope withdrew his suspension of the Grand Inquisitor – Philip's confessor – Guillaume de Paris. In fact Clement left the brethren's enemies in full control, for the French Church was packed with royal agents. Philip forced the appointment of one of his creatures, Philip de Marigny, to the archbishopric of Sens. As his suffragan, the Bishop of Paris had to obey the new archbishop. Immediately seventy-two Templars were brought to Poitiers, where they repeated their 'confessions' *en masse* before a horrified Clement. The pope interrogated Fra' Jacques and the Grand Preceptors of Cyprus, Normandy and Aquitaine, who admitted their guilt. All were gagged by dread of reprisals as they knew that Clement was weak and were already appalled by his failure to rescue them. Only when safe in the commission's hands would they dare tell the truth; it is possible that most brethren had received instructions from their superiors. Unfortunately these first confessions left an indelible impression on Clement, who always remained convinced of the brethren's guilt. Most historians credit the pope with a total lack of scruple, but Clement was not only frightened, he was also ill and tired, not only vacillating by nature, but cursed with a weak man's obstinacy.

From Spain and Cyprus came news that the Templars were innocent, while investigations in the empire too found them guiltless. Pressure could be brought to bear on England, but here many prisoners had escaped, and when the remaining fifty were interrogated nothing could be extracted; a second inquiry in 1310 examined 228 brethren with no more result. Finally Clement ordered Edward II to use torture. Eventually King Edward agreed, stipulating that there must be no 'mutilations, incurable wounds or violent effusions of blood'. Out of more than 200 Templars, including *confratres* and retainers, examined in 1310 and 1311, all of whom were subjected to excruciating agonies, only four admitted to spitting at the cross. The Grand Preceptor begged his examiners 'for the love of God and as you hope for salvation judge us as you will be judged before God'. But there was no mercy.

The commission finally assembled in August 1309. The seven members sat in the Bishop of Paris's palace; their chairman, the Archbishop of Narbonne, was Philip's man. At first the Templars were uncertain that it really was the commission for which they waited. Then the Preceptor of Paris retracted his confession and on 26 November the Master came before the commissioners. Vehemently he retracted his confession, rejecting categorically 'wicked and false accusations by the Order's enemies'. Later the Master growled how he wished France had the custom 'as among Saracens and Tartars, of beheading perjurers'.[11] He declared that no other Order had such rich churches or beautiful relics, or priests who celebrated Mass with more dignity and devotion, adding that 'no Order has fought more determinedly, more bravely, given its blood more generously in Palestine for Christianity'. Fra' Jacques also made a simple but moving declaration of faith. Nogaret interrupted: 'the Order's corruption is notorious . . . a chonicle at St Denis states that when the Templars were beaten Saladin blamed the defeat on their vice and sodomy, on betraying their own religion'.[12] The Knight answered that he had heard no such tale before; of course there had been alliances, to save Outremer. The court was impressed. Yet the commissioners could not credit false witness of such magnitude. On the other hand this man seemed so sincere – he had begged to be shriven and for communion. Jacques de Molay was asked if he would conduct his Order's defence. Then the Master made two fatal mistakes.

First he demanded to see Pope Clement, for now that the commission had assembled he could speak without fear. Unfortunately Fra' Jacques had been *too* subtle; after that first shattering interview Clement had made up his mind once and for all. Molay's second error was refusing to undertake the brotherhood's defence. To begin with, he told the court he would be a 'poor creature' if he did not, but he needed money and lawyers. However, on reflection, Fra' Jacques declined, realizing that royal agents might intimidate the defending counsel. Alone it was impossible, as Molay, who was unlettered,[13] was entirely dependent on secretaries. He staked everything on the pope; with really free access he could convince Clement and save his brethren. But the pope had no intention of seeing him. Cunningly the chairman adjourned the commission until February 1310; by then the Templars would have heard of their Master's refusal and be entirely demoralized. In March, at his final appearance before the commission, Molay again refused and asked to see the pope.

Probably Philip and his advisers anticipated no more trouble. Yet though dispersed and confined for two nightmarish years, there is a strong likelihood that somehow brethren, though gyved and bound, had managed to communicate and agree on a common policy. Suddenly in April brother after brother retracted his confession, over 500 of them offering to defend the Temple. The court had to take them seriously; the prisoners were assembled in the garden of the commissioners' palace to choose four representatives – two chaplains and two knights – the most capable being the priest, Fra' Pierre de Boulogne, once Preceptor of Rome. On 7 April he appeared in front of the commission and produced a statement for the pope, affirming the Order's innocence. The preceptor demanded that his brethren be removed from royal custody, that laymen – Philip's agents – be excluded from the court and that the accused be supplied with funds. He showed a remarkable grasp of the legal situation, pointing out that if his brethren agreed to plead before the court this did not mean they recognized its legality. Pierre argued his case with fluency and logic. How could Templars deny Christ when so many had died in Palestine rather than do this very thing? The commission were visibly shaken.

But Philip's creature, the Archbishop of Sens, controlled the ecclesiastical machinery of Paris; fifty-four Templars were handed over to the secular authority to be burnt as relapsed heretics. More torture, bribes, the pleading of relatives, could not cow them. All met an agonizing death with determination, shrieking that they were guiltless. Even so, one brother, Amaury de Villiers-le-Duc, 'pale and terrified', broke down in front of the papal commissioners. Fifty years of age and thirty years a Templar, he may well have been a Palestinian veteran.[14] Fra' Amaury cried that his tortures had been so terrible he would have confessed anything and begged the tribunal not to tell his jailers what he had said – faced by the fire, he 'would swear to murdering God himself'[15] if necessary. As the account occurs in the official report, available to royal agents, one prefers not to speculate on his subsequent fate. By the end of May, 120 Templars had been burnt. The Archbishop of Sens demanded that Reynaud de Pruino, Pierre de Boulogne's colleague, be handed over for examination. The commissioners were beginning to panic; on 30 May they adjourned, surrendering Reynaud and Pierre to the council of Sens. Every brother withdrew both his retraction and his offer to defend the Order.

Perhaps the Templars' worst anguish was spiritual – it must have seemed that God Himself had died – and probably many brethren went mad. Yet the wildest rumours circulated, for French public opinion undoubtedly believed in the brethren's guilt. They were supposed to have summoned devil women from hell and slept with them, while bastards were roasted in front of images smeared with children's fat, and cats were worshipped. The commission reassembled to examine witnesses who offered no defence.

Philip was apprehensive of the General Council of the Church, soon to assemble. The propaganda campaign against Clement was resumed. He was forced to try Boniface posthumously, the late pontiff being accused of every imaginable iniquity, including black magic. This preposterous charade had the same object as the Templar plot – to tarnish the papacy, bringing it more firmly under French control. However, the prosecution was discredited by its own absurdity and the trial was abandoned in return for papal condemnation of its former Praetorian Guard. When the council met at Vienne in October, however, it invited the Templars to defend themselves once again. Seven Poor Knights, bearded, wearing full armour and the red cross habit, appeared from nowhere. Clement was appalled; such monsters of guile might well convince foreign bishops of their innocence. Hastily he adjourned the council. These trusting brethren were arrested, and a massive hunt was started for their comrades, 1,500 of whom were supposed to be concealed in the neighbouring Lyonnais.

In February 1312 the French Estates' General demanded the Order's condemnation. Finally, in March, Clement, in private consistory (that is, with his advisers *in camera*), formally pronounced the Poor Knights of the Temple of Solomon to be guilty of all charges made against them. When the council reassembled on 3 April they were presented with a *fait accompli*, the bull, *Vox in excelso*, declaring the Order dissolved. The pope explained his reasons; canonically the Templars could not be convicted on the evidence, but he himself was convinced of their guilt and had therefore exercised his prerogative to condemn them. The General Council accepted his decision without demur. On 2 May a further bull disposed of the brotherhood's lands, which were given to the Hospitallers. Those brethren who had retracted confessions – or refused to confess at all – received life imprisonment, while those who had stuck to their confessions were released on a minute pension, most of them ending up as beggars. Clement waited before sentencing the high officers, Jacques de Molay (still pleading for an interview), the Treasurer and the Preceptors of Maine and Normandy.

The Hospitallers watched their rival's destruction with mixed feelings. They could not altogether repress their pity for men who had so often been comrades-in-arms; English Hospitallers always referred to Grand Preceptor de la More, who died in the Tower, as 'the Martyr' and their Prior, William de Tothale, drew up a list of the Temple's Masters to pray for their souls. However, even the most sympathetic looked forward to getting his hands on their wealth. But the kings had seized the preceptories and were reluctant to disgorge; Philip kept all revenues till his death, claiming that the Templars had owed him the cost of their trial, while in England Edward II had already shared out the spoils, and the Order of St John found itself faced by countless lawsuits from the occupants and the descendants of the original donors. Even when an Act of Parliament recognized the Hospitallers' title in 1324, it took years before this was properly implemented – the Strand Temple was recovered only in 1340, the remainder being let to lawyers. In Europe one half of the Poor Knights' possessions was lost to the laity.

None the less, this was an immense accession of wealth for the Hospitallers.* In Germany the vast estates of the Templars enabled the *Herrenmeister* of the Brandenburg *Ballei* of the '*Johanniterorden*' to become semi-autonomous. Hitherto the Hospitallers' strength in the German-speaking lands had been in Austria, Silesia, the Breisgau and Switzerland. Now they acquired great estates in Brunswick and Halberstadt.

English commanderies had to be drastically reorganized to absorb new lands; sometimes the commandery itself was transferred to a former preceptory, as at Egle in Lincolnshire. Scotland was in such chaos that the Apostolic Decree dissolving the Scots' Temple was never ratified, but it is untrue that the Templars continued as part of a combined Order, even if a few Poor Knights may have been received as Hospitallers. Some English brethren were taken in as pensioners; in 1338 a former Templar was still living at Egle.[16] Finally, after years of litigation, the number of St John's English houses rose to fifty-five. In 1338 their brothers numbered thirty-four knights, forty-eight sergeants and thirty-four chaplains.

Even the greediest Hospitaller must have been shaken by the

---

* Even in Aragon, after sufficient had been taken to found the new Order of Montesa, enough Templar property fell into the hands of the kingdom's *Hospitalarios* to make it necessary to divide the Castellanry of Amposta (i.e. priory of Aragon) and erect a new priory of Catalunya.

last act. On 14 March 1314 the four Templar great officers were paraded on a scaffold outside Notre-Dame to hear their sentence – life imprisonment. Then Molay spoke from this macabre rostrum, the Templars' ultimate battleground:

I think it only right that at so solemn a moment when my life has so little time to run [he was nearly seventy] I should reveal the deception which has been practised and speak up for the truth. Before heaven and earth and with all of you here as my witnesses, I admit that I am guilty of the grossest iniquity. But the iniquity is that I have lied in admitting the disgusting charges laid against the Order. I declare, and I must declare, that the Order is innocent. Its purity and saintliness is beyond question. I have indeed confessed that the Order is guilty, but I have done so only to save myself from terrible tortures by saying what my enemies wished me to say. Other knights who have retracted their confessions have been led to the stake; yet the thought of dying is not so awful that I shall confess to foul crimes which have never been committed. Life is offered to me but at the price of infamy. At such a price, life is not worth having. I do not grieve that I must die if life can be bought only by piling one lie upon another.

Two of his brethren listened fearfully, but the Preceptor of Normandy, Fra' Geoffroy de Charnay, rallied to the Grand Master, speaking with equal defiance. Next morning the two brothers in religion were burnt alive over a slow charcoal fire on an island in the Seine, shouting their innocence through the flames. A legend grew up that Fra' Jacques had summoned Philip and Clement to come before God for judgement; certainly the pope was dead within a month, the king by the autumn, and his three sons and successors all died young.

One must not see the attack on the Templars as an isolated incident. Accusations of such viciousness were made against the Teutonic Knights that they transferred their headquarters from Venice to Prussia, while the crisis confirmed the Hospitallers' decision to move to Rhodes, hastening their development into a federation of national brotherhoods; Philip attempted, unsuccessfully, to stop this reorganization, which made a French takeover impossible. It also perpetuated the Leper Knights' division; in 1308 King Philip took Fra' Thomas de Sainville, the Master General of the Knighthood of St Lazarus, and all his Order's possessions under royal protection, but when Thomas died in 1312 his successor was not recognized by Naples and in 1318 Pope John XXII gave the priory of Capua full independence – henceforth there were two distinct branches of St Lazarus – Burton Lazars supporting Boigny.

Sometimes the Roman Church has proved an unnatural mother, savaging those who love her best – like the eighteenth-century Jesuits – but seldom as gullible or as cruel as in the bull *Vox in excelso*. As Hilaire Belloc said, 'When one remembers how the Catholic Church has been governed, and by whom, one realizes that it must be divinely inspired to have survived at all.' Some Castilian Templars were so horrified that they fled to Granada[17] and turned Moslem. The Poor Knights' most lasting achievement, their contribution towards the overthrow of the Church's attitude to usury, was economic. No medieval institution did more for the rise of capitalism. Yet the Templars deserve to be remembered not as financiers but as the heroes of Acre.

RHODES AND THE SEA KNIGHTS

Unlike the Templars, the Hospitallers responded brilliantly to the challenge of new conditions. Rhodes had become a nest of pirates, Greek, Italian and Saracen, a Levantine Tortuga disrupting Christian trade throughout the Aegean. Initially the brethren occupied the island for this reason alone, but the attack on the Templars shocked them into making it their headquarters. In 1306, after spies had brought glowing reports, Master Foulques de Villaret, formerly the Order's first admiral, sailed for Rhodes in June with two galleys and some transports carrying only 35 knights and 500 infantry. En route he was joined by a Genoese adventurer, Vignole de' Vignoli, who brought two more galleys. The great port beat off their first assault, but in November the key fortress of Philermo was taken and the brethren invested Rhodes in earnest. Though Greek troops joined the outlaw garrison, for the Byzantine emperor had no wish to forfeit his nominal sovereignty, the little army hung on grimly, Fra' Foulques borrowing money to hire more soldiers. Finally the city was stormed and its defenders fled to the hills. This probably took place in early 1307, the convent being transferred two years later.[1]

This hilly island, forty-five miles long, twenty-two miles wide and divided by mountains, was famed for an idyllic climate and fertile crops, though there was no town other than Rhodes itself, which the brethren had made the safest trading base in the Levant, its landlocked harbour fortified by chains, booms and moles. Egypt and the Anatolian emirates would have to suffer endless raids; not without reason did they name the Hospitaller lair 'stronghold of the hounds of Hell'. Crusading states are usually limited to six, but Rhodes has some claim to be the seventh.

Sweeping reforms dealt with new maritime duties; from 1299 the admiral ranked as a conventual bailiff while the Turcopolier, now responsible for coastal defences, was similarly promoted. Their survival was no less spectacular than their rivals' fall. Then the threat of Philip IV acted as a catalyst for a structural revolution; even in the thirteenth century there had been an embryonic division into *langues*, those speaking the same tongue. The Order was now divided into seven of these *langues*, each comprising several priories under a Grand Priory and with its own *auberge* (hall of residence): at Rhodes, Provence, Auvergne, France, Italy, Spain, England (with Ireland) and Germany (including Scandinavia and Bohemia–Poland). Because of the large number of Gallic brethren, France was given three *langues*, while in the fifteenth century Spain would be divided into Aragon (with Catalonia and Navarre) and Castile (with Crato, i.e. Portugal). Though he ranked lower than his nation's Grand Prior, at Rhodes a brother commanding a *langue* was one of the conventual bailiffs, and styled a *pilier*: Provence was under the Grand Commander, the Master's lieutenant administering the brotherhood's properties; Auvergne had the Marshal, senior military officer; France the Hospitaller; Italy the Admiral; Spain the Drapier; England the Turcopolier; Germany the Grand Bailiff.

The Chapter General included all brethren from the Master to the humblest serving brother, but as its meetings were stormy and often riotous, it met less and less. Day-to-day government was administered by the Venerable Council, a quorum of senior officers, though the most important constitutional body was the Sacred Council, an assembly of bailiffs – conventual, Syrian (nominal except for Armenia) and European. Italy possessed seven priors, the Iberian peninsula five (the castellan of Amposta ranking as prior of Aragon). England had four members: the Turcopolier, the priors of England and Ireland, and the commander – styled bailiff – of Egle. All *langues* shared the Syrian posts and the seven Cypriot commanderies. To become a bailiff it was necessary to spend fifteen years at Rhodes. As great officers they were distinguished by a larger cross and called 'bailiffs grand cross', receiving especially rich commanderies – the English prior, for example, occupied four besides Clerkenwell.

The fourteenth century was to prove a difficult one for the Order of St John, for the concept of the crusade was dying, while Italian merchants were strangling the Latin East with their capitalist tentacles, averse to alienating Moslem business interests. Despite the Templar properties there was a steady decline in revenues, and the Order was hard hit by the Black Death. It had already suffered great financial losses when the Florentine banks had failed in the 1340s. There were also severe internal dissensions, even at Rhodes. Fra' Foulques, able but overbearing, became increasingly dictatorial and then went to pieces, womanizing and drinking. In 1317 angry brethren, led by an elderly, embittered commander, Fra' Maurice de Pagnac, tried to murder him, but he escaped to the castle on the acropolis of Lindos.[2] In 1319 John XXII confirmed Fra' Foulques's deposition and he retired to a commandery in Languedoc.[3] Pagnac had died, and so the brothers elected Fra' Elyon de Villeneuve as their superior.

Yet life on Rhodes remained monastic. Brethren ate and slept in their *langue*, saying Office in its chapel. Altogether the *auberges* constituted one convent, and all brothers attended chapters in the magistral palace, keeping important feasts in the Order's church where novices made their solemn profession to the Master. Several hundred knights lived on Rhodes – two hundred in 1330, twenty-eight of them English – so a single house was impracticable. Rhodian coins show the Master kneeling before a crucifix, proclaiming both his religious status and his role as 'Guardian of the Poor'. All brethren worked in the great hospital, with its 1,000 beds where the sick slept between linen sheets and ate off silver plates, drinking wine from silver cups. Patients included casualties in battle, merchants, pilgrims and the island's poor. Every evening at sunset in the 'Palais des Malades', chaplain brethren recited the great prayer for 'Our Lords the sick': 'Seigneurs Malades, pries pour pais que Dieu la mande de ciel en terre. Seigneurs Malades, pries pour le fruit de la terre que Dieu

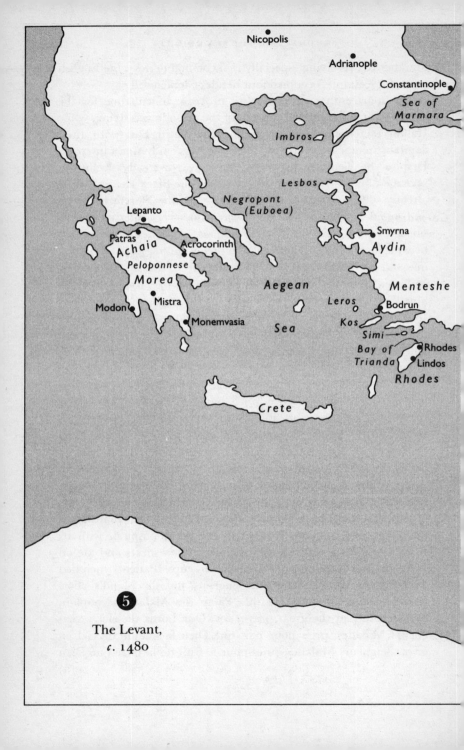

The Levant,
c. 1480

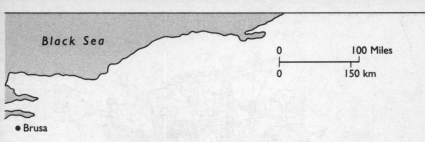

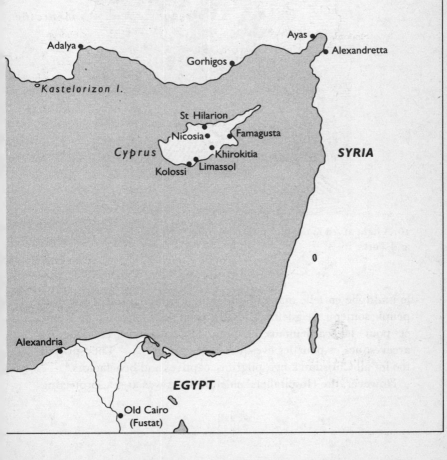

10. A fight at sea in the fifteenth century between Knights of Rhodes and Turks

le multiplie en telle manière que saincte église en soit servie et le peuple soutenu. Seigneurs Malades, pries pour l'apostell de Rome et pour les cardennaus et pour les patriarchs et pour les arcevesques et pour les evesques et les prelate . . .' They prayed too for all Christian kings, pilgrims, captives and benefactors.[4]

However, the Hospitallers' chief business was at sea, protecting

Christian merchantmen or waylaying Moslem traders. They themselves ran a fleet of cargo vessels and pilgrim transports. Their battle flotilla seldom contained more than a dozen galleys, yet these were the hardest-hitting warships of their day, small but extremely fast, usually carrying twenty-five men-at-arms with rather more crossbowmen. Their torpedo was the iron ram which stove in timbers, and mangonels were the artillery – a heavy boulder could crash through a ship's bottom while fireballs, naphtha or incendiary arrows set her alight. Such techniques crippled rather than sank and the enemy ships were immobilized – holed below the water-line, their oars smashed, transfixed by a metal beak or tethered with grappling hooks – so that the knights could board, their arbalestiers shooting down on the crew. Rhodes was often lashed by sudden storms and the brethren made themselves excellent sailors, the best fighting seamen of their age; in Edward Gibbon's majestic prose: '. . . under the discipline of the Order that island emerged into fame and opulence; the noble and warlike monks were renowned by land and sea; and the bulwark of Christendom provoked and repelled the arms of the Turks and Saracens'.

Mameluke Egypt remained strong and threatening, while Asia Minor was now a mass of small Turkish emirates ruled by *ghazis* (warriors for the faith). The largest groupings were the Karamans, ruled by the Grand Karaman at Konya, and the Germaniyans, but a succession of superb leaders had transformed the small Osmanli clan into the dominating tribe, under whose horsetail standard all ambitious *ghazis* hastened to enrol. In 1326 Orhan – 'Sultan, son of the Sultan of the Ghazis, Ghazi son of the Ghazi, Marzuban of the Horizons, Hero of the World' – captured Brusa, and, in 1329, Nicaea. It was only a matter of time before Osmanli *spahis* conquered the Balkans.

Of Christian neighbours Greece – 'Romania' – was a mosaic of small, violently inimical states. The Palaeologan revival waned until the Byzantine Empire entered its final decline with the civil wars of the mid-fourteenth century. Every hilltop and island was ruled by an independent lord – Greek, French, Spanish or Italian

– while Genoese and Venetians possessed a multitude of trading posts. The Hospitallers had several commanderies, the Teutonic Knights a few isolated ones. Cyprus was Rhodes's chief neighbour. Hugh IV (1324–58) and his descendants were each crowned King of Cyprus at Nicosia, King of Jerusalem at Famagusta nearest the mainland, and their sons styled Prince of Antioch or Tyre. Despite nostalgia for *la douce Syrie* – Frankish ladies always wore black in mourning for the lost kingdom – Cypriot nobles with names evocative of Outremer – Ibelins, Gibelets, Scandelions – led a sybaritic existence in delightful villas amid rose gardens and vineyards. To Hospitallers the Cypriot monarch was the most important sovereign in Christendom but, as Jacques de Molay had written to Pope Clement, his army was too small. Then there was Armenia, hard pressed by Mamelukes. When the last Hethoumid died in 1342, the Cilicians chose Hugh IV's nephew, Guy de Lusignan, as their king. But these ferocious mountaineers were unreliable; not only did they quarrel – Guy was murdered in 1344 – but they reacted violently at tactless attempts to Romanize the Gregorian Church with its hooded prelates, crowned *vartapets* (archpriests) and dramatic liturgy. Even when their country was reduced to its capital, Sis, with a string of coastal fortresses and a few mountain strongholds inland, the proud, warlike barons held out among their wild glens and clifftops. Yet for all their courage 'Erminie' was doomed.

The sea-knights won victory after victory. Those of their victims who escaped limped home with horrific tales of these fiendish dogs from Gehenna. In 1319 the Grand Commander Albrecht von Schwarzburg was escorting the Genoese governor of Chios to his island when he was attacked by a Turkish fleet, which he routed. Only six enemy vessels escaped, by night, while most of the Faithful were drowned. The *ghazis* wanted revenge, and in June 1320 Rhodes was blockaded by eighty warships. But the pugnacious Albrecht sailed out to meet them with the Order's battle-squadron of four galleys and twelve other vessels. Most of the enemy's ships were boarded or sent to the bottom, while their entire assault force, which had landed on a nearby island, was captured.[5] In 1334 a fleet of Hospitaller, papal, Cypriot, French and Venetian crusaders ambushed Yakshi, emir of Marmora, off the island of Episkopia on the Negropont coast, and, during a running battle which lasted nine days, outsailed and outfought the Turks, who lost over 100 vessels.[6]

In 1344 Clement VI, learning that Umur of Aydin was building an armada of landing craft, formed the Latin League, comprising Cyprus, Venice and Rhodes. Their combined fleet of twenty-four galleys, commanded by the Prior of Lombardy, Fra' Gian de Biandra, stormed Umur's stronghold of Smyrna in October, burning his entire navy of 300 ships at anchor. All Christendom rejoiced, and a crusading army of 15,000, mainly French, arrived in 1346. Another victory was won, off Imbros, in 1347 by the Catalan prior, Pere-Arnal de Peres Tortes, in which the Turks lost 100 galleys, while the following year Umur himself was killed during a gallant attempt to retake his beloved Izmir. Now the brethren held it for the pope.[7] This crusading resurgence, however, was checked by bubonic plague. In Cyprus only the fortress of St Hilarion – where the royal family took refuge – was immune, and the mortality was so terrible that for years afterwards visitors were deterred by the island's reputation for disease and poisoned air.

After the Templar dissolution the Hospitallers were weakened by brethren hurrying back to Europe in hope of some rich commandery. The General Chapter of 1330 ordained that before promotion all brothers must serve five years 'in the convent', including three caravans, each constituting a year's active service. In 1342 the pope had complained to Fra' Elyon about his Order's laxity, threatening to create a new brotherhood with its surplus revenues. By the end of the fourteenth century few European commanderies contained more than one brother, the commander himself. In England conventual life ceased, save at Clerkenwell, postulants entering the novitiate at Rhodes. The St Lazarus and St Thomas brotherhoods were moribund. After the Black Death there was a remarkable decline in leprosy. Formerly houses like Burton Lazars with separate cells for each leper, and medicinal baths, took in only those suffering skin disease; now ordinary sick were admitted, though the 'Governor, Warden and Master of Burton Lazars' conducted visitations until well into the fifteenth century, sometimes acting as Lieutenant in Scotland for the Master at Boigny.[8] The last-known Knight of St Thomas, Fra' Richard de Tickhill, was professed and given the habit by the preceptor of Cyprus, Fra' Hugh de Curteys, in 1357 at the Church of St Nicholas of the English in Nicosia.[9]

Rhodes possessed two ports, the outer or 'Harbour of the Galleys' formed by a long, curving neck of land, the inner a landlocked bay whose narrow entrance was guarded by moles on which stood the towers of St Jean and St Michel. The city was built in a semi-circle round this inner port, protected by a double wall with thirteen towers and five projecting bastions – one of which was allotted to the English brethren – and also by a rampart along the harbour front. Though the great cathedral of St Jean, begun in 1310, had been built in a hybrid, Catalan– Italian style, other churches such as St Catherine's were flamboy- ant with ogee arches and wild tracery, while the rich merchants' houses next to the *collachium* were both imposing and luxurious and, like the brothers', swamped in a sea of flowers – roses, oleanders, bougainvillaea, Turkish tulips, mimosa and jasmine. Inland, as far as the eye could see, was a rich green vista of gardens, orchards, vineyards, farms, with an abundance of fig, nectarine and peach trees. Everything in the city, even its ram- parts, was built of honey-coloured stone. The markets sold every luxury known – silks, spices, scent, sandalwood, damascene metal- work, precious stones, jet, furs, amber and slaves – for this embattled port commanded the Levant trade-routes. In its narrow, cobbled streets, through the Gothic gateways, swarmed not only Greeks and westerners but Christian Copts from Egypt, Armenian refugees, Syrians of *poulain* or Jacobite origin and even Georgians, besides Jews from the ghetto. Yet Rhodes was their home and they were loyal to their lords, the sons of country gentlemen in Yorkshire, the Limousin or Westphalia, the Cam- pagna, Castile, or any other land in Western Europe.

The *collachium* was the compound which cloistered the 'convent' proper, including the Magistral palace, the Order's church, the Sacred Infirmary and the *auberges* in the '*rue des Chevaliers*'. By now every *langue* owned one, though in the previous century the Catalan prior, Pere-Arnal de Peres Tortes, recorded that when he arrived he 'had to beg his lodging in the streets', after which he erected a fine Aragonese *auberge*. Naturally some *langues* were better represented than others, particularly the French, while Poles and Scandinavians must have felt lonely in the German house. The total strength of knights in the convent was raised from 200 to 350 in 1466, to 400 in 1501 and finally in 1514 to 550,[10] but the number of English brethren never rose to more than a dozen. Despite this disparity, the system worked well enough, apart from occasional squabbles over precedence. Many were stationed outside the convent. On the island itself there were fortresses inland protecting little country towns, and a castle on the bay of Trianda, a few miles west of Rhodes, as well as the acropolis of Lindos, a fortified table-mountain whose garrison included twelve brothers under a commander. The Order ruled the entire Dodecanese archipelago, Kos – or Lango – being the most important island, with a flourishing town often described as a miniature Rhodes. Symi and Leros were defended by strong towers, while a hundred miles to the east, just off the Anatolian mainland, was Kastelorizon or 'Châteauroulx'. All had harbours in which the brethren's galleys could shelter and revictual. No doubt knights posted to these isolated outposts pined for the convent, where not only did they eat off silver but their diet included nutmeg, cinnamon and pepper in quantities unknown in Europe save at the greatest tables, while sugar was a commonplace. Persimmons, dates and pomegranates were served in that age when oranges and lemons were an exotic luxury to the West, as well as those sweet wines beloved by the medieval palate. Brethren returning from the stench of bilge and galley slaves knew the pleasure of hot baths. For relaxation there was hawking and buck hunting, and no doubt sailing and fishing. Visitors were always welcome and occasionally there was the excitement of royal guests, Byzantine or Cypriot, besides Turkish and Egyptian embassies. Yet the *collachium* made Rhodes a real monastery, spiritual duties being enforced with a heavy hand; sometimes wilder spirits, who found it too severe, fled to the fleshpots of Cyprus.

Hugh IV of Cyprus abdicated in 1358 to make way for his son, Pierre I, a visionary who was determined to win back Jerusalem. His reign began with a series of spectacular victories. As Armenia had appealed to Rome for help, in 1361 Pierre garrisoned the hard-pressed *Haiot* port of Gorighos, after which, assisted by the crew of four Hospitaller galleys, he stormed the pirate city of Adalya.[11] Soon the Turks learnt to dread this fierce king, who dragged captured *ghazis* 'at the horse's tail'; but Pierre left for Europe to plead for a crusade, travelling to Venice, Avignon, France, England, Germany, Bohemia and Poland. By 1364 it was time he returned; Cyprus had been laid waste by Turkish raiders, and hitherto friendly emirs were growing menacing. In June 1365 the king sailed with his crusaders from Venice to Rhodes, where the Cypriot fleet joined him in August.

Together with the Hospitaller flotilla of sixteen galleys carrying 100 brothers and their mercenaries under the Order's admiral, Fra' Ferlino d'Airasca, this armada – 165 vessels in all – set out for Alexandria.[12] It included flat-bottomed landing craft from which horsemen could ride out on to the beach. The destination was kept secret and the Mamelukes were taken by surprise. Pierre de Thomas, the papal legate, harangued his flock: 'Soldiers of Christ take comfort in the Lord and his Holy Cross and fight His War bravely – have no fear of the enemy and pray to God for victory. The gates of Paradise are open.'[13] The Egyptians defended their walls vigorously with cannon, vats of boiling oil and molten lead, flame-throwers – wooden tubes discharging jets of naphtha – and even gas bombs, inflammable discs which emitted dense fumes of sulphur and ammonia to drive blinded attackers reeling back, vomiting and choking. At first the Christians were beaten off, their scaling ladders thrown down, then some sailors crawled through a drain to open a gate, and the besiegers swept into the great city. Many brethren fell during the assault and Fra' Robert Hales, Bailiff of Egle, performed prodigies of valour.

> O worthy Petro, king of Cypre, also
> That Alisaundre wan by heigh maistrye . . .

The glory was tarnished by massacre: 20,000 men, women and children died in the sack.

Unfortunately the crusaders, gorged with plunder, exhausted from rape, refused to march on Cairo, and Pierre, heartbroken, was forced to evacuate hard-won Alexandria. A tyrannical disposition and a vigorous private life had made him many enemies at home, including the queen (although Pierre spread her nightdress over his bed every night he spent away from her!). One evening in 1369, as the king lay asleep with his favourite mistress, some dissident noblemen burst in and killed him. Then the kingdom's Turcopolier castrated the royal corpse; the Lusignan vitality died with Pierre.

An old comrade suffered a worse fate. European kings had begun to employ Hospitaller priors as ministers, and in 1380 Robert Hales, the hero of Alexandria and Prior of England, became Richard II's treasurer. Alas, 'Hob the Robber's' poll tax provoked the Peasants' Revolt. After burning Clerkenwell the mob prised Fra' Robert and the Archbishop of Canterbury out of the Tower, hacked off their heads, which were then stuck on poles, and nailed the archbishop's mitre to his skull.

Juan Fernández de Heredia became Master in 1374. Born in 1310, this penniless scion of a great Aragonese family entered religion after being widowed twice. Hitherto his career had been a scramble for power – and money to leave to the children adopted by his brother. Ingratiating himself with successive popes, he became captain of the papal guard. He fought at Crécy in 1346 – questionable conduct for the Pontiff's envoy, even if he saved the French king's life – and was regarded with deep disapproval by many brethren. However, in the papal court at Avignon friends bought him promotion and ultimately the Mastership.

As soon as he was Master, he leased Achaia for five years, paying its pretender 4,000 ducats. After leaving Rome in 1377, he helped the Venetians storm Patras, where he was first over the wall and personally beheaded its emir in single combat, an extraordinary feat for a man of sixty-seven. He then retook Lepanto, on the other side of the Gulf of Corinth, recently captured by Albanian tribesmen, but was ambushed by them and sold to the Turks, to spend a year in captivity. When Navarrese mercenaries invaded Achaia shortly afterward, he decided to evacuate the Order's troops.

Juan's later years were troubled by the papal schism, with Urban VI reigning at Avignon, 'Clement VII', the anti-pope, at Rome. The Master, with the French and Spanish kings, supported the latter, and Urban therefore nominated an anti-Master, Fra' Ricardo Carracciolo, Prior of Capua. Some brethren turned pirate, like Fra' Guillaume de Talebart who, in 1391, boarded two Aragonese merchant ships off the Sardinian coast and seized a valuable cargo of coral.[14] However, the convent remained loyal to Heredia, who had become a much-loved superior, until his death at Avignon in 1396.

As a keen humanist Heredia commissioned the first translation of Plutarch into a vernacular language – Aragonese – as well as part of Thucydides' *Peloponnesian War*, Marco Polo's *Travels* and some oriental works.[15] Indeed the Hospitallers did include intellectuals, such as Jean Hesdin, dean of the theological faculty of Paris, an enthusiastic classicist and the spokesman for the French party during the controversy over the papal return to Rome, who was attacked by Petrarch.[16] Several brethren were masters of canon law, a necessary qualification for dealing with the Roman bureaucracy.

Brother knights were called, of course, to be Men of God – 'that with this rule of life we may merit the reward of eternal life'. Every day these tough seamen recited the Little Office, the Office of the Dead or 150 'Pater Nosters'. Their habit remained the black tunic and cloak, and though it is unlikely that knights joined in singing the full Roman Office like Spanish *freyles caballe-*

ros, on great feasts they attended Canonical Hours at the conventual church, where non-military brethren acted as canons, the Master presiding from an abbatial throne. Even on caravans the sea-knights chanted their 'Pater Nosters', led by the ship's chaplain, while the galley was halted to say the 'Angelus', and slaves rested thankfully on their oars. It was not enough for Hospitallers to substitute 'the defence of the Holy Catholic faith against the infidels and the enemies of the Christian religion' in place of 'the defence of the Holy Land'; there must be a double profession. The Church had hallowed secular knighthood with a ritual in which sword, belt and spurs acquired a quasi-sacramental quality. The Hospitallers made this ceremony a preface to the old, non-military rite of profession when the candidate received the habit, to stress the dual vocation. Those who found the life difficult faced Draconian penances. A brother guilty of negligence or calumny could incur the *septaine*; one week's confinement to the *auberge*, where he ate bread from the floor – fighting off the dogs – and drank water, while every twenty-four hours he was scourged 'with thongs' before the High Altar of the conventual church. Graver offences, gambling and dining in low taverns, earned forty days of the same treatment – the *quarantaine*. 'The crime of fornication', concubinage, duelling or simony were punished by incarceration in the convent's prison *and* flogging. All brethren had to confess to the Order's priests of whom there were two grades, chaplains at Rhodes under their conventual prior and priests-of-obedience in Europe – an inferior class who did not have to furnish proofs of nobility and rarely obtained commanderies. The brotherhood's real spiritual superior was the Reverend Grand Master, 'servus pauperum Christi et custos Hospitalis Hierusalemis'.

Often the crew of an Egyptian carrack, becalmed off some exquisite Aegean island, would wake at sunrise to see beneath the violet sky a galley darting out from a silent cove. The noise in itself was terrifying: huge oars beating the water in a rhythmic stroke sounded by shrill whistle-blasts or banging on a gong. There was a jarring crash when the prow's iron beak buried itself in ship's timbers and then, through the smoke, along the ram or over a boarding bridge, swarmed the steel-clad brethren.

All knights were anxious to complete the caravans necessary for promotion. A voyage lasted several months, and they lived in acute discomfort, fitting themselves into the machinery of an instrument built for speed and fighting. Brethren and their *patrons* slept huddled together under a tent on the stern platform, and their provisions were restricted to oil-soaked biscuit and watered wine. The real horror was the stench of rowers, and brothers sometimes plugged their noses. These poorly fed oarsmen, criminals or Saracen prisoners, were chained to their benches, lashed by overseers and only when in port were sheltered by a sailcloth awning. Yet shipmasters saw to a bare minimum of health, as starved or scurvy-ridden rowers could not produce an adequate rate of knots. Ships now mounted guns – breech-loading lombards, unreliable and dangerous but effective enough at short range. The Order's sea-going hierarchy consisted of the General of the Galleys on permanent duty with the battle squadron and the *patrons* or ships' captains, who were frequently bailiffs. A fixed complement of brethren manned the guardship which patrolled outside Rhodes night and day.

The whole of the Latin East was failing, even Cyprus. After the coronation banquet of 1372, several Genoese were killed in a brawl, whereupon the republic invaded the island. Eventually a bitter peace was concluded, with Genoa retaining Famagusta. Jacques I, released from imprisonment in an iron cage, isolated the port with a ring of fortifications, but the monarchy was ruinously weakened despite his coronation as King of Armenia in 1393, for the last Haiot strongholds had been overrun by the Mamelukes. The Turks were swallowing Greece; Adrianople became their capital in 1366. The kingdom of Bosnia, the empire of the Serbs and the tsardoms of the Bulgars were soon conquered. In 1394 Bayezid proclaimed himself 'Sultan of Rum' (Rome). His army was invincible, its key troops being *spahis* (bowmen equipped with steel helmet, mail shirt, shield, lance and yataghan) who were supported by similarly armed feudal troops under beys. Tactics were still the arrow storm and lightning charge.

The pope succeeded in launching the greatest expedition since the days of St Louis. Philippe de Mézières, once Pierre I's chancellor, had wandered all over Europe for nearly half a century preaching Holy War. The Balkans could be reached without a dangerous sea voyage while at hand there were powerful allies, Hungary–Croatia and Wallachia. Jean de Nevers brought 10,000 Burgundians and Frenchmen, the Earl of Huntingdon 1,000 English. From Germany came 6,000 men, and there were also Czechs, Poles, Spaniards and Italians. All met at Buda in July 1396, where King Sigismund of Hungary had assembled 60,000 Magyars and Transylvanians with 10,000 Vlachs under their Prince, Mircea the Old. Most of the western contingents were *gens d'armes* in grotesque *hounskull* helmets with 'pig face' visors and *jupons* (short cloth tunics worn over mail shirts). However, the majority of eastern Europeans were light cavalry or spearmen. By September, besides whoring and drinking bad wine, they had invested the Bulgarian city of Nicopolis and spent a fortnight trying to starve its Osmanli garrison into surrender. They were joined by the Venetian, Genoese and Hospitaller contingents, the latter under Master Philibert de Naillac, whose galleys had sailed up the Danube from the Black Sea.

On 25 September 1396 Bayezid *Yilderim* ('Lightning') appeared with an equally large army, 100,000 men, including a force of Christian Serbs under their despot, Stefan Lazarović. The sultan's first line of battle was light auxiliaries – *akinjis* (horse) and *azebs* (foot) in front of rows of pointed stakes. These sheltered his real infantry of archers and axemen. Behind them, completely hidden by a range of low hills, were the *spahis* and feudal cavalry. The French chivalry hurled themselves at the Turks' light troops. After killing at least 10,000, they dismounted to pull out the stakes and get at the bowmen, who fled up the hill. The knights pursued on foot, climbing the steep incline in their heavy armour. Suddenly '40,000' *spahis* galloped over the crest, charging down on the sweating men-at-arms still toiling up towards them. It was a massacre, and even the unwounded rolled down the hill to lie prostrate at the bottom. Sigismund and his Magyars, with the Germans and the brethren, rode forward to meet the Turks, though their Romanian allies had fled. They slew 15,000 infidels and for a moment it seemed Bayezid might be defeated, but then the Serbs came to his rescue with a ferocious charge. Sigismund and Philibert escaped in boats down the Danube, while archers galloping along the bank shot at them until they were picked up by a Venetian galley. Most Hungarians, however, died beside their German comrades and many brethren fell with them. Next day, apart from 300 great nobles rich enough to pay extortionate ransoms, the captured knighthood was slaughtered 'from morning till Vespers'. Nicopolis was the Latin East's death sentence.[17]

Bayezid then besieged Constantinople for seven years, but the Hospitallers were needed elsewhere; in 1400 they bought Mistra and Acrocorinth from the despot of the Morea, who had fled to Rhodes. Mistra refused to admit the brethren, as the Turks had now withdrawn from the Peloponnese, but Acrocorinth, which was more exposed, welcomed them. However, after four years the Master sold these Greek possessions to the empire. Bayezid had indeed intensified his siege of Constantinople in 1402, uttering threats of massacre and extermination, but was himself overwhelmed the same year by Tamberlane at Chibukabad.

Tamberlane invested Smyrna on 2 December 1402. The first day a white flag flew over the Khan's tent, signifying that if the city surrendered the lives of all would be spared; the second day the flag was red, promising mercy for the common people but not their rulers; the third day it was black – no man, woman or child would be spared. The besiegers numbered tens of thousands and had brought every conceivable siege-engine. The captain of Smyrna, Fra' Iñigo d'Alfara,[18] his 200 brethren and their few mercenaries had to man the ramparts under a sky black with missiles, while sappers tunnelled ceaselessly beneath their feet. Even so, a contemporary Persian historian wrote that the Tartars, victors from Delhi to the Don, thought that they fought 'like a band of enraged devils'. After a fortnight a Hospitaller fleet was sighted but the besiegers redoubled their efforts and breached the city walls. The remnants of the garrison cut their way through to the jetties and swam out to the galleys. In the ensuing orgy of extermination the triumphant horde fired the heads of fallen brethren at the Christian ships.

Smyrna had protected Black Sea shipping, and a few years later, therefore, Fra' Philibert occupied the Turkish castle of Bodrun on a mainland peninsula opposite Rhodes, building a great stronghold, Fort St Pierre, with seven lines of fortification and a secure harbour.[19] He was an unusually able Master who reunited the brethren, even though the papal schism continued. Probably his worst problems were financial, as receipts from European commanderies dwindled alarmingly. He travelled to many western capitals on fund-raising expeditions, visiting London in 1410. The brethren increased their commercial activities, investing in Italian enterprises or trading direct with Alexandria and Damietta. But even if they negotiated treaties with Egypt, their caravans continued to sweep the Levantine seas.

Fortunately for Rhodes, Cairo regarded Cyprus as its chief enemy. The island was weakened by recurrent outbreaks of plague, by swarms of locusts and by the declining authority of an impoverished monarchy. Yet King Janus saw himself as another Pierre. Frequent raids were made on the Egyptian coast and Moslem merchantmen attacked without mercy, for Janus would not restrain his privateers. In Pierre's day the Mamelukes had been crippled by a shortage of ship's timber, but now they possessed the Cilician forests. In 1426 Sultan Barsbei dispatched an armada of 180 galleys, carrying cavalry and Turcoman regulars, which landed in late June. The king, woefully incompetent, was surrounded and routed at Khirokitia;[20] his horse was killed under him and he proved too fat for any remounts available. The Mamelukes then burnt Nicosia to the ground and laid the whole kingdom to waste. In Cairo the wretched Janus was paraded through the streets on a donkey, his bare feet shackled beneath its belly save when jeering guards made him dismount to kiss the ground. After a year the king 'who never smiled again' was released on payment of the enormous ransom of 200,000 ducats, to which the Order contributed 30,000.[21]

Henceforth Cypriot kings were the sultan's vassals and almost overnight an aggressive crusader state had changed into a harmless trading base. Royal authority all but disappeared and the estates of both king and magnates never recovered. Indeed, the Order of St John, the largest landowner in the country, found its houses nearly bankrupt: in 1428 Grand Commander Hermann von Ow leased Kolossi to two brethren for seven years at a nominal rent of four ducats on condition they put the commandery on its feet – the normal income was 12,000 ducats.[22] In 1440 the Order reached an agreement with Cairo whereby Cyprus would not be involved in any future hostilities. The brethren could expect little help from the shattered kingdom's scanty forces and could certainly not afford to defend it, while both sides were anxious to safeguard their mercantile interests. Now Rhodes was the sole heir of crusader Jerusalem.

THE THREE SIEGES

The convent's growing peril heightened its brethren's sense of dedication. Significantly Hospitallers began to use the term 'our holy Religion' more often when referring to their Order, and the official adoption of the style 'Grand Master' by Fra' Antonio Fluvian, elected in 1421, reflects renewed purpose as much as worldly grandeur. Rhodes was the new kingdom of Jerusalem, where warriors guarded a consecrated citadel under the patronage of the Holy Virgin of Philermo. But they no longer had rivals to fight at their side.

The Templars had gone and St Lazarus was disappearing. In England there was no mention of Locko after 1351, though its revenues continued to be enjoyed by Burton Lazars, and Chosely had gone by 1458. In 1450 the pope granted the petition of Master William Sutton that no further confirmation was needed once Burton Lazars had elected its superior. Scotland stayed loyal to Boigny a little longer, though in France too preceptories were degenerating into sinecures. The Leper Knights of Outremer would have had difficulty in recognizing their incumbents as brethren.[1]

Rhodes was always ready for an attack. The guardship patrolled the coast ceaselessly, there was a tall watchtower on Simi, and not only were Hospitaller consuls active in Egypt but Rhodian merchants knew every rumour circulating in Cairo or Alexandria. Fortunately the brethren's seamanship often enabled them to outsail and outfight far larger forces. This was dramatically evident in 1440 when Sultan Jakmak of Egypt, increasingly incensed by the pirate monks' depredations, sent a fleet against them. After destroying the villages on Kastelorizon his eighteen galleys, 'extremely well furnished with soldiers, oarsmen, cannon and ammunition', went on to attack the convent itself. As soon as they were sighted, the marshal of the Order, Fra' Louis de Saint Sebastien, led out his entire battle-squadron, eight galleys and four armed cargo vessels, firing his guns and playing martial music. So unnerved were the Egyptians by this unexpectedly aggressive reception that they ran close in to the shore, lying alongside each other and turning their poops seaward. Here they held off the brethren with a barrage of cannon-shot and Greek fire until nightfall. They then hurriedly set sail – apparently bound for Turkey. But Fra' Louis learnt from a captured Mameluke that their real destination was Lango. Sailing hard throughout the night, he managed to intercept them. Again the horrified Egyptians refused battle, taking refuge in an uninhabited harbour 'which the Turks call Carathoa'. They thought themselves safe enough in its sandy shallows, for the Hospitaller carracks drew too much water to follow. Swiftly Fra' Louis transferred the latter's men-at-arms aboard his galleys and then went into the attack. A 'great and bloody battle' ensued, in which the Mamelukes lost 700 men against 60 Rhodian casualties. Only nightfall and a rising sea saved them from annihilation.

The wasps' nest was never disturbed with impunity. In the summer of 1444 an Egyptian armada landed 18,000 men, who devastated the island before investing the city and its convent. Luckily, small reinforcements had just arrived from Burgundy and Catalonia. After six weeks the Mameluke guns breached the massive curtain-walls and the Grand Master, Jean Bonpars de Lastic, realized that a general assault was imminent. Before dawn on 24 August he assembled his troops silently in the darkness, outside the ramparts, with knights and pikemen in the centre, arbalestiers on the wings. In those days brethren fought on foot in brigandines (leather coats sewn with metal studs) and steel hats or *sallets* while, as seamen, their favourite weapon seems to have been the boarding pike. Among Englishmen present was the Turcopolier, Fra' Hugh Middleton. At first light the charge was sounded, whereupon, with trumpets braying, kettledrums and cymbals clashing, the formidable little army smashed its way into the sleeping Mameluke camp, roaring the old battle cry 'St Jean, St Jean'. It was over quickly: the enemy bolted to their ships, though not before hundreds had been cut down by exulting brethren, who captured the entire siege-train. Jakmak was so disheartened that he made peace in 1446.[2]

But if the convent had weathered its first great siege it would soon be confronted by a far more terrible foe. The Turks were steadily overrunning Greece; the Latin lords of the archipelago and the mainland frequently sent desperate appeals to the bailiff of the Morea, while the empire itself was very near the end, reduced to Constantinople and a few towns. In 1451 the most ferocious of all sultans ascended the Osmanli throne – Mehmet II, who on several occasions swore he would conquer Rhodes after Constantinople. Probably the fall of Byzantium and the hero's death of the eighty-first Roman emperor in 1453 were more keenly mourned by the knights than anyone, if only as apocalyptic confirmation of the Latin East's doom. Grand Master Jacques de Milly launched a series of highly successful raids on the Turkish coast while Mehmet was busy subjugating the remnants of Romania. Then in 1462 Pius II's crusade failed to materialize. Broken-hearted, the pope died. Holy War was dead. Although the brethren foiled an Egyptian attempt to conquer Cyprus, the kingdom's affairs were deteriorating, and it was no doubt a growing sense of isolation which caused the increase of the convent to 400 knights in 1466. Careful thought had been given to their deployment; in 1460 the garrison of Bodrun was raised to fifty and that of Kos to twenty-five, while forty were assigned to guardship duty. Fortunately the Turks were distracted by a long war with Venice, which continued until 1479.

The Grand Commander of Cyprus in 1467 was Fra' John Langstrother, an English brother of boundless ambition whose early history was a good example of a successful career in the Order. Born in 1416, by 1448 he was a commander and Lieutenant-Turcopolier, castellan of Rhodes in 1453, Bailiff of

Egle in 1464 and Grand Prior of England in 1469. Fra' John had already been appointed the kingdom's treasurer by the Earl of Warwick, who had taken over the government from Edward IV. Edward later dismissed Langstrother, but in 1471 'My Lord of St John's' supported Henry VI, commanding part of the Lancastrian van at Tewkesbury. After the defeat he took refuge in the abbey, but was dragged out and beheaded.[3]

The case of Ireland shows just how anarchic and unprofitable were some European priories. Here most commanderies were farmed out to laymen, while Irish brethren were never seen at Rhodes, being far too involved in tribal politics. The nadir was reached during the lordship of Edward IV, when Fra' James Keating became prior. Little better than a bandit, on one occasion he seized Dublin Castle. He ignored the General Citation of 1480 and in any case never sent Responsions (revenues) to the convent. Grand Master d'Aubusson declared him deposed in 1482 but, when Fra' Marmaduke Lumley came to take his place, Keating promptly imprisoned his unwary brother. Fra' James was still disastrously active in Henry VII's reign.[4]

Most brothers were *petite noblesse* – in England, gentry. English brethren rarely bore great names, though even if their fathers had been merchants who purchased land and arms or their brothers were apprenticed to a trade there was a very real gap between knight and burgess. Perhaps the fifteenth century had not evolved the meticulous stratification of *seize quartiers*, but in that strange pageant world a man's occupation had almost mystical symbolism, and all military brethren enjoyed the glamour of aristocracy.

Chivalry still flourished in northern Europe, but as an aesthetic cult whose devotees belonged to court orders such as the Golden Fleece, the Star, the Porcupine, the Garter. Living an Arthurian dream and taking fantastic vows, their arena was the tournament rather than the battlefield. If these exotic fraternities met at 'Chapters', clad in 'habits', and attended corporate services in their own churches, their ideals were those of the 'Morte d'Arthur', not the cloister. Brethren at Rhodes living hard, simple lives bore small resemblance to the weird *incroyables* of the Burgundian court.

If there were sinners among them, weak 'from the strength of evil passions', they remained essentially men of God. In the *Liber Missarum ad usum Ecclesiae Hospitalis Sancti Johannis*, compiled at Rhodes in 1465, the feast of St John was celebrated with three Masses – the last pontifical – at midnight, at dawn and at full light; a liturgical distinction normally reserved for Christmas Day.[5] Before the end of the century a Cardinal Master would preside in the conventual church wearing cope and mitre. Even today a modern chaplain of the Religion can write, 'for the knight the poor are nothing less than Christ, incarnate in their suffering and in them he takes care of Christ'.[6]

The net, however, was closing. In 1463 the Lord of Lesbos sent a desperate appeal for help, but, though the brethren rushed to defend his capital, Mytilene, it fell by treachery. In 1470 the Turks descended on Euboea (Negropont), whereupon the Order sent a flotilla under Fra' Pierre d'Aubusson to relieve its Venetian garrison – without success, as the republic's admiral lost his nerve. The knights concentrated on strengthening their own island. They had to face formidable new troops, the *yeni cheri*. These Janissaries were recruited from a compulsory tribute of Christian boys, but developed into a crack unit employed for assaults or forlorn hopes; before 1500 they never numbered more than 2,000. Not only did they forgo wine, gambling and whores but they were forbidden to marry and they slept in dormitories, being affiliated to the Bektashi sect of dervishes whose originator, Haji Bektash of Khurasan, had blessed their foundation. Armed with spear and yataghan, they presented a strange, disturbing appearance when attacking, led by their chief officers the *Chorbaji* (soup-maker) and the *Kaveji* (coffee-maker) in an odd, minuet-like marching step – three paces forward, a pause, then three paces forward again – to the sound of a braying military band, the *Mehtar*. Over mail shirts they wore a uniform of green-and-yellow cloaks with white ostrich plumes and tassels hanging from high white mitres; their standard was a flowing banner of white

11. Fra' Guillaume Caoursin (an eye-witness) presents his bestseller account of the siege of Rhodes in 1480 to the Grand Master Fra' Pierre d'Aubusson

silk hung with horsetails. But their performance was no less remarkable than their appearance.

By 1479 Mehmet was ready to settle accounts. He had a worthy opponent in the Grand Master, Pierre d'Aubusson. Born in 1423, this fifth son of a great Limousin family had entered the Order in his late twenties, having already seen military service against the English.[7] Despite his northern origins, he probably by now had more in common with the princes of Renaissance Italy than with those of late medieval France or ducal Burgundy – he was enough of a *Quattrocento* intellectual to employ the humanist poet Gian Maria Filelfo as Latin secretary. Remarkable as soldier, administrator and diplomat, Fra' Pierre's greatest gifts were realism and leadership, and he combined magnetic appeal with a magnificent appearance. Both brethren and Rhodians were devoted to him. Mehmet sent an ambassador to lull the brethren's suspicions, but Pierre was not deceived. In all he could muster perhaps 600 brethren with 1,500 mercenaries, Rhodian militia and privateer sailors, while since his election he had been strengthening fortifications, deepening ditches, demolishing buildings close to the city walls, installing artillery and laying up stocks of food and ammunition.

Turkish agents, however, considered the garrison hopelessly inadequate. Mehmet appointed an apostate member of the Byzantine imperial family, Misac Palaeologus Pasha, as Vizier and commander of the expedition. In April 1480 lookouts on Rhodes sighted enemy warships, and on 23 May 70,000 men landed at the bay of Trianda while the port was blockaded by fifty galleys. Misac pitched camp on the hill of St Etienne, overlooking Rhodes. The key to the siege was Fort St Nicholas on the promontory flanking the outer harbour: once it had fallen, Rhodes could be starved into surrender. A large Turkish battery was built on the opposite shore, mounting three brass 'basilisks', the period's howitzers, discharging stone balls over two feet in diameter.

These guns were directed by Meister Georg, a German artillery expert, who suddenly appeared before the walls claiming sanctuary 'for the sake of conscience'. In fact he was a double agent spurred on by bribes to discover where artillery fire would do most damage, and he tried to panic the garrison by describing the besieging army's vast size and ferocity. All believed that if Rhodes fell they would be impaled alive, for the Turks had brought large quantities of sharpened stakes. But the Grand Master saw through this feigned deserter and later hanged him.[8]

When his guns had battered a wide breach in the fort's walls, the Vizier ordered the first assault. Turkish galleys sailed in to land troops on both sides of the mole. Wading ashore, their feet were impaled on ships' nails and old knives set in baulks of timber laid on the sea bed.[9] Halting in confusion, they made excellent targets for hand gunners and arbalestiers, while in the breach they were decimated by cross-fire from flanking batteries, before meeting a counter-charge led by d'Aubusson. His helmet knocked off by a cannon ball, Fra' Pierre joked about improving prospects of promotion and then returned to the fight. Eventually the enemy galleys fled before a flotilla of fire ships, whereupon Misac called off his thoroughly demoralized men, leaving 600 dead.

The distance between Fort St Nicholas and the opposite shore was hardly 150 yards. The Turks therefore constructed a pontoon, and one night a small boat fastened an anchor in the rocks under the mole round which a cable was passed to haul the floating bridge across. However, an English sailor dived in and removed the anchor. Next came an assault by night, on 18 June, the Turks attacking all along the mole in a swarm of light craft and towing their pontoon into position, galleys pounding away at the fort. The darkness was lit up by the weird glow of naphtha and molten lead, flickering gunfire and the flames of incendiary ships; several enemy galleys were set alight, garrison artillery sinking at least four. The battle raged from midnight until ten o'clock the following morning. It was reported that the Turks lost 2,500 men – including the officer who had led the storming party, a son-in-law of the sultan. Misac was so discouraged that he did nothing for three days but sit, brooding, in his tent.

He had ordered a general bombardment at the beginning of the siege before concentrating on the south-eastern section of the ramparts, which contained the Jewish quarter. Even if the Master's palace was in ruins, strategically the building was unimportant – though the destruction of the magistral wine cellar upset some brethren – but here the walls were old and not very solid. The enemy's batteries thundered ceaselessly, protected by

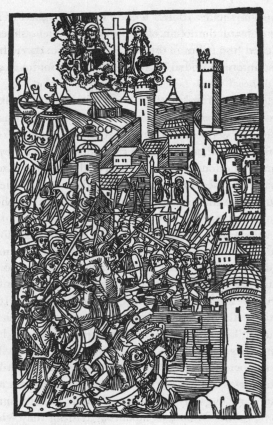

12. The Siege of Rhodes, 1480

earthworks and timber shelters, the largest mounting eight brass
basilisks, while their sappers undermined the foundations. As the
walls soon began to crumble, d'Aubusson built a ditch and a
brick wall behind them. Everybody took a hand in the work,
citizens and knights toiling day and night, the Master himself
setting an example. A rain of incendiary arrows and grenades
started fires all over Rhodes, so he sent women and children into

the cellars or a shelter roofed with baulks of timber. He also ordered the construction of an old-fashioned trebuchet;[10] sardonically christened 'the tribute', this devilish machine threw rocks so large they splintered wooden battery shelters like matchwood and opened up mines.

Some Italian brethren lost their nerve and found a spokesman in the magistral secretary, Filelfo, who begged d'Aubusson to negotiate. The Master called them together, saying coldly that it was still possible for a galley to run the blockade and they could leave at once, then bullied and coaxed them into a tougher mood. Misac resorted to Byzantine methods; two 'deserters', an Albanian and a Dalmatian, were sent into the city with the news that Mehmet was on his way with 100,000 men. D'Aubusson refused to believe it, and they attempted to enlist Filelfo in an attempt to murder him. Immediately the Italian informed his Master, and the wretched men were lynched by the garrison.

All this time the bombardment of the south-east wall continued. One battery was stormed under cover of darkness by the Italians, who returned with Turkish heads on their pikes, but the Vizier had the moat filled with rubble. After six weeks only a heap of collapsed masonry with a breach wide enough for cavalry to ride through stood between the brethren and their enemies. Misac's envoy, Suleiman Bey, came to the breach, declaring a good defence had earned good terms: by surrendering, the garrison could become Sultan Mehmet's allies, by resisting they would be annihilated – the breach was open, 40,000 crack troops waiting. Fra' Antoine Gautier, castellan of Rhodes, answered that if the walls were down there were fresh defences behind them, that attackers could only expect the same reception they had had on the St Nicholas mole, that the sultan had an odd way of making friends and that anyway his brethren were ready for an assault. For a day and a night every Turkish gun available pounded the breach. After the bombardment had stopped, an hour before dawn on 28 July, a single mortar was fired as signal, and scaling parties crept forward silently. The exhausted, deafened garrison was asleep and the few guards easily rushed – within minutes the

Turks had captured not only the breach but the bastion of Italy, sending word to the Pasha to bring up more troops.

Fra' Pierre was there at once, gripping a half-pike, shouting to his brethren that they must save Rhodes or be buried in its ruins. First up the ladder on to the mound of rubble, he was knocked down twice but climbed back. Soon knights and Turks were at each other's throats all along the shattered rampart. Usually armour made up for lack of numbers; great elbow guards could catch and snap a sword and at close quarters a man-at-arms would rip his lightly armed opponent to shreds. However, now it seemed that the defenders, reeling from fatigue, would be pushed off the walls. Elbowing forward in his gilt armour[11] followed by three standard-bearers and a handful of brethren the Master used himself as a living banner to rally the convent, whereupon Misac sent in a squad of Janissaries with orders to kill him.

Soon the Grand Master was almost down, wounded in three places; the tide turned as brethren rushed to his rescue, but not before he collapsed with two more terrible wounds, including a punctured lung. Brethren hurled themselves on the astonished Turks, who suddenly broke; not only were they swept off the ramparts and out of the breach – where many were jammed in and killed – but the Vizier's camp was stormed and his standard captured.

Misac gave up in despair. The garrison claimed that 3,500 Turks who had fallen swelled his casualties to 9,000, the defenders having killed more than twice their own number, not to mention 30,000 wounded. Even if the Vizier had known that more than half the brethren had died, including most bailiffs, the news that the Master's wounds were not mortal was sufficient disappointment.[12] His army's spirit was broken and, when a Neapolitan carrack and a papal brigantine ran the blockade, the humiliated Turks burnt their stores and set sail, three months after investing the port.

Plainly the Turkish defeat was a miracle, and as at Marienburg the brethren had seen Our Lady with a host of angels, accompanied by a familiar figure in camel hair – John the Baptist; the vision was gratifyingly corroborated by tactful prisoners. Pierre d'Aubusson recovered to find himself the hero of Europe.[13]

Mehmet, infuriated, began preparations for a fresh expedition, but died in May 1481. Though he had intended his younger son Djem to succeed him, the elder Bayezid was more popular and reduced his brother to hiding in the Karamanian mountains. Djem took the desperate step of begging d'Aubusson for refuge, and a galley was sent to collect him; he arrived at Rhodes in mid-summer, to be received with the honours due to a reigning sovereign. Cruel, treacherous and a born soldier, this Osmanli was as formidable as his father and, had he gained the throne, would have turned on his hosts without compunction. Bayezid II was the best sultan the brethren could hope for, a pious Moslem preoccupied with building mosques, and naturally peaceable. Understandably the Grand Master expected diplomatic capital and shortly afterwards sent Djem to France, where he stayed in distinguished confinement at the larger commanderies. Pierre obtained a pension for him from Bayezid of 30,000 gold ducats – besides an annual indemnity of 10,000 for the Religion. Finally in 1488 this *fainéant* sultan was handed over to Pope Innocent VIII, and in 1495 died, reputedly poisoned by the Borgia pontiff, Alexander VI.

In 1485 Fra' Pierre was made cardinal and papal legate. Not only did he build a church in thanksgiving for his miraculous victory but he tightened the Religion's discipline. Some brethren had begun to dress in silks and velvets with gold chains and jewelled scabbards; these were rigorously proscribed and they had to wear their habit, black cassock, cloak and skullcap, with a small white cross on the cloak's left breast. European commanders might have lived as rich country gentlemen yet the visitor to Rhodes knew he was in a monastery; contemporary illustrations show a habited, monkish community in chapter, listening to the scriptures in the refectory or working in their hospital. Meanwhile the city's walls were rebuilt and new towers added. Fort St Nicholas became a great star-shaped bastion, its angled gun-emplacements making frontal assault impossible. Heavier cannon were installed, while the convent raised its permanent garrison to 450 brethren in 1501. That year all Jews were expelled as constituting a potential fifth column. Pierre's criterion was survival and, for the same reason that he expelled Hebrews, he courted Rhodians, admitting them to the Religion, even to bailiwicks.

The convent was on good terms with most European sovereigns, who tended to nominate grand priors. Clerkenwell escaped this fate, though the English priory had its troubles: in 1515 the great house of canonesses at Buckland severed its connection with the Order,[14] while Cardinal Wolsey prised a lease of their richest manor, Hampton Court, out of Prior Docwra. But on the whole relations with England were excellent. Henry VII was named 'Protector of the Religion' and English grand priors continued to attend parliament and head embassies to Rome or Paris.

In 1494 Charles VIII of France, who idolized d'Aubusson, invaded Italy with the avowed object of going on to conquer Constantinople and Jerusalem. Next year he was crowned at Naples as Emperor of the East and King of Jerusalem, while Pope Alexander VI organized a Holy League against the Turk with Pierre as generalissimo; it included Emperor Maximilian, and the kings of Spain, Portugal and Hungary, as well as Charles's successor, Louis XII, and the Doge of Venice. The convent made extensive preparations but the crusade never materialized. Fra' Pierre 'died of chagrin' in 1503, eighty years old and worn out by ceaseless vigilance. Rhodes gave him the funeral of a great monarch; a grieving procession marched through the silent city, led by four brethren carrying his personal banners, while two more bore his Red Hat and legate's cross. Greek as well as Latin bishops and clergy walked in the cortège.

We owe our knowledge of the siege to an eyewitness, the Vice-Chancellor Fra' Guillaume Caoursin, a Frenchman from Douai who was Aubusson's secretary. He wrote the Grand Master's dispatches to the pope and the emperor, then incorporated them in his book *Obsidionis Rhodie Urbis Descriptio* which (first printed just four months afterwards) became a bestseller. Its popularity is understandable, since Western Europe was terrified of the threat posed by Ottoman expansion. Only a few days after raising the siege of Rhodes, the Turks had captured and sacked Otranto on the Adriatic coast of southern Italy, which they occupied for a whole year – beheading everyone who refused to convert to Islam. The Sultan Mehmet had intended to conquer both Rhodes and the entire Italian peninsula, but the brethren had saved the Italians by decimating his army. They were an inspiration to all Christendom.

There were never more than a handful of English Knights on the island, perhaps fewer than twelve out of the 550 brethren at Rhodes. In 1514 the Langue of England numbered a mere twenty-eight Knights, and the majority had to stay at home. It was incumbent on the Grand Prior of England, the Prior of Ireland and the Prior of Scotland to do so – like the Grand Prior in England, the latter sat in the Scots Parliament – while most middle-aged and elderly brethren were needed to administer the commanderies. There were also one or two 'Knights of Honour', to whom the Grand Master had given the gold 'cross of devotion'.

Among these honorary brethren were Thomas Stanley, 2nd Earl of Derby, who was received in 1517, and Charles Somerset, 1st Earl of Worcester, received at the same time. They never visited the island.

However, humbler Englishmen, unconnected with the Order, went out to Rhodes. After the fall of Constantinople it had become a refuge for Greek scholars, who attracted students eager to learn their language. One such student was to be the first headmaster of St Paul's School in London, William Lily.

The Knights themselves included highly educated and even learned men. Caoursin possessed some knowledge of the Classics, while the last Grand Chancellor at Rhodes, Fra' Andrea d'Amaral, was said to know the works of Pliny as well as most men knew their own names. Fra' Sabba da Castiglione, professed at Rhodes in 1505, was a keen antiquarian who spent his spare time scouring the Aegean for classical statuary, which he sent home to Mantua.

To the conquerors of Rum the very existence of Rhodes was an insult, and in 1503 the corsair Jamali raided the island to terrorize its inhabitants. The brethren, however, placed squadrons of cavalry at strategic points, and the raiders moved on to Leros. This islet-rock had only two knights in its tiny castle – the elderly bedridden commander and a young brother, Paolo Simeoni, eighteen years of age. The latter and their few servants manned the guns, but by the first evening enemy artillery brought part of the walls crashing down. Next morning the infidels were astonished to see a large contingent of brethren waiting for them in the breach and hastily they set sail; Fra' Paolo had dressed the island's entire population, men and women, in the Order's red surcoats.[15] In 1506 seven Egyptian 'flutes' – extremely fast and unusually long and narrow galleys with very large sails – attacked Kos. A pair were sent ahead as scouts, but two Rhodian warships suddenly appeared from behind a promontory, cutting them off, whereupon the Mamelukes beached their vessels and fled inland. The brethren put a crew on board the flutes, and they decoyed the remainder of the flotilla into a bay where the Order's galleys lay in wait; all five were captured and the prisoners sold as slaves.[16] Even more spectacular was the taking of 'the great carrack of Alexandria' in 1509. Every year this treasure-ship, named 'Queen of the Seas', plied between Tunis and Constantinople with wealthy merchants bringing fabulous luxuries from India. The *Mogarbina* was a gigantic vessel with seven decks, whose mainmast 'needed the arms of six men to circle it' and, defended by '100 guns and 1,000 soldiers', the traders confidently ventured their richest wares, for the carrack had repulsed the brethren on several occasions. Commander de Gastineau, a wily Limousin, waylaid the leviathan off Crete. Under pretence of parleying, he laid the Order's own great carrack alongside and then mowed down the captain and officers on the poop with one murderous salvo of grapeshot. The leaderless crew struck their colours and the knights boarded to find a staggering consignment of silver and jewellery as well as bales of silk, cashmere and carpets, and quantities of pepper, ginger, cloves and cinnamon. On the way home the brethren captured three smaller cargo ships, and the entire treasure was eventually sold in France, its owners being held to ransom or sent to the slave market.[17]

In August 1510 Sultan Qansuh al-Ghawri of Egypt sent his nephew with twenty-five sail to 'Laiazzo' – Ayas near Alexandretta on the coast of Asia Minor – to bring back a badly needed consignment of ship's timber. The Order's spies sent word of the expedition to Rhodes. Suddenly, out of the blue, the brethren appeared before Ayas with four galleys under Fra' Andrea d'Amaral and eighteen armed carracks and feluccas under Fra' Philippe Villiers de l'Isle Adam (a shared command which one day would bear bitter fruit). The Mamelukes rashly sailed out to meet them, in order of battle. After a particularly bloody hull-to-hull fight, the brethren won a glorious victory, capturing four war-galleys and eleven other vessels. It was the greatest of all their Rhodian sea-battles and a triumph for their espionage system. In addition there were political overtones. The timber had been intended for a new Egyptian fleet, which was to have joined the Turkish navy in driving the Portuguese out of the Red Sea – the abortive alliance was the last between Mameluke and Osmanli, who soon turned on each other. In 1516 the Turks defeated and killed Qansuh al-Ghawri, hanging the last Mameluke sultan the year after. Above all, the battle off Ayas had been an uncomfortable reminder to the Porte that Rhodes was an increasingly formidable sea power.

The gentle Bayezid was made to abdicate in 1512 and was poisoned by his own son Selim I, 'the Grim', in whom bloodlust and treachery reached manic intensity. He was a brilliant soldier and won many victories, equipping his Janissaries with arquebuses. The convent trembled, but fortunately Selim was occupied with wars in Hungary, Persia and Egypt. Then in 1517 he added Cairo and the caliphate to his possessions; the convent was encircled. However, just as he was about to set out for Rhodes in 1521, Selim died. His successor, Suleiman the Magnificent, most attractive and most formidable of Turkish emperors, inherited a campaign-hardened army accustomed to victory. Anatolia was now the Osmanli heartland, yet only a few miles off its coast lay that hornet's nest of idolatrous pirates, described by the contemporary chronicler Kemal Pashazade as 'this source of sin and gathering place of twisted religion'. Until it was extinguished, Turkey needed all warships for home waters and could never be a great maritime power herself.

The magistral election of 1521 was contested by Fra' Thomas Docwra, Prior of England; by the Portuguese Prior of Castile, Fra' Andrea d'Amaral; and by Fra' Philippe Villiers de l'Isle Adam, Prior of Auvergne. The third was chosen, to the noisy dismay of Amaral, who shouted, 'This will be the last Grand Master of Rhodes.' Receiving a letter from the new sultan congratulating him on his election, Fra' Philippe wrote a sardonic reply tantamount to a challenge, for his spies had infiltrated Suleiman's seraglio and he knew that an attack was imminent.[18] Europe ignored his appeals for help but a resourceful serving brother managed to hire 500 Cretan arbalestiers, despite their Venetian rulers' prohibition, disguising them as merchants or deckhands.[19] Best of all, he recruited Gabriele Tadini de Martinengo, the greatest military engineer of the day, who evaded frenzied attempts to stop him reaching Rhodes. Once there, the devout Martinengo was so impressed that, being unmarried, he asked to join the Order. Delighted, Philippe not only accepted this gifted postulant as a Knight of Grace but also made him a Grand Cross, whereupon the new bailiff enthusiastically set about strengthening defences: ravelins – arrow-shaped double trenches – were dug in front of each bastion and 'fascines and gabions' – wooden bundles and baskets of earth – heaped near any danger point, while every battery, protected by mantelets of wood or rope, was sited to command maximum fire. Philippe's garrison was little bigger than d'Aubusson's – he had 500 brethren, 1,000 men-at-arms and some militia – but his fortifications were stronger and his fire-power immeasurably superior.[20]

On 26 June 1522, two days after the feast of St John, a Turkish armada of 103 galleys with 300 other vessels was sighted. Every Rhodian flocked to the conventual church where, 'when the sermon was done a ponthyficall mass was celebrate with all solempnytees', and 'the reverent lorde grete mayster'[21] laid the city's keys on the altar, entrusting them to St John. Finally he personally elevated the Host, blessing the island and its garrison. Then in gilt armour he rode through the streets, whilst brethren stood to their posts. He had already allotted sectors, as well as inspecting each langue's contingent in full battle order outside their respective auberges.

Contemporaries believed that the besiegers numbered 140,000 soldiers and a labour force of 60,000 Balkan peasants.[22] Their commander was Suleiman's brother-in-law, Mustafa Pasha, brave but inexperienced − 'plus brave soldat qu'habile général'.[23] Even though his chief of staff, Pir Mehmed Pasha, was a seasoned old Aga, veterans of Selim's campaigns had little confidence in this young courtier. Pir wrote to Suleiman, stating that morale was low, that the sultan must come himself if the faithful were to take Rhodes; and on 28 July the Grand Signor arrived with 15,000 troops.

Throughout August the Turks concentrated on the ramparts between the bastion of Aragon and the sea. Their bombardment was more scientific than that of 1480 and the artillery included mortars for vertical fire. Mines now used gunpowder, besides being dug more quickly − with the greater number of pioneers available − though Martinengo detected many by means of drum parchment seismographs with little bells.[24] Methodically, guns demolished carefully selected areas and two huge earth ramps − 'marvellous great hills' − were built as high as the walls, to shoot down into the city. On 4 September two great gunpowder mines exploded under the bastion of England and twelve yards of rampart came crashing down, filling the moat − a perfect breach. The Turks assaulted at once and soon held the gap. Philippe was saying office in a nearby church. Taking its opening words 'Deus in adjutorium meum intende' for inspiration, he seized his half-pike and rushed out to see seven horsetail standards waving from the ruined wall. Mercifully the English brothers under Fra' Nicholas Hussey held an inner barricade, from which Philippe led a counter-charge to such effect that the Turks deserted both breach and standards, though Mustafa slashed with his own sword at those who fled. The magistral standard-bearer, the English Fra' Henry Mansell, was mortally wounded, but the besiegers had lost many men, including three sanjak beys.[25]

Twice more Mustafa repeated his assault on the badly damaged bastion of England. Columns of the Children of the Prophet, a thousand deep, came roaring over the barricades, but the Turcopolier Fra' John Buck counter-charged from the rubble. The enemy gave ground, and Mustafa himself rushed to their support. However, the English now had help – German brethren under Christoph von Waldner – while cannon arrived, easily transportable sakers and falconets (six- and three-pounders), to cut bloody swathes at close range. The Pasha fought like a lion until his men dragged him away. The convent's casualties also were high, including Buck and von Waldner with many English and German brothers.[26] Mustafa decided to risk everything in a general assault on 24 September, which Sultan Suleiman watched from a convenient hillock. Four bastions, those of Aragon, England, Provence and Italy, were pounded mercilessly, and then through the smoke came the *yenicheri*, racing for the walls. The Aragonese began to fail – they faced the Aga of the Janissaries – but the Grand Master came up with 200 fresh troops and the Aga was hurled back. Suleiman sounded the retreat; his warriors were about to break. Never had they met men like these, fanatics fiercer than the wildest dervish. Over 2,000 Turkish corpses remained.

Burning with shame, the sultan paraded the entire army to see his brother-in-law shot to death with arrows, sparing him only after old Pir Mehmed had pleaded for mercy. Suleiman was about to raise the siege when an Albanian deserter claimed that so many brethren had been killed that Rhodes could not face another assault, whereupon he appointed a new commander-in-chief, Ahmed Pasha, an elderly engineer general with great experience. 'Hakmak Bashaw's'* strategy was one of attrition.

Philippe's powder was running short, and though a makeshift mill was built there was insufficient saltpetre. Steadily Ahmed's guns demolished the walls; every day fewer fighting men were on their feet. Winter storms prevented the priories' contingents from leaving Messina; an English ship carrying the Bailiff of Egle was overtaken by a tempest in the Bay of Biscay and sank with all hands. Then a Turkish girl slave persuaded fellow slaves to fire the city, but they were caught and executed. A Jewish doctor was found shooting messages into the enemy camp. Even more alarming, Andrea d'Amaral's servant was discovered communicating with the Turks by the same means. Under torture he implicated his master, Prior of Castile and Grand Chancellor. 'Put to the question', Amaral denied the charge though he may have attempted to negotiate privately. None the less, if not a turncoat this bitter old man's defeatism had unnerved the whole garrison. He was solemnly degraded from his vows and then beheaded.[27]

The Turks, protected by huge wooden shields, had dug trenches up to the walls. During an attack on the bastion of Aragon the invaluable Gabriele Martinengo was shot in the eye – the bullet passing through his head. The Master moved into the crumbling tower, which he did not leave for five weeks, sleeping on a straw mattress amid the rubble. Desperate watchmen scanned the horizon for relief. Finally, Philippe ordered the garrisons of the archipelago and Bodrun to run the blockade in feluccas, with twelve knights and 100 men.[28] By the end of November bombardment had so destroyed the bastion of Italy that two churches were demolished to build barricades, while the bastions of England and Aragon had hardly one stone standing on another. When the next general assault came, Martinengo was on his feet again, and he and Philippe were everywhere, urging on their exhausted troops. Fortunately it rained and the Turks' ramps

---

* Fra' Nicholas Roberts's rendering of his outlandish name – see p. 263.

became a sea of mud, their powder useless, with the Janissaries beaten off once more with heavy casualties.

Vertot, who knew his Order, comments: 'On est bien fort et bien redoutable quand on ne craint point la mort.' Suleiman despaired. He had lost over 50,000 men – so the brethren believed – besides thousands dead from plague and cold. An officer was sent to the walls offering good terms, telling the garrison it was doomed. 'Brethren of St John only do business with their swords,' shouted a commander. The English brother Nicholas Roberts afterwards wrote '. . . Most of our men were slain, we had no powther nor . . . manner of munycone nor vitalles, but all on by brede and water; we wer as men desperat determyned to dye upon them in the felde rather than be put upon the stakes, for we doubted he would give us our lyves considering ther wer slain so many of his men . . .'[29] Winter set in with howling gales and snowstorms. The Grand Master, although determined to die fighting, summoned the council.

An eye-witness account of this dramatic meeting survives. It was written by an elderly commander who had been caught in Rhodes by accident, having come there on business, not to fight. 'Frère Jacques, Bastard de Bourbon' as he engagingly styled himself – he was a natural son of the Prince-Bishop of Liège – says that all senior officers reported disastrous losses. Martinengo was particularly blunt. 'Le capitaine frère Gabriel' reported to the very reverend Master and very reverend lords of the council that

having seen and considered the great pounding the town has suffered, having seen how large the breach is and how the enemy's trenches are inside the town to a depth of 100 feet with a breadth of more than 70 feet, having also seen that they have broken through the wall in two other places, that the greater part of our men-at-arms – both knights and all the others – are dead or wounded and supplies exhausted, that mere workmen are taking their place, it is impossible to resist any longer unless some relief force comes to make the Turk strike camp.

The Bastard adds that an excited debate followed as to which was better – 'die to the last man or save the people'. Many argued that 'ce fut bien et sainctement fait de mourir pour la foy', though others pointed out that the sultan's terms did not require them to deny Christ.[30] Suddenly the Greek bishop and a delegation of weeping citizens appeared, begging the brethren to capitulate. Fra' Philippe 'fell downe allmost ded'.[31] Recovering, he and the bailiffs finally agreed 'it would be a thing more agreeable to God to sue for peace and protect and the lives of simple people, of women and children'.

A truce was arranged, but within a week it was broken. Then on 16 December Fra' Nicholas Fairfax ran the blockade in a brigantine, bringing all he could find – a cargo of wine and 100 Cretan arbalestiers.[32] By now the city's walls were mounds of rubble, the brethren's remnant living in muddy holes where they sheltered from snow and sleet. On 17 December the Turks attacked, and again the day after. Powderless, weak from cold and hunger, reeling brethren still managed to hurl them back. Perhaps it was during this last ghastly struggle that a slain English brother's Greek mistress cut their two children's throats, donned his armour, took his sword and went to the trenches, where she fought until killed. But other Rhodians were deserting, despite summary executions. On 20 December the Grand Master asked for a fresh truce.

Suleiman's terms were generous: in return for Rhodes, its archipelago with Bodrun and Kastelorizon, the brethren were free to leave with all their goods. The Turks would even supply ships. No churches would be turned into mosques and Rhodians would have freedom of worship, besides being dispensed from all taxes for five years. After the Grand Master had been entertained in the sultan's 'red pavilion', Suleiman, disdaining an escort, visited the ruined city, where Philippe showed him the pathetic barricades. Asked to enter Turkish service, he replied, 'a great prince would be dishonoured by employing such a renegade'. Later the sultan remarked how sorry he was to make 'that fine old man' leave his home.[33]

On the night of 1 January 1523 a single trumpet sounded and

then, to the besiegers' amazement, the brethren marched out in parade order, armour burnished, banners flying and drums beating. Then they embarked for Crete, with their most precious relics (the icon of Our Lady of Philermo and the hand of St John the Baptist), their archives and the key of the City of Rhodes. From the Grand Master's galley there flew at half-mast a banner of the Sorrowing Virgin, holding the dead body of her Son, and bearing the words *Afflictis tu spes unica rebus* – 'in all which afflicts us thou art our only hope'. Yet though the Emperor Charles V might comment 'nothing in the world was so well lost as Rhodes', the Hospitallers who sailed away into the snowy darkness knew that Jerusalem had fallen once again.

VI

THE LAST CRUSADE
1523–1571

Malta, Lepanto and the Counter-Reformation

So they are seen to be a strange and bewildering breed,
meeker than lambs, fiercer than lions. I do not know whether
to call them monks or knights because though both names
are correct, one lacks a monk's gentleness the other a
knight's pugnacity.

Bernard of Clairvaux, *c.* 1128, 'De Laude Novae Militiae'

THE BATTLE FOR THE
MEDITERRANEAN

It seemed unlikely that the Order of St John would survive, its homeless brethren wandering anxiously from refuge to refuge – from Messina to Cumae, from there to Civita Vecchia, thence to Viterbo, then Cornetto, and Villefranche, and finally to Nice. In 1524 the Emperor Charles V offered Malta and Tripoli, but the religion had not yet abandoned all hope of Rhodes. Then in 1527 Henry VIII announced that the English langue would become a separate brotherhood with the task of defending Calais, and the alarmed Grand Master came to England; Henry was upset that he had not been consulted about the Order's future. However, Fra' Philippe flattered him with the title 'Protector of the Religion', besides agreeing to retain the Turcopolier designate John Rawson[1] as Irish prior because of his success 'in civilizing the natives', while in return the king allowed Fra' William Weston to be installed as Grand Prior of England.[2] The Master held deep misgivings about the emperor's offer, which entailed swearing fealty, but, after his captain-general failed to hold Modon in the Morea despite its capture, was compelled to accept in 1531. Many years would elapse before the brethren were reconciled to Malta.

This new kingdom, even smaller than Rhodes – seventeen miles by eight – was arid and treeless, its thin soil criss-crossed by dry stone walls and bare ravines. There were no rivers, not even streams. Gozo was no better, Comino and Cominetto hardly more than rocks. Most of the 20,000 inhabitants spoke 'a sort of Moorish' though their nobles were Aragonese or Sicilian. Neither the capital, Citta Notabile – modern Mdina – 'an old, deserted town', or the few mean villages held any charm for Aegean exiles.

Inside Grand Harbour two rocky spits divided by a deep creek project from the eastern shore. On the northern one was a fishing village, Birgu, guarded by a ramshackle tower mounting three old cannon, Fort St Angelo. Later the creek would become the Harbour of the Galleys, the southern spit Senglea. A hilly peninsula, Monte Sceberras, separated Grand Harbour from another large bay, Marsamxett.[3]

The convent was established in Birgu, protected by earthworks rather than ramparts. Auberges, installed in little houses, were for reasons of economy occupied only by young knights, who slept in dormitories. Commanders were expected to buy their own houses with revenues or prize money, though they must say office and hear Mass every day, dining 'in hall' four times a week. Outside, brethren retained the habit only for formal or conventual occasions, but their new dress was clerical enough – a white linen cross sewn on the black doublet and a white enamelled cross hanging from their necks. The make-shift convent's scattered buildings were uncloistered by a *collachium*, and whoring and duelling were not unknown. Serious crime earned incarceration in the peculiarly grim dungeons of St Anthony, or 'loss of the habit'. When an English brother murdered his Maltese mistress at the same time as a chaplain-novice was caught pilfering jewels from Our Lady of Philermo's shrine, the miserable pair were tied in sacks, rowed out to sea and thrown overboard. In 1532 a gentleman-in-waiting of the Prior of Rome killed a Provençal knight in a duel; uproar broke out, with a pitched battle in the streets between the French, Italian and Spanish langues. Nomadic life had unsettled the Order.

In 1534 Grand Master de l'Isle Adam, who was over seventy-five and quite worn out, died, still homesick for Rhodes. He left a formidable fleet. Its basic warship continued to be the galley, best suited for a small navy's hit-and-run tactics. The great carrack of the Religion, bluff-bowed, four-masted and square-rigged, some-times accompanied caravans, though her purpose was essentially defensive, to convey a valuable cargo or important embassy. Sailing from Candia to Messina in 1523, Fra' William Weston had commanded such a vessel, capable of carrying 500 men with provisions for six months, her hull lead-plated against gunfire, like the six-decked 1,700-ton *Santa Anna*, built for the Order in 1530. Other ships included brigantines – light, deckless, square-rigged two-masters useful as troop carriers – besides a swarm of feluccas and tartans, the *saettas* ('arrows') who nosed out prey for galleys. Despite vows of poverty, brethren were allowed to keep a portion of their prize money, the *spoglio*, though, except for one-fifth which could be willed away, their fortunes reverted to the Religion when they died. In its straitened circumstances the convent now sold knights the privilege of fitting out their own galleys.

In 1535 the emperor attacked Tunis, recently seized by Khair ed-Din Barbarossa, Dey of Algiers; his ships were commanded by the redoubtable Andrea Doria, while the Religion sent four galleys, the great carrack and eighteen brigantines under its Vice-Admiral, Fra' Ottavio Bottigella, Prior of Pisa. Though garrisoned by 6,000 Turks, Goletta was quickly stormed, the knights leading the assault, while, as soon as Barbarossa marched out from Tunis, some brethren among his prisoners (led by Paolo Simeoni, the hero of Leros) overpowered their jailers and captured the citadel, whereupon the Moslem army outside the walls fled and Simeoni opened the gates to the imperial troops. The brethren entertained Charles to a victory banquet on board the *Santa Anna*; finding the splendour of their table *équipage* and air of magnificence unedifying, he muttered sarcastically, 'What do they do for God?' Bottigella broke in: '*They* go before God without weapons or uniform, but in sandals, a plain habit and a hairshirt – they do not stand, they prostrate themselves. If your Majesty joined them you'd be given a choir stall, a black cowl and a rosary.'[4]

The Reformation was beginning to sap the brethren's strength. In 1545, when the Margrave of Brandenburg turned Protestant, the *Johanniterorden* was lost. Ironically the indirect architect of the English langue's destruction, Clement VII, had once been Fra' Giuliano de' Medici, Grand Prior of Capua. In May 1540 the

English priory was dissolved and its brethren pensioned off. Irish houses, most of which had been held by Prior Rawson himself, were also confiscated. Only the Scots priory remained, with its single commandery at Torphichen. The ten English brethren at Malta obtained funds from the common treasury, but English bailiwicks were not refilled as they fell vacant.[5] In 1539 Fra' Thomas Dingley, commander of Baddesley, had been beheaded together with a Knight of Honour, Adrian Fortescue,[6] for denying the Royal Supremacy; then in 1541 another professed brother, Fra' David Gunston, was hanged, drawn and quartered. Two more professed brethren, William Salisbury and John Forest, died in prison, providing five martyrs in all. Their langue numbered fewer than fifty and Knights of Honour were even fewer, yet St John gave more lives for the papacy than any Order in England save the Carthusian. In Fuller's words, 'The Knights Hospitallers, being gentlemen and soldiers of ancient families and high spirits, would not be brought to present to Henry VIII such puling petitions and public recognitions of their errors as other Orders had done.'[7]

Adrian Fortescue, born in the 1470s, became the protomartyr and patron of the English Knights of Malta. His daughter had married the tenth Earl of Kildare, 'Silken Thomas', whose uncles, James and John FitzGerald, were Knights of Honour, and it was probably they who recruited Sir Adrian into the Order in 1532. Two years later his son-in-law proclaimed himself King of Ireland, besieging Dublin; defeated, he was hanged in chains at Tyburn with his uncles. Such relatives cannot have endeared Fortescue to Henry VIII. However, when he was executed in 1539, it was for refusing to take the Oath of Supremacy.

His maxims reveal something of his personality.

Above all things love God with all thy heart. Desire his honour more than the health of thine own soul . . . Repute not thyself better than any other person, be they never so great sinners, but rather judge and esteem yourself most simplest. Judge the best. Use much silence, but, when thou needs must, speak. Delight not in familiarity of persons unknown to thee.

Be solitary as much as is convenient with thy estate . . . Pray often . . . Be pitiful to poor folk and help them to thy power, for then thou shalt greatly please God. Give fair language to all persons, and especially to the poor and needly . . . Continue in dread and ever have God before thine eyes . . . If by chance you fall into sin, despair not.

An early seventeenth-century painting by an unknown artist, now in the Palazzo Malta at Rome, portrays Sir Adrian with his head miraculously reunited to his body – the sword still in his neck. He was beatified in 1970. His feastday is 9 July, the anniversary of his execution on Tower Hill.

At Burton Lazars, 'a very fair hospital and collegiate church' with a Master and eight brethren, St Lazarus's statue and holy well still attracted pilgrims. In 1540 Dr Thomas Legh, 'of a very bulky and gross habit of body', an agent of Cromwell in the Dissolution of the Monasteries, became its last Master; the Duke of Norfolk wrote: 'alas what pity it were that such a vicious man should have the governance of that honest house' – by 1544 Burton Lazars was dissolved.[8] Its community had long ceased to be Knights. However, St Lazarus continued a shadowy existence in France and Piedmont.'

Each year more *korsanlar* raided the Mediterranean coast, almost within sight of the Eternal City itself. Tripoli was in particular danger, and as late as 1551 St John considered transferring the entire convent to this cluster of oases, hemmed in by burning sand and stony hills. Torghut was now the most dreaded corsair and installed himself at Mahedia between Tunis and Tripoli, where he became such a nuisance that in 1550 the emperor sent an expedition, including 140 brethren, to burn out this wasp's nest. Torghut, 'Sword of Islam', swore vengeance. In July 1551 he cast anchor in the Marsamxett. Birgu was too formidable so he besieged Mdina, devastating the island. The Turcopolier, Fra' Nicholas Upton, optimistically appointed on the death of Henry VIII, rode out with thirty knights and 400 local horse to inflict casualties; the victory was marred by Upton, an immensely fat man, expiring from heat stroke. The corsair then set sail for Tripoli, where an inadequate garrison sweltered in a rickety castle. Its governor, the Marshal Gaspard de Vallier, fought bravely, but no relief, not even a messenger, came, and he surrendered. He returned to a grim welcome. There had been criticism in the convent of Grand Master d'Omedes, who gave way to senile rage, and the marshal was deprived of the habit and imprisoned; had not a courageous brother remonstrated, the infuriated old man would have beheaded him.[10]

Yet caravans were increasingly successful. The Religion's naval hierarchy had taken on its final form with a Grand Admiral – sometimes represented by a Vice-Admiral – and a Captain-General of the Galleys. The *Patrons*, now called captains, were each assisted by a lieutenant and a ship-master, the latter a hired mariner. Moslem traders dreaded Strozzi and Romegas no less than Christian merchantmen feared Torghut. Leone Strozzi was appointed captain-general when young but left the Order to fight Charles V, after his father, a prisoner of the emperor, had committed suicide. A bitter, quarrelsome man, he had eventually to leave France, but Omedes refused to take back this stormy petrel, who set up as corsair, calling himself 'the Friend of God alone'. Strozzi's little fleet became a byword, for he was a superb seaman who feared nothing, and the religion gladly reinstated him when he next applied; but Fra' Leone resigned once again to wage a vendetta on the Medici, dying in an obscure raid on the Tuscan coast. In his *Memoirs* Benvenuto Cellini says of Strozzi, 'That excellent officer was one of the greatest men of the age in which he lived and at the same time one of the most unfortunate', while that fierce old soldier, Blaize de Montluc, described the Prior of Capua as 'one of the bravest men that these hundred years have put to sea'.[11] The most famous of the Order's sailors was Mathurin d'Aux de Lescout Romegas, who never attacked an enemy ship without taking or sinking it, frequently engaging half a dozen Turkish vessels singlehanded. He was indestructible. On the night of 23 September 1555 a terrible storm struck Malta, sinking every ship in Grand Harbour. Next morning, knocking was heard from the keel of Romegas's galley, floating bottom up;

planks were prised loose, whereupon out crawled the ship's monkey, followed by the redoubtable captain.[12]

Omedes decreed that postulants must show four proofs of nobility, though the Order admitted aspirants with insufficient quarterings, the usual fault being a rich mother of plebeian origin, as Knights 'of Grace'; later, these inferior brethren were barred from promotion to bailiff, though many became Knights 'of Justice' (i.e. by right of birth) by papal dispensation. The Religion's sisters had also to produce proofs of nobility, Sigena in Aragon attracting the daughters of the greatest families in Spain, while a convent was established at Malta. Their red habit was replaced by a black one in mourning for Rhodes, though the white cross was still worn; at Sigena the cross was red and the coif white, nuns carrying silver sceptres in choir on great feasts.[13] *Confratres*, or Knights of Honour, had to have the same qualifications as professed knights, but Donats formed two classes, the plebeian being indistinguishable from serving brethren, those of noble birth aspirant Knights of Justice. Even chaplains and servants-at-arms must never have worked with their hands or engaged in shop-keeping and usually belonged to the haute bourgeoisie or the obscurer ranks of the *petite noblesse*. Serving brethren were non-commissioned officers, 'demi-chevaliers', rather than orderlies, some of the bravest being promoted to Knights of Grace. Many brothers came to Malta as pages, no more than twelve years old, though they had to be fifteen before entering the novitiate, which lasted a year and was undergone in a special house supervised by the Novice Master. However, a good number made their professions at home, to a knight of the local priory.

Fra' Claude de la Sengle became Grand Master in 1553 and devoted himself to fortifying the convent. The star-shaped Fort St Elmo was built on Monte Sceberras, commanding the entrances to Grand Harbour and the Marsamxett, though Fra' Claude concentrated his chief efforts on the peninsula opposite Birgu, Fort St Michel being strengthened and bastions erected; grateful brethren surnamed the promontory 'Senglea'. In 1557 Fra' Jean

Parisot de la Valette was elected Grand Master. A devout Gascon from Quercy born in 1494, this tall nobleman, bearded like a patriarch, silver-haired and burnt brown by the sun, 'in temperament rather melancholy',[14] possessed complete self-control, invariably speaking in a low voice. 'Fra' Jehan' had never left the convent since his solemn profession – normally knights who had completed four caravans (eight cruises) and spent three years at Malta could expect to retire to their commandery for a well-earned holiday. This was not the case with Valette, who sailed on caravan after caravan. In 1541 his galley, the *St Jean*, was taken by the Turks and he survived a year as a galley slave. Now that he was Master, duelling, gambling and whoring were rigorously punished and conventual observance enforced, brethren being required to hear Mass and say office daily, besides attending Matins and Vespers at the convent church on important feasts. Financial administration was thoroughly overhauled. But Fra' Jean's main reforms were defensive, as befitted a veteran of Rhodes; Birgu's buildings were strengthened while a boom of steel links 200 metres long was forged at Venice to bar the Harbour of the Galleys.

Queen Mary had revived the English langue in 1557; Clerkenwell was restored under Grand Prior Thomas Tresham[15] with ten commanderies, the three bailiffs – Turcopolier, Prior of Ireland and Bailiff of Egle – reappointed and the little auberge in Birgu reoccupied by five brethren. But Elizabeth became queen and by 1559 the langue had again broken up. In 1564 the last Scots prior, Fra' James Sandilands,[16] turning Protestant, was given his commandery by the Crown and became Lord Torphichen. The only English brother left in Malta was Oliver Starkey, Lieutenant Turcopolier and commander of Quenington, a quiet scholarly man who lived alone in a house in Majjistral Street next to the deserted auberge. Later he was made Latin Secretary to La Valette, a post which entailed drafting all diplomatic correspondence.

The Religion was heartened by the advent of a new brotherhood. In 1561 Cosimo I of Tuscany founded the Knights of San

Stefano, their rule 'Benedictine', their mission war on corsairs. There were four classes: knights with four proofs of nobility who took vows of poverty, *charity* and obedience, wearing a white cloak lined with rose, a gold-edged red Maltese cross on the left breast; chaplains in white soutane and cape, their cross edged with yellow; serving brethren in white serge with a plain red cross; and canonesses. The Grand Dukes were hereditary Masters, knights could marry, and conventual duties were part-time – bailiffs, comprising Constable, Admiral, Grand Prior, Chancellor, Treasurer, Conservator and Conventual Prior, being elected for three years.[17] Cosimo endowed his brethren magnificently, engaging the painter-architect Giorgio Vasari to build an ornate church and convent at Pisa, the first hung with Turkish trophies, the latter adorned with frescoed ceilings commemorating Lepanto.[18] However, these knights of the latterday Renaissance were not only ornamental; many bachelor brothers lived in the convent, and their galleys co-operated enthusiastically with Malta.

In 1564 Romegas waylaid a great Turkish carrack on her way from Venice to Constantinople with a cargo valued at 80,000 Spanish ducats.[19] As this ship belonged to the Kustir Aga, Chief of the Black Eunuchs, and the 'imperial odalisques' had shares in her cargo, there was great uproar in the seraglio. Meanwhile an aged Turkish 'lady of high rank', who had previously been captured, was sending piteous letters from Malta. Suleiman, old now, saddened by a son's rebellion and the death of his favourite wife, was easily angered; 'Allah's Bestower of Earthly Peace' could no longer tolerate pirate unbelievers in the Turkish *Mare Nostrum*. Torghut, the brethren's implacable foe, exaggerated their weakness, so the sultan sent his generals to attack Malta with fewer than 30,000 men. They were, however, the cream of the imperial army: headed by 6,000 hand-picked Janissaries carrying long damascened muskets, there followed 9,000 crack Spahis in vivid contrast, feudal levies, who probably resembled the regiments maintained by the Porte, clad in crimson, yellow or dark-blue brocade, horsemen using the horn bow, though they also had guns and knew how to fight on foot. There were 6,000 corsairs and sailors, less luxuriously armed, and 3,500 rapacious *akinjis*, volunteers who served for plunder. Grimmest of all were 4,000 dervish *ghazis*, berserk with hashish.[20]

This force had two commanders: the aged Mustafa Pasha – a veteran of Rhodes – and the young Piyale, a Serbian foundling who had married an Osmanli princess and become *Kapudan Pasha*, admiral-in-chief of the Turkish navy. Their staff included Ali el-Uluji, the future hero of Lepanto, and many famous corsairs, but, despite such talents and the presence of Suleiman's personal standard – a great silver disc with its gold ball and crescent surmounted by all-conquering horsetails – the expedition was to be handicapped by this divided command. However, the cannon of 1565 were more effective than before and musketry had improved, for Janissaries had become skilled marksmen; their long-barrelled wheel-locks, made at Constantinople by German gunsmiths, could not be as quickly loaded as the shorter European arquebus but were more accurate. Spies reported that artillery would blast Malta's makeshift defences out of existence within a few days.

The Religion's agents could not fail to notice the seething activity in Constantinople's dockyards and arsenals. Brethren were summoned from Europe and large supplies of food and powder stored in cellars dug in the rock beneath St Angelo. Malta was not a country off which besiegers could live; peasants stripped it of crops, poisoning the wells with hemp and rotting offal. Mdina, well fortified and garrisoned by militia, was left to fend for itself. Fra' Jean had 600 brethren – the resident community of 474 brother-knights and 67 serving brethren and, in addition, new arrivals – with 1,200 Italian and Spanish mercenaries and 3,000 Maltese militia. Other troops available, including galley-slaves and Greeks resident in the island, numbered 1,300. In all, his total strength was 6,000 men, of whom fewer than half were professionals.[21] Furthermore, the Sicilian Viceroy had given Philip II's word that 25,000 men would relieve the convent.

Militia and mercenaries fought as pikemen or arquebusiers, though all carried swords. The mercenaries, as professionals, were

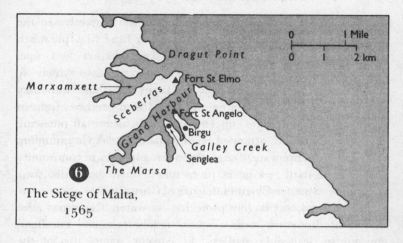

The Siege of Malta, 1565

armoured with high-crested morion helmets, 'breast-and-back', and tassets (articulated thigh plates). Militia had only helmets and leather jerkins. Their knight officers carried sword and dagger, the former a broadsword or rapier, though some brethren preferred the great German two-hander. A few may have had the hand buckler, a small shield with a spike. On the walls many wielded hooked halberds or boarding pikes. 'Harness' was still an advantage in hand-to-hand combat; most brethren must have worn *armatura de piede*, half-armour for fighting on foot, while some wore a thickened 'bullet-proof' breastplate, others the brigantine of metal-studded cloth. Over all was the scarlet sopravest, the battle habit, something like a herald's tabard, its great white cross square-ended instead of eight-pointed. The Grand Master's sopravest was of cloth-of-gold.

The Religion was not an ordinary army but a monastery at war which followed its *reverendissimus magister*, his leadership resting on spiritual foundations – brethren who disobeyed him disobeyed Jesus Christ; they were still convinced that by dying in battle against the infidel they gave their lives for the Saviour as He had for them. La Valette understood his children perfectly. In the spring they were assembled in chapter to hear him preach a noble sermon: 'Today our Faith is at stake – whether the Gospel must yield to the *Koran*. God is asking for the lives which we pledged to Him at our profession. Happy are those who may sacrifice their lives.'[22] Then he and his habited brethren went in solemn procession to the conventual church, where all renewing their vows confessed, attended High Mass and took Communion; this was the corporate Communion of a religious community rededicating itself to God as its members must soon fulfil their vocation – to die for Christ in defence of Christians.

The convent was largely protected by water. Ramparts were inadequate but earthworks – moats, trenches, ramps – excellent, covered by well-sited artillery. St Angelo, at the tip of the northern peninsula, was garrisoned by 500 troops with fifty brethren under La Valette himself who made it his command point, and had two tiers of batteries. The rest of the peninsula was guarded by the walls of Birgu and several small bastions linked by trenches, though the landward side was weak, dependent on earthworks manned by the French langues, the German taking the shores, while the Castilian held the vulnerable angle to the south. Between this bastion of Castile and the Hospital was 'the Post of England' – knights from several nations under Oliver Starkey. Senglea, the southern peninsula, even better served by the sea, had four bastions in Italian charge, while the Aragonese manned Fort St Michel on the landward approach. Fort St Elmo, at the foot of Monte Sceberras, shaped like a four-pointed star, was built of poor-quality stone but strengthened by a raised gun-emplacement (or 'cavalier') on the seaward side and an outwork of trenches, a 'ravelin' facing the Marsa. Normally manned by only eighty men, its garrison was raised to 300, Fra Luigi Broglia, the old bailiff in command, being joined by a brother scarcely less aged, Fra' Juan de Eguaras, Bailiff of Negropont.

On 18 May 1565, the infidel armada was sighted: 180 warships besides cargo vessels and transports, with nearly 30,000 eager troops, and a floating arsenal of cannon.[23] It anchored in the exposed bay of Marsaxlokk. Mustafa was in favour of storming Mdina but Piyale feared for his ships and insisted that St Elmo, which commanded the entrance to Marsamxett, a perfect haven, must first be taken. The little fort was invested and on 25 May batteries opened fire; their guns included ten 80-pounders and a basilisk hurling balls of 160 lb. Jean rushed in 64 brethren and 200 mercenaries under Fra' Pierre de Massuez Vercoyran – 'Colonel le Mas'. Old Broglia, suffering heavy casualties, soon asked La Valette for more reinforcements; his messenger, Fra' Juan de la Cerda, told the Sacred Council that St Elmo would quickly fall.[24] The angry Master announced his intention of taking command himself, but eventually sent Fra' Gonzalez de Medran with 200 troops and 50 knights. By 29 May the Turks had captured the outermost trench. Then, on 2 June, Torghut, eighty years old, arrived with 1,500 corsairs and more cannon. He deplored Piyale's plan of concentrating on St Elmo, yet he knew that to abandon it would have a disastrous effect on morale. His guns were mounted on Gallows Point, subjecting the tiny stronghold to an even fiercer pounding.

On the night of 3 June Turkish sappers found the ravelin unguarded and knifed the sentries; Janissaries nearly succeeded in storming St Elmo itself before the portcullis could be lowered and were only halted by two small cannon. The Turks continued to attack until noon next day. Fire-throwers and boiling oil supplemented the fort's cannon while there was a large supply of fiery *cercles* and grenades: the former were huge hoops, bound with inflammable wadding, set alight and hurled with tongs – a lucky throw could ring three infidels to turn them into flaming torches. Hand-bombs were earthenware pots packed with combustibles, four fuses projecting from the spout to make sure it exploded. Morale was epitomized by Fra' Abel de Bridiers de la Gardampe who fell, shot in the chest; a brother bent over him but he muttered, 'Go away – don't think I'm alive – your time's better spent helping the others,' and then crawled away to the fort's chapel to die at the foot of the altar.[25] Five hundred Turks were dead as against 20 brethren and 60 mercenaries, but without the ravelin the fort's besiegers could now build a ramp and fire down on the defenders. A sortie failed to retake it. By 7 June the barrage was rocking the fort 'like a ship in a storm', and Gonzalez de Medran brought Fra' Jean the message that the considered opinion of Broglia and Eguaras was that the bastion was doomed; he himself believed that further defence of this outpost would waste good troops.

La Valette disagreed, certain that relief must come if only he could hold on long enough, for the Sicilian viceroy, García de Toledo – a *frey-caballero* of Santiago – considered Malta the key to Sicily. Further, the viceroy's son, 'a promising youth who took the Habit', was in the convent.[26] St Elmo would buy time. He was therefore thunderstruck when on the night of 8 June, after a major assault, Fra' Vitellino Vittelleschi appeared with a round robin signed by fifty-three of his beleaguered brethren – though not by Broglia or Eguaras – which stipulated that, unless evacuated at once, they would sally out to die a holy death. Three brothers were immediately sent to investigate. One, Fra' Constantino de Castriota, reported that St Elmo could resist for many days and offered to lead a relief force. Only fifteen brethren with 100 militia, all volunteers – including, to the general wonderment, two Jews – were allowed to go, but a shrewdly phrased letter told the garrison they were welcome to return to a safer place; all stayed. Meanwhile the bombardment continued; it was not a question of demolishing ramparts but of clearing debris. The Turks assaulted relentlessly, by night as well as by day. On 18 June Torghut and Mustafa ordered a general assault. 'So great was the noise, the shouting, the beating of drums and the clamour of innumerable Turkish musical instruments, that it seemed like the end of the world.'[27] Their troops too were equipped with grenades, limpet wildfire bombs which clung to armour. Four thousand arquebusiers blasted every gap in the rubble with a storm of lead while culverins from Monte Sceberras and Gallows Point hurled cannonballs – iron, bronze or stone. Then the dervishes went in, mad with prayer and hashish, frothing at the mouth, followed by Spahis and finally by Janissaries. This was the chosen élite of an army accustomed to victory from Persia to Poland.

The Grand Master, however, had ferried over quantities of ammunition and barrels of reinvigorating wine; and so, when the enemy came yelling through what was left of the walls, cannon tore into them; as for limpet bombs, the knights had great vats of sea water into which to jump.[28] After six hours this assault was called off. One thousand Turkish bodies littered the blood-soaked ground, while 150 defenders had died, including Medran, cut down as he seized a horsetail banner. The wounded were ferried back to the Hospital, where the period's best medical skill soon restored them. Torghut began to build new batteries on Monte Sceberras just before he was mortally wounded by stone shrapnel – and soon it became impossible to reinforce or to evacuate St Elmo. On 22 June the faithful launched the fiercest assault yet. The walls, reduced to their foundations, were heaped with rocks, earth, palliasses, baggage, corpses, anything that would serve as a barricade. In six hours the attackers lost 2,000 men and then withdrew in amazement. But they had killed 500 Unbelievers. A swimmer got through to St Angelo and Fra' Jean tried unsuccessfully to send one last detachment of volunteers – but it could not pass the enemy's hail-storm of shot.

At midnight on the morning of 23 June – the Eve of St John – Mass was said in the tiny chapel, the only surviving building. Two chaplain brethren heard each man's confession, then everyone received the Body of the Lord he was soon to meet. Finally the chaplains buried their chalices and burned the chapel's furnishings; all night long these two priests tolled its bell – as a Passing Bell. Just before first light the soldiers of Christ took up their positions; there were only sixty left. The senior officers, Eguaras, 'Colonel Mas', and a Captain Miranda were too badly wounded to stand, so they sat, Eguaras weak from loss of blood and Miranda horribly scorched by wildfire, in chairs at the main breach, Mas, whose leg was smashed by bullet wounds, sitting on a log.[29] At six a.m. the entire Turkish army attacked; even galleys sailed in to bombard the stinking mound of rubble and rotting corpses, regardless of fire from St Angelo. Yet for four hours the defenders answered them with guns and grenades, until at last they stormed in. Juan de Eguaras, hurled from his chair, jumped up with a boarding pike before a scimitar took his head off, while Mas, sitting on his log, slew several Turks with his great two-handed sword. An Italian lit a beacon to tell his Master it was over. Only nine brethren – probably mortally wounded – were taken alive, though a handful of Maltese swam to safety. It had cost an army, acknowledged as the best of its time, nearly five weeks, 18,000 rounds of cannon-shot and 8,000 men to gain this little fort.[30]

'Allah,' said Mustafa, looking across at St Angelo, 'if this small son cost so much, what do we pay for his father?'[31] Each brother's corpse was decapitated, a crucifix hacked in its chest, nailed to a wooden cross and pushed out to sea. Next morning, on the feast of the Religion's patron, the tide brought in four mutilated bodies. Fra' Jean burst into tears. At once he ordered all prisoners to be beheaded; suddenly Pasha's troops heard gunfire, then their comrades' bleeding heads were bouncing all over the camp.[32] Meanwhile the Grand Master reminded his brethren of their vocation as they renewed their vows on that Baptist's Day: 'What could be more fitting for a member of the Order of St John than to lay down his life in defence of the Faith,' he preached; the dead of St Elmo 'have earned a martyr's crown and will reap a martyr's reward'. Nor did he forget the militia and the mercenaries: 'We are all soldiers of Jesus Christ like you, my comrades,' he told them.[33] A reinforcement reached the convent on 3 July, a 'little relief' or *piccolo soccorso* consisting of 700 soldiers led by 42 brethren and 'gentlemen volunteers' under Frey Melchior de Robles of the Order of Santiago.[34] Two of them were English, John Evan Smith and Edward Stanley, and no doubt they received a warm welcome from Fra' Oliver Starkey at the 'Post of England'. Meanwhile dysentery and malaria had broken out among the Turks, whose water came from poisoned wells. The Pasha offered terms, to receive a contemptuous refusal.

Mustafa then had eighty galleys hauled by slaves from Marsamxett over the narrowest stretch of Monte Sceberras into Grand Harbour; the Senglea promontory could be attacked by the army from the landward side, by the navy from the seaward. Hastily Frà' Jean constructed a coastal boom – iron chains fastened on stakes set in the sea bed – while he built a pontoon bridge between Birgu and Senglea. On 5 July seventy Turkish cannon opened fire on Senglea, killing women and children in the streets. Sappers swam in with axes to destroy the boom but were driven off by Maltese knifemen who grappled with them in the water. Hassem, the young Dey of Algiers, now arrived with 2,500 veteran corsairs who sneered at the Turks' performance at St Elmo; Mustafa allowed them to lead a general assault on 15 July. Of the enemy troops, Turkish, Algerian and Corsair, Balbi, an eyewitness, wrote: 'Even the rank and file wore scarlet robes and there were many in cloth-of-gold and of silver and of crimson damask. Armed with fine muskets of Fez, scimitars of Alexandria and Damascus, they all wore splendid turbans.'[35] Hassem, with half his force, tried to rush Fort St Michel where Robles tore them to shreds with grapeshot; his other troops waded ashore on the seaward side, but La Valette sent reinforcements over the pontoon. Mustafa then dispatched ten boatloads of Janissaries to land on an unguarded stretch of Senglea. He did not know of a hidden battery under St Angelo. As the boats approached, its commander trained five culverins – loaded with stones, chains and spiked iron balls – at a range of 150 yards and blew them out of the water with a single salvo. The few survivors drowned. This repulse saved the day. Meanwhile, after five hours' fearful carnage Hassem began to withdraw, whereupon St Michel's garrison sallied out in pursuit; 'Remember St Elmo,' shouted brethren and Maltese. The infidels left 4,000 dead, including those who drowned.[36] The Grand Master laid up six captured Turkish standards in a church and ordered the singing of a 'Te Deum'.

The Turks would not give up – they knew that the defenders were desperate. The garrison had been decimated, supplies almost exhausted. Relentlessly the enemy hammered away. The heaviest cannonade of the siege began on 2 August – it could be heard in Sicily. Then came another general assault on Senglea; the Faithful charged Fort St Michel five times in six hours – Maltese women helped drive them off with tubs of boiling water. On 7 August came another general assault; Piyale attacked Birgu with 3,000 men, rushing into a breach in the bastion of Castile to be decimated by crossfire. Mustafa attacked Senglea simultaneously, cheering on his troops as they finally stormed St Michel. This time the bastion of Castile had been well mined and besiegers poured into the yawning breach. Amid the smoke and confusion many believed it was the end. Snatching a helmet and a half-pike, Fra' Jean ran to the breach. A grenade exploded, wounding him in the leg, but he refused to leave: 'I am seventy-one – how can it be possible for a man of my age to die more gloriously than among my brethren and my friends in the service of God, in defence of our holy Religion?'[37] The storming party was thrown out, but Senglea and Birgu were collapsing. Every casualty at the Hospital who could walk had to man the walls. Suddenly, the retreat was sounded; the Pasha thought that his enemy's relief had come. In fact a few cavalry had ridden out from Mdina to massacre the Turkish wounded. For ten days their enraged comrades attacked daily before launching yet another general assault on 18 August. On 20 August, 8,000 Turks were again thrown back from Fort St Michel. Three days later the entire Sacred Council was in favour of withdrawing to Fort St Angelo. But Fra' Jean would not abandon 'his loyal Maltese, their wives and their families', while Turkish batteries in Birgu would soon demolish St Angelo – 'here we die together or drive out our enemies'.[38] Then he blew up the bridge between Birgu and St Angelo.

The assaults and the bombardment continued mercilessly. Yet if the garrison were desperate so were the Turks: food and ammunition were running out, for supply ships were waylaid by Christian corsairs. This was an excessively hot summer – fever raged among the besiegers and plague was feared. Guns were wearing thin, and so was morale; it was rumoured that *djinn* and *affrit* had been seen at La Valette's side – he was a magician in

Satan's pay. The attackers had to be driven on by other officers. Mustafa called off an assault on Mdina, whose governor had manned the walls with townsmen in red sopravests and loosed off every gun available. On 8 September a Christian fleet passed St Angelo, each ship firing a three-gun salute, and Piyale's navy was too demoralized to attack. 'I don't think any music has ever soothed the mind of man quite so much as the pealing of our bells on 8 September 1565, the Nativity of Our Lady,' wrote Francesco Balbi, who was present throughout the siege and left a vivid account. 'The Grand Master ordered them to be rung at the time when the call to arms was normally sounded and for three months we had heard nothing but the call to arms. On that morning, however, they summoned us to Mass, a pontifical High Mass sung very early, to thank God and his Blesed Mother for the mercies they had bestowed upon us.' (The Knights of Malta still attend a '*Vittoria*' Mass every September.) The relieving force which landed further north was at most 10,000 strong but included knights from all over Europe, even another English brother. When Mustafa, who had set sail, realized how few they were, he landed again, at St Paul's Bay. But his men were already beaten: Christian troops smashed into them and total rout was averted only by Mustafa's leadership. Grimly he and Piyale sailed for Constantinople; Osmanli sultans seldom forgave failure – death was the usual penalty. And of the 40,000 besiegers – Turks, Algerians, Berbers – only 10,000 survived. Suleiman was enraged, shouting, 'Only with me do my armies triumph – next spring I will conquer Malta myself.'[39] But he spared his trembling generals.

La Valette received the dilatory viceroy with every honour. Only 600 fighting men were on their feet to greet him; over 2,500 mercenaries had died with 250 of the brethren, besides 7,000 Maltese men, women and children.[40] But they were the heroes of Europe. Pius V offered Fra' Jean a Red Hat, which he declined gracefully as it meant visiting Rome and he would not leave the convent. Even the Archbishop of Canterbury ordered services of thanksgiving. King Philip sent a sword of honour with 15,000 troops to guard the island until it was re-fortified; Catholic sovereigns gave many handsome contributions for this purpose.

Now a real convent could be built. Monte Sceberras was the site for *Humilissima Civitas Valettae*, work beginning in March 1566. Fra' Jean was refounding Jerusalem, the Rhodes of his youth; church, hospital, palace and auberges were to be simple, with a *collachium* as in that lost but still beloved Aegean island. A portrait of the Very Reverend Grand Master shows a curiously reflective face, an abbot's face, and indeed Valetta was intended first and foremost as a monastery, the mother house of a great Order. He lived another two years, watching his dream — which he 'loved like a daughter' — take shape, before dying of a stroke in August 1568. He was buried in his brothers' new home. Oliver Starkey wrote an epitaph: 'Here lies Valette, worthy of eternal honour, he that was formerly the terror of Asia and Africa and the shield of Europe, whence by his holy arms he expelled the barbarians, the first buried in this beloved city of which he was the founder.'

Yet the siege had decided nothing, and the Turks completed their conquest of the Levant. Venetian Cyprus fell in 1571, and even the Serene Republic joined Pius V's Holy League of Spain, Genoa, Tuscany and Malta. In August of that year its fleet gathered at Messina under Philip II's bastard brother, the young Don John of Austria, assisted by Frey Luís Zúñiga y Requesens, Santiago's grand commander of León. Their armada had 202 galleys, seventy small sailing ships and eight large Venetian galleasses (a kind of galleon with oars). Of the Order's contingents San Stefano's was the biggest — twelve galleys — but Malta's was the most formidable — three galleys under the Religion's Admiral, Pietro Giustiniani, with Romegas.

By now the galley had reached its final form, as much as 180 feet in length if one includes raked poop and prow; such a vessel might have a beam of less than twenty feet, shallow draughted and rolling horribly. But in calm water, propelled by thirty oars a side and two lateen rigged masts, its average speed was two knots — over four for short distances. Normally a 48-pounder culverin and four 8-pounder sakers were mounted on the prow, with smaller guns elsewhere.

Crusaders and faithful met in the Gulf of Corinth off Lepanto on 7 October 1571. Ali, the Kapudan Pasha, had 216 war-galleys, thirty-seven galliots (small galleys) and various lesser vessels.[41] The crusader line of battle was Venetians on the left flying yellow banners, Genoese on the right flying green, and Don John and his ships with the papal galleys in the centre flying azure, and behind them a reserve – probably including San Stefano's squadron – flying white; Malta's vessels flanked Don John's right. Along his front line he spaced the galleasses, where their big guns' cross-fire could do most damage. Confidently the young admiral sailed forward to music from his minstrels' gallery, unfurling the blue banner of the Holy League, embroidered with the figure of Christ crucified. The Turks were spread out over six miles in poor formation which deteriorated under fire; a galley sank at the third salvo.

Ali Pasha and his red banner emblazoned with the prophet's sword went straight for the *Reale*, the League's flagship, guns blazing; his iron ram penetrated to the fourth rowing bench – for a moment her crew feared she would settle. But now Don John's bowchasers raked Ali's own flagship. Then the troops, 300 Janissary marksmen with 100 archers against 400 Spanish arquebusiers, set to; the prince would not shoot until he 'could be splashed with his enemies' blood'. Many Christian oarsmen left their benches and grabbed boarding-pikes. The struggle surged from one ship to the other until the papal commander, Colonna, who had just captured the Bey of Negropont, came up, blasting the Turks from stem to stern. Don John's men boarded for the third time; not one enemy soldier survived. Elsewhere the entire Christian centre had been victorious. On the left the issue was more in doubt. Chuluk Ali – 'Sirocco' – had attacked savagely and, though he was killed, his ships outflanked the League's line, passing between it and the coast. However, fighting like fiends, the Venetians drove them aground, Christian galley-slaves breaking loose to slaughter their masters. It was very different on the right. That superb seaman Ali el-Uluji, Dey of Algiers, made a wide sweep as though to take the Christians in the rear, and the Genoese drew back to forestall him. A galley, by stopping one bank of oars and double stroking the other, could turn in its own length. Suddenly the corsairs swung in, racing for the now isolated squadron of Malta. The brethren fought with habitual ferocity but were hopelessly outnumbered; their flagship was overwhelmed and the great banner of St John torn down, only three knights surviving – an Italian, an Aragonese who lost his arm and half of one shoulder from a single sword-cut, and the admiral himself, found beneath a pile of Turkish dead. The Order's other galleys would have been taken too, had not the reserve come to their rescue, followed by Don John and then the Genoese. Surrounded, el-Uluji battled on magnificently for another hour before cutting his way out with twelve ships. His Moslem comrades had lost 210 vessels – 40 sent to the bottom – and 30,000 men, including nearly all senior officers.[42]

Constantinople and Islam had lost the Mediterranean at Lepanto. The Ottoman navy's fire power had been destroyed by the wholesale elimination of its bowmen. These specialist archers were irreplacable since a lifetime was needed to learn their skills, passed down from generation to generation.

VII

BAROQUE PALADINS
1571–1789

'Chi la pace non vuol la guerra s'abbia'
('Who wills not peace, let war his portion be.')

Tasso, *Gerusalemme Liberata*

BAROQUE PALADINS

The Counter-Reformation replaced the military religious orders with new shock-troops: Jesuits. As a Spaniard, the founder of the Jesuits, Ignatius Loyola, was very much aware of Santiago, Calatrava, Alcántara and Montesa, whose brethren undoubtedly contributed to his inspiration. Even so, monks of war continued to do battle with the Infidel until Napoleonic times. Nor did the Knights of Malta forget their other, hospitaller, vocation. Significantly, several new brotherhoods emerged to join the ranks of the monks of war.

This chapter is a general survey of the military religious orders during the seventeenth and eighteenth centuries, a period in which many of their members showed that the calling retained a good deal of its original vitality.

Throughout the age of the Baroque, the monks of war displayed all their old Crusader zeal. When the twenty-year siege of Candia in Crete came to an end in 1668, Knights of Malta had held the half-demolished gate of Sant'Andrea for three months against relentless attacks by the Turks. After the twenty-nine brethren who remained on their feet finally withdrew, the Venetian general reported in a dispatch to his Council at Venice, 'I lose more from the departure of these few superbly brave soldiers than from all the rest put together.' During the previous year they had been heartened by the arrival of a detachment of white-cloaked Teutonic Knights under Johann-Wilhelm von Metzenhausen, Komtur of Coblenz.[1] In 1687 the Order of Malta helped Francesco Morosini's Venetians conquer the Morea, while two years later a *Malteserorden* force marched with the Imperial army on the campaign to retake Belgrade.

In 1631 there were 2,000 professed members of the Order of Malta, of whom 1,746 were Knights. The Order even acquired colonies. In 1653 Grand Master Lascaris bought the Caribbean islands of Tortuga, St Croix and St Barthélemy, to be administered as a bailiwick; but the venture proved a failure, and after twelve years they were sold to the French West India Company.[2] However, Malta grew steadily richer, its European revenues supplemented by the *spoglio* – prize money from Moslem shipping captured by the *corso*, the sea caravans of the Knights.

13. Capturing a Barbary Corsair in the seventeenth century

The General of the Galleys – 'The Venerable Bailiff, General of the Armies of the Religion on the Sea', to give him his full title – commanded a formidable navy. (Although technically his superior, the Order's admiral was a desk-bound officer who never put to sea, rather like the old First Sea Lord and the British Navy.) Until 1700 its principal warships continued to be a battle fleet of seven black-and-red galleys. There was also a *'gran galeone'* of never less than seventy guns, together with the invaluable *saettas* (feluccas used for scouting) and the tartans which sometimes mounted as many as twenty-two guns. The Knights were famous for their gunnery and their ability to dismast an enemy ship with a single salvo.

The General's *'Capitana'* (flag-ship) flew the Order's Great Banner, red with a white cross and bearing the motto *'Vias tuas, Domine, demonstra mihi'* – 'Show unto me thy ways, O Lord'. There was a banner of the Blessed Virgin flying from every mainmast, banners of St John the Baptist fore and aft. There was also a life-sized gilded statue of the Baptist on each poop-rail, the highest point of the stern, dominating the ship. (Brethren often had his likeness or a prayer to him engraved on their armour and weapons.)

Yet the galleys of Malta were as uncomfortable as ever. There was no means of cooking food while the Knights still slept on the poop deck, catching lice from the *ciurme* or oarsmen, the reek of whose sweat and excrement must have been overpowering beneath a hot Mediterranean sun. If magnificent fighting machines, in foul weather such narrow, cramped vessels were a nightmare, unwieldy and easily capsized. However close together they might sail, they often lost sight of one another in the big seas which frequently swamped them – the oarsmen shrieking and cursing above the storm, straining on the chains which bound them to their benches, voiding themselves from fear. Any captain who lost his galley in a shipwreck, even though blameless, could expect a lengthy spell in the dungeons of St Elmo after appearing before the Sacred Council – which, among its many functions, acted as an Admiralty court. When his vessel the *Santo Stefano* ran aground off Leghorn, Fra' Denis de Polastron de la Hilière saved her by his fervent prayers – eyewitnesses reporting that a miracle took place, the wind changing immediately and lifting her off the rocks.

'The Most Eminent and Reverend Lord the Grand Master of the Sacred Religion and Most Illustrious Order of the Hospital of

St John and of the Holy Sepulchre in Jerusalem, Guardian of the Poor of Jesus Christ, Prince of Malta, Gozo and Rhodes, Lord of the Royal Domain of Tripoli' was very much a monarch. In 1607 he was made a Prince of the Empire, while after 1630 his rank at Rome was equated with that of a Cardinal Deacon. (He is still called 'Altezza *Eminenza*' today.) He addressed kings as 'Mon Cousin', receiving ambassadors from Rome, Vienna, Paris and Madrid. In the eighteenth century Grand Master Pinto would place a royal crown over his arms.

A grand master had several roles and, judging from their portraits, some holders of the office preferred one role more than another. Fra' Alof de Wignacourt (1601–22) was painted by Caravaggio as a warrior; a magnificent study shows him in a parade armour and another in his choir-dress. His successor, Fra' Luis Mendez de Vasconcellos, liked to be portrayed as a monk-hospitaller, in a habit and holding a towel, with a breviary in front of him. By contrast, Fra' Manoel Pinto de Fonseca (1741–73) made Favray paint him as a sovereign in ermine-trimmed robes of state, with a crown next to him.

Yet all grand masters were formed by the Order's novitiate. As soon as he reached Malta, each young novice had to familiarize himself with the heroic deeds of his predecessors, soldiers for Christ. He did so through the chronicles of Giacomo Bosio and of Fra' Bartolomeo dal Pozzo. The former's *Istoria della Sacra Religione et Illustrissima Militia di San Giovanni Gierosoloimitano* was commissioned by the Sacred Council and published in 1594; by order of the Council it was read in the refectory of every auberge. Bosio had access to material now lost and, if often inaccurate and too full of pious legend, his book is still of value. Dal Pozzo's *Historia della Sacra Religione Militare di S. Giovanni Gerosoloimitano* of 1703–15 is the sequel, dealing with the seventeenth century.

Another inspiring work which novices were encouraged to read was Goussancourt's *Martyrologie des Chevaliers de Sainct Jean de Hierusalem, dits de Malte*. Published at Paris in 1643, this tells of the sufferings borne by captured Knights, who refused to embrace Islam – of how they had steadfastly endured the terrible life of a

T.III. p. 84

14. A Knight of Malta, still wearing the Crusader surcoat in 1721

galley-slave, with its daily floggings, or of their tortures in the dungeons of Constantinople or Tripoli. The martyrology listed by name an impressive selection of brethren who had fallen in battle against the Infidel, giving a brief account of how each had met his death, together with a picture of his coat of arms. Thus, Fra' Jean Jacques de Harlay 'had expired of a wound from a poisoned assegai while fighting the Turks of Zagiora near Tripoli, in the year 1550'. (An assegai was a Berber javelin long before it became a Zulu spear.) This sort of death, which continued to await a surprising number of Knights during the seventeenth and even eighteenth centuries, merited the martyr's palm. For they were still Crusaders.

In itself Valetta was sufficient testimony to the Knights' achievement. The conventual church of St John was deliberately built low so that defending cannon should not have their field of fire restricted seaward. The auberges were barracks, with guardrooms, stores and slave-quarters, and the Grand Master's palace had been designed as a command-post. The city had been designed as a soldiers' cantonment, its streets on a grid pattern with boxlike blocks of houses which could easily be held against Turkish or Moorish invaders.

This grim military exterior concealed a wealth of Baroque splendours, of noble halls and elegant apartments. They were lined by Gobelin tapestries and Oriental rugs, furnished with rich cabinets, antique bronzes, Chinese vases and an abundance of silver plate. As was fitting, the greatest splendours were in the conventual church. Its gilded ceiling framed scenes from the Baptist's life, while its chapels were adorned with superb statuary; that of the Langue of Italy contained paintings by Caravaggio, who was briefly and ingloriously a Knight. (Another important Baroque artist, Mattia Preti, was also a member of the Order – known as '*Il Cavaliere Calabrese*', he became Commander of Syracuse.) Even the church's floor was magnificent, marquetried by plaques commemorating dead Knights, whose arms were picked out in jasper, porphyry, agate, onyx and lapis lazuli.[3]

The Sacred Infirmary, whose great ward measured 185 feet by

34, sheltered 350 patients on average. Its vast staff included doctors, surgeons, nurses and pharmacists, while the food was specially chosen (vermicelli and chicken for the weak, wine and game for the strong), served on silver dishes. There were clinics for outpatients, with one for leprosy and another for venereal disease, slaves and beggars receiving free prescriptions. An external nursing service tended the old in their own homes. (During his novitiate, each Knight had to serve in the Hospital for one day a week, as did the Grand Master and the bailiffs on great feast-days.)

Under the Order's benevolent despotism the Maltese grew rich from the Levant trade and from cotton. An English tourist, Mr Brydone, wrote of Valetta's streets in 1770 as being 'crowded with well dressed people who have all the appearance of health and affluence'. Bread was cheap, its price carefully controlled. The streets were swept and policed, health regulations were far in advance of their day, and the penal code was surprisingly enlightened. There were almshouses for the aged poor and an orphanage. This benevolence extended to the European mainland. In the 1770s Henry Swinburne came across a hospice in Puglia which the Order had recently founded for humble travellers, offering them free food, beds and stabling.

Throughout the eighteenth century the Knights of Malta continued to see plenty of action at sea, ships of the line supporting the galleys after 1704 though never replacing them. In 1716 the Order joined Venice and the Papacy in a last Holy League, which made a gallant attempt to save the Morea. Between 1723 and 1749 Fra' Jacques de Chambray sailed on thirty-one caravans, taking over eleven prizes and amassing a *spoglio* of 400,000 *livres*. Fra' Pierre-André de Suffren de Saint-Tropez, formerly captain of a galley, served with the French Navy during the American War of Independence, outsailing and outgunning a British fleet far larger than his own in the Indian Ocean in 1782-3. (He was rewarded with the title of Vice-Admiral of France and has been called with some justice the greatest of all French naval tacticians.) The Order's own navy sailed with those of Spain and

Portugal in 1784 to shell Algiers, while until the last decade of the century its caravans patrolled the Mediterranean and guarded the Italian coast.

Part of the Adriatic coast of southern Puglia is known as the '*Difesa di Malta*' on account of its contribution to the island. (In 1775 the Knights built a *masseria* or fortified manor house of that name near Ostuni; it still stands amid the olive groves.) The Order owned particularly rich estates in this area, shipping wine, corn, oil and almonds to their island home, together with valuable revenues. The locals did not begrudge them. For centuries Moslem slave-raiders had come here in search of prey, no woman daring to walk along a lonely beach. Nothing reassured the Pugliesi more than a glimpse of a black galley flying a red flag with a white cross.

Some historians claim that the reduced activity of the Order's navy during the late eighteenth century indicates decline. The reverse is true. It was inactive because it had been so successful. The pirate states of North Africa no longer bothered to build large ships because they knew that these would inevitably be caught or sunk by Maltese galleys. As soon as the Knights left Malta, Algerian piracy revived, becoming a major threat to merchant shipping in the Mediterranean – an eloquent tribute to the Knights' policing.

The Order of Malta's standing remained high in every Catholic country, its priors and bailiffs ranking with the great nobles of the land. If the Prince Grand Prior of Germany ruled only a very modest little state at Heitersheim (near the Alsatian border in what is now Baden Württemberg) and was overshadowed by the Hoch und Deutschmeister, his opposite numbers in France, Spain and Portugal were scions of the reigning dynasty; in the ill-starred year of 1789 the Duc de Berry became Grand Prior of France, while Charles III of Spain made his son Prior of Castile, and in Portugal Dom Miguel, grandson of Mary I, became Prior of Crato. At a more modest and local level, an important bailiff such as the Prior of St Gilles in Provence or the Prior of Barletta in Puglia enjoyed enormous influence.

The Knights still saw their life as a spiritual calling. On Malta during the last decades of the seventeenth century half a dozen of the older brethren lived permanently in a retreat house created for them by the Jesuits, serving 'Our Lords the Sick' daily in the Sacred Infirmary, saying the Office punctiliously and practising mental prayer. The *Vie de Messire Gabriel Dubois de la Ferté*, published at Paris in 1712, is the life of their leader. Born in 1644, he served in Louis XIV's army as well as in the Order's navy during the campaigns of Crete and the Morea, captaining a galley, before being given shore jobs on Malta. Having received the minute commandery of Le Breil-aux-Francs in the depths of the French countryside, he found it in ruins but soon made it a centre of prayer and alms-giving. He said Office in its chapel every morning, giving food and medicine to beggars before going out to nurse the lonely and forgotten. He sat by the bedsides of men whose maladies stank so horribly that no priest could bear to go near them.

A man who slept in a hayloft and who was known to hand his shirt to a tramp, Fra' Gabriel none the less lived up to his social position, dining with the local gentry. When he died in 1702 they mourned him deeply and believed he had been a saint. A committed hospitaller, his life showed what the vocation could mean. Under a contemporary engraving of Fra' Gabriel is written

> *De la Croix du Sauveur, je tire ma Noblesse –*
> *J'en fus le Religieux, l'Enfant et le Soldat.*
> *J'en fis tous mes plaisirs et toutes mes richesses*
> *Par elle je vainquis le Grand Turc au combat.*

('From the Saviour's Cross I draw my noble blood – from it, as page and as soldier I was a monk. I accounted it all my joy and all my riches – by it I overcame the Grand Turk in battle.') This is the authentic voice of the true Knight of Malta.

Among other brethren of this type, Fra' Gaspard de Simiane la Coste (who lived half a century before Fra' Gabriel) stands out.

He built a hospital for galley-slaves at Marseilles, nursing them himself and preaching the Gospel. He refused to leave them when the plague came in 1649 and died of it.

The Order inspired a highly readable historian in the Abbé Vertot, whose *Histoire des Chevaliers Hospitalliers de S. Jean de Jérusalem* was published in 1726. He wrote for the general public, adapting Bosio and dal Pozzo, and is often inaccurate, but he provided an enjoyable introduction to the story of the Knights. His book had great success and was even admired by Edward Gibbon.

The Teutonic Order survived the loss of Livland and also that of its rich Venetian commandery in 1595. During the same year, 1595, the then Hoch und Deutschmeister, Archduke Maximilian of Austria, was able to send 100 Knights to Hungary at the head of 400 horsemen – to fight the Turks. He summoned a chapter-general to Mergentheim in 1606, which inaugurated a revival of the Order's spiritual vocation. Henceforward, brethren had to perform their novitiate at specified houses, while every command-ery had to have a resident priest.

During the seventeenth century a Teutonic Knight's military calling became that of an officer in the Holy Roman Emperor's army, serving against the Turks in the wars to free the Balkans. They helped to defend Vienna in 1683, and twelve years later founded the famous 'Hoch und Deutschmeister Regiment'. During the eighteenth century the brethren produced some distin-guished field marshals, notably Guido von Starhemberg, Philipp von Harrach and Maximilian von Merveldt.

A Westphalian, born in 1764, Count Max von Merveldt served as a hussar against the Turks before entering the Order in 1791. He then fought in the Revolutionary Wars against the French, winning the coveted Maria-Theresa Cross for his gallantry at Neerwinden. During the Napoleonic Wars he was prominent as both cavalry commander and diplomat, becoming *Feldmarschall Leutnant* and Austrian ambassador to St Petersburg. In 1808, after his commandery had been secularized by the French, he was dispensed of his vows and married. Merveldt died in 1815 when he was Austrian ambassador to London, his widow declining the offer of a state funeral at Westminster Abbey.

Although bereft of its Baltic lands, the Teutonic Order retained enormous prestige in Germany and the Habsburg domains, where it still possessed twelve bailiwicks. The Hoch und Deutschmeister took precedence over Prince Archbishops, while the Komtur of Coblenz and the Komtur of Altshausen ranked *ex officio* as Counts of the Empire. Admission was much sought after – magnificent commanderies in the Rhineland, Westphalia, Austria or Bohemia made enviable homes for pious bachelor noblemen – but required sixteen quarterings of German nobility. The Order's little state on the Tauber river in Württemberg, ruled from Mergentheim (now Bad Mergentheim), consisted of some forty square miles of farmland with perhaps 200,000 inhabitants. Like that of most princely courts in Germany during the Age of the Baroque, life at the Hoch und Deutschmeister's court was a comfortable round of religious services, card games and hunting parties. His imposing '*Fürstenhof*' at Mergentheim was a massive schloss, patrolled by a handful of white-uniformed lifeguards.

The Teutonic Knights never forgot their lost lands, making a formal protest when the Elector of Brandenburg took possession of East Prussia on the extinction of his cousin Duke Albrecht's line in 1618, and again when the Elector crowned himself 'King in Prussia' at Königsberg in 1701. They too found a fine historian. In 1784 the Komtur Wilhelm Eugen Josef de Wal published the first volume of his monumental history of the Teutonic Order, which was dedicated to the Hoch und Deutschmeister of the time, Archduke Maximilian Franz. Wal, who wrote in French, is the Teutonic Vertot. His purpose was to justify the Knights' historic calling and to glorify their achievements. The Komtur was more scientific and less of a popularizer than Vertot, going straight to the primary sources, such as the chronicles of Petrus von Dusburg or Pusilge. In his view, articulate brethren had a duty to make known their order's traditions. He is still surprisingly readable.

During the seventeenth and eighteenth centuries the military orders of Spain and Portugal turned into convenient civil lists which provided their Knights with titles and pensions, even if in theory they were bound to recite a simple daily Office. Despite their decline, they remained prominent in Iberian life for many years to come. In 1625 there were 949 Knights of Santiago, 306 of Calatrava and 197 of Alcántara. Twenty years later, together with the Knights of Montesa, they founded the *Regimento de los Ordenes*, which survived in the Spanish army into the present century. Grandees continued to wear the *habito* or choir mantle with pride – in his self-portrait, Velasquez ostentatiously placed the red sword-cross of Santiago on his doublet. Clerigos and commanders lived according to their rules until the eighteenth century, when they grew impoverished and their priories fell into ruin. (The castle of Montesa was destroyed by an earthquake in 1748.) The military tradition was preserved by insisting that Knights must be army officers with eight years' service – many were Irish émigrés. Candidates had to show four generations of paternal and maternal nobility.

In Tuscany the Order of Santo Stefano was active until the late seventeenth century. One of its grand masters, the Grand Duke Ferdinand II (1621–70), sent galleys manned by his Knights to raid Greece and North Africa. He had statues of himself and of the Order's founder, Cosimo I, cast from captured Turkish cannon and placed outside the conventual church at Pisa, which was already filled with infidel trophies: standards, scimitars and shields. The island of Elba became the order's naval base. However, when the Tuscan Knights sailed with the Holy League in 1684, it was not only their first expedition for many years but their last. The cause of their decline was the pathological inertia of the effete Medici Grand Dukes. Even so, they retained a certain prestige, the title of Count being conferred on those who founded commanderies – which was how the Count of Monte-Cristo supposedly acquired his title in Dumas' novel.

Three new 'religions' were active in the Mediterranean during the seventeenth century. They were modelled on Santo Stefano, their Knights being allowed to marry. The Order of SS Maurice and Lazarus, established in 1572, was based on the leper-knights' former commanderies in Piedmont. The dukes of Savoy provided grand masters. Its Knights, who wore green cloaks with a white-and-green cross 'botonny', equipped and manned galleys, besides financing lazar houses. (Membership was a prerequisite for anyone who hoped to become a Knight of the august Piedmontese court order of the Annunziata.) In France the old leper knight commanderies were appropriated by Henri IV to create an 'Order of Our Lady of Mount Carmel and St Lazarus'. Louis XIV tried in vain to make it a rival of Malta, appointing as its Grand Master the Marquis de Dangeau, whose principal achievement was to devise 'habits' of white satin enhanced by purple cloaks.

The most interesting newcomer was the Constantinian Order of St George. Although claiming Byzantine origin, this had been founded in the sixteenth century by a family of Greek exiles from Albania called Angeli, who persuaded the Papacy to recognize its head as Pretender to the Eastern Empire. In 1680 some of its Knights fought for King John III Sobieski of Poland against the Turks at the relief of Vienna. In 1698 the grand mastership of the Order was bought from the last of the Angeli by Francesco Farnese, Duke of Parma. From 1717 to 1719, a Constantinian Regiment of 2,000 musketeers and grenadiers in royal-blue uniforms with red facings, officered by ten Knights, campaigned against the Turks in Dalmatia and Albania – the only time it went into action. In 1734 the grand mastership passed to the royal house of the Two Sicilies. Its cross was a gold-edged red cross fleury with a gold chi-rho monogram, its choir mantle sky-blue.

The last military religious order to be founded was the Bavarian Order of St George, Defender of the Faith, in 1729. The founder was the Elector Charles Albert (later the Holy Roman Emperor Charles VII) and the statutes were approved by Pope Benedict XIV. They were later amended by the Elector Charles Theodore in 1778. The Grand Masters were the Heads of the House of Wittelsbach, in later years kings of Bavaria, while the Grand Priors were Princes of the Blood. The membership consisted of 100 of Bavaria's most distinguished Catholic noblemen, who had to show thirty-two quarterings. The Order's cross was eight-pointed like that of Malta, with a gold ball at each point and a white border, a gold medallion in the centre bearing a representation of St George.

Whatever some historians may imply, the seventeenth and eighteenth centuries were far from being a Baroque sunset for military orders. They flourished right up to the destruction of the *ancien régime*. If less austere than when they were in the Holy Land or on the Baltic, they nevertheless continued to produce not only fine soldiers and fighting seamen but dedicated religious as well.

VIII

SURVIVAL –
AGAINST ALL ODDS
1789–1995

'The last aristocrats, men from a single social and even religious caste whose very existence is not suspected by the man in the street.'

Roger Peyrefitte, *Chevaliers de Malte*

SURVIVAL – AGAINST ALL ODDS

Although the military religious orders no longer wage war, most of them survive in some form. They have done so despite a savage and sustained onslaught by the French Revolution, by Napoleon, by Hitler and by Marxist Socialism, not to mention intermittent attacks by a whole host of lesser enemies. The Knights of Malta have proved best at weathering cruel storms, not least because of their hospitaller tradition and religious calling. Ironically, another of the reasons for their survival also explains why they have acquired so many enemies: the fact that they provide the last defendable bastions of hereditary nobility. They alone preserve the mystique of rank and birth in a world which finds aristocracy not merely alien but incomprehensible. For the military orders are the final refuge of the *ancien régime*.

Predictably, the French Revolution was hostile to military orders. There were demands for the suppression of French commanderies, numerous pamphlets attacking 'monks in arms'. The commanderies survived for a time because of the value of France's trade with Malta, but in 1791 it was discovered that the Order of Malta had subsidized Louis XVI's unsuccessful flight to Varennes. The suppression of the three French Grand Priories which ensued, and the consequent loss of revenue, were a very serious blow to the Knights.

In 1797, when he was planning his expedition to Egypt, General Bonaparte reported

400 knights and at most a regiment of 500 men are the only defence of La Valette's city. The inhabitants, numbering more than 100,000, are

well disposed towards us and hate the Chevaliers who can no longer feed themselves and are dying of hunger. I have purposely had their Italian property confiscated. With Malta and Cyprus we will be masters of the Mediterranean.

It would give the Corsican parvenu – who once described the Order as 'an institution to support in idleness the younger sons of privileged families' – real pleasure to destroy this maritime Bastille. On 9 June 1798 a French fleet appeared off Valetta with 29,000 troops on board.

If the shrewd and courageous Emmanuel de Rohan had still been Grand Master, Malta might well have survived even an attack by Napoleon Bonaparte. But Rohan had died in 1797 and his successor, Fra' Ferdinand von Hompesch zu Bolheim, titular Bailiff of Brandenburg, was little more than a petulant figurehead whom the Knights elected merely because he was a German, in the vain hope that this would endear their Order to the Habsburg Emperor at Vienna. Hompesch announced that he had no military skills, handing over the defence's conduct to the Congregation of War, which meant that the Knights were led by a war office instead of a general. Moreover, there were enemies within the walls; not French, as has been claimed by Francophobes or misinformed historians, but Spaniards whose country was an ally of France. The Spanish envoy ordered Spanish Knights not to fight, and they refused to take any part in the defence. Later the envoy welcomed the invaders.

Although many of the 250 brethren on the island were too old to bear arms, others were ready to fight to the death, and especially French Knights embittered by the Revolution. Their mistake was attempting to defend all Malta and Gozo instead of withdrawing inside their impregnable fortifications, where they could have held out for three months or until the English Mediterranean fleet arrived. Had they done so, the attackers would certainly have sailed on. But early reverses in small engagements demoralized the Maltese, who began to desert. Some Knights were undismayed, such as the Bailiff de La Tour du Pin and 16 young brethren who manned the guns themselves when their troops fled, or the Bailiff Tommasi who tried to make a stand with unarmed men, or the bedridden old Bailiff de Tigné who had himself carried on to the walls. Then the Maltese mutinied, and the citizens begged the Grand Master to make peace. Hompesch lost his nerve, asking for an armistice. (La Tour du Pin was convinced that German freemasons had ordered him to surrender.) Bonaparte entered Valetta on 12 June and the Knights were swiftly evicted from Malta. If anyone was to blame for their humiliating collapse, it was the Grand Master Hompesch.

Although Hompesch never abdicated, in 1799 a group of Knights illegally elected the Emperor Paul of Russia as Grand Master. When this bizarre episode was ended by his death in 1801, the restoration of Malta to the Knights seemed assured, but the English, who had captured the island from the French, refused to give it up. The Spanish Grand Priories were confiscated in 1802, those of Germany, Venice and Lombardy in 1806, those of Rome, Capua and Barletta in 1808 and those of Russia in 1810. The handful of Knights who formed the ruling body of the Order took refuge in Sicily but the Sicilian Grand Priory was lost in 1826. The Grand Priory of Crato in Portugal went in 1834. Only the Grand Priory of Bohemia remained in the Order's possession, together with the Austrian commanderies of the former Grand Priory of Germany. It looked as though there was very little future indeed for the Knights of Malta.

In 1786 there were still a hundred Teutonic Knights with nearly fifty conventual chaplains. But in 1802 they lost most of their Rhineland commanderies, and in 1809 the rest of their German lands were confiscated by Napoleon, Mergentheim going to the King of Württemberg. The Teutonic Order was reduced to two bailiwicks in Austria. Perhaps Napoleon's dislike was fuelled by the knowledge that Archduke Charles, who defeated him briefly at Aspern in 1810, had been Hoch und Deutschmeister from 1801 to 1804.

At the beginning of the nineteenth century the four Spanish Orders of Santiago, Calátrava, Alcántara and Montesa possessed some 200 commanderies among them. Often these were ruinous, but they were surrounded by rich estates whose revenues provided excellent incomes. There were also numerous houses of clerigos and commanders. Most were sacked more than once during the Peninsular War. It was the same with the three Portuguese Orders of Aviz, São Tiago and Christ.

Everywhere the political climate was implacably hostile towards the heirs of the monks of war.

Nevertheless, when the Napoleonic Wars ended, the Sovereign Military Order of Malta refused to despair. If Venice, the *Serenissima*, had vanished beyond recall, Valetta the *Humilissima* could be restored in exile, since new citizens could be found for it from among the nobles of Catholic Christendom. The age of Sir Walter Scott sympathized with the Knights, despite the politicians. (It was Scott who said that Valetta was a city for gentlemen built by gentlemen.) At least one politician was well disposed, the Austrian chancellor Prince Metternich, a member of the Order and for decades the most powerful man in Europe. The Grand Priory of Rome was re-established in 1816. As early as 1806 Gustavus IV of Sweden – who had been made a Knight of Malta by Tsar Paul – wished to give the Knights the Baltic island of Gotland, while in 1815 Metternich suggested Elba but with the unacceptable proviso that the Habsburgs should have the right to nominate Grand Masters. In the 1840s Ferdinand II of Naples (Grand Master of the Constantinian Order) offered them Ponza off the Neapolitan coast, but their fighting days were over.

When Lieutenant Master Busca left Sicily in 1825, Pope Leo XII, a former member of the Order, gave him a convent at Ferrara. Nine years later, Gregory XVI told the Lieutenant Master Candida to install himself in the Order's former embassy at Rome, a palazzo at the foot of the Spanish Steps. Candida re-established the novitiate, taking over a hospice at the Ponte Sisto where once again novices served 'My Lords the Sick' as in the days before 1798. The Grand Priories of Barletta, Capua and Messina were restored in 1839 as the Grand Priory of Naples and Sicily, as were those of Lombardy and Venice in the same year, also as a single Grand Priory. New commanderies were endowed in Italy and Austria, while national associations were founded all over Europe. Everywhere there was a return to hospitaller ideals. Neapolitan Knights financed an operating theatre at Naples from 1859. German and Austrian Knights organized nursing in the Danish War of 1864, the Austro-Prussian War of 1866 and the Franco-Prussian War of 1870, while the Order was represented at the Second International Red Cross Conference in 1869.

In 1878 Pope Leo XIII appointed the first Grand Master since 1805, Fra' Giovanni-Battista Ceschi a Santa Croce. The Order's sovereignty was recognized by several Catholic states; Austria had never ceased to do so. Its nursing services increased steadily. During the First World War it ran field-hospitals and hospital trains for the Austro-Hungarian and Italian armies. By 1921 it was supporting homes and clinics at Rome, Naples, London and Paris, and near Jerusalem. It numbered 1,800 members of all grades, including forty Knights of Justice in vows and 250 Knights of Honour and Devotion – not in vows but with the necessary proofs of nobility.

The Teutonic Knights also recovered during the nineteenth century. In 1834 Emperor Francis I gave them sovereign status within Austrian territory. Yet while the Order retained impressive commanderies, such as the castle of Bozen (Bolzano) in the Tyrol or the Deutscheshof at Vienna with its beautiful Gothic church, his gesture seemed a little hollow, since there were only eleven Knights. It looked as if the Order might die out. However Archduke Maximilian Joseph, who became Hoch und Deutschmeister in 1835, initiated a restoration of hospitaller and pastoral activities. Hospitals and schools were founded, sisters being recruited to staff them; the order's priests took on parish work, living together in community. Archduke Wilhelm, who succeeded Maximilian in 1863, introduced the *Ehrenritter* or Knights of Honour, modelled on those of Malta and recruited from the greatest German families of the Habsburg monarchy. There were

15. Book plate of the last Hoch und Deutschmeister, *c.* 1894

also the '*Marianer*' or distinguished friends of the Order, who wore a neck cross very like that of the Knights.

Professed Knights continued to form the heart of the Teutonic Order. In 1914 there were twenty of them, together with thirty Knights of Honour. They had to show sixteen quarterings, that each great-great-grandparent had been of German noble birth, and they took vows of poverty, chastity and obedience. They grew beards as the rule stipulated. The habit was a white tunic with a large black cross and a white cloak with a similar cross, black thigh boots and a plumed black hat being worn on ceremonial occasions. All were serving or former serving officers of the Imperial and Royal army like their superior, who remained colonel of the *Hoch und Deutschmeister* Regiment. A crack infantry corps, this had many battle honours and a famous band. On the eve of the First World War, the Order supported nine hospitals, seventeen schools and fifty parishes, run by two congregations of priests and four of sisters.

Archduke Eugen, who became Hoch und Deutschmeister in 1887, was both a devout religious and an Austrian general who played an important role in defeating the Italians at Caporetto in 1917. Throughout the Great War, like the Order of Malta the Teutonic Order financed and staffed field-hospitals, the Marianer serving as ambulance-drivers or stretcher-bearers.

After the fall of the monarchy, the Austrian republic resented the Teutonic Order as a 'Habsburg fiefdom'. In 1923, in order to ensure its survival, Archduke Eugen handed over his powers to the priest brethren, who accepted his abdication with the utmost reluctance. Six years later they reorganized the Order as a mendicant brotherhood of priests, one of whom was elected Hochmeister – no longer Hoch und Deutschmeister. No more Knights were professed, though Knights of Honour (who no longer needed proofs of nobility) were sometimes created. The priest brethren retained the white cloak with its great black cross.

In 1874 Pope Pius IX united the four Spanish orders under a conventual prior at Ciudad Real in La Mancha, who was nominated by the king. Each order preserved some degree of autonomy and kept its distinctive cross. Open only to great noblemen, the membership of all four, including *freyles caballeros* and *clerigos*, amounted to fewer than 200.

In 1916 Alfonso XIII took the title 'Master of the Four Orders', a title of which he was extremely proud. Not only did he wear the white *habito* with the four crosses during their ceremonies at Ciudad Real, but he had the crosses embroidered on the inside breast-pocket of all his suits.

By contrast, the Portuguese military orders, dispossessed in the 1830s, never recovered. They survived vestigially in the form of national orders of merit. As their Master, on state occasions the King of Portugal wore an enamelled badge which bore the three crosses of Aviz, Christ and São Thiago. A similar badge is still worn by the Portuguese president.

Persecution came again in the 1930s. After the *Anschluss* Hitler dispersed the Teutonic Order, confiscating its property and harrying its members because of its Habsburg associations. The Spanish orders had fallen into abeyance when King Alfonso abdicated. During the Civil War two of Calatrava's convents of commendadoras were sacked, but luckily their other house was safe at Burgos. The Order of Malta's most famous convent of nuns in Spain, Sigena, was destroyed by Republicans in 1936.

The Knights of Malta weathered the mid-twentieth century, though they lost their ancient commanderies in Bohemia. There was talk of giving them Rhodes during the 1930s and again in the late 1940s, of Ibiza in the 1950s, talk which sadly came to nothing. However, they enjoy excellent relations with the government of Malta and once more occupy Fort St Angelo.

The Palazzo Malta (the Order's headquarters) in Via Condotti at Rome and its villa on the Aventine are extra-territorial – the world's smallest sovereign state. The Order exchanges ambassadors with more than forty countries, issuing passports. (King Umberto of Italy travelled on an Order of Malta passport.) The Grand Master and the bailiffs who govern the some 10,000 Knights, Dames and Chaplains are mainly Knights of Justice – noblemen who take vows of poverty, chastity and obedience.*

In Europe recruitment is balanced between the old ruling class and the new élite, but the emphasis remains aristocratic. At the time of writing the President of the French Association is Prince Guy de Polignac, and almost every French bailiff descends from men who held government office under the *ancien régime* or the Restoration. King Juan Carlos's present successor as President of the Spanish Association is the Marqués de Pelerinat, Grandee of Spain. The President of the Portuguese Knights is the Marquez de Monfalim. Don Francesco Colonna, Duke of Garigliano, has

---

* A Knight of Justice in Britain must show that all his four grandparents had inherited arms or that his family has been noble in the male line for three hundred years. Nobility is defined as possession of a coat of arms on record at the College of Arms in England or at the Lion Court of Chivalry in Scotland.

been succeeded as President of the Italian Association by Don Giovan-Pietro dei Duchi Caffarelli. The President of the German Knights is Prince Johannes Loewenstein-Wertheim-Freudenberg. The Prince Grand Prior of Austria is Fra' Wilhelm Prince Liechtenstein (whose Knights include ten Habsburg Archdukes). The Lieutenant of the Grand Priory of Bohemia, where the Order has recovered its commanderies, is Franz Prince Lobkowicz. The President of the Polish Association is Count Tarnowski, of the Belgian the Prince de Ligne.

The 'Recusants', those old Catholic landed families who have always stayed faithful to Rome, form the backbone of the British Association. In the New World, however, the Associations of the United States and Australia consist almost entirely (though not exclusively) of Knights of Magistral Grace, who are not asked for proofs of nobility. Mainly of Irish-American descent, they are frequently men of great wealth and influence.

The heart of the Order continues to be the professed Knights of Justice, of whom there are about forty. The rite of profession – the taking of solemn vows of poverty, chastity and obedience – is the living link with the men who died at Hattin or at Acre, and who triumphed at Malta in 1565. The sword is blessed before Mass, sprinkled with holy water and presented to the kneeling, red-coated candidate, who is told: 'Wound no man unjustly.' The candidate is then girded with a sword-belt, exhorted to be chaste and to practise the cardinal virtues: prudence, justice, fortitude and temperance. Golden spurs are fastened to his heels, a 'spur for the heart', reminding him to hold gold in contempt.

The new Knight is then made a monk. Clothed with the black habit, he is told that it commemorates the Baptist's camel-hair and must be worn as a penance for sins, that the points of its cross stand for the eight beatitudes. He is given a stole embroidered with emblems of the Crucifixion to keep him always in mind of the 'Bitter Passion of Our Lord Jesus Christ'. On ceremonial occasions he wears a red military uniform with white facings under a black choir-mantle with a white eight-pointed cross on the left shoulder. (Those not in vows have similar uniforms, with black facings, but generally wear black habits or 'choir-mantles' with a white cross in outline on the breast.)

Professed Knights live a monastic life in the world, while in some ways Knights not in vows resemble Franciscan tertiaries. The Order's hospitaller activities range from Peru to Pakistan, from California to Eastern Europe – funding and administering hospitals, providing ambulance brigades and sending medical supplies to areas stricken by natural disaster. German Knights sponsor the *Malteser Hilfendienst*, one of the largest relief and rescue operations in the world.

16. Hospitallers practising their vocation

However, the first precept of all Knights of Malta is *'tuitio fidei'*. Membership of the Order imposes the solemn duty, at all times and in all circumstances, of defending the Faith as enshrined in the teachings, doctrines and traditions of the Holy Roman Catholic and Apostolic Church, and of owing a particular personal loyalty to His Holiness the Pope as Christ's Vicar on earth and the supreme authority of his 'Religion' – the Order. This duty takes precedence of every other obligation. The Knights have never forgotten that, nearly nine hundred years ago, they were founded by a papal bull.

In recent years British members of the Order of Malta have been delighted by the election of the first English Grand Master for seven centuries and by the restoration of the ancient Grand Priory of England. In 1988 Fra' Andrew Bertie became the 78th Grand Master. He is a collateral descendant of Sir Edward Bellingham, Knight of Malta and last Commander of Dinmore in Herefordshire from 1530 to 1540. The Italian press's fascinated interest in the election of the *'papa crociato'* – the Crusader Pope – underlined the Order's enormous prestige in modern Italy. In 1993 the pope gave permission for the restoration of the Grand Priory of England, founded during the twelfth century but dissolved by Henry VIII and again by Elizabeth I. A minimum of five Knights of Justice is required by the Code de Rohan (the Order's legal code) for the establishment or re-establishment of a Grand Priory. Fortunately there were now seven English Knights in vows or preparing to take vows. The 55th Grand Prior of England is Fra' Matthew Festing, the Field Marshal's son.

After the Second World War the Teutonic Order proved highly successful at re-establishing itself in Austria and in northern Italy in its new clerical form. Currently (1995) it numbers about forty priests, ten brethren preparing to be priests and ten lay-brothers, with nearly 300 sisters, and has a fine hospital in Carinthia. The Hochmeister is Pater Dr Arnold Wieland OT.

The last professed Teutonic Knight died in 1970 – he had become a priest of the Order – and there is very little prospect of his ancient vocation being revived. However, there are twelve Teutonic Knights of Honour (among them Prince Franz-Josef of Liechtenstein) who wear the white cloak. There is also an Association of Friends (*Familiaren*) of the Teutonic Order, whose 600 members have taken the place of the *Marianer*. On ceremonial occasions they wear a black cloak with a white Teutonic shield and the old *Marianer* neck-cross.

The Order's headquarters are at the Deutscheshof in Vienna, with its beautiful Gothic church and treasury. In 1957 the Order recovered another historic commandery, the Sachsenhaus at Frankfurt. (The Marienburg, destroyed by Russian bombardment in 1944, has been magnificently rebuilt and restored by the Polish authorities.) Until a few years ago, a handful of the Order's priests in the Tyrol used horses to visit their mountain parishes, and it was oddly moving to see horsemen ride by who were clad in the Teutonic Knights' white cloak with its great black cross.

In Spain new *freyles caballeros* of Santiago, Calatrava, Alcántara and Montesa were at last admitted in 1986, the first for fifty-six years. The Grand Master and Perpetual Administrator of the Four Orders is, of course, King Juan Carlos, who appoints a Dean-President of the Council. The first was the king's father, the late Count of Barcelona, who has been succeeded by HRH Prince Carlos de Borbon y Borbon. The Prior is the Bishop of Ciudad Real, whose cathedral is the church of the Priorate of the Military Orders. The heir to the throne, Don Felipe, Prince of the Asturias, is a Knight of Santiago and has been clothed with the white *habito*, which still bears the red sword-cross of St James. Once again there are a Clavero of Calatrava and Clavero of Alcántara, each with the gold key of his office. Four quarterings of nobility are required for admission, and membership is restricted to Spain's proudest families, those of the Grandees – there are fewer than 150 *freyles caballeros* and *novicios*. The Knights promise to place their personal fortunes at the Grand Master's disposal, to observe marital chastity, and to defend the doctrine of the Immaculate Conception.

The Constantinian Order of St George is one of the last links with the old Kingdom of Naples, its 28th Grand Master being HRH Prince Ferdinand Maria, Duke of Castro, Head of the Royal House of Bourbon Two Sicilies. It is deeply respected throughout Italy and not just in the Mezzogiorno, with over 1,000 members. A former President of Italy, Francesco Cossiga, was a Grand Cross while the Italian government allows its diplomats and army officers to wear the insignia. To some extent it is an international order; among its Knights are the Pretenders to six thrones, nine Nobel prizewinners, a former Secretary-General of NATO and several members of the House of Lords. There is a British Association whose President is Lord Mowbray, Segrave and Stourton. Relations with the Church are excellent, over twenty Cardinals having accepted its Grand Cross. There are also close links with the Order of Malta. The Constantinian Knights support specific charitable works, those in Britain contributing to the relief of drug addicts and alcoholics.

Like the Order of Malta, the Constantinian Order is now a stronghold of what might be called Italy's 'old establishment'. So too is another dynastic military order, that of SS Maurice and Lazarus, whose Grand Master is Crown Prince Victor Emmanuel, although, unlike the last two, it is not recognized by the Italian government. From having become a national order of merit under the kings of Italy, this has now reverted to its origins and has been transformed into a redoubt for the Piedmontese aristocracy and a focus of sympathy for the House of Savoy. It too has a small British Association, whose President is the Earl of Erroll, hereditary Lord High Constable of Scotland.

Yet another Italian order of this sort, which is showing signs of revival, is that of Santo Stefano in Tuscany, the present Grand Master being the Grand Duke Sigismondo.

In Germany the Bavarian Order of St George continues to thrive. Its Grand Master is HRH Albrecht, Duke of Bavaria (Stuart Pretender to the throne of England). The Grand Prior is

Crown Prince Franz of Bavaria and the commanders are all Wittelsbach princes. The Order has 100 Knights, each with thirty-two quarterings, and supports a hospital. It is very much respected in Bavaria, where a good deal of monarchist sentiment still exists. The Order of St George's headquarters are at the royal palace of Nymphenburg.

Monks booted and spurred, carrying swords – much about the military religious orders may seem strange and alien. Perhaps this is why their achievements have never received the recognition they deserve, whether as the first properly staffed and officered troops in Western Europe since Roman times, or as colonists and fighting seamen.

The Knights of today's orders no longer go out to battle but concentrate on their hospitaller calling. So long as they keep their traditions and their patrician character, they will survive. Should they abandon either, however, they will soon die – having lost that cachet which attracts recruits, to fade away as short-lived imitations of the Red Cross. But if the Knights remain steadfast, then they will enter the second millennium to serve Our Lords the Sick for centuries to come.

APPENDICES:
ORDERS OF ST JOHN
IN THE MODERN WORLD

APPENDIX I

THE GRAND PRIORY OF ENGLAND

The Order of Malta restored its Grand Priory of England in 1993, with the Vatican's permission, after being in abeyance for nearly 450 years. Henry VIII had dissolved the Order in England in 1540, confiscating its property. The Priory had been briefly restored by Queen Mary, only to be have its lands seized again by Elizabeth I in 1559.

Despite the Reformation, there were always English, Scots or Irish Knights of Malta. Until the end of the eighteenth century most of the Englishmen and Irishmen tended to join the Langue of Italy, while Scotsmen usually joined the French Langues. Titular Grand Priors were appointed, together with titular Priors of Ireland and Bailiffs of Egle.

Several attempts were made to restore the Grand Priory. The first was by Sir Nicholas Fortescue, a descendant of Blessed Adrian Fortescue, who became a Knight of Justice in 1639; but, although he secured the support of Queen Henrietta Maria, the Civil War put an end to the project. The Duke of Berwick – James II's natural son by Arabella Churchill – who joined the Order in 1687, made a second attempt and was appointed titular Grand Prior by Grand Master Carafa. When his father was deposed, Berwick raised a red-coated force to fight for him in Ireland: it was known as the Grand Prior's Regiment. The Duke was followed as Grand Prior by two of his sons, Lord Peter and Lord Anthony Fitzjames. (At least two-thirds of today's British Knights have Jacobite ancestors, direct or collateral, who fought for the Stuarts in the '15 or the '45, or who served in the armies of the Catholic powers with commissions signed by James III.) The Anglo-Bavarian Langue, established in 1782 and composed mainly of Germans and Poles, was recognized as the successor of the Langue of England but came to an end in 1806. The last titular Grand Prior of England was appointed in the same year, Fra' Girolamo Laparelli, 54th Grand Prior, who died in 1815.

The Order was never without British Knights, even if not all of them were Knights of Justice. Two prominent examples during the first half of the nineteenth century were Prince Nugent (1777–1862), an Austrian field marshal and titular Prior of Ireland, and the last Catholic Earl of Shrewsbury, who founded a commandery. Sir George Bowyer, Bt., MP, became a Knight of Justice in 1851 and established the Order's British Association in 1875, building the church which is now in St John's Wood. Among its early presidents were Lord Ashburnham and the Earl of Granard, Master of the Horse – from whom Queen Victoria's son, later to be Edward VII, received the honorary cross of a Bailiff Grand Cross in 1882; he wore it during a visit to Malta after his accession to the throne. (His father, the Prince Consort, had also received an honorary cross.) Those in this century have included Lord North, Viscount FitzAlan of Derwent (the last Viceroy of Ireland), the Earl of Iddesleigh, the Earl of Gainsborough, Major-General Viscount Monckton of Brenchley, Sir Peter Hope and Lord Craigmyle.

In 1946 Pope Pius XII encouraged the Order to restore the Grand Priory of England, but, although six English novice Knights of Justice were available, this attempt too came to nothing. In 1972 the Sub-Priory of Blessed Adrian Fortescue was founded, with Lord Robert Crichton-Stuart as Regent. Subsequent Regents included the future Grand Master, Fra' Andrew Bertie, Fra' Anthony (Viscount) Furness, the Earl of Gainsborough and the present Grand Prior, Fra' Matthew Festing.

The Order's statutes stipulate that five Knights of Justice, monk-knights, are needed for the erection of a Grand Priory. By 1993 there were seven such Knights in England, together with nearly twenty Knights of Obedience – who make a single promise of obedience instead of taking vows. The new Grand Prior of England, Fra' Matthew, had entered the Order in 1977, taking his solemn vows in 1992. (His father, the late Field Marshal Sir Francis Festing, had also been a member of the Order.) Fra' Matthew is the fifty-fifth in succession to Fra' Walter, who was appointed Prior in 1144.

APPENDIX 2

THE ORDER OF MALTA
IN NORTH AMERICA

Several Knights of Malta played a most distinguished role in early Canadian history. They included Samuel de Champlain's first sponsor and three of his comrades. Among them were the first governors of both New France and Acadia (Nova Scotia), the first '*seigneur*' in Acadia and the founder of the settlement at La Hève. A Knight was also the first to propose a settlement at Chebucto – now Halifax.

Aymar de Clermont de Chaste of the Langue of Auvergne, Vice Admiral of France, was appointed Lieutenant-General of New France by Henry IV in 1602 but died the following year, though not before sponsoring Champlain's first exploration of the St Lawrence River. In 1632, on behalf of the Company of New France, the Commander Isaac de Razilly (a kinsman of Cardinal Richelieu) organized an expedition of settlers to Quebec and to Acadia, assisted by Champlain and two other Knights, Marc-Antoine Brasdefer de Chateaufort and Charles-Jacques Huault de Montmagny. A veteran soldier, Fra' Isaac had lost an eye during the siege of La Rochelle and had campaigned in Morocco. During the same year of 1632 he was appointed Viceroy of New France, Governor of Acadia and Seigneur of the Île Sainte-Croix and of Port-Royal. He wrote to Grand Master Paule, suggesting that a Priory of the Order should be established at Port-Royal (later Annapolis) or at Chebucto, but the proposal was not accepted. He died in Acadia in 1635, being buried at the gate of Fort Sainte-Marie-de-Grâce in his settlement of La Hève. Fra' Isaac had been devoted to Canada which he described as 'an earthly paradise'.

Chateaufort was interim governor of Quebec from Champlain's

death in 1635 until the arrival of Montmagny, the following year. Montmagny – a fine seaman who had fought a notably successful action against the Turks off Rhodes in 1627 – built the second château of Saint-Louis, adorning its walls with the order's eight-pointed cross; the battered stone bearing the cross is now on the main gate of the Château Frontenac Hotel, which stands on the site of the former residence of the Governors of New France. During his governorship, which lasted until 1648, Montmagny's Lieutenant was another Knight, Fra' Antoine Brehaut de l'Isle, who commanded the garrison at Trois-Rivières. Montmagny died in 1653 on the Isle Sainte-Christophe (St Kitts-Nevis), when it was part of the Order's short-lived Caribbean colony.

Other members of the Order prominent in New France during the seventeenth century were Fra' Hector d'Andigné de Grandfontaine, Governor of Acadia from 1670 to 1673; Fra' Thomas de Crisafy, who commanded Canada's troops and died at Montreal in 1696; and Mgr Jean-Baptiste de Saint-Vallier, who became the second Bishop of Quebec – a prelate whose influence on Canadian Catholicism can be felt even today.

During the eighteenth century the Commander Constantin-Louis d'Estourmel, a Knight of the Langue of France, commanded the French fleet which carried out an expedition to recapture Louisbourg from the British in 1746. Fra' Félicien de Bernetz, Colonel of the Royal-Roussillon regiment, played a leading role in the defence of Quebec against the English and Americans in 1759. Another Knight of Malta who took an important part in the defence of Quebec was François-Claude de Bourlamaque, Colonel of Infantry. The son of their general, the heroic Marquis de Montcalm, entered the Order in 1744.

Although there had always been one or two Canadian Knights, the Order's Canadian Association was not founded until 1952. One of its presidents, Quintin Jeremy Gwyn, became Grand Chancellor of the Order and was the first Knight from the New World to be elected to the Sovereign Council. However, the best-known modern Canadian Knight is undoubtedly General Georges P. Vanier (1886–1967) who was Governor-General of Canada at the time of his death, having previously served with great distinction in Canada's army and diplomatic corps. A most saintly man, his cause is being considered for beatification.

The Canadian Association now numbers about 250 members. So far, it is unique among the Order's Associations in both the Old World and the New in having had a Knight of Justice as its President, Fra' John MacPherson. It concentrates on support for gerontologic institutes and assessment centres besides helping refugees from south-east Asia and eastern Europe. There is also the Quebec Service of Order of Malta Auxiliaries.

It is not too much to say that a Knight of Malta was largely responsible for winning the American War of Independence. In 1781 Admiral de Grasse made it impossible for the British Navy to relieve Yorktown, ensuring General Cornwallis's surrender. (The Admiral had entered the Order as a boy but did not take vows in order to marry.) Many of the best sailors in the old French Navy, the '*Marine Royale*', learnt their seamanship in the Order of Malta's galleys. The greatest of them all, the Bailli de Suffren, was France's other outstanding Admiral during the War of Independence. Among the professed Knights who commanded French ships of the line during that war were Pierre-Louis de Sambuçy and Jean-Louis-Charles de Coriolis d'Espinousse – the latter being one of Admiral de Grasse's *chefs-d'escadron* at Chesapeake Bay and at Yorktown.

Over twenty Knights fought in the war, fourteen becoming members of the Society of Cincinnati, founded by George Washington for officers of the American Continental Army and their descendants. One of the Order's Chaplains of Obedience, the Canadian-born François-Louis-Eustache Chartier de Lotbinière, served as a Catholic chaplain in the very largely Protestant Continental Army and received a pension from Congress.

In 1794 Grand Master Rohan explored the possibility of the Order acquiring a small territory in the United States, his intermediary being Fra' Jean de Cibon of the Priory of Aquitaine, who had been the Order's *chargé d'affaires* in Paris. In return, the

Knights offered to protect all American shipping in the Mediterranean from the still very real threat of Algerian piracy. However, the American minister at Paris, the future President Monroe, proved uncooperative.

During the nineteenth century, several Knights from the United States entered the Order. The Americans have always possessed an aristocracy though, for historical reasons, it has never been armigerous as in Europe. An American Association was founded in 1927, based in New York, which became renowned for spectacular fund-raising under the influence of the formidable Cardinal Spellman. Today it has over 1,700 members. Among its charitable activities is AmeriCares, which provides aid on a very lavish scale to many countries, especially in Latin America. For many years its President has been J. Peter Grace, who is also an extremely active member of AmeriCares. The senior chaplain is HE Cardinal O'Connor, Archbishop of New York.

The Western Association was formed in 1953, based in San Francisco, and now has 520 members, its president being the Knight of Obedience Peter Nigg. Among many fine works of charity, this association sends large parties of sick on the Order's annual pilgrimage to Lourdes despite the enormous distance and expense. It finances clinics and retirement homes and supports a hospital, the O'Connor Hospital, where it also gives assistance. The two senior chaplains are Mgr John Quinn, Archbishop of San Francisco, and HE Cardinal Roger Mahony, Archbishop of Los Angeles.

The third association in the United States, the Federal Association, was founded in 1974 and is based on Washington. It has 455 members, the President being the Hon. James A. Belson. It supports hospitals and clinics and encourages volunteer hospital visiting on a large scale, besides sending vast quantities of medical aid to Africa, the Caribbean and Central America. It too sends parties of the sick on the Lourdes pilgrimage, regardless of distance or expense. The chaplain is HE Cardinal James Hickey, Archbishop of Washington.

In January 1989 President Ronald Reagan accepted the Collar of the Order *pro Merito Melitensi*, which was conferred on him for his firm stand against abortion. The President was invested by the Prince and Grand Master himself, HMEH Fra' Andrew Bertie, at the American Association's annual dinner in New York. This was the first formal acknowledgement of the Order of Malta by a serving President of the United States of America. During a second visit to the United States in 1991, Fra' Andrew was received at the White House by President George Bush.

APPENDIX 3

THE JOHANITTERORDEN

The Protestant orders in Germany, Sweden, Holland, Finland and France, known collectively as the 'Alliance Orders of St John', claim descent from the old Hospitaller bailiwick of Brandenburg. While the Order of Malta cannot accept them as Knights of Malta, it acknowledges them as 'recognized orders of St John' – a formula propounded by the *Johanniter* themselves.

During the later Middle Ages the commanders of the Brandenburgh Ballei acquired considerable independence, with the right to elect their own *Herrenmeister*, whose seat was at Sonneberg from 1428. When the local Hohenzollern ruler turned Lutheran in 1538, most commanders followed suit and married but retained their commanderies, which they bequeathed to their heirs. From the end of the sixteenth century the office of Herrenmeister was generally held by a Hohenzollern. (The Order of Malta recovered five of the commanderies in 1648, so that there was also a Catholic Bailiff of Brandenburg.) During the seventeenth century the Herrenmeister became an ornament of the court at Berlin, commanding the Electress's Life Guards. In 1763 the then Herrenmeister Prince Ferdinand of Prussia, Frederick the Great's uncle, sent responsions (dues from his commanderies) to Grand Master Pinto, which were graciously accepted. Although never recognized as Knights of Malta, the commanders of the Brandenburg Ballei went on sending responsions and in 1787 began to wear the Order's red uniform.

In 1810 Prussian reformers persuaded King Frederick William III to abolish the Brandenburg Ballei as a 'feudal encumbrance', replacing it by a decoration called the Prussian Order of St John. However, in 1852 Frederick William IV, a romantic with a nostalgia for the Middle Ages, restored the Brandenburg Ballei; in the following year the Ballei's few survivors – none had been created since 1800 – met at Sonneberg to elect the king's nephew, Prince Frederick Karl, as Herrenmeister. He promptly wrote to the Order of Malta's Lieutenant Master, Fra' Philip Colloredo, demanding recognition. When this was refused, he formed a new order, the 'Knightly Order of the Hospital of St John of Jerusalem (Brandenburg Ballei)', recruiting 500 members from the noble families of north Germany. By 1890 it had founded nineteen hospitals.

The fall of the Hohenzollern monarchy in 1918 was a serious blow for the Johanniter, on account of its association with the dynasty. (It had become, and remains even today, a semi-dynastic order.) The Swedish Knights seceded, to form a separate order under their own sovereign. Nevertheless, the main branch survived very well in Weimar Germany, President Hindenburg proudly wearing the Johanniter cross on his uniform at all state occasions, as did many army officers. The climate changed under the Third Reich, Nazi Party members and their families being forbidden to belong to the Order; a dozen of its Knights were hanged in the aftermath of the 1944 plot, martyred for their opposition to Hitler. Then, as a result of the Russian invasion of 1945, the Johanniter lost its hospitals in East Germany where it had originated. It seemed that Sonneberg had gone for ever.

However, immediately after the war, the Allies were faced by the urgent need to provide emergency services in Western Germany, where hospitals and nursing services had collapsed. Since they found the Red Cross to be largely staffed by former members of the Nazi Party, the Allies turned to the two aristocratic hospitaller organizations, the Order of Malta and the Johanniter Order – the latter's Herrenmeister being Prince Oscar of Prussia, a younger son of the Emperor William II. The Federal Republic followed the Allies' example, recognizing the two orders as charities which had become national institutions. They continue to run jointly the republic's main ambulance service.

Today the Herrenmeister is HRH Prince Wilhelm-Karl of

Prussia, who presides over some 3,000 Knights of the Lutheran or Reformed faith. In addition to the ambulance service, they maintain nineteen old people's homes (sheltering 2,000 souls) as well as fifteen large hospitals with 3,500 beds. Annual government funding is in the region of DM 500 million. Although noble proofs are no longer demanded, most of the Order's senior officers bear names which would have been familiar enough at the old Prussian court. Following the reunification of Germany in 1989, they have recovered many of their hospitals and historic buildings in what was East Germany, including Sonneberg.

The Johanniterorden has a flourishing commandery in Austria, and a sub-commandery in Canada. There are autonomous Johanniter commanderies in Finland, Switzerland, Hungary and France.

The Order's full title is *Die Balley Brandenburg des ritterlichen Ordens St Johannis vom Spital zu Jerusalem.*

(For an account of its members' heroic contribution to the plot against Adolf Hitler, see Wilhelm-Karl Prinz von Preussen and Bernt Baron Freytag von Loringhoven, *Johanniter und der 20 Juli 1944*, Nieder-Weisel, 1985/1989.)

APPENDIX 4

THE VENERABLE ORDER OF ST JOHN

The Venerable Order of St John was founded in 1888 as an order of the British Crown. Its Sovereign is the Monarch, its Grand Prior the Duke of Gloucester, while it has a membership strong in Lord Lieutenants and Chief Constables. But though it occupies the old priory of the Knights of Malta at Clerkenwell and bears their eight-pointed cross as its insignia, it has no historical continuity whatever from the Order of Malta or the medieval Hospitallers. Far from being 'the oldest order of chivalry in the world', it is one of the newest.

Its early history is shrouded in obscurity. In *The Venerable Order of St John in the British Realm*, published at Clerkenwell in 1967, the late Sir Harry Luke – a senior bailiff – provided the fullest account which has yet appeared. He writes:

The activities of the Grand Priory of England were temporarily dislocated in 1540 when King Henry VIII, by an Act of his amenable Parliament, sequestrated its properties at the Dissolution of the Monasteries. What remained of the properties was restored to the Grand Priory in 1557 but was re-appropriated by the Crown under Queen Elizabeth I in 1559. Since Queen Mary's Letters Patent were never revoked, and Queen Elizabeth never formally dissolved the Order in England, the Grand Priory is properly to be regarded as having remained dormant until it was resuscitated in 1831, within the framework of the Church of England, on the initiative of a representative body of Knights of the SMOM known as the Capitular Commission. The continuity is in fact expressly defined in paragraph 1 of the Schedule to the Charter of Queen Victoria in the following terms: 'the Grand Priory of England is the Head of the Sixth or English Language of the Venerable Order of the Hospital of St John of Jerusalem'.

He continues:

The French body termed the 'Capitular Commission' consisted mainly of members of the three French tongues of Provence, Auvergne and France who for some years after the Napoleonic Wars represented the only effective force within the Sovereign Order, that Order which had not only lost its territorial possessions of the Maltese islands but had otherwise been despoiled and dispersed by the French Revolution and its aftermath.

The Grand Priory of England thus revived, and perforce separated from the original stem, became a British Order of Chivalry still dedicated to its original humanitarian objects, when Queen Victoria granted it her Royal Charter in 1888.

In a summarized and slightly modified account which Sir Harry contributed to the 1970 *Encyclopaedia Britannica*, he says of the alleged revival, 'The Sovereign Military Order at Rome at first accepted the step, then repudiated it in 1858.'

His account is based on serious misconceptions, though apparently it is still the Venerable Order's official version of its origins. For a more accurate picture, it is necessary to know the Order of Malta's history during the first quarter of the nineteenth century, and especially that of the 'Capitular Commission'.

The 'Commission of the French Langues' was certainly not 'the only effective force within the Sovereign Order'. Since the death of Grand Master Tommasi in 1805 it had been ruled by Lieutenant Masters, first from Catania in Sicily and then from Ferrara. (The Lieutenancy did not establish its seat at Rome until 1834.) The Order was still recognized as sovereign by the Holy See and by the Austrian Empire, whose all-powerful Chancellor, Prince Metternich, was a bailiff of the Order.

The French Commission was set up in 1814 to recover the Order's French estates, confiscated during the Revolution. In December of that year Louis XVIII approved legislation permitting the return to the Knights of property (mainly woodland) valued at 29 million francs, as soon as the Order acquired a territory which constituted an independent state. However, the Congress of Vienna declined to restore Malta to the Knights, while Metternich's offer of Elba was unacceptable since it entailed giving the Austrian Emperor the right to nominate a Grand Master. The legislation therefore remained in abeyance. Even so, the French government instructed the Chancellery of the Legion of Honour (which regulated orders and decorations in France) to grant official recognition to new Knights created by the Order.

In 1821 the Commission's secretary, the Commander Jean-Louis de Dienne from the former Langue of Auvergne, decided to retire on account of his great age. As his successor he nominated a mysterious figure whom Dienne (according to his niece) 'loved more than his own self', an adventurer of a type familiar enough in today's false orders of St John. This was the self-styled 'Marquis de Sainte-Croix-Molay', alias 'Duc de Santo-Germanie' or 'Sante Germiny', titles which do not appear in any *armorial* of the French nobility. Nor is he listed in the register at the Grand Magistery. His real name is still unknown. Although he may have received a cross from his Commission, it is unlikely that he was ever recognized as a Knight of Malta by the Lieutenancy, which referred to him in correspondence as 'the so-called [*soi-disant*] Marquis de Sainte-Croix-Molay'. Living under an assumed name, he could not produce evidence of his own identity, let alone furnish noble proofs.

The Commission had been supporting itself on passage money, fees charged for admission to the Order. French Knights (of whom about 700 were admitted between 1814 and 1825) had to pay 6,000 gold francs, donats 4,000. In consequence it was able to install itself in a resplendent 'Hôtel de la Chancellerie' at Paris. Soon Molay, promoted from Secretary to Chancellor, was planning to sell several thousand more crosses.

In 1823 Molay proposed that the Order of Malta should send a naval expedition to reconquer Rhodes, led by himself in the capacity of General of the Galleys; and he began negotiating with the Greeks. He seems to have interested the Comte de Villèle, the French Prime Minister, later claiming that the French government had offered him 'two ships of the line, two frigates, 500 half-pay officers, ammunition from Toulon and all sorts of assistance'. In order to finance the expedition, Molay and his associates (notably the 'Chevalier' Philippe Chastellain and a Mr Donald Currie) attempted to raise a loan of £640,000 on the London money-market through the bankers Hullet Bros. They also had a scheme for recruiting 4,000 new Knights of Malta and, without bothering to obtain the Lieutenancy's permission, set up a 'Priory of the Morea' for Greek Orthodox Knights, who were each to be charged 500 Venetian gold sequins for their knighthoods. (Among the few Greeks enlisted was 'Petros Bey, Prince of the Maniots'.)

Since it would destabilize the Ottoman Empire still further, the project was calculated to infuriate Prince Metternich, the Austrian Chancellor. Only in the Habsburg lands did the Order of Malta continue to flourish, retaining all its ancient Bohemian and Austrian commanderies, its palaces at Prague and Vienna. Lieutenant Master Busca dared not antagonize Metternich. Through the Order's *chargé d'affaires* at Vienna, he instructed the Austrian Chancellor's confidential bankers, Messrs Rothschild, to inform the London newspapers that the loan was unsound and thus effectively killed the scheme.

Some French historians take Molay's scheme seriously, but it bore no relation to reality. Whatever the case might have been during the Middle Ages, in the 1820s the Orthodox Greeks of Rhodes would scarcely have welcomed full-scale colonization by Catholic Frenchmen. The Vice-Chancellor Vella had good reason to write from Catania in March 1824 to the *chargé d'affaires* at Vienna that '*Le plan de guerre est ridicule, il ne manque rien, même pas un Don Quixote, Ste Croix* [Molay] . . .'

Vella noted in the same letter that the French Commission had disowned both the loan and the negotiations with the Greeks – '*elle rejette le crime sur le soi-disant Marquis de Ste Croix*'. Forced to resign, Molay had complained in a wildly unbalanced letter to the Lieutenancy of 'anarchy and sedition' in both Sicily and France. He also complained that the Commission was making Knights and Dames – the latter being given the title of Countess – 'without any of the accustomed formalities'. (He seems to imply that it was dispensing with noble proofs, though he can scarcely have been in a position to provide proofs of his own.) He prophesied that soon the Commission would consist only of 'legal advisers and married Knights'.

Busca ordered his envoy at Paris, the Bailiff Baron de Ferrette, to send a dossier on the Commission's activities to the French Foreign Minister and to ask him to stop them. The response was a royal decree in April 1824, announcing that henceforward the Chancellery of the Legion of Honour would recognize as Knights of Malta only those who had entered the Order in the time of the Grand Masters. However, in July the French government formally recognized the Lieutenancy, and the Chancellery agreed to acknowledge as Knights those who could produce diplomas issued from Catania; it refused to accept 'illegal nominations made by a pretended commission which sits at Paris'. M. de Villèle was offered and accepted the Grand Cross of Devotion.

Busca forbade the Commission to reassemble, or to reconstitute itself under any other name. Ignoring this explicit prohibition, the Commission reappeared early in 1826 as a 'Council', its members including Dienne, with Molay as *Grand* Chancellor. In April it convened a 'Chapter General' at Paris, where there was wild talk of nominating another Lieutenant Master in place of Busca but, since the Council had no legal existence, it could do nothing. (One historian, Cecil Torr, says that the meeting was broken up by the police.) Even so, it continued to sell admission to the Order, sending Busca letters in which it begged him to authorize these 'knighthoods' – letters which received no reply.

However, Molay refused to abandon his Rhodian scheme, for the climate of international politics looked more promising despite Prince Metternich's opposition. In 1826 the British Foreign Secretary, George Canning, proposed that France, Russia and England should help the Greeks to win their independence, and in

July 1827 the three governments signed a treaty with a secret clause in which they promised to use their navies jointly against the Turkish fleet.

In order to attract British support, Molay hit upon the idea of reviving the Grand Priory of England 'in Protestant form', the blueprint being presumably his stillborn 'Priory of the Morea' with its Orthodox brethren. His principal agent across the Channel was Mr Donald Currie, 'Colonial and General Outfitter of Regent Street, London', who had played a key role in trying to raise the loan. In 1826–7 a group of interested Englishmen visited Paris, where they were apparently introduced to Molay by a genuine Knight of Malta, Denis O'Sullivan, who had entered the Langue of France in 1783. The only one of these Englishmen whose name has survived is the Reverend Sir Robert Peat, absentee vicar of New Brentford in Middlesex.

Unlike the Marquis de Sainte-Croix-Molay and the Chevalier O'Sullivan, we know a good deal about Sir Robert Peat. Born in about 1770 in County Durham, he was the son of a watchmaker and silversmith in the Hamsterley area, and had been a 'Ten Year Man' at Trinity College, Cambridge – which meant acquiring a degree for money without the irksome obligation of having to read for it. He had served as a military chaplain during the Peninsular War and, although never presented to him, had been appointed 'chaplain extraordinary' to the Prince Regent. There were over 100 such chaplains but few, if any, of the others can have received the accolade as had Sir Robert, who derived his title from his questionable possession of the Polish Order of St Stanislas. A small, dandified man, he had some surprisingly unclerical ways. One source says that he was a heavy gambler, while he was undoubtedly a fortune-hunter. According to his obituary in the *Gentleman's Magazine* for October 1837, he had married and abandoned a very rich lady a quarter of a century older than himself. This was the grotesque and half-crazy Miss Jane Smith of Herrington House, County Durham, who had settled £1,000 a year on him before their wedding in 1815.

Why Peat wanted to be Grand Prior of England is unknown,

though obviously he was obsessed with orders of chivalry. (Someone who met him in about 1815 noticed that he was wearing three gold orders on his coat.) What is perfectly clear, however, is that he was convinced that the Council of the Three Langues had full authority to revive the Grand Priory.

'Articles of convention' were drawn up, dated 11 June 1826, and 24 August and 15 October 1827, authorizing the 'revival'. A similar document was produced to authorize a new loan on the London money-market, perhaps the main reason for 'reviving' the Grand Priory. Elegantly printed on the finest paper, with beautifully embossed seals, their wording is a masterpiece of equivocation:

We, Bailiffs, Grand Priors and Commanders composing the Venerable Council Ordinary of the Sovereign Order of St John of Jerusalem, representing the Langues of Provence, of Auvergne and of France, the Provincial Chapters and the Grand Priories, statutorily constituted under the Protection and Spiritual Authority of Our Lord His Holiness Pope Pius VII, in virtue of the Pontifical Bull of 10 August 1814, the Authorisation of the Lieutenant of the Magistracy and the Sovereign decisions of the Great and Sacred Council sitting at the headquarters [chef-lieu] at Catania of 9 October in the same year, to our Venerable Brethren, Greetings in Jesus Christ. Forasmuch as that from this we have the right and the power . . .

The 'bull' of 1814 had been a brief (Papal letter) and not a bull, bestowing no more than a formal blessing, while, as has been seen, the Lieutenant Master and the Sacred Council had *withdrawn* their authorization. But Peat and his friends were completely taken in by the articles of convention, which would one day be seen as the title deeds of the 'Grand Priory of England in Protestant Form'. London bankers were less trusting, and the loan failed to materialize; no doubt Messrs Rothschild had dispelled any illusions. There was no reconquest of Rhodes, and for three years nothing more was heard of the revival.

In 1830 Molay came up with a fresh plan. Algiers was about to be conquered by the French – could it not be given to the Order of Malta as a colony? The Papal Nuncio at Paris, Lambruschini (a member of the Order), was enthusiastic until told by the French Prime Minister, the Prince de Polignac, that Algiers was going to need a garrison of 20,000 troops. Anxious for British support, Molay announced that some English gentlemen were urging their own Prime Minister, the Duke of Wellington, to revive the Grand Priory, but no evidence has been found to support this statement. The Algerian plan ended abruptly with the July Revolution, since the new Orléanist regime had no time for Knights of Malta.

Now that the market had finally dried up in France, Molay was understandably eager to proceed with the revival of the Grand Priory. At London on 31 January 1831 Molay's 'delegate', M. Philippe Chastellain (a future drawing-master at Edinburgh and inmate of a debtors' prison), solemnly invested Sir Robert as 'Grand Prior of England'. Money changed hands, though the amount is not known. Confusingly, during the 1830s another group in Britain, headed by a 'Count Mortara' and possibly set up by the enterprising M. Chastellain, called itself the 'Grand Priory of England'. There was also a group which claimed to be the Anglo-Bavarian Langue though the real Anglo-Bavarian Langue had ceased to exist in 1806.

Early historians of the Venerable Order state that Peat took an oath of office in the King's Bench on 24 February 1834, swearing to keep and obey the statutes of the Sovereign Order, and to 'govern the Sixth Language as Prior thereof under the provision of the statute of the 4th and 5th Philip and Mary'. A later, Protestant, historian, Cecil Torr, commented: 'By the statutes of the Order (which he promised to keep and obey) he was neither qualified for appointment nor appointed by the proper authority ... There is no statute [Act of Parliament] of 4 & 5 Philip and Mary relating to the Order, only Letters Patent; and these make no provision for the government of the Language or the Priory. So he only bound himself to discharge the duties of an impossible office under an imaginary statute.' As for the Venerable Order's claim that the oath was recorded, 'It would certainly be on the record, if it was sworn in the King's Bench, as 9 George IV, cap 17, was then in force,' Torr observes, writing in 1921. 'I had the record searched: it was not there.' Even so, the Langue's members were convinced that Peat had taken such an oath. Yet the Letters Patent merely allowed the Order to act as a corporation in England so that it could sue, hold land and have a common seal. If Peat really did take the oath, it was, as Torr says, a meaningless gesture.

Until our own day, the 'revival' has been widely accepted. So respected a historian of the Knights of Malta as Roderick Cavaliero could write in 1960 (in *The Last of the Crusaders*) that 'A number of Roman Catholic gentry established an English Priory under Sir Robert Peat who became Prior in 1831, but when it was not accepted in Rome financial stringency forced it to recruit Protestants.' Peat has even been styled '55th Grand Prior'. Such misconceptions have arisen in the absence of any proper account of the 'revival'.

Peat's first four 'Knights' were certainly not Roman Catholics. They were Lord Dunboyne, an impoverished Irish peer living at Calais; 'Sir' John Phillipart, a government clerk with a Swedish Order; 'Sir' James Lawrence, a journalist who claimed to have become a Knight of Malta in 1789 as a boy during his holidays from Eton; and Admiral Sir William Johnstone Hope, who had been made a Knight of Malta by the Emperor Paul of Russia. Later, however, one or two Catholics would be recruited by the Langue.

Molay continued his fantastic career for another decade. During the summer of 1837 he made a short visit to London in his capacity as 'Grand Chancellor of the French Langues', staying in Harley Street, where he was visited by the new Grand Secretary of the English Langue, Dr Bigsby. Molay's visit was 'exclusively devoted to [the Order of Malta's] affairs, and he was about to proceed with similar objects to Vienna', says the trusting Bigsby, who adds: 'I believe he wore out his life in fruitless services on behalf of the Order.' In 1840–41 the 'marquis' tried to persuade the unsavoury Honoré V of Monaco to offer Monte Carlo to the Knights of Malta in return for the Grand Mastership.

Molay seems to have died shortly afterwards, for in September 1841 a member of the English Langue took the documents supposedly authorizing its revival to Paris, where in return for a further payment they were endorsed by the Chevalier Taillepied de la Garonne, 'Secretary-General *ad interim* of the Venerable Langues of France'. In October the Langue received a most plausible letter from Baron Notret de Saint-Lys, 'Mandatory-General for the Langues of France to the *Chef-Lieu*', in which he lamented that there were now a mere eighty French Knights, only eight of whom were aged under thirty. According to its third secretary, Richard Broun, the Langue stayed in touch with the 'Venerable Langues of France' until the 1848 Revolution, when it lost contact.

The 'English Langue' remained blissfully unaware that it had been the victim of an elaborate confidence-trick, its members being wholly convinced that they were genuine Knights of Malta. Their activities appear to have been purely convivial, apart from some vague talk of erecting a '*Hospitallarium*' which never materialized. Their inspiration was fancy-dress chivalry of the Eglinton Tournament sort, embodied by the two Grand Priors after Peat. As King's Champion, Sir Henry Dymoke (1837–47) had ridden into Westminster Hall in full armour during George IV's coronation banquet, while he had tried to claim the barony of Marmion. Sir Charles Lamb (1847–60) was Knight Marshal of England and had officiated at the Eglinton Tournament; a man of pleasure, according to rumour his health had been ruined by debauchery. The 1911 *Encyclopaedia Britannica* was not entirely inaccurate in describing the Langue as 'a characteristic sham-Gothic restoration of the Romantic period'.

The Langue's first Grand Secretary (or Vice-Chancellor), John Philippart, was a somewhat shadowy figure who lived at Hammersmith, being for many years chairman of the Fulham and Hammersmith District Board of Works. Incorrectly, he called himself 'Sir John' on account of having received the Swedish Order of

Vasa. Philippart was succeeded by the far from shadowy Dr
Robert Bigsby of 1, Elm Villas, Elm Grove, Peckham, an antiquarian writer and poet, who took the title 'Grand Seneschal' and
wrote an epic entitled *Ombo, or the Knights of Malta. A Dramatic
Romance, in Twelve Acts.* His first period of office seems to have
ended after an episode straight out of *The Pickwick Papers*: unable
to pay the costs of an action for libel which he had brought
against the headmistress of a boarding school, he had been
immured in a debtors' prison.

Later, during a second period of office, Dr Bigsby published a
memoir of the Langue in which he listed his many honours.
Among other distinctions, he was a Knight of the Golden Militia
of Rome and a Count Palatine of the Lateran, a Chevalier
d'Honneur de l'Ordre Souverain du Temple, the Grand-Maître
Conservateur de l'Ordre Impérial Asiatique de Morale Uni-
verselle, a Commandeur Baron de l'Ordre Noble d'Épire, and an
Honorary Doctor of Glasgow University. (The Ordre Impérial
Asiatique was probably the same Asiatic Order which, so *The
Times* of 8 September 1858 informs us, had been founded by an
impostor calling himself 'Aldina del Dir, Sultan of Mongolia'.) In
1864 Bigsby was to become an Honorary Colonel in the 'Armée
Chrétienne d'Orient', a force organized by the 'Junte Gréco-
Albanaise'. Dr Bigsby – as he preferred to be known, rather than
as Colonel Count Bigsby – was highly esteemed by the Langue,
who in 1867 presented him with a silver cup on the occasion of
his retirement from a second period as Grand Secretary, Registrar
and Judge-of-Arms.

The third Grand Secretary was Sir Richard Broun, Bart, who
lived in lodgings at Sphinx Lodge, Chelsea. The 'projector of the
London Necropolis and National Mausoleum at Woking', he was
also author of 'various works on heraldry, agriculture, colonization, sanitation &c.'. As honorary secretary of the Committee of
the Baronetage for Privileges, he achieved a certain notoriety
from his campaign to prove that every baronet had a right to a
seat in Parliament. (Disraeli caricatured him in *Sybil* as 'Sir
Vavasour Firebrace'.) Broun too published informative memoirs

of the Langue, one in 1837 and another twenty years later – the *Synoptical Sketch*.

In July 1857 Broun informed a member of the Langue who lived on Malta, John James Watts, that he had been nominated 'Commissioner for the Langue of England to Southern Europe'. During the following summer Watts visited Rome, where he called at the Palazzo Malta. Here he learnt that the Lieutenancy had never received any formal notification of the Langue's creation. 'The surviving chiefs of the [French] Commission having grown old and incapable,' he was told, 'its affairs fell into the hands of an unprincipled secretary [Molay] and his associates, who embezzled money, sold crosses and forged documents, and in other words made a most illegal and dishonest use of the Commission.' Watts realized that Peat had been duped by, as he later put it, 'a small knot of swindling Frenchmen'.

Even so, Watts was able to report to Broun (in a letter of 19 June 1858) that he had persuaded the Lieutenancy to explore the possibility of restoring the Grand Priory of England, to which an Association of Protestant noblemen could be attached. 'If you are willing to be with us on the terms proposed, not only will we meet you half-way but we will come all the way to you,' Watts was told by Lieutenant Master Colloredo's secretary, Count Luca de Gozze, who added, 'Not only will we hold out the right hand of fellowship but both hands.' The idea must have seemed far from implausible after the revival of the Johanniterorden in 1852, which had been welcomed by the Lieutenant Master – the new Herrenmeister had written to inform him of his appointment, and Colloredo had sent the Herrenmeister his congratulations, applauding the restoration of a bastion against the baneful tendencies of the age.

The Lieutenancy envisaged the restoration of the pre-Reformation Grand Priory of England, soundly funded and engaged in hospitaller work. As soon as it was functioning, an English non-Catholic priory (i.e. the Langue) would be established as an integral part of the Order. However, when the enthusiastic Count de Gozze came to London to investigate in August 1858, he soon

347

realized that the scheme was unworkable, partly because of the Langue's attitude and partly because of its membership.

For the Langue had something very different in mind. It wanted a small and purely titular Catholic Grand Priory, under its authority, whose sole function would be to give the Langue the historical continuity and legitimacy which it lacked. The 'English branch' declined to be in any way subordinate to the Lieutenancy, which it always referred to solemnly as the 'Italian branch'. Broun, who handled the negotiations for the Langue in his capacity as Grand Secretary – Grand Prior Lamb was too ill to be involved in them – proved to be a difficult, not to say impossible, man to deal with; and they quickly foundered. Poor Broun died of a stroke, apparently brought on by rage at their failure. Afterwards de Gozze wrote of negotiating with him as *'ce mauvais rêve'*. (On purchasing Broun's papers from his landlady at Sphinx Lodge – she had impounded them as security for arrears of rent – the Langue was pained to learn that its Grand Secretary had had his *Synoptical Sketch* printed on credit and that its members would have to foot the bill.)

In any case, Count de Gozze did not at all care for what he was able to learn of the Langue's membership. The Protestant English 'Knights' were certainly very different from the Lutheran junkers of the Johanniterorden. While accepting that some of them were undeniably distinguished, de Gozze described the Langue (in a rueful letter of 24 September) as an association in which *'on trouve des gens qui [ne] sont décidément pas "Gentlemen"'*. He can scarcely have been reassured by the use of questionable titles by several members. Even the tolerant Dr Bigsby admitted that although Dr Burnes, the 'Preceptor of Scotland', was a Knight of the Guelphic Order of Hanover, he had no right to call himself 'Sir James'. Philippart, the former Vice-Chancellor, continued to be 'Sir John'. There was also the Langue's Receiver-General, 'Baron de Bliss', the son of a well-known London omnibus proprietor and horse-dealer, who had changed his name from Aldridge to de Bliss and who had somehow acquired a Portuguese barony. Worst of all, there was the 'Count de Melano'.

It was embarassing to say the least that, during de Gozze's visit to London, *The Times* of 3 and 8 September (quoting the French legal journal *Le Droit*) should have chosen to report the 'investigations which are being made into the trafficking in titles and decorations' in Paris. According to *The Times*, the ring-leader was 'a Piedmontese established at London, and who calls himself Count Antonio de Melano'. The bogus orders which he had been peddling included those of the Four Emperors of Germany, St Hubert [of the Ardennes], the Lion of Holstein, the Golden Spur and the Asiatic Order. 'He was in constant communication with men engaged in the same traffic as himself in Spain, Germany, Italy, and especially in France,' reported *The Times*. Among the agents of Melano in Paris whom it named was 'a person calling himself Baron Notret de Saint-Lys, Commander of the Order of the Four Emperors'. (This was the 'high official member of the French Council Ordinary' – Bigsby's description – with whom the Langue of England had corresponded in 1841.) Those of the gang held in French custody were fined or sentenced to terms of imprisonment.

The three genuine Knights of Malta (members of the 'Italian branch') then in England ensured that de Gozze was aware of the lurid reports in *The Times*. In the circumstances it was therefore peculiarly unfortunate that 'Colonel Count Antonio Laurent de Melano de Calcina' should be a Knight Commander of the English Langue. Living in Park Road, New Wandsworth, London SW, he was a neighbour and seemingly a close friend of Dr Bigsby; he does not appear to have been unduly disturbed by the unflattering references to him in *The Times*. A few years later Bigsby recorded his name among those of deceased members of the Langue and did so with obvious pride.

Another member of the English Langue whose name cropped up during the trial was the 'Duke Ludovico Riario-Sforza', described by Broun as 'Bailiff Mandatory in Italy' of the Order of the Golden Spur – one of the orders which had been peddled. (Since 1841, bestowal of the Golden Spur had been reserved exclusively to the Holy See.) Riario-Sforza was a Knight Grand

Cross of the Langue and had been its 'Commissioner to Italy'. Bigsby tells us that he was 'uniformly regarded by his more intimate acquaintance as an accomplished, high-spirited, ingenuous and amiable man'.

Other members of the Langue besides Dr Bigsby were taken in by Melano and Riario-Sforza, proudly wearing their bogus orders. Some dabbled in similar business. According to *Notes and Queries* (3rd S., III, 342), one of them had inserted the following advertisement in the London newspapers during November 1857:

A person who has held a high appointment under one of the European royal families, and who possesses considerable influence at several foreign courts, is willing to use that influence with a view to obtain the title of MARQUIS, COUNT or BARON, for a Catholic gentleman. The title would be of great service for a family desiring high position, or about to visit Rome or the Continent.

Significantly, Gozze (in his letter of 24 September 1858) also observed, with a certain sarcasm, that 'Sir' James Burnes was *'Parmi les franc-maçons, dont il était un des plus hauts dignitaires en Écosse.'* It was common knowledge that Burnes was a former Grand Master for Western India where, so the *Dictionary of National Biography* informs us, he had established 'a lodge for natives'. Even if the Langue's members had been otherwise totally acceptable, from the start its links with freemasonry doomed the project for a Protestant branch of the Order in England. Peat had himself been introduced as a member of St John's Lodge (No. 80) at Sunderland in July 1829. (Sainte-Croix-Molay's name, presumably assumed after much careful thought, hints at both Rosicrucianism and a pretended descent from the last Templar Master, Jacques de Molay.) Dr Bigsby's memoir of the Langue, first published in 1864, contains a list of members since the 'revival', from which it is clear that at least a third of them were masons. Bigsby was one himself – when he died in 1873, his obituary appeared in *The Freemason*.

Such links scarcely made for ecumenical relations. In those

days Catholics were terrified of freemasonry. Rome lived in dread of another great mason, Garibaldi, future Grand Master of the Orient for Italy, who had occupied the Eternal City in 1849 and who was a sworn enemy of the Roman Church. Indeed, in 1864 in the encyclical *Quanta Cura*, Pope Pius IX would solemnly declare freemasonry to be damned, '*damnantur clandestinae societates*'. At that time the Church did not appreciate that British free-masonry was very different from the Latin variety and in no way hostile to Christianity, and that British masons made a most valuable contribution to charity. (Since then the Catholic Church has greatly modified its attitude.)

Eventually the Langue despaired of obtaining recognition from the Lieutenancy. Unwilling to accept that Peat had been duped, in 1862 it set up as an independent order, the 'Sovereign and Illustrious Order of St John of Jerusalem, Anglia'. As a recent writer, G. S. Sainty – a member of the modern Venerable Order – has admitted frankly, 'without the recognition of the Lieuten-ancy, the early nineteenth-century English Priory was a purely private organization'. So too was its successor, the Sovereign and Illustrious Order. They were what would today be termed false Orders of St John.

However, the new order somehow secured the patronage of the Duke of Manchester, the first English peer to join it, who became Grand Prior. It then began to acquire genuinely dedicated mem-bers, notably Sir Edward Lechmere, who realized its potential. In consequence, what had hitherto been no more than a fancy-dress dining-club for cranks and dealers in bogus honours was transformed into a great national institution, performing humani-tarian work of vital importance. In 1872 Lechmere was respon-sible for purchasing the gatehouse of the pre-Reformation Priory of St John at Clerkenwell, formerly *The Old Jerusalem Tavern*, where the Langue had held its chivalric dinners. Fascinated by the Sovereign Order's history, he sympathized with many of its ideals. Not only did he start a splendid collection of books, paintings and armour associated with it, but he initiated a noble hospitaller tradition. The origins of the St John ambulance movement date from 1872.

Invited by the Duke of Manchester, the Princess of Wales joined the Order in 1876, as did the Duke of Albany in 1883. Other members of the royal family followed. They seem to have been inspired to some extent by the example of the Johanniter-orden, since close links existed between the British and Prussian courts. In 1888 Queen Victoria granted the Order a charter which reconstituted it as an order of the Crown, the Prince of Wales becoming Grand Prior.

In 1961 the Venerable Order became one of the 'Alliance Orders of St John', signing a convention with the German, Dutch and Swedish branches of the Johanniterorden. Two years later it signed a *concordat* with the Sovereign Military Order, which relegated 'to the realm of academic discussion' the dispute as to 'whether the Most Venerable Order was the lineal descendant of the old Grand Priory of the Sovereign Order'. Relations have grown cordial between the Venerable Order and the Sovereign Order's British Association, who co-operate in various charities and are sometimes represented at each other's services.

Today the 'Grand Priory in the British Realm of the Most Venerable Order of the Hospital of St John of Jerusalem' has some 25,000 members, 1,500 being Knights or Dames. Its many hospitaller works include the Ophthalmic Hospital at Jerusalem (founded in 1882); the St John Ambulance Brigade (1887); and the St John Ambulance Association (1877). The Order also has Priories with large memberships in South Africa, New Zealand, Canada and Australia, and a Society in the United States.

SOURCES

The Tongue of England, 1858-9, 1859-60 (unpublished letter books in the possession of the Sovereign Military Order of Malta).

REDFORD, W. K. R., and HOLBECH, R., *The Order of the Hospital of St John of Jerusalem* (London, 1902).

BIGSBY, R., *Memoir of the Illustrious and Sovereign Order of St John of Jerusalem* (Derby, 1867).

BROUN, R., *Hospitallaria, or a Synopsis of the Rise, Exploits, Privileges, Insignia, etc, of the Venerable and Sovereign Order of St John of Jerusalem* (London, 1837).

——, *Synoptical Sketch of the Illustrious and Sovereign Order of Knights Hospitallers of St John of Jerusalem and of the Venerable Tongue of England* (London, 1857).

LUKE, Sir H., *The Venerable Order of St John in the British Realm* (London, 1967).

PIERREDON, M. DE, *Histoire Politique de l'Ordre Souverain de Saint-Jean de Jérusalem (Ordre de Malte) de 1789 à 1955*, vol. 2 (Paris, 1963).

SAINTY, G. S., *The Order of Saint John* (New York, 1991).

TORR, C., *Small Talk at Wreyland*, vol. 2 (Cambridge, 1921).

(An account of the Rev. Sir John Peat may be found in W. Brockie's *Sunderland Notables* (Sunderland, 1895).)

APPENDIX 5

SELF-STYLED ORDERS
OF ST JOHN

Most, though not all, self-styled 'Orders of St John' base their pretensions on an alleged Russian provenance.

After the fall of Malta in 1798, members of a recently founded Grand Priory of Russia, together with exiled French Knights, elected Tsar Paul I as Grand Master. The Tsar's favourite reading had been Vertot's history of the Order of Malta, and he accepted joyfully. The election was totally invalid. Not even a Catholic, let alone a professed Knight in vows, Paul was never recognized as Grand Master by the Holy See. However, he secured *de facto* recognition from most Catholic powers.

The Tsar set up a council of the Order at St Petersburg, modelled on the former Sacred Council at Valetta. Besides the Catholic Grand Priory of Russia, founded in 1797 by agreement with Grand Master de Rohan, he established a Grand Priory for Knights of the Orthodox faith. Soon there were 250 Russian Knights, besides members of the imperial family and ladies upon whom Paul had bestowed the Cross. (Among the latter was Lady Hamilton, Nelson's friend.) Paul also encouraged the endowment of *ius patronatus* commanderies, the founder's family enjoying the right of nominating the commander; a commander had to have belonged to the Order for five years and to have served in the Russian Army.

After Paul's murder in 1801, his son, Alexander I, told the Knights who had taken refuge in Sicily to elect a new Grand Master. When the Pope appointed the Bailiff Tommasi in 1803, the 'Sacred Council' at Petersburg recognized him at once and voted its own dissolution. In 1810–11 the Tsar confiscated the estates of the Russian Grand Priories, Catholic and Orthodox, formally confirming their complete dissolution in 1817. The commanderies' lands were given back to the families of the founders.

Because of the dissolution's vagueness and lack of co-ordination, and from a mistaken belief that hereditary commanderies had been founded, attempts have been made to revive the Russian Grand Priories. At the beginning of this century an American citizen, Colonel William Lamb, announced that he was a descendant of a General Ivan Lamb, whom he alleged to have been a member of Tsar Paul's Russian Grand Priory. In 1908 he held a meeting in New York at the Waldorf Astoria Hotel which, so it is claimed, was attended by eight descendants of Russian ex-commanders, who supposedly formed a Grand Priory of America. In 1911 this organization registered itself as the 'Knights of Malta Inc.', later establishing a headquarters at Shickshinny, Pennsylvania. Little was heard of it for many years. However, since the late 1950s, at least 30 so-called 'Orders of St John' have appeared, most of them basing their claims to 'authenticity' on descent from the Shickshinny group, and each one with a Grand Master, Prior or Protector – in one or two cases, members of the former ruling houses of Russia or Yugoslavia. Some of these groups have attempted, not without success, to sell titles and even false passports.

Not all these 'Orders' have based their claims on Russian descent. A Danish group has insisted that it is the Order of St John in Denmark, mainly on the grounds that the Danish Crown never abolished the Order in their country.

In order to combat the activities of such organizations and to stop them using its name and insignia, the Sovereign Order has set up a False Orders of St John Commission. Besides those from the Sovereign Order, the commission includes representatives from the 'Alliance Orders of St John' (the Johanniterorden in Germany, together with its commanderies in Austria, Finland, France, Switzerland and Hungary, the Johanniter Orde in the Netherlands and the Johanniterorden in Sweden), and also from the Venerable Order of St John in Great Britain.

The definitive study of the Order of Malta in Russia is Fra'

Cyril Toumanoff's *L'Ordre de Malte et l'Empire de Russie* (Rome, 1979), while the best introduction to the labyrinthine world of the self-styled orders of St John is by A. Chaffanjon and B. Gallimard Flavigny, *Ordres et Contre-Ordres de Chevalerie* (Paris, 1982). The world expert on such orders is generally acknowledged to be Professor Jonathan Riley-Smith, Librarian of the Venerable Order of St John.

NOTES

CHAPTER 2: THE BIRTH OF A NEW VOCATION

1. Fulcherius Carnotensis, 'Historia Hierosolymitana', *R.H.C. oc.*, vol. III, p. 468.

2. See F. Macler, 'Armenia', *Cambridge Medieval History*, vol. IV.

3. See R. C. Smail, *Crusading Warfare 1097–1193* (Cambridge University Press, 1957).

4. 'The foot, on both the line of march and the battle-field, were usually placed between the enemy and the knights . . . a living barrier armed with spears and bows.' ibid., p. 130.

5. Dr Smail believes that sergeants fought as foot soldiers. ibid., p. 91.

6. ibid., p. 75, 'Turkish tactics'.

7. Smail (op. cit., p. 87 n. 6) quotes William of Tyre on the Egyptians in one disastrous campaign. 'The vile and effeminate Egyptians ['Egyptiis vilibus et effeminatis'] who were more of a hindrance and a burden than a help . . .' See 'Historia rerum in partibus transmarini gestarum', *R.H.C. oc.*

8. For the Frankish charge, see Smail, pp. 112–15, 200–201: 'on many occasions the divisions of the army charged in succession' (i.e. attacked in echelon).

9. Sir Ernest Barker, *The Crusades* (Oxford University Press, 1949), p. 48.

10. For the earliest account of the Templars' origin see William of Tyre, op. cit., bk. 12, ch. VII, pp. 520–21, 'Ordo militiae templi instituitur'. Jacques de Vitry, *Historia orientalis seu Hierosolymitana*, adds details, such as those about the gift of the Temple, which he must have had from the brethren themselves.

11. For the Hospitallers' origins see William of Tyre, op. cit., bk. 18, ch. 4, pp. 822–3, 'Describitur, unde habuit ortum et initium domus

Hospitalis' (in the 'Estoire d'Eracles', a thirteenth-century French translation, this is charmingly rendered *'Comment li Hospitalier orent petit commencement'*). Also Riley-Smith, *The Knights of St John in Jerusalem and Cyprus*, p. 32 *et seq.*, where all traditions and sources concerning the order's origins are fully examined.

12. Delaville le Roulx, *Cartulaire Général des Hospitaliers de Saint Jean de Jérusalem 1100–1310*, vol. I, cart. no. 30.

13. 'The Papal bull of 1113, *Pie postulatio voluntatis*, was the foundation charter for the new order.' Riley-Smith, op. cit., p. 43.

14. 'Un document sur les débuts des Templiers', ed. J. Leclercq in *Revue de l'histoire ecclésiastique*, LII (1957).

15. See H. de Curzon, *La Règle du Temple* (Paris, 1887). For a résumé of its principal statutes see Melville, *La Vie des Templiers*, pp. 42–7. (Marion Melville does not consider the rule to be St Bernard's despite its Cistercian form – p. 20.) For the Templar translation of the *Book of Judges* see Melville, pp. 81–3, who comments that it transforms scripture into 'une sorte de roman de Chevalerie'.

16. The best easily available description of the brethren's daily life is in Melville, op. cit., ch. XVII.

17. 'De Laude Novae Militiae' in *S. Bernardi Opera*, vol. III (*Editiones Cistercienses*), ed. Dom J. Leclerq and Dom H. M. Rochais (Rome, 1963).

18. See Lees, *Records of the Templars in England in the Twelfth Century*.

19. Other great officers were the Gonfanonier (Standard Bearer), the Vice-Marshal and the Turcopolier. For a more detailed account of the Templar hierarchy see Melville, op. cit., pp. 84–101.

20. Until recently this bull was ascribed to 1139, but Dr Riley-Smith has shown that it cannot be earlier than 1152 – and also that in that year the Templars were still not yet exempt from the partriarch's jurisdiction. See *English Historical Review* (April 1969).

21. Ekkehard of Aura in 'Hierosolymitana', *R.H.C. oc.*, vol. V.

22. Trans. G. Webb and A. Walker, quoted in L. Bouyer, *The Cistercian Heritage* (Mowbray, 1958).

23. Professor Riley-Smith considers that fighting was an auxiliary activity – 'an extension of its charitable duties' (op. cit., p. 55) – which did not become as important as the latter until the thirteenth century.

24. See King, *The Rule, Statutes and Customs of the Hospitallers, 1099–1310*.

25. See Riley-Smith, op. cit., p. 257. Vainer brethren seem to have spent their regulation pocket money on clothes of better cloth, embroidered with gold thread, or on silk turbans etc.

26. See ibid., pt. II.

27. Grand Commander in the West was an office occasionally bestowed on a great bailiff like the Prior of St Gilles (southern France), ibid., p. 366.

28. ibid., pp. 334–5.

29. H. de Curzon, op. cit.

30. See J. Nichols, *History of the County and Antiquities of Leicestershire*, vol. II, pt. I (London, 1759); also 'The Hospital of Burton Lazars', *V.C.H. Leicestershire*, vol. 2, pp. 36–9; the founder's charter is in Dugdale, *Monasticon Anglicanum*, vol. VI (2), p. 632.

31. See Delaville le Roulx, 'L'Ordre de Montjoie', *Revue de l'Orient Latin*, vol. I (Paris 1893); this article is still the definitive study.

CHAPTER 3: THE BULWARK OF JERUSALEM

1. For the death of Bernard de Tremelay see the 'Estoire d'Eracles', *R.C.H. oc.*, vol. I, bk. 17, ch. XXVII, p. 805.

2. 'Marseilles, indeed, as the centre of transport from France to the Holy Land, had in 1253 and 1255 to pass statutes to regulate the traffic. Not more than fifteen hundred pilgrims were to be taken in any one ship. First-class passengers, with deck cabins, were to pay 60 sous; second-class, between decks, 40; third-class, on the lowest deck, 35; and fourth-class, in the hold, 25. Each pilgrim received a numbered ticket . . .' Joan Evans, *Life in Mediaeval France* (Phaidon, 1969), p. 98.

3. See William of Tyre, op. cit., bk. 20, ch. XXVI, p. 990 – 'Milo Armenus, frater domini Toros' – 'De la grant desloiauté Meslier le frere Toros'.

4. See Delaville le Roulx, *Les Hospitaliers*, pp. 65–76 and *Cart. Gen.* no. 402 – the charter which confirmed this great gamble.

5. On Gautier de Mesnil, Etudes de St Amand and King Amalric, see Melville, op. cit., pp. 103–4, and William of Tyre, op. cit., bk. 20, ch. XXX, pp. 997–9.

6. See Gibbon, *The Decline and Fall*, ch. LIX.

7. William of Tyre says that the Master literally *breathed* fury – 'spiritum furoris habens in naribus' – op. cit., bk. 21, ch. XXIX, p. 1057.

8. A famous description of the splendid establishment at the Temple of Jerusalem was written by an enthralled Franciscan priest, Johann von Würzburg, who visited it in the 1170s. See 'Johannis Wirburgensis Presbyterii Descriptio Terrae Sanctae', *M.P.L.*, ch. CLV.

9. See 'L'Estoire de Eracles Empereur et la conqueste de la terre d'outremer'. *R.H.C. oc.*, bk. 28, ch. XXVI, p. 40.

10. *R.H.C. oc.*, II, bk. 23, ch. XXXV, p. 52.

11. *R.H.C. oc.*, II, bk. 23, ch. XLIII, p. 65 – 'En cele bataille fù la Sainte Crois perdue'. Marion Melville makes much of a story that a Templar escaped with the True Cross, which he buried in the sand; later he returned but could not find it. Yet Arabic sources definitely state that the Cross was captured.

12. The main source for these details is Ralph de Diceto's *Ymagines Historiarum*. See 'The Historical Works of Master Ralph de Diceto, Dean of London', ed. Stubbs, *Rolls Series*, vol. II (London, 1876), p. 80.

13. See Legge, *Anglo-Norman Literature and its Background*, p. 191.

14. See Riley-Smith, op. cit., pp. 272-3.

15. For contemporary writers who admired the Templars, see Melville, ch. XVI, 'Un archevêque et deux trouvères' (Jacques de Vitry, Guiot de Provins, and Christien de Troyes).

16. For Wolfram von Eschenbach's admiration for the Templars, see Melville, p. 182.

17. See Masson, *The Emperor Frederick II of Hohenstaufen*, p. 147.

18. Until very recently it was supposed that Frederick crowned himself king but it has now been shown that this was not the case – he merely wore the imperial crown. See H. E. Mayer, 'Das Pontifikale von Tyrus and die Krönung der Lateinischer Koenige von Jerusalem', *Dumbarton Oaks Papers*, no. 21 (1967).

19. Only Matthew Paris mentions this plot. See Riley-Smith, op. cit., p. 168.

20. An oddly haunting inscription was found in the Great Gallery of Krak:

SIT TIBI COPIA
SOT SAPIE(N)CIA
FORMAQ(UE) DET(UR)
INQ(UI)NAT O(MN)IA SOLA
SUP(ER)BIA SI COMI(TETUR)

– wealth may be yours, wisdom too, and you may have beauty, but if pride touch them, all will turn to dross. See Deschamps, *Le Crac des Chevaliers*, p. 218.

21. 'The acquisition or successful defence of strong places was the highest prize of warfare, besides which success in battle was of secondary importance.' Smail, op. cit., p. 139.

22. ibid., pp. 60, 61 – castles 'served as residences, as administrative centres, as barracks and as police posts'. Dr Smail also believes that they were centres of colonization and economic development.

23. Behaviour in the refectory was not always decorous – brethren would sometimes beat or throw bread and wine at the paid servants who waited on them. See Riley-Smith, op. cit., p. 254.

24. 'Quingentas marcas' (50 marks), a very large sum for the period. See Matthew Paris, *Chronica Majora*, ed. Luard, vol. III, p. 490.

25. A Templar, Fra' Roger l'Aleman, taken prisoner, apostatized but then escaped; he was expelled from the Order. Melville, p. 206.

26. See Matthew Paris, op. cit., vol. IV, p. 342.

27. Writing in 1250 of the last fifty years' main events, Matthew Paris noted: 'The houses of the Temple, of the Hospital, of St Mary of the Germans, and of St Lazarus have twice been taken prisoner, killed and scattered.' He was referring to La Forbie and the disasters of St Louis. Paris, op. cit., vol. V, p. 192.

28. See Joinville, *Histoire de Saint Louis*, p. 300.

CHAPTER 4: ARMAGEDDON

1. See Matthew Paris, *Chronica Majora*, vol. V, p. 745.

2. 'In the magistracy of Bertrand de Comps between 1236 and 1239, brother knights were given precedence over the priests and it was later said that Bertrand had done more for them than any other Master.' Riley-Smith, op. cit., p. 238. See *Chronica Magistrum Defunctorum*, XVII.

3. It was laid down by the Hospitallers' Chapter-General of 1262 'that no Prior nor bailiff nor other brother knight receive a brother unless he who is to be knighted should be the son of a knight or of knightly family'. Delaville le Roulx, *Cartulaire Générale*, vol. 3, p. 42 (trans. from 'The Thirteenth-Century Statutes of the Knights Hospitallers', ed. King).

4. '. . . ces Césars mamelûks, bêtes de proie traîtresses et féroces, mais soldats de génie, connaisseurs et manieurs d'hommes . . .' Grousset, vol. III, p. 615.

5. Fra' Guillaume de Beaujeu was '. . . a great nobleman ("mout gentilhome"), a cousin of the King of France, so generous, openhanded and charitable that he was famous for it'. This, at any rate, was the opinion of his secretary, the Templar of Tyre. *R.H.C. arm.*, II, p. 779.

6. See 'Les Gestes des Chyprois', *R.H.C. arm.*, II, p. 793.

7. loc. cit.

8. ibid., p. 808, '. . . le Mensour ce est a dire le Victorious'.

9. ibid., p. 812, '. . . une grant nacare . . . quy avoit mout oryble vois'.

10. ibid., p. 816, '. . . frere Mahé de Clermont . . . come chevaliers preus et hardis, bon crestiens. Et Dieus ait l'arme de yaus!' It is worth remembering that this account of the Marshal's last stand was written by the Templar of Tyre who spoke to eye-witnesses. The Hospitaller Master wrote later of the Marshal '. . . estoit nobles et preus et sage as armes. Diex li soit deboinaires!' See Delaville le Roulx, vol. III, cart. no. 4157.

11. ibid., p. 813, 'Et il lor respondy hautement que chascun l'oy: Seignors, je ne peu plus, car je suy mort – vées le cop.'

12. In the letter quoted above which the Master of the Hospital afterwards wrote to the Prior of St Gilles, '. . . en larmians souspirs et en très grande tristece, vous anonchons le maleuret trebucement d'Acre, le boine cité, hec! con grande doleur . . .', he says that 'nous meymes fume en cel jour feru à mort d'une lance entre les garites . . .'

13. Grousset tells the story particularly well, vol. III, pp. 760 *et seq.*

CHAPTER 5: THE CRUSADE ON THE BALTIC

1. Dusburg, 'Chronica Terre Prussie', I, 1.

2. 'This man was eloquent, affable, wise, careful and far seeing, and glorious in all his actions.' Dusburg, op. cit., I, 5.

3. See Herder, *Der Orden Schwertbrüder* (Cologne, 1965), who identifies the origins of a surprisingly large number of Sword Brethren.

4. 'Among the Knighthood's brethren at that time there was a certain Wigbert whose heart was far more inclined to love the world rather than religious discipline and who had caused much discord among his brothers . . . he was a real Judas . . . like a wolf among sheep . . . in the upper room where he had gone on the pretext of communicating some secret, suddenly, with the axe ['bipenne'] which he always carried, he struck off the Master's head . . .' Heinrich von Lettland, p. 132, 'Chronicon Livonicum vetus' in *S.R.L.*, vol. I. (Balthasar Rüssow, 'Chronica der Provintz Lyfflandt', *S.R.L.*, vol. II, p. 13, mistakenly dates the murder to 1223.)

5. '. . . there arrived unexpectedly from Livonia Gerlac the Red announcing that Master Wolquin with many brethren, pilgrims and people of God had been killed – slain in battle'. Dusburg, op. cit., III, 28.

6. '. . . terram horroris et vaste solitudinis.' Dusburg, op. cit., II, 10.

7. They mistook every created thing for God, says Petrus, '. . . the sun, the moon and the stars, thunder and lightning, and even four-legged beasts, down to the toad'. ibid., III, 5. The Order never forgot this gruesome paganism: An eighteenth-century knight historian wrote 'La Prusse, vaste pays encore plongé alors dans les ténèbres de l'idolatrie' – Wal, vol. I, p. 194.

8. '. . . castrum dictum Vogelsanck quod dicitur latine cantus avium . . .' seems to be a ponderous joke on Petrus's part. Dusburg, op. cit., II, 10.

9. Treitschke, op. cit., p. 40. At least one great victory was won over the Prussians 'tempore hyemali, cum omnia essent gelu intensissimo indurate'. Dusburg, op. cit., III, 11.

10. In fact Master Wolquin had been negotiating for the incorporation of his brotherhood into the Teutonic Order for the last six years. See Dusburg, op. cit., III, 28.

11. However, in Pomerellen the brethren left the native Slav nobility in possession of its lands since it was firmly Christian.

12. *'in errores pristinos sunt relapsi'*, Dusburg, III, 89.

13. On one occasion Martin von Gollin (probably a *halbbruder*) seized a Lithuanian ship and sailed back down the rivers to Thorun, 250 miles away. Petrus tells us that Martin always attacked Prussian villages at dusk, to catch the warriors in their saunas. Dusburg, op. cit., III, 199.

14. '. . . and all the tribes in the said land had been conquered or driven out [*expugnate essent et exterminate*] so that not one was left who would not humbly bow his neck to the Most Holy Roman Church'. Dusburg, op. cit., III, 221.

15. The Engelsburg commandery took its name from the 'angelic life' led by its brethren – no doubt the Prussians had another name for it.

16. The rite of profession contains a sword blessing, *'Benedicio ensis ad faciendum militum'*. See Perlbach, p. 129, who gives French, Low German and Dutch versions as well as Latin and German – in the early days admission was not restricted to Germans.

17. The Landmeister's banner depicted the Blessed Virgin in Glory, according to Banderia Prutenorum in *S.R.P.*, vol. IV.

CHAPTER 6: THE ORDENSLAND

1. This point is made by Carsten in *The Origins of Prussia*, p. 7.
2. ibid., pp. 30 and 52.

3. Only about 100 knightly families received estates from the Order during its first 50 years in Prussia; ibid., p. 54.

4. 'As late as the fifteenth century one of the Grand Masters was "neither doctor nor clerk", that is to say he could neither read nor write.' Treitschke, *Das deutsche Ordensland Preussen*, trans. Eden and Cedar Paul, p. 97.

5. 'In this essentially political world, only one science was diligently fostered, that of historiography.' ibid., p. 98.

6. 'Not all these classes, however, were represented. Only knights and a few townsmen were found in the Eastern Baltic lands.' See Hermann Aubin, 'The lands east of the Elbe and German colonisation eastwards', *Cambridge Early History*, vol. I, pp. 367–8.

7. 'In the year 1343 when the aforesaid Master [Burkhardt von Drei-leve] had descended upon the schismatics [i.e. Russians] with an armed fleet, behold, on the eve of St George's Day the converts of the diocese of Reval fell back into their old religion; they killed their own lords and all Germans including little children, dashing babies against rocks or throwing them into the water or into fires, and doing to women that of which I am ashamed to speak, cutting them open with swords and impaling on spears the infants hiding in their wombs . . .' Hermann von Wartberge, 'Chronicon Livoniae', *S.R.P.*, vol. II, p. 70.

8. '. . . Rutenos . . . subditores et co-operatores paganorum . . .' Hermann von Wartberge, op. cit., p. 115.

9. A *reysa* in 1387 is described by Hermann von Wartberge. 'On the sixth day before St Valentine's, Wilhelm [von Freimersen] the Master of Livonia went briskly ('strenue ivit') with his men against the Lithuanians at Opython where for nine days he killed, burnt, laid waste and destroyed all things.' ibid., p. 115.

10. 'Wynricus de Knyprode . . . vir decorus et personatus, magne relligiositatis [*sic*] et multe prudentie.' See 'Historia Brevis Magistrorum Ordinis Theutonici Generalium', *S.R.P.*, vol. IV.

11. For a brief but illuminating summary of Templar and Hospitaller possessions in Pomerania and Brandenburg, see Carsten, op. cit., p. 13.

12. See 'Le Livre des faicts du Marechal Boucicaut: Comment messire Boucicaut alla la troisème fois en Prusse, et comment il voulut venger la mort de messire Guillaume de Duglas', *S.R.P.*, vol. II.

13. 'A.D. 1390. In this yer Ser Herry, erl of Derby, sailed into Prus, where with help of the marschale of Prus and of a kyng that hite Witot, he ovyrcam the kyng of Lettow and made him for to fle. Thre of his dukes he took and foure dukes he killed with many lordes and knytis and swieris mo than thre hundred.' (King Henry's contribution has been somewhat exaggerated!) See John Capgrave, *Chronicle of England*, ed. Hingeston (London, 1858).

14. See Metcalfe, *A Great Historic Peerage, the Earldom of Wiltes* and *Burke's Landed Gentry* – 'Scrope'. Sir Geoffrey's brother was the future Archbishop Scrope of Shakespeare's *Henry IV* who was executed for high treason.

15. So folk songs called him, according to Treitschke, op. cit., p. 85.

16. '. . . the man whose heart was as hard as his name, Henning Schindekopf'. ibid., p. 75.

17. '. . . une secte que après leur mort ils se font ardoir en lieu de sepulture, vestus et aournez chascun de leurs meilleurs aournemens, en ung leur plus prochain boi ou forest qu'ilz ont, en feu fait de purain bois de quesne . . .' See *Guillebert de Lannoy et ses voyages en 1413, 1414 et 1421*, ed. J. Lelewel (Brussels, 1844), p. 38.

18. 'Crist ist enstandin' – see Johann von Pusilge in 'Annalista Thorunensis' III–IV, *S.R.P.*, vol. III, p. 316.

19. See 'Banderia Prutenorum', *S.R.P.*, vol. IV, compiled in 1448 by the Pole, Johannes Dlugosz, at Cracow where the captured banner was probably still hanging.

20. However, it was identified and brought back to the Marienburg for burial even if '. . . the Tartars and the Cossacks practised their hideous tricks of mutilation upon the Grand Master's body'. Treitschke, op. cit., p. 115.

21. 'They besieged the castle with every kind of siege engine, bombards and other weapons of great strength and power, day and night for two months or more.' See Conrad Bitschin, the fifteenth-century continuer of Petrus von Dusburg, *S.R.P.*, vol. III, p. 485.

CHAPTER 7: THE CRUSADERS WITHOUT A CAUSE

1. The former Hochmeister was accused of scheming to regain power with Polish assistance in 1414 and imprisoned for nine years. Even Treitschke (op. cit., I, p. 125) believed this charge to have been unjust.

2. Though written over 400 years later, the epic *Konrad Walenrod* by the great Polish Romantic poet Adam Mickiewicz reflects his countrymen's traditional hatred of the Order. The Hochmeister is made to say of *Litwa*:

Burned are its towns, a sea of blood is spilled:
These are my deeds, my oath I have fulfilled.

3. The plague was dysentery – one casualty was the Livonian Land-meister himself, Cysus von Rutenberch. See Dyonisius Fabricius, 'Livoni-cae Historiae compendiosa series', *S.R.L.*, vol. 2, p. 460.

4. See Conrad Bitschin, op. cit., p. 502.

5. There is a brief account of this episode in the late Professor R. W. Seton-Watson's *History of the Roumanians* (Cambridge University Press, 1934), p. 35.

6. 'The Emperor and the Empire looked on inert while the impotence of a theocracy that had been too rigid and the lawless arrogance of the mercantile patriciates and the squires were betraying New Germany to the Poles.' Treitschke, op. cit., p. 135.

7. 'The rough fellows broke into the cells, tied up the knights, and proceeded to cut off their beards.' Treitschke, op. cit., p. 133.

8. Boswell, *Cambridge Mediaeval History*, vol. VIII, p. 578.

9. 'He gathered together a vast army for the purpose, up to 100,000 men, such as none of the Masters before him in Livonia had been able to do.' See Dyonisius Fabricius, op. cit., p. 461. This figure is hardly credible.

10. Two hundred years later he was still remembered. 'Walter Pletten-berg is the Man, whom those Nations prefer to all their other Heer-Meisters for Valour, Wisdom and Good Fortune.' Blomberg, *An Account of Livonia*, p. 11.

11. 'The Livonians waged a fierce and famous war against the Russians ... against the hereditary enemies of pious Catholics ...' Levenclavius, 'De Moscovitarium bellis adversus finitimos gestis', *H.R.S.E.*, vol. I.

12. There is a good summary of the war in J. Fennell's *Ivan the Great of Moscow* (Macmillan, 1961).

13. There is a dramatic account in Wal, op. cit., vol. 6.

14. For Plettenberg's campaigns, see Levenclavius, op. cit.

15. See *The Travels of Sir Jerome Horsey, Kt.*, ed. A. Bond (Hakluyt Soc., 1856).

16. Ivan was merely treating Livland in the way that he was accustomed to treat his own rebellious subjects. For the Russian point of view see I. Grey, *Ivan the Terrible* (Hodder & Stoughton, 1964).

17. For Caspar von Oldenbock see Balthasar Rüssow, 'Chronica der Provintz Lyfflandt', p. 65. Also Dyonisius Fabricius, op. cit., p. 476, who says that the Russians retired 'cum ignominia'.

CHAPTER 8: THE RECONQUISTA

1. For Calatrava, see J. F. O'Callaghan, 'The Affiliation of the Order of Calatrava with Cîteaux', a series of articles in *Analecta Sacri Ordinis Cisterciensis*, which is the only comprehensive study of this brotherhood.

2. ibid., vol. 16, p. 285. 'There should be no hesitation in affirming that it [the spirit of Calatrava] was essentially a Cistercian spirit based not only upon the fundamental texts of the Benedictine Rule and the *Carta Caritatis*, but also upon the less tangible principles of twelfth-century chivalry, seen by the Cistercians as another means of reforming and purifying the lives of men . . .'

3. See O'Callaghan in *Analecta*, vol. 16, pp. 33–8.

4. ibid., vol. 16, p. 31.

5. The definitive modern work is Lomax, *La Orden de Santiago 1170–1275*.

6. A thirteenth-century Castilian translation of the Rule of Santiago is printed in Lomax, op. cit., p. 221.

7. See Lomax, p. 238, for a deed of 1190 in which Vitalia, wife of Frey Vitalis de Palombar, is received into the Order.

8. See J. F. O'Callaghan, 'The Foundation of the Order of Alcántara', *Catholic Historical Review*, vol. 47.

9. See Joseph da Purificão, 'Catalogo dos Mestres e administradores da illustre e antiquissima Ordem Militar de Aviz', *C.A.R.H.P.*, vol. 2.

10. The Master of the Portuguese Templars, Gualdim Paes, who reigned for nearly half a century and died in 1195, achieved almost folk-hero status by his exploits against the Moors. See 'Catalogo dos Mestres da Ordem do Templo Portugueza, e em outras da Hespanha', *C.A.R.H.P.*, which credits him with 'immortal gloria'.

11. As in other military brotherhoods, *caballeros* who sought a more contemplative life could, with their Master's permission, transfer to a house of *clerigos* or to another Order. Lomax (op. cit., p. 94) cites the examples of Maestre Fernando Díaz, who became a canon of Santiago, and of a brother who joined the notoriously severe hermit Order of Grandmont.

CHAPTER 9: THE GREAT ADVANCE

1. Rades, 'Discordia y scisma en la Orden', *Chrónica de Calatrava*, p. 21.

2. Iberian Hospitallers frequently failed to send Responsions (revenues) to the convent and often ignored the Grand Master, so occasionally one of their priors was nominated 'Grand Commander in Spain', with authority over all peninsular brethren of St John. See Riley-Smith, op. cit., p. 369.

3. See Cocheril, 'Essai sur l'Origine des Ordres Militaires dans la Péninsule Ibérique'.

4. There is a colourful account of this battle in Rades, *Chrónica de Calatrava*, pp. 28–30.

5. This point, that brethren protected colonists and aided agriculture, is made by Almeida, *Historia da Igreja em Portugal*, vol. I, p. 552.

6. 'In fine, he acted the part of a good Man and a Just Prince' – John Stevens, *The General History of Spain* (London, 1699).

7. Fighting did not make them forget religious duties; in 1245 the Cistercian Chapter-General described Calatrava as 'membrum nobile et speciale Ordinis Cisterciensis'. See O'Callaghan, op. cit., vol. 16, p. 287.

8. Significantly, this Master was long remembered in his Order as 'el Josue español'. See Lomax, 'A Lost Mediaeval Biography: the Crónica del Maestre Pelayo Pérez', in *Bulletin of Hispanic Studies*, XXXVIII (1961).

9. There was of course some rivalry, with inevitable wrangling over lands and jurisdiction. See Lomax, op. cit., ch. VI, under 'La rivalidad con Calatrava' and 'disputas territoriales y fiscales'.

10. An agreement between these bankers – Don Bono, Don Jacobo and Don Samuel – and the Master of Santiago is printed in ibid., pp. 270–71.

11. São Thiago was not properly independent until John XXII's bull of 1317. See F. de Almeida, op. cit., vol. I, p. 330.

12. 'Thus, the Reconquista degenerated into a series of tournaments between Christian and Moorish knights, while the ideal of the monk-warrior "religioso-guerrero" which had inspired the brethren changed slowly into the courtier knight of the romances.' Lomax, op. cit., p. 99.

13. See Rades, 'Deposicion del Maestre', *Chrónica de Alcántara*, p. 15.

14. Almeida, op. cit., vol. I, p. 340.

15. During the many revolts in fourteenth-century Aragon '. . . among the few who firmly supported the king were the Castellan of Amposta, the Master of Montesa and the *comendador major* of the Order of Santiago in Aragon'. See Luttrell, 'The Aragonese Crown and the Knights Hospitallers of Rhodes 1291–1350'. The same authority makes the point that by the mid-fourteenth century the Aragonese Hospitallers, firmly controlled

by the king, had almost become a national as well as an international Order, pp. 17–18.

16. See Rades, *Chrónica de Calatrava*, pp. 50–51 – 'vn llano cerca de Vaena'. Also O'Callaghan, op. cit., vol. 16, p. 260.

17. See Rades, *Chrónica de Alcántara*, p. 23 – '. . . le hizo degollar y aun hizo quemar su cuerpo'. Also Stevens, op. cit., p. 261 – 'D. Gonzalo Martínez or Núñez of Calatrava was impeach'd of several hainous Crimes and being Summon'd to appear and answer for himself, fled to the King of *Granada* . . . Nevertheless in the Spring the King went into *Andaluzia* and besieg'd the Master of *Calatrava* in *Valencia* a Town within the Bounds of the Antient Lusitania. He was taken, condemn'd as a Traytor, Beheaded and Burnt for a Terror to others.' (Here Mariana has confused Calatrava with Alcántara.)

18. Torres y Tapia, *Crónica de la Orden de Alcántara*, vol. II, p. 50.

19. See Russell, *English Intervention in Spain and Portugal in the time of Edward III and Richard II*.

CHAPTER 10: KINGS AND MASTERS

1. Doña Leonor de Guzmán retained the seal of Santiago on behalf of her son, after the death of her brother, the Master Alonso Meléndez de Guzmán. See Ayala, *Crónica del Rey Don Pedro* (1779), vol. I, p. 22. A footnote cites the Bullarium of Santiago.

2. Rades, *Chrónica de Alcántara*, p. 25 – Don Fernán Pérez Ponce was Doña Leonor's cousin.

3. See Rades, *Chrónica de Calatrava*, p. 54 – 'Don Iuan Núñez de Prado degollado'.

4. ibid., p. 56 – 'El Rey mato a don Pedro Estevañez'. Rades says that King Pedro 'le dio de estocadas delante de la Reyna su madre, y fue luego muerto'. However, Ayala (op. cit., p. 208) says that he was clubbed to death with a mace by the squire of his rival as Master, Diego García de Padilla, outside the castle.

5. Ayala, op. cit., pp. 240–42 – the slave was 'un mozo de su camera'.

6. 'El Rey Bermejo' and his court seem to have been shot to death with javelins. See Ayala, op. cit., p. 347 – '. . . E el Rey don Pedro le firio primera de una lanza . . .'

7. In 1362, ibid., p. 336, also Rades, *Chrónica de Calatrava*, p. 57 – 'El Rey Moro [Abu Said] hizo el Maestre muy amoroso recibimiento y le trato muy honrradamente' because he was a brother of Blanche de Padilla.

8. Diego García de Padilla had been asked to advocate. Rades, op. cit., p. 58.

9. Ayala, op. cit., vol. 2, pp. 21, 22 – 'que el Rey Don Enrico le guardaria al seguro que le avia fecho'.

10. Yet a contemporary critic of Juan Núñez of Calatrava had written 'Fué este maestre muy disoluto acerca de las mujeres'. O'Callaghan, op. cit., vol. 16, p. 25.

11. See 'Catalogo dos Grampriores do Crato da Ordem de S. João de Malta' in *C.A.R.P.H.*, vol. 4.

12. See Torres y Tapia, *Crónica de la Orden de Alcántara*, vol. II, p. 179 – '. . . eran tantos los dardos, saetas, y lanzas que los Moros arrojaban, que se escaparon pocos de sus manos, y á ellas murio el Maestre.'

13. In 1444 abbot John VI of Morimond conducted a visitation of Montesa and found novices so poverty-stricken that he ordered all future postulants to obtain this sum from their relatives, to maintain them until they acquired a commandery. O'Callaghan, op. cit., vol. 16, p. 14, n. 6.

14. 'Their Badge a Red Cross with a white Twist in the middle.' Stevens, op. cit., p. 248.

15. See MacDonald, *Don Fernando de Antequerra*.

16. 'The increasing laxity in the Order of Calatrava must be traced chiefly to the admission to the ranks of men unworthy and unsuited to wield the spiritual and temporal swords in defence of Christendom . . . There were two major inducements: the opportunities for satisfying both personal ambition and greed.' O'Callaghan, op. cit., vol. 16, p. 285.

17. See Múñoz de S. Pedro, *Don Gutierre de Sotomayor, Maestre de Alcántara*.

18. See Highfield, 'The Catholic Kings and the Titled Nobility of Castile'.

19. See MacDonald, op. cit.

20. Rades, *Chrónica de Calatrava*, p. 66. 'This don Enrique de Villena, Master of Calatrava, was greatly learned in the human sciences, that is to say in the liberal arts, astrology, astronomy, geometry, arithmetic and the like; in law and necromancy so much so, as is said and written with such admiration by so many people, that he is thought to have made a pact with the Devil.'

21. See O'Callaghan, 'Don Pedro Girón, Master of the Order of Calatrava 1445–66', *Hispania*, vol. 21, 1961–2.

22. 'His Manners and course of Life were wholly addicted to Debauchery and Lewdness.' Stevens, op. cit., p. 381.

23. 'Then a Cryer proclaimed Sentence against the King, laying to his Charge many horrid Crimes. While the sentence was reading they leasurely stripped the statue of all its Robes, and at last with Reproachful Language threw it down from the Scaffold.' ibid., p. 407.

24. 'Not long before the Master's Death, in the Territory of Jaén, there appeared such a multitude of Locusts that they hid the sun.' ibid., p. 408.

25. Rades, *Chrónica de Calatrava*, p. 78. 'Aqui yaze el muy magnifico y muy virtuoso Sennor el noble don Pedro Girón, Maestre de la Cauallería de la Orden de Calatrava, Camerero Mayor del Rey de Castilla y de León, y del su conseio: el equal en veynte annos que fue maestre, en mucha prosperidad esta orden rigio, defendio, y acrescento en muy grand puianza. Desta presente vida fallescio a dos dias de Mayo, Anno del Sennor De MCCCCLXVI.'

26. Rades, *Chrónica de Alcántara*, p. 45. 'Ocasion de las discordias entre el Maestre y el Clauero.'

27. ibid., p. 49. 'Dan al Maestre unos grillos de hierro por principio de la cena.'

28. ibid., p. 47. 'Duquesa de Plasencia pretende el Maestradgo para su hijo.'

29. *'Coplas que fizo por la muerte de su padre'*. See *Oxford Book of Spanish Verse* (1965), p. 43. The translation is from Gerald Brenan's *The Literature of the Spanish People* (Oxford University Press, 1951), p. 99.

CHAPTER II: TRIUMPH AND NEMESIS

1. Rades, *Chrónica de Calatrava*, p. 81. 'En tiempo de paz siempre residio en al Convento de Calatrava; y alli continuava el Choro y guardara en todo la vida reglar come buen reglar.'

2. Pope Sixtus IV allowed *freyles caballeros* to wear clothes of whatever colour they wished, but they retained the white cloak with its distinguishing cross. O'Callaghan, op. cit., vol. 16, p. 37.

3. These figures, which are often quoted, are those given by Marineo Siculo in *Obra de las Casas Memorables de España*.

CHAPTER 12: READJUSTMENT AND THE TEMPLAR DISSOLUTION

1. This was Fra' Foulques de Villaret, later Master. Riley-Smith, op. cit., p. 330.

2. ibid., p. 328.

3. ibid., pp. 210–13.

4. See 'The Preceptory of Locko', *V.C.H., Derbyshire*, vol. 2, pp. 77–8.

5. See 'St Thomas of Acon', *V.C.H., London*, vol. 1, pp. 491–5.

6. It has been said that the abbey of St Thomas in Dublin belonged to the Order but the editor of this house's cartulary believed that the abbey was one of Victorine (Augustinian) Canons from its foundations. See *The Registers of the Abbey of St Thomas, Dublin*, ed. P. Gilbert (London, 1889).

7. Runciman, *History of the Crusades*, vol. III, p. 436.

8. In 1309 the Count of Armagnac would write to the King of Aragon '. . . I have just learnt that the King of Granada proposes to invade and ravage your kingdom with a vast multitude of Saracens, Jews and Templars converted to the Saracen creed'. See Finke, op. cit., vol. 2, p. 188 (no. 105).

9. See Schottmueller, vol. 2, for documents of the investigations in Cyprus.

10. See Schottmueller, *Der Untergang des Templer-Ordens*, vol. 1, p. 441. *Wild- und Rheingraf* was a title signifying 'Count of the Forest and the Rhine'.

11. Michelet, op. cit., I, p. 34, '. . . quod observatur a Saracenis et Tartaris contra tales perversos'.

12. ibid., p. 44, '. . . quod in cronicis, quae erant apud Sanctum Dionisium, continebatur quod tempore Saladine . . . Templarios fuisse dictum adversitatem perpessos, quia vicio Sodomitico laborabant, et quia fidem suam et legem prevericati fuerant . . .'

13. ibid., p. 42, '. . . miles illiteratus . . .'

14. ibid., p. 275, '. . . dictus testis, palidus et multum exterritus'.

15. ibid., p. 276, '. . . et quod eciam interfecisset Dominum, si peteretur ab eo'.

16. See Larking and Kemble, *The Knights Hospitallers in England*.

17. Occasionally fugitive *freyles* of Santiago turned Moslem – see Lomax, op. cit., p. 95, on Chapter of 1251.

CHAPTER 13: RHODES AND THE SEA KNIGHTS

1. Riley-Smith, op. cit., p. 216.

2. The *Chronica Magistrum Defunctorum* (XXIV) says that these brethren would have murdered Foulques in his bed ('in suo lecto interfecissent') had not his chamberlain helped him to escape.

3. He died in poverty – 'Obiit frater simplex et egenus'. ibid.

4. L. Le Grand, 'La Prière des Malades dans les Hôspitaux de St Jean', *Bibl. de l'École des Chartes*, LVII (Paris, 1896).

5. Delaville le Roulx, *Les Hospitaliers à Rhodes*, pp. 78, 79.

6. ibid., p. 89.

7. ibid., pp. 94, 95, 108, 109.

8. *V.C.H., Leicestershire*, vol. 2, p. 36.

9. Stubbs, *The Mediaeval Kingdoms of Cyprus and Armenia.*

10. King, *The Knights of St John in the British Realm*, p. 52.

11. Delaville le Roulx, *Rhodes*, p. 141.

12. ibid., p. 152.

13. Luttrell, *The Crusade in the Fourteenth Century.*

14. Delaville le Roulx, 'Deux aventuriers de l'Ordre de l'hôspital – les Talebart', *Mélanges sur l'Ordre de St Jean de Jérusalem.*

15. For his career, see Delaville le Roulx, *Les Hospitaliers à Rhodes*, and Herquet, *Juan Ferrandez [sic] de Heredia, Grossmeister des Johanniterordens.* The latter work has an appendix dealing with his literary activities.

16. See Luttrell, *Jean and Simon de Hesdin – Hospitaller Theologians.*

17. See Atiyah, *The Crusade of Nicopolis.*

18. See Delaville le Roulx, 'L'Occupation Chrétienne à Smyrne, 1344–1402', *Mélanges.*

19. Delaville le Roulx, *Rhodes*, p. 309.

20. ibid., vol. 2, pp. 478–80. There was a Hospitaller commandery at Khirokitia.

21. Bosio, op. cit., vol. II, p. 146.

22. ibid., p. 147, and Hill, *A History of Cyprus*, vol. 2, p. 487.

CHAPTER 14: THE THREE SIEGES

1. *V.C.H., Leicestershire*, p. 37.

2. Belabre, p. 28, gives this account but does not quote his sources. Bosio (op. cit., pt. II, pp. 162, 163) gives few details save that after forty days the Egyptians, having done much damage with their artillery, were then driven back to their ships by a sortie. It is also known that Lastic and Middleton were in the convent.

3. See King, *The Knights of St John in the British Realm.*

4. See R. Bagwell, *Ireland under the Tudors* (London, 1885).

5. See Ducaud-Bourget, *The Spiritual Heritage of the Sovereign Military Order of Malta*, p. 153.

6. ibid., p. 154.

7. See Bouhours, *The Life of the renowned Peter d'Aubusson.*

8. '. . . a diabolical hypocrite . . .' – see Taaffe, op. cit., vol. 3, p. 50.

9. See Caoursin, *Obsidionis Rhodiae Urbis Descriptio*, trans. Kay, p. 14, '. . . and thereabout the sea is at every tide, flow and ebb, wherefore there were thrust down pipes and tuns and tables full of nails . . .'

10. ibid., p. 24, '. . . an engine called a Trebuchet, like a sling, which was great, high and mighty and cast great and many stones'. Bosio, op. cit., pt. II, p. 331.

11. See Bosio, op. cit., pt. II, p. 338.

12. Caoursin, op. cit., p. 30. 'But the Lord Master had five wounds of the which one was jeopardy of his life . . . but through the Grace of God and help of leeches and surgeons.'

13. The Master wrote a letter with a lively account of the siege to the Emperor Frederick III which is printed in Taaffe – the Latin original is in bk. 4, app. CLXXII and a translation in bk. 3, p. 53.

14. See Knowles and Hadcock, *Mediaeval Religious Houses.*

15. Bosio, op. cit., pt. II, p. 488.

16. ibid., p. 489.

17. ibid., p. 491.

18. Suleiman's letter is printed in Vertot, op. cit., II, p. 456.

19. Bosio, op. cit., pt. II, p. 525.

20. Bosio gives a complete list of the names of brethren present, many misspelt – pt. II, p. 533 *et seq.*

21. See 'The begynnynge and foundacyon of the holy hospytall, & of the ordre of the knyghtes hospytallers of saynt Iohan baptyst of Ierusalem. (Here foloweth the syege, cruell oppugnacyon, and lamentable takynge of the cyte of Rodes.) Imprynted by Robert Coplande: London, the xxiii of Iuly 1524.'

22. These are Bosio's figures – op. cit., pt. II, p. 544.

23. Vertot, op. cit., vol. II, p. 482.

24. Bosio, op. cit., pt. II, p. 558.

25. ibid., p. 559.

26. ibid., p. 560 and 563; Vertot, op. cit., vol. II, p. 482.

27. For the Amaral affair, see Bosio, op. cit., pt. II, pp. 576, 577.

28. ibid., p. 578.

29. Roberts's letter is printed in Taaffe, op. cit., bk. 4, app. CCIV.

30. Bourbon, op. cit., p. xxxviii.

31. Taaffe, op. cit., bk. 4, app. CCIV.

32. Bosio describes Fairfax as 'Huomo molto spiritoso e prudente', op. cit., pt. II, p. 578.

33. ibid., pt. II, pp. 589, 590; Baudoin, op. cit., vol. I, pt. 267; Taaffe, op. cit., bk. 3, p. 25.

CHAPTER 15: THE BATTLE FOR THE MEDITERRANEAN

1. For John Rawson, see the *Dictionary of National Biography*.

2. For William Weston, see the *Dictionary of National Biography*.

3. For the unenthusiastic report of the commissioners whom the Order had sent to investigate Malta, see Vertot, op. cit., vol. III, p. 41 *et seq.*

4. Schermerhorn, *Malta of the Knights*, p. 108, who takes the story from *La Soberana Orden Mil. de S. Juan de Jer; por Un Caballero de la Orden.*

5. By 1548 English brethren in Malta were reduced to pawning their plate. See Scicluna (ed.), *The Book of Deliberations of the Venerable Tongue of England 1523-1567.*

6. For Adrian Fortescue, see the *Dictionary of National Biography*.

7. Fuller, *The Historie of the Holy Warre* (Cambridge, 1640).

8. For Thomas Legh, see the *Dictionary of National Biography*; for the houses' surrender, *V.C.H. Leicestershire*, vol. 2, p. 38.

9. Bertrand de la Grassière, *L'Ordre Militaire et Hospitalier de Saint-Lazare de Jérusalem.*

10. See Vertot, op. cit., vol. III, p. 291 *et seq.*

11. Cellini, *Memoirs*, p. 396; Montluc, *Commentaries*, p. 288. For Strozzi's career, see Brantôme, *Les vies des hommes illustres et grands capitaines françois*, vol. 2, p. 352.

12. For Romegas, see Vertot, op. cit., vol. III, p. 411 *et seq.* For his miraculous escape, see Bosio, op. cit., pt. III, p. 367.

13. There is a colourful account of Sigena in modern times – before its sack and destruction in 1936 by Spanish Republicans when the entire community was murdered – in Sir Sacheverell Sitwell's *Monks, Nuns and Monasteries* (Weidenfeld & Nicolson, 1965).

14. Balbi, op. cit., p. 27.

15. For Thomas Tresham, see the *Dictionary of National Biography*.

16. For James Sandilands, see the *Dictionary of National Biography*.

17. See Helyot, 'De l'Ordre Militaire de Saint Étienne Pape & Martyr en Toscane', *Histoire des ordres religieux*, vol. VI, p. 248.

18. Einar Rud, *Vasari's Life and Lives; the first art historian*, trans. Spink (Thames & Hudson, 1964), p. 74.

19. See Balbi, op. cit., pp. 28–31, and Vertot, op. cit., vol. III, pp. 421, 424.

20. Balbi, op. cit., p. 36 – I have accepted Balbi's figures.

21. ibid., p. 41.

22. Vertot, op. cit., vol. III, p. 436.

23. ibid., p. 444.

24. Balbi, op. cit., p. 56.

25. Vertot, op. cit., vol. III, p. 461.

26. ibid., p. 432.

27. Balbi, op. cit., p. 81.

28. Bosio, op. cit., pt. III, p. 561.

29. ibid., pp. 572, 573; Vertot, op. cit., vol. III, p. 490.

30. Balbi, op. cit., p. 91.

31. Vertot, op. cit., vol. III, p. 492.

32. ibid., p. 492.

33. ibid., vol. IV, p. 3.

34. Balbi, op. cit., p. 101.

35. ibid., p. 111.

36. ibid., p. 117.

37. Vertot, op. cit, vol. IV, p. 51.

38. ibid., p. 61.

39. ibid., p. 80.

40. Balbi, op. cit., p. 189.

41. Dal Pozzo, *Historia della Sacra Religione Militare di S. Giovanni Gerosolimitano*, vol. I, p. 19.

42. ibid., p. 30.

CHAPTER 16: BAROQUE PALADINS

1. For the Teutonic Knights at Candia, see Voigt, *Geschichte des deutschen Ritterorden in seinen zwölf Balleien in Deutschland* (Berlin, 1857–9), vol. II, p. 387.

2. See D. D. Macpherson, *De Poincy and the Order of St John in the New World* (St John's Gate, 1949).

3. See Scicluna, *The Church of St John in Valetta*.

GLOSSARY

adelantado – governor of a province
alcalde – governor of a castle
bailiff – senior officer
bailiwick – senior officer's command
balleien – bailiwicks
cadi – Moorish magistrate
cavalgada – cavalry raid
chapter-general – council attended by all brethren
chevauchée – cavalry raid
clavero – key bearer (i.e. castellan)
cofradias – confraternities
confrater – honorary knight brother
Deutschritter – Teutonic Knights
domi conventuales – houses in which the rule was observed
encomienda – commandery (Castilian)
escudero – squire
espada – the red sword-cross emblem of Santiago
familiares – associates and employees
frares cavallers – knight brethren (Catalan)
frares clergues – priest brethren (Catalan)
freyles caballeros – knight brethren (Castilian)
freyles clerigos – priest brethren (Castilian)
ghazi – warrior for the faith (Muslim)
gomeres – negro knifemen
grosskomtur – grand commander
halbbruder – honorary knight brother
hauskomtur – house commander
hermandad – brotherhood
hermangilda – guild
hidalgo – nobleman

Hoch und Deutschmeister – High and German Master

jinetes – light horse

komturei – commandery

landkomtur – district commander

landmeister – provincial Master

langue – 'tongue' (i.e. national association)

largetto – 'lizard' – a popular name for the red sword-cross of Santiago

latifundio – great agricultural estate

maestrazgo – mastership (Castilian)

Maestre – Master (Castilian)

mestrat – mastership (Catalan or Portuguese)

Mestre – Master (Catalan or Portuguese)

mudéjar – Moor subject to Christian rule

Office – prayers and psalms to be said or sung at specified times of the day

Ordensmarschall – Marshal of the Order

Pfleger – commander

preceptor – commander

professed – having taken the monastic vows of poverty, chastity and obedience

rabito – garrison of a ribat

razzia – raid

ribat – fortified Moslem 'monastery'

ricos-homems – noblemen (Portuguese)

Schwertbrüder – Sword Brethren

sergeant – man-at-arms

taifa – petty state

trezes – the Council of Thirteen (of the Order of Santiago)

Turcopolier – general commanding native light horse

vogt – commander (of the Sword Brethren)

BIBLIOGRAPHY

See Abbreviations on p. 13.

1. Bullaria, Cartularies, Rules, Statutes, Chronicles, Documents and Contemporary Histories of the Orders

GENERAL

AMMAN, J., *Cleri totius Romanae ecclesiae* (Frankfurt 1585).

BUONANNI, F., *Ordinum Religiosorum in ecclesia militanti catalogus* (Rome 1714).

GIUSTINIANI, B., *Historie Cronologiche degl'Ordini Militari e di tutte Religioni Cavalleresche*, 2 vols. (Venice 1692).

HELYOT, P., *Histoire des ordres religieux, monastiques et militaires*, 7 vols. (Paris 1714–21).

HERMANT, J., *Histoires des Religions ou Ordres Militaires* (Paris 1696).

JONGELINUS, *Originis equestrium militarium ordinis Cisterciensis* (1640).

RADES Y ANDRADA, F., *Chrónica de las tres Órdenes y Cavallerías de Sanctiago, Calatrava y Alcántara* (Toledo 1572).

ALCÁNTARA

Difiniciones [sic] y Estableciementos de la Orden y Cavalleria de Alcántara (Madrid 1609).

ORTEGA Y COTES, I. J., *Bullarium Ordinis Militiae de Alcántara, Olim Sancti Juliani de Pereiro* (Madrid 1759).

TORRES Y TAPIA, A. DE, *Crónica de la Orden de Alcántara*, 2 vols. (Madrid 1763).

AVIZ

PURIFICÃO, J. DA, 'Catalogo dos Mestres e administradores da illustre e antiquissima Ordem Militar de Aviz', *C.A.R.H.P.*, vol. 2.

CALATRAVA

Diffiniciones de la Orden y Cavallería de Calatrava (Valladolid 1603).

ORTEGA Y COTES, I. J., *Bullarium Ordinis Militiae de Calatrava* (Madrid 1761).

ORDER OF CHRIST

Definiçoes e estatus da ordem de Christo (Lisbon 1746).

MALTA

BALBI, F., *The Siege of Malta*, trans. E. Bradford (Folio Society 1965).

BOSIO, G., *Dell'istoria della Sacra religione et Illma. Militia de San Giovanni Gierosolimitano*, 3 vols. (Rome 1594).

—, *Histoire des Chevaliers de l'Ordre de S. Jean de Hierusalem*, trans. and ed. by J. Baudoin (Paris 1629).

BOURBON, J. DE, *La Grande et merueilleuse et très cruelle oppugnation de la noble cité de Rhodes prinse naguères par Sultan Séliman à present grand Turq ennemy de la très saincte foy Catholique que redige par escript par excellent et noble chevalier Frère Jacques bastard du Bourbon commandeur de Sainct Mauluiz, Doysemont e fonteynes au prieuré de France* (Paris 1525).

CAOURSIN, G., *Obsidionis Rhodiae Urbis Descriptio* (Ulm 1496), trans. John Kay, ed. H. W. Fincham (St John's Gate 1926).

The Cartulary of the Knights of St John of Jerusalem in England, ed. M. Gervers (London 1982).

'Catalogo dos Grampriores do Crato da Ordem de S. João de Malta', *C.A.R.H.P.*, vol 4.

Chronica Magistrum Defunctorum in Dugdale, vol. VI.

DELAVILLE LE ROULX, J., *Cartulaire Général des Hospitaliers de Saint Jean de Jérusalem 1100–1310*, 4 vols. (Paris 1894–1906).

The Knights Hospitallers in England, being the report of Prior Philip de Thame to the Grand Master Elyan de Villanova for A.D. 1338, ed. L. B. Larking, introd. J. M. Kemble (Camden Soc., London 1858).

LE GRAND, L., 'La prière qui se doit dire au Palais des Malades (à Chypre)', *La prière des malades dans les hôpitaux de l'ordre de Saint-Jean de Jérusalem*, in Bibliothèque de l'École des Chartes LVII (1896).

POZZO, B. DAL, *Historia della Sacra Religione Militare di S. Giovanni Gerosolimitano*, 2 vols. (1703, 1715).

SCICLUNA, H. P. (ed.), *The Book of Deliberations of the Venerable Tongue of England 1523–1567* (Malta 1949).

VERTOT, G. AUBERT DE, *Histoire des Chevaliers Hospitaliers de S. Jean de Jérusalem*, 4 vols. (Paris 1726).

MERCEDARIANS

Regula et constitutiones Fratrum Sacri Ordinis Beatae Mariae de Mercede Redemptionis Captivorum (Salamanca 1588).

MONTESA

RADES Y ANDRADA, F., *Diffiniciones de la sagrada Religion y Cavalleria de Sancta María de Montesa y Sanct Iorge d'Alfama* (Valencia 1573).

SAMPER, H. DE, *Montesa Ilustrada*, 2 vols. (Valencia 1669).

SANTIAGO

Bullarium Equestris Ordinis S. Iacobi de Spatha (Barcelona 1719).

Regla y Establescimientos de la orden de la Caualleria de San Sanctiago del Espada (1555).

SWORD BRETHREN

ALNPEKE, DIETLEB VON, 'Die Riterlichen Meister und Brüder zu Leiflant', *S.R.L.*, vol. I.

LETTLAND, HEINRICH VON, 'Chronicon Livonicum Vetus', *S.R.L.*, vol. I.

RÜSSOW, BALTHASAR, 'Chronica der Provintz Lyfflandt', *S.R.L.*, vol. II (Bart 1584).

WARTBERGE, HERMANN VON, 'Chronicon Livoniae', *S.R.P.*, vol. II

TEMPLARS

ALBON, MARQUIS D', *Cartulaire général de l'ordre du Temple 1119–1150. Recueil des chartes et des bulles relatives à l'ordre du Temple* (Paris 1913).

'Catalogo dos Mestres da Ordem do Templo Portugueze e em outras da Hespanha', *C.A.R.H.P.*, vol. 2.

CLAIRVAUX, BERNARD OF, 'Liber ad Milites Templi de Laude Novae Militiae', in Leclercq, J. and Rochais, H. M., *S. Bernardi Opera*, vol. III (Editiones Cistercienses, Rome 1963).

CURZON, H. DE, *La Règle du Temple* (Paris 1887).

—, *La Maison du Temple à Paris* (Paris 1888).

LECLERCQ, J., 'Un document sur les débuts des Templiers', *Revue de l'histoire ecclésiastique*, vol. LII (1957).

LIZERAND, G., *Le Dossier de l'Affaire des Templiers* (Paris 1923).

MICHELET, J., *Procès des Templiers*, 2 vols. (Paris 1841–51).

UPTON-WARD, J. (trans.), *The Rule of the Templars: the French text of the Rule of the Order of Knights Templar* (London 1992).

TEUTONIC KNIGHTS

BITSCHIN, CONRAD, 'Chronica Terrae Prussiae', *S.R.P.*, vol. III.

BLUMENAUE, L., 'Historia de Ordine Theutonicorum Cruciferorum', *S.R.P.*, vol. IV.

Chronicon Equestris Ordinis Teutonici (Netherlands 1738).

Das grosse Amterbuch des Deutschen Ordens (Danzig 1921).

DUELLIUS, E., *Debita seu statuta Equitum Theutonicorum* (1724).

'Historia Brevis Magistrorum Ordinis Theutonici Generalium ad Martinum Truchses continuata', *S.R.P..*, vol. IV.

DUSBURG, PETRUS VON, 'Chronica Terre Prussie', *S.R.P.*, vol. I.

—, *Chronicon Prussiae . . . cum incerti auctoria continuatione usque ad annum MCCCCXXXV* (Frankfurt and Leipzig 1679).

MARTIN, K., *Minnesänger* (Baden-Baden 1953) – illuminated miniatures from the Manessa Codex.

PERLBACH, M., *Statuten des Deutschen Ordens* (Halle 1890).

PUSILGE, JOHANN VON, 'Annalista Thorunensis', *S.R.P.*, vol. III.

STREHLKE E., *Tabulae Ordinis Teutonici* (Berlin 1869).

WAL, G. DE, *Histoire de l'Ordre Teutonique*, 8 vols. (Paris and Rheims 1784–90).

2. Other Contemporary Sources

AYALA, P. LOPEZ DE, *Crónicas de los reyes de Castilla*, 2 vols. (Madrid 1778–80).

BORCH, M. J., *Lettres sur la Sicile et sur l'Isle de Malte* (Turin 1782).

BRANTÔME, P. DE BOURDEILLE DE, *Les Vies des Hommes Illustres et Grands Capitaines estrangers de son temps* (Amsterdam 1665).

—, *Les Vies des Hommes Illustres et Grands Capitaines François de son temps*, 4 vols. (Amsterdam 1666).

BRYDONE, P., *A Tour through Sicily and Malta* (London 1773).

CELLINI, B., *The Memoirs of Benvenuto Cellini* (Oxford University Press 1961).

CHARTRES, FULCHER OF, 'Historia Hierosolymitana. Gesta Francorum Iherusalem peregrinantium', *R.H.C. oc.* 3.

DICETO, RALPH DE, 'Ymagines Historiarium', *The Historical Works of Master Ralph de Diceto, Dean of London*, ed. W. Stubbs, 2 vols. (Rolls Series, London 1876).

HILL, ROSALIND (ed.), *Gesta Francorum* (Nelson 1962).

HORSEY, J., *The Travels of Sir Jerome Horsey, Kt.*, ed. A. Bond (Hakluyt Soc. 1856).

IBELIN, JEAN D', 'Le Livre du Jean d'Ibelin', *R.H.C. Lois.* I.

JOINVILLE, J. DE, *Histoire de Saint Louis*, ed. N. de Wailly (Paris 1874); trans. M. R. B. Shaw, *Chronicles of the Crusades* (Penguin 1963).

LELEWEL, J. (ed.), *Guillebert de Lannoy et ses voyages en 1413, 1414 et 1421* (Brussels 1844).

MARIANA, J. DE, *Historiae de rebus Hispaniae* (Toledo 1592–1610), trans. John Stevens, *The General History of Spain* (London 1699).

MONTLUC, B. DE LASSERAN-MASSENCOME DE, *Commentaires de Messire de Monluc*, 2 vols. (Lyons 1593), trans. C. Cotton, *The Commentaries of Messire Blaize de Montluc* (London 1674).

PARIS, MATTHEW, *Chronica Majora*, ed. H. R. Luard, 7 vols. (Rolls Series, London 1872–83).

STUBBS, W. (ed.), 'Itinerarium peregrinorum et gesta regis Ricardi', *Memorials of the Reign of Richard I* (Rolls Series, London 1869).

VILLEHARDOUIN, G. DE, *La Conquête de Constantinople*, ed. E. Faral, 2 vols. (Paris 1938–9), trans. M. R. B. Shaw, *Chronicles of the Crusades* (Penguin 1963).

VITRY, JACQUES DE, *Historia orientalis seu Hierosolymitana*, ed. J. Bongars (Hannau 1611).

3. Later Sources and Studies of the Orders

ALCÁNTARA

O'CALLAGHAN, J. F., 'The Foundation of the Order of Alcántara', *Catholic Historical Review*, vol. 47 (1961–2).

S. PEDRO, M. MÚÑOZ DE, *Don Gutierre de Sotomayor, Maestre de Alcántara* (Caceres 1949).

AVIZ

OLIVIERIA, M. DE, 'A Milicia de Evora e a Ordem de Calatrava', *Lusitania Sacra* I (1956).

CALATRAVA

GUTTON, F., *L'Ordre de Calatrava*, Commission de l'ordre de Cîteaux, P. Lethellieux (Paris 1955).

O'CALLAGHAN, J. F., 'The Affiliation of the Order of Calatrava with Cîteaux', *Analecta Sacri Ordinis Cisterciensis*, vols. 15 and 16 (1959–60).

—, 'Don Pedro Girón, Master of the Order of Calatrava 1445–66', *Hispania*, vol. 21 (1961–2).

CONSTANTINIAN ST GEORGE

SEWARD, D., *Italy's Knights of St George: the Constantinian Order* (Gerrards Cross 1986).

GENERAL

BRASIER, L., and BRUNET, J., *Les Ordres Portugaises* (Paris 1898).

CLINCHAMPS, G. DU PUY DE, *La Chevalerie* (Paris 1961).

COCHERIL, M. M., 'Essai sur l'Origine des Ordres Militaires dans la Péninsule Ibérique', *Collectanea ordinis Cisterciensium Reformatorum*, vols. 20 and 21 (1958–9).

Encyclopaedia Britannica: articles on Order of St John of Jerusalem, Teutonic Knights and Templars.

FOREY, A., *The Military Orders from the twelfth to the early fourteenth century* (London 1992).

Grande Enciclopedia Portuguesa e Brasileira: articles on Alcántara, Aviz, Calatrava, Order of Christ, Santiago, etc.

LLAMAZARES, J. FERNANDEZ, *Historia Compendiada de las Cuatres Órdenes Militares* (Madrid 1862).

LOMAX, B. W., *The Reconquest of Spain* (London 1978).

MACKAY, A., *Spain and the Middle Ages* (London 1977).

NICHOLSON, H., *Templars, Hospitallers and Teutonic Knights: Images of the Military Orders* (Leicester 1994).

SALLES, F. DE, *Ordres Religieux de Chevaliers*, 2 vols. (Paris 1887–9).

MALTA

BASCAPE, G. C., *L'Ordine di Malta e gli Ordini Equestri della Chiesa nella Storia e nel Diritto* (Milan 1940).

BELABRE, F. DE, *Rhodes of the Knights* (Oxford 1908).

BERTINI FRASSONI, C. A., *Il Sovrano Militare Ordine di S. Giovanni di Gerusalemme, detto di Malta* (Rome 1929).

BOISGELIN, P. M. C. DE, *Ancient and Modern Malta and the History of the Knights of Jerusalem* (London 1805).

BOUHOURS, A., *The Life of the renowned Peter d'Aubusson* (London 1679).

BRADFORD, E., *The Great Siege* (Hodder & Stoughton 1961).

BREMOND D'ARS, A. DE, *Le Chevalier de Téméricourt* (Paris 1904).

CAMPO BELLO, CONDE DE, *A Soberan Militar Ordem de Malta e a sua acção em Portugal* (Lisbon 1931).

CAVALIERO, R., *The Last of the Crusaders* (Hollis & Carter 1960).

CHAFFANJON, A., and GALLIMARD FLAVIGNY, B., *Ordres et Contres-Ordres de Chevalerie* (Paris 1982).

DAUBER, R., *Die Marine des Johanniter-Malteser-Ritterordens* (Vienna 1989).

DELAVILLE LE ROULX, J., *Les Hospitaliers en Terre Sainte et à Chypre (1100–1310)* (Paris 1904).

—, *Les Hospitaliers à Rhodes jusqu'à la mort de Phillibert de Naillac (1310–1421)* (Paris 1913).

—, *La France en Orient au XIVe siècle. Expéditions du Maréchal Boucicaut*, 2 vols. (Paris 1885–6).

—, *Mélanges sur l'ordre de St Jean de Jérusalem* (Paris 1910).

DESCHAMPS, P., *Les Châteaux des croisés en Terre Sainte. Le Crac des Chevaliers* (Paris 1934).

DUCAUD-BOURGET, F., *The Spiritual Heritage of the Sovereign Military Order of Malta* (Vatican City 1958).

EASSON, D. E., *Mediaeval Religious Houses – Scotland* (Longmans, Green 1957).

FIGUERIDO, J. A., *Nova Historia da Miltar Ordem de Malta . . . en Portugal* (Lisbon 1800)

GABRIEL, A., *La Cité de Rhodes* (Paris 1921 and 1922).

GAEA, M., *German Knights of Malta* (Valetta 1986).

GATTINI, M., *I Priorati, i baliaggi e le commende del Sovrano Militare Ordine di San Giovanni nelle provincie meridionali d'Italia* (Rome 1928).

HERQUET, K., *Juan Ferrandez [sic] de Heredia, Grossmeister des Johanniterordens (1337–99)* (Mulhausen i. Th. 1878).

HUMPHREY-SMITH, C., *Hugh Revel, Master of the Hospital of St John of Jerusalem 1258–1277* (Chichester 1994).

JURIEN DE LA GRAVIÈRE, J. E., *Les Chevaliers de Malte et la Marine de Philippe II* (Paris 1887).

KING, E. J., *The Knights Hospitallers in the Holy Land* (Methuen 1931).

KING, E. J. and LUKE, H., *The Knights of St John in the British Realm* (St John's Gate 1967).

KNOWLES, D. and HADCOCK, R. N., *Mediaeval Religious Houses – England and Wales* (Longmans, Green 1953).

LACROIX, A., *Déodat de Dolomieu* (Paris 1921).

LAVIGERIE, O., *L'Ordre de Malte depuis la Révolution Française* (Paris 1889).

LUTTRELL, A., 'The Aragonese Crown and the Knights Hospitallers of Rhodes 1291–1350', *English Historical Review*, vol. 76 (1961).

—, 'Jean and Simon de Hesdin – Hospitaller Theologians', *Recherches de Théologie Ancienne et Mediévale*, vol. 31 (1964).

—, *The Hospitallers in Cyprus, Rhodes, Greece and the West 1291–1440* (London 1978).

—, *Latin Greece, the Hospitallers and the Crusades 1291–1440* (London 1982).

MIFSUD, H., *Knights Hospitallers of the Venerable Tongue of England in Malta* (Malta 1914).

LA VARENDE, J., *Tourville et son Temps* (Paris 1943).

L'Ordre Souverain, militaire et hospitalier de Saint Jean de Jérusalem, de Rhodes et de Malte (Paris 1963).

MICHEL DE PIERREDON, COUNT G., *Histoire Politique de l'Ordre Souverain de Saint-Jean de Jérusalem (Ordre de Malte) de 1789 à 1955*, 3 vols. (Paris 1956–90).

PORTER, W., *History of the Knights of Malta* (London 1858).

PROKOPOWSKI, C., *L'Ordre Souverain et Militaire Jérosolymitain de Malte* (Vatican 1950).

RILEY-SMITH, J., *The Knights of St John in Jerusalem and Cyprus, 1050–1310* (Macmillan 1967).

ROSSI, E., *Storia della Marina dell'Ordine di S. Giovanni di Gerusalemme, di Rodi e di Malta* (Rome 1926).

SAINTY, G. S., *The Orders of St John* (New York 1991).

SCHERMERHORN, E. W., *Malta of the Knights* (Heinemann 1929).

—, *On the Trail of the Eight-Pointed Cross* (New York 1940).

SCICLUNA, H. P., *The Church of St John in Valetta* (Rome 1955).

SIRE, H. J. A., *The Knights of Malta* (Yale University Press 1994).

SPAGNOLETT, A., *Aristocrazie e Ordine di Malta nell'Italia Moderna* (Rome 1988).

TAAFFE, J., *History of the Order of St John of Jerusalem* (London 1852).

WIENAND, A. (ed.), *Der Johanniterorden, Der Malteserorden* (Cologne 1988).

SANTIAGO

LOMAX, D. W., *La Orden de Santiago, MCLXX–MCCLXXV* (Madrid 1965).

—, 'The Order of Santiago and the Kings of León', *Hispania* vol. 18 (1958).

MONTHERLANT, H. DE, *Le Maître de Santiago* (Paris 1947).

ST LAZARUS

CIBRARIO, G. A. L., *Précis historique des Ordres Religieux et militaires de S. Lazare et de S. Maurice avant et après leur réunion*, trans. H. Ferrand (Lyons 1860).

GRASSIÈRE, P. BERTRAND DE LA, *Histoire des Chevaliers Hospitaliers de Saint Lazare* (Paris 1932).

—, *L'Ordre Militaire et Hospitalier de Saint-Lazare de Jérusalem* (Paris 1960).

'The Hospital of Burton Lazars', *Victoria County History: 'Leicestershire'*, vol. 2 (Oxford University Press 1954).

NICHOLS, J., *History of the County and Antiquities of Leicestershire*, 2 vols. (London 1795).

'The Preceptory of Locko', *Victoria County History: 'Derbyshire'*, vol. 2 (Constable 1907).

Regi magistrali provvedimenti relativi all'ordine dei santi Maurizio e Lazzaro (Turin 1855).

ST THOMAS

FOREY, A., 'The Military Order of St Thomas of Acon', in *English Historical Review* xciii (1977).

'St Thomas of Acon', *Victoria County History: 'London'*, vol. 1 (Constable 1909).

STUBBS, W., *The Mediaeval Kingdoms of Cyprus and Armenia* (Oxford 1878).

WATNEY, J., *Some Account of the Hospital of St Thomas Acon in the Cheap, London, and of the Plate of the Mercers' Company* (London 1892).

SWORDBRETHREN

BLOMBERG, C. J. VON, *An Account of Livonia with a Relation of the Rise, Progress and Decay of the Marian Teutonick Order* (London 1701).

BUNGE, F. G. VON, 'Der Orden der Schwertbrüder', *Baltische Geschichtstudien* (Leipzig 1875).

HERDER, J. G., *Der Orden Schwertbrüder* (Cologne 1965).

LEVENCLAVIUS, JOHANNES, 'De Moscovitarium bellis adversus finitimos gestis', *H.R.S.E.*, vol. 1.

SCHURZFLEISCH, H., *Historia Ensiferorum Ordinis Teutonici Livonorum* (Wittemberg 1701).

TEMPLARS

ADDISON, C. G., *The Knights Templars* (London 1842).

BARBER, M., *The Trial of the Templars* (Cambridge 1978).

—, *The New Knighthood: A History of the Order of the Temple* (Cambridge 1993).

BORDONOVE, G., *Les Templiers* (Paris 1963).

BOUYER, L., *The Cistercian Heritage* (Mowbray 1958).

CAMPBELL, G. A., *The Knights Templars* (Duckworth 1937).

DESSUBRÉ, M., *Bibliographie de l'Ordre des Templiers* (Paris 1928).

EDWARDS, J., 'The Templars in Scotland in the thirteenth century', *Scottish Historical Review*, V, no. 17 (October 1907).

FINKE, H., *Papstumm und Untergang des Templerordens* (Munster 1907).

LIZERAND, G., *Jacques de Molay* (Paris 1928).

MARTIN, E. J., *The Trial of the Templars* (Allen & Unwin 1928).

MELVILLE, M., *La Vie des Templiers* (Paris 1951).

OURSEL, R., *Le Procès des Templiers* (Paris 1955).

PARKER, T. W., *The Knights Templars in England* (Tucson 1963).

PIQUET, J., *Les Banquiers du Moyen Âge: Les Templiers* (Paris 1939).

PRUTZ, H., *Entwicklung und Untergang des Tempelherrenordens* (Berlin 1888).

SCHOTTMUELLER, K., *Der Untergang des Templer-Ordens*, 2 vols. (Berlin 1887).

SIMON, E., *The Piebald Standard* (Cassell 1959).

TEUTONIC KNIGHTS

BOOCKMANN H., *Der Deutsche Orden* (Munich 1981).

BOSWELL, A. B., 'The Teutonic Order', *Cambridge Mediaeval History*, vol. VII (1932).

CARSTEN, F. J., *The Origins of Prussia* (Oxford University Press 1954).

CHRISTIANSEN, E., *The Northern Crusades: the Baltic and the Catholic Frontier 1100–1525* (Macmillan 1980).

FABRICIUS, DYONISIUS, 'Livonicae Historiae Compendiosa series', *S.R.L.*, vol. II.

HALECKI, O., *Borderlands of Western Civilisation* (New York 1952).

KOCH, H.W., *History of Prussia* (Longmans 1978).

LAVISSE, E., 'Chevaliers Teutoniques', *Revue des Deux Mondes*, vol. 32 (1879).

MICKIEWICZ, A., *Konrad Walenrod* (California 1925).

SALLES, F. DE, *Ordres Religieux de Chevalerie*, 2 vols. (Paris 1887–9).

SCHUMACHER, E., *Die Burgen in Preussen und Livland* (1962).

SIENKIEWICZ, H., *The Teutonic Knights* (trans. ed., London 1943).

TREITSCHKE, H. VON, *Das deutsche Ordensland Preussen* (Leipzig 1915); trans. E. and C. Paul, *Treitschke's Origins of Prussianism* (Allen & Unwin 1942).

TUMLER, P. M., *Der Deutsche Orden im Werden, Wachsen und Wirken bis um 1400* (Vienna 1955).

VOIGT, J., *Geschichte Preussens*, 9 vols. (Koenigsberg 1827–39).

VOIGHT, J., *Geschichte des deutschen Ritterordens in seinen zwölf Balleien in Deutschland*, 2 vols. (Berlin 1857–9).

WAL, G. DE, *Recherches sur l'ancienne constitution de l'Ordre Teutonique* (Mergentheim 1807).

WIESER, K. (ed.), *Acht Jahrhunderte Deutscher Orden* (Bad Godesberg 1967).

INDEX

Brethren/Knights from the early Mediaeval period (to Chapter 4) are entered under their first names. Thereafter, the surname is used.

Metzenhausen, Johann-
Wilhelm von 293
Mewe commandery 116
Mézières, Fra' Philippe
de 239
Middleton, Fra' Hugh
244
Miguel, Dom, Prior of
Crato 300
Milly, Fra' Jacques de
245
Mindaugas of Lithuania,
King 100, 105–6
Miranda, Captain 283
Misac Palaeologus
Pasha, Vizier 249,
250, 252–3
Mistra 240
Mleh, Fra' 48, 60
Mogarbina 257–8
Molay, Fra' Jacques de
19, 209, 211, 212,
214, 215, 216–17,
219, 221, 230
Molay, 'Marquis de
Sainte-Croix-' 338–
45 passim, 347, 350
Monckton of Brenchley,
Major-General
Viscount 326
Monfalim, Marquez de
316
Mongka Khan 79
Mongols 77, 78–9, 82,
84, 104
Monroe, President
James 331
Monroy, Frey Alfonso
de 189, 190
Montalban
commandery 170
Monteiro, Frey Fernaõ
Rodrigues 158
Montesa castle 170, 304
Montesa, Order of 170,

176, 179, 220n, 293,
304, 311–12
Montfort (Starkenberg)
castle 68, 69, 81–2,
98, 108
Montgisard battle
(1177) 51
Montherlant, Henri de:
Le Maître de Santiago
19
Montiel battle (1369)
176
Montjoie castle and
Lady of Montjoie
Order 42
Montluc, Fra' Blaize de
274
Montmagny, Charles-
Jacques Huault de
328, 329
Monzon stronghold 145,
214
More, Fra' William de-
la 214, 219
Morfia, Queen 25
Morimond 150, 176, 188
Morosini, Francesco 293
Moventi, Frey García de
157
Mowbray, Segrave and
Stourton, Lord 321
Muhammad II of
Granada, Sultan
167
Muhammad III ibn-
Yakub, Caliph 158
Muhammad VI of
Granada, Sultan
178, 180
Muhammad VII of
Granada, Sultan
185
Muhammad ibn-al-
Ahmar, Caliph 164
Muhammed ibn-Yusuf

ibn-Ahmed ibn-
Nasr (al-Ahmar)
166–7
Muley Hassan, Sultan of
Granada 193, 194,
195
Múñiz, Frey Pedro 178
Murcia 162, 164, 180
Mustafa Pasha 260, 261,
278, 281, 282, 284–
7 passim
Myriocephalum battle
(1176) 50
Mytilene fall (1463) 247

Nablus massacre (1242)
73
Naillac, Fra' Philibert de
239, 240, 241
Nájera battle (1367) 176
Naples and Sicily Grand
Priory 312
Napoleon I, Emperor
309–11
Narbonne, Archbishop
of (cit. 1309) 216
Nasr, Caliph 47–8
Navarre 143, 154, 224
Nestorians 79
Neva river battle (1240)
105
Nevers, Fra' Jean de 239
New Zealand:
Venerable Order of
St John 352
Nicaea capture (1329)
229
Nicholas IV, Pope 208
Nicopolis battle (1396)
239–40
Nieszawa 127
Nigg, Peter 331
Nogaret, Fra' Guillaume
de 210–11, 213, 216
Nolasco, Frey Pere 163